JAZZ SELLS

Jazz Sells: Music, Marketing, and Meaning examines the issues of jazz, consumption, and capitalism through advertising. On television, on the Internet, on the radio, and in print, advertising is a critically important medium for the mass dissemination of music and musical meaning. This book is a study of the use of the jazz genre as a musical signifier in promotional efforts, exploring how brand, jazz music, and jazz discourses come together to create meaning for the product and the consumer. At the same time, it examines how jazz offers an invaluable lens through which to examine the complex and often contradictory culture of consumption upon which capitalism is predicated.

Mark Laver is an Assistant Professor of Music at Grinnell College, where he teaches classes on jazz and popular music. His work has been published in *Popular Music and Society, Popular Music, Black Music Research Journal*, and *Critical Studies in Improvisation*. Dr. Laver is also a busy saxophonist who has performed with Lee Konitz, William Parker, and Dong-Won Kim, among many other leading international artists.

Transnational Studies in Jazz

Series Editors: Tony Whyton and Nicholas Gebhardt

Jazz Sells: Music, Marketing, and Meaning
Mark Laver

The Cultural Politics of Jazz Collectives: This is Our Music
Edited by Nicholas Gebhardt and Tony Whyton

JAZZ SELLS

Music, Marketing, and Meaning

Mark Laver

Routledge
Taylor & Francis Group

NEW YORK AND LONDON

First published 2015
by Routledge
711 Third Avenue, New York, NY 10017

and by Routledge
2 Park Square, Milton Park, Abingdon, Oxon, OX14 4RN

Routledge is an imprint of the Taylor & Francis Group, an informa business

Library of Congress Cataloging-in-Publication Data
Laver, Mark, author.
 Jazz sells : music, marketing, and meaning / Mark Laver.
  pages cm — (Transnational studies in jazz)
 Includes bibliographical references and index.
 1. Jazz—Social aspects. 2. Branding (Marketing)—History.
3. Advertising—History. 4. Jazz—History and criticism. I. Title.
II. Series: Transnational studies in jazz.
 ML3506.L38 2015
 306.4'84250973—dc23
 2015001116

ISBN: 978-1-138-01875-4 (hbk)
ISBN: 978-1-138-01876-1 (pbk)
ISBN: 978-1-315-77954-6 (ebk)

Typeset in Bembo
by Apex CoVantage, LLC

Senior Editor: Constance Ditzel
Senior Editorial Assistant: Elysse Preposi
Production Editor: Bonita Glanville-Morris
Marketing Manager: Chris Jacobs
Copy Editor: Nicola Prior
Cover Design: Jayne Varney

For Erin, Nora, and Finnegan

CONTENTS

List of Illustrations   *ix*
Series Foreword   *x*
Preface   *xi*
Acknowledgments   *xiii*

1   Introduction   1

Mass Production, Mass Mediation, and the Emergence
    of the Consumer-Citizen   3
Music in Advertising: An Overview   12
Studying Music and Advertising: Reviewing the Field   22
Theoretical Framework   26
Methodology   30
Chapter Outline   34

2   Pimps, Rebels, and Volkswagens   40

"You've Taken My Blues and Gone": Jazz, Commerce,
    and the Culture Industries 1920–1960   42
"You My Audience . . .:" Charles Mingus, Dissent,
    and Commodification   56
Mingus Sells Jettas: Improvisation and the Open Road   70
Conclusion   78

3   Autoeroticism: Sex, Cars, and Jazz   84

Joyrides, Jazzy Tendencies, and the Decline of America   87

American Dreams: Jazz, Cars, and Consumerism 93
Jazz Economies: Plymouth, Honda, and Globalization 106
"This is My Car:" Chrysler, Pop-Jazz, and Diana Krall 120
Conclusion 137

4 The New Sound of Cola 142

Developing the New Sound of Cola 144
"Coming Together": Diversity and the Omni-American Cola 158
"Jazz Up Your Life": Pepsi Jazz and Consumer Agency 166
Conclusion: Indulge Yourself With Jazz 170

5 "The Bank of Music" 177

Buying Goodwill: Sponsorship as Advertising 180
A Brief History of Jazz Festivals 186
Comfort and Community: Jazz Festivals as Brand Fit 194
Corporate Social Responsibility: Ethical Marketing,
    Marketing Ethics 210
Conclusion: Jazz Festivals and the Spectacle of Community 219

6 Conclusion 228

Index 237

ILLUSTRATIONS

1.1 Clicquot Club Ginger Ale bottle, ca. 1914   7

2.1 Cover of *The Clown* (Atlantic, 1957)   57

2.2 Charles and Sue Mingus (courtesy Sue Mingus)   60

2.3 *Beneath the Underdog* (Alfred A. Knopf, 1971 [Vintage Books, 1991])   65

2.4 Nick Drake   71

3.1 Cadillac with Elvis plate (Niels Gerhardt/Shutterstock.com)   85

3.2 1940 De Soto advertisement (Hartman Center for Sales,
     Advertising, and Marketing History, Margaret Fishback
     Papers, Box OV12)   95

3.3 Dinah Shore with family (Grey Villet, The LIFE Picture
     Collection/Getty)   98

3.4 Dinah Shore in 1942 (Bob Landry, The LIFE Picture
     Collection/Getty)   100

3.5 Plymouth Valiant ad, 1959 (courtesy Chrysler Group LLC)   108

3.6 Plymouth Valiant ad, 1959 (courtesy Chrysler Group LLC)   108

3.7 Plymouth Valiant ad, 1959 (courtesy Chrysler Group LLC)   109

3.8 Honda Jazz (courtesy Honda UK)   112

4.1 Cola Wars (Nenov Brothers Images/Shutterstock.com)   145

5.1 Under the Granville Street Bridge   178

5.2 Dave Brubeck, *Jazz Impressions of Eurasia* (Columbia, 1959;
     Sony BMG, 2008)   183

5.3 Groove and Graffiti, TD Toronto Jazz Festival (2010)   197

5.4 TD FEF booth in Gastown district, Vancouver (2010)   199

5.5 TD *Place Confort* in Montreal (2010)   203

5.6 TD Stage in Gastown   206

5.7 Vancouver Sun Stage in Gastown   207

SERIES FOREWORD: TRANSNATIONAL STUDIES IN JAZZ

Since the 1990s the study of jazz has changed dramatically, as the field continues to open up to a variety of disciplinary perspectives and critical models. Today, as the music's meaning undergoes profound changes, there is a pressing need to situate jazz within an international research context and to develop theories and methods of investigation which open up new ways of understanding its cultural significance and its place within different historical and social settings.

The *Transnational Studies in Jazz* series presents the best research from this important and exciting area of scholarship, and features interdisciplinary and international perspectives on the relationships between jazz, society, politics, and culture. The series provides authors with a platform for rethinking the methodologies and concepts used to analyze jazz, and will seek to work across disciplinary boundaries, finding different ways of examining the practices, values, and meanings of the music. The series explores the complex cultural and musical exchanges that have shaped the global development and reception of jazz. Contributors will focus on studies of the music, which find different ways of telling the story of jazz, with or without reference to the United States, and will investigate jazz as a medium for negotiating global identities.

PREFACE

Jazz has historically been a difficult genre of music to pin down. While insiders debate musical specifics—eighth note syncopation, ride cymbal patterns, instrumentation, and the centrality of improvisation, for instance—the discussions in popular culture at large are far more diffuse. So-called "jazz" festivals commonly include big-ticket artists such as Sting, Bruce Springsteen, and De La Soul. In everyday speech, the word "jazz" can function as a noun or a verb: it can be something you listen to, of course, but it can also be something that you do (as in "get jazzed," or "jazz it up"), or indeed, a generic substitute for the word "stuff" ("all that jazz"). It gets even messier when we think about the way that jazz gets deployed in advertising and branding. Recent television spots have used jazz soundtracks or iconography to advertise UK-based "Drench" spring water (featuring a band of musical hamsters) and North American iShares financial investment services. As a brand name, "jazz" has referred to everything from a Pepsi diet soft drink, to an in-ear thermometer, to instant microwavable potatoes. Clearly, once you move outside the community of jazz musicians, critics, and aficionados, the definition of "jazz" doesn't rest on the ride cymbal. The popular usages of jazz are so varied and so disparate that it is difficult to determine if "jazz" means anything at all.

In *Jazz Sells: Music, Marketing, and Meaning* I seek to make sense of that collection of discourses about jazz in order to piece together what it might mean in 21st century popular culture. I do so by talking to some of the central authors of popular culture—the advertisers and marketers behind some of the most noteworthy English-language jazz advertisements and brands that have appeared over the last two decades, particularly in the United States, Canada, Australia, and the UK. I situate their remarks—together with my own readings of the various advertisements, marketing activities, and brands that they have produced—in the overlapping 20th and 21st century discourses around jazz, America, capitalism, and consumer culture. As the book unfolds, it becomes clear that, as strangely disconnected as Pepsi Jazz and Potato Jazz may seem from discussions about syncopation and improvisation, even the most apparently incomprehensible jazz brands and advertisements in fact emerge from the *longue durée* of jazz history. Indeed, jazz's efficacy as a branding and advertising theme is specifically (if not always explicitly) predicated upon key historical moments and discursive formations. In other words, jazz history is the reason that jazz sells.

Of course, the crucial relationship between jazz history and current jazz-based advertising and marketing also represents something of a paradox. How is it possible that a musical practice that has commonly (if not always accurately) been linked to countercultural and anti-capitalist movements—indeed, that has itself been discursively constructed as extra- or anti-commercial to a considerable extent—can be so readily put to use in service of both everyday commerce and the broader ideology of capitalism? With that in mind, it is worth noting that *Jazz Sells* is not a thoroughgoing history of uses of jazz in advertising, nor does it pretend to comprehensively survey every iteration of jazz advertising and branding around the world, although it is international in scope. Rather, the core project of the book is to examine the paradox of jazz advertising in order to develop a better understanding of both the position of jazz in popular culture, and the affective dimensions of the ideologies that undergird consumer capitalism.

A Note on the Website

The website, www.jazzsells.com, an independent website hosted by the author, is intended to serve as a valuable supplement to your reading. The site includes video and audio examples of many of the ads discussed in the book, links to other useful resources, discussion forums that will allow you to interact with me and with other readers, and a blog in which I (along with occasional guest authors) offer further commentary related to the central themes and questions raised in this book. My hope is that *Jazz Sells* will spark an ongoing conversation, and that the website will provide a place for us to develop that conversation together. I'll look forward to hearing from you!

Mark Laver, August 2014

ACKNOWLEDGMENTS

The fact that mine is the only name to appear on the cover pages of this book is misleading; from the start, this project has been a truly collaborative effort, and I am deeply indebted to more people than I can possibly name here.

I would first like to thank my mentors from my career as a graduate student and postdoctoral fellow: James Kippen, Ken McLeod, Josh Pilzer, and Jeff Packman from the University of Toronto, Timothy Taylor at UCLA, and Ajay Heble and Daniel Fischlin from the University of Guelph. I have depended heavily on the encouragement and criticism of Ken, Josh, Jeff, Tim, and Daniel throughout the process of researching and writing this project. Their capacity to offer new insights, and to show me new ways of listening to and thinking about music has been seemingly limitless. Ajay Heble has become one of the most influential people in my life during the last three years, two spent as a postdoctoral research fellow with the Improvisation, Community, and Social Practice research initiative in Guelph, Ontario. As an artist, a researcher, a writer, and an educator, Ajay is one of the people whom I most wish to emulate in my career. James Kippen, meanwhile, has been my mentor and friend since I started my undergraduate degree in jazz performance at the Faculty of Music in Toronto in 2001. He taught me what ethnomusicology is and showed me how to do it. Throughout my university studies and my academic career, he has never let me forget why it is so important to study music and learn from the people who make and use it.

I would like to thank my many colleagues who have offered crucial feedback and moral support over the years as this project has come together: Kara Attrep, Stephanie Conn, Andy Hillhouse, Keith Johnston, Pete Johnston, Carolyn Ramzy, Colleen Renihan, Nate Renner, Jeremy Strachan, Rob Wallace, Chris Wilson, and Alexa Woloshyn have been inspiring colleagues, and even better friends.

As I became increasingly immersed in my research over the past number of years, I more or less had to stop practicing the saxophone. Nevertheless, despite my deteriorating technique, some of my favorite musicians (and people) in the world kept calling me for gigs, and kept answering the phone on those rare occasions when I called. I especially want to thank Ali Berkok, Jay Burr, Alex Coleman, Tania Gill, Chris Hunt, Pete Johnston, Jason Logue, Dave MacDougall, Alex Samaras, Tim Shia, Mike Smith, Vince Spilchuk, and Carrie Wiebe. There are many more—too many to mention, but you know who you are. Thank you for always reminding me that making music is just as important as thinking about it.

Jazz Sells came together in part through a somewhat miraculous combination of serendipity and generosity. Without my friend Rob Carli, I never would have been able to connect with David Fleury, who in turn introduced me to my key research collaborators for my research on the Chrysler campaign: Pearl Davies, Steve Denvir, Rob Quartly, and Mike Smith. Without Josh Grossman—a very old and very dear friend and musical colleague who is also the Artistic Director of the Toronto Jazz Festival—I never would have been able to speak with my collaborators from the Toronto Jazz Festival and the TD Bank: Alan Convery, Michele Martin, D'Arcy McDonald, Aileen Le Breton, and Pat Taylor. Similarly, Pete Johnston introduced me to his friends at the Halifax Jazz Festival: Chris Elson, Adam Fine, and Dustin LindenSmith. Finally, my Pepsi Jazz research was the result of a cold call to OMD Communications Director Gail Stein. Through Gail's expansive network, I was able to get in touch with current and former DDB employees Howard Finkelstein, Kathryn Harvey, Elizabeth Hodge, Pepsi brand manager Lauren Scott, and Expansion Team composers Alex Moulton and Genji Siraisi. Without the kindness (and guest bedrooms) of beloved friends Rob Mosher and Daniel Pencer, I would have had a much more difficult time completing critical research in New York and Montreal. I am extremely grateful to all of these individuals—along with Todd Barkan, Sue Mingus, Phil Nimmons, Terry Promane, Paul Read, Kate Saxton, Scott Thornley, and Hugh Wakeham—for their insights and their generosity.

In August of 2010, I spent a fruitful week at the John W. Hartman Center for Sales, Advertising & Marketing History at Duke University. I would like to thank the excellent staff at the Hartman Center for all of their assistance during my visit, and for their continued support in the years that followed.

To my editors at Routledge—Constance Ditzel, Nick Sorensen, and Tony Whyton—thank you for your tremendous guidance and support, and for recognizing when I needed a little bit of friendly-but-firm pressure to keep the project on the rails.

To my extended family—the Coxes/Robertses, the Parsons, the Quongs/Chases, and the Wainwrights—thank you so much. To my in-laws—Fred, Mary, Ken, Robin, Jane, Sean, Kyle, and Clare—naturally, I knew almost right away that marrying my wife would be a good idea, but I didn't immediately realize that it would mean that I would also get to be part of such a remarkable (and remarkably hilarious) family. Thank you for welcoming me into your lives, and for your support.

To my immediate family—Tom, Margaret, John, and Serena—this book is as much yours as it is mine. You have taught me everything, made me everything, and supported me in everything. I could never express the depths of my love and my gratitude.

To Finnegan: thanks for taking me on all those walks. It's a little weird when you want to curl up behind me on the chair, but I guess it's ok.

To Nora: you make me want to make the world better. I hope that this book will go some small distance towards making that happen.

Finally, to my wife Erin: I'm not totally sure why you have stayed with me while I have disappeared to different cities and countries for weeks on end, into the office for months at a stretch, or into my own brain off and on for the better part of ten years, but I promise to spend the rest of my life trying to make it worth your while, and trying to show you that you are always on my mind. This work—like everything I ever have done and ever will do—is for you.

This research was funded by a Joseph-Armand Bombardier Canada Graduate Scholarships Program Doctoral Scholarship, administered by the Social Sciences and Humanities Research Council of Canada.

1

INTRODUCTION

Most jazz isn't really about jazz, at least not in terms of how it is actually consumed.
Krin Gabbard, "Jammin' at the Margins: Jazz and
the American Cinema" (Gabbard, 1996)

This book may never have been written if I hadn't gone grocery shopping at just the right time. On a brisk autumn night, sometime in November of 2006, I left my apartment on Bathurst Street in Toronto to buy a carton of 1 percent milk from Steven's grocery store. To get to the dairy section at the back of the store, I always walked through the well stocked junk food aisle (a much more interesting route than the adjacent condensed soup aisle). While I rarely ever bought anything, I would always let my eyes rove idly over the gleaming chocolate bar wrappers and potato chip bags on the one side, pop bottles on the other, reminiscing about my misspent, Coca-Cola and Dorito-fueled youth; simpler times when I worried less about grown-up concerns such as milk fat percentage. On this particular evening, my eye was drawn to an unusually shiny bottle in the pop fridge. The caramel-colored foil wrapper screamed "Jazz" in large, italicized letters, with the familiar red, white, and blue Pepsi logo underneath.

As a jazz saxophonist, I was intrigued, and more than a little bemused. I grabbed two bottles, one for myself and one for my roommate—a jazz bassist with a similar sense of humor—and went back home, having forgotten all about the milk. Neither of us was able to get through more than a few sips of our bottles, repulsed by the overwhelmingly sweet, "Caramel Cream" flavor. Despite barely making it through the bottlenecks, the drink provided us with many days' worth of fodder for conversation. How could the music to which we had dedicated so much of our lives be distilled into a soft drink? What on earth did diet cola have to do with jazz? And, above all, why did it taste so bad?

After my Pepsi Jazz encounter, I started noticing jazz-based advertising and branding everywhere: in Canada, I found a "Jazz" hair salon in Toronto; a "Jazz" printing and photocopying shop in Vancouver; and of course Air Canada Jazz, an airline specializing in regional travel. My favorite product (conceptually at least; at the time of writing, I haven't yet worked up the nerve to taste it) is "Potato Jazz," an instant, microwavable potato product by Edmonton, Alberta-based "The Little Potato Company."[1]

But the phenomenon is not uniquely Canadian. In Greece, I found a brand of women's shoes called "Jazz." From New Zealand, I heard about a variety of apple called "Jazz." International computer giant IBM has developed a software integration system called "Jazz." I searched on YouTube (still a relative novelty in 2007) and found a variety of advertisements for jazz products, including a cologne by French fashion house Yves St. Laurent called "Live Jazz," as well as the television spot for "Diet Pepsi Jazz." I soon discovered that I wasn't alone in my interest in the bizarre panoply of things called "Jazz." Through a friend, I found a Tumblr page operated by BBC radio producer Russell Finch called "things called jazz that are not jazz."[2]

Finch's list included several products that I had heard of, in addition to a number of others with an exceedingly tenuous connection to jazz music: the Keeler "Jazz" in-ear diagnostic thermometer, a "Jazz" blood glucose monitoring system (featuring Bluetooth wireless capability), an aerosol spray pump called "Jazz," a keypad auto-lock by American lockmaker Schlage called "Jazz," and a 90-meter "Jazz" "super yacht" by German shipbuilder Bluhm+Voss. As I found more and more of these products and thought about them further, my attitude gradually changed from bemusement to curiosity, and my questions became more nuanced: rather than incredulously asking, "what on earth do cola, potatoes, and super-yachts have to do with jazz?", I began to wonder, "what is it about jazz that has made it appealing to advertisers and marketers as an advertising and branding tool in these contexts, and for these products?"

Jazz Sells works towards answering that question. Of course, given the extraordinary diversity of "jazz" products, there is no single answer. If jazz can simultaneously be a seasoned potato, a diet cola, an in-ear thermometer, and a super yacht, if it can cost anywhere from US$1 to £300 million, its core meaning is exceptionally elusive, if it has any singular core meaning at all. Indeed, if we expand our scope to consider brands that are connected to jazz in other ways—brands that use jazz soundtracks in advertising, or brands linked to jazz via festival, concert, or artist sponsorships—the waters become incredibly muddy. The astonishing diversity of brands and commodities that have been articulated to jazz speaks both to its remarkable semiotic fluidity as a cultural touchstone, and to the creativity of the various marketers and advertisers who have imagined such a bewildering array of things that jazz could potentially *mean*, tenuous though many of those articulations may be.

Every branding and advertising context uses jazz in a slightly different way, working to draw out a different set of musical or (more often) sociocultural themes from the music to best suit the product. Hence, rather than seeking to draw out a single, overarching theme—working to expose the singular essence of jazz's utility as an advertising tool, and concomitantly, its cultural significance—each chapter in this book moves principally along three related trajectories, linked by a central concept.

In each chapter, I elucidate the key themes that are at play in a given example of an articulation of jazz and commodities through advertising or branding. Second, I situate these themes historically, examining how jazz advertising is predicated on jazz discourses that have emerged from a variety of sectors (chiefly musicians, critics and, somewhat tautologically, advertisers and marketers themselves), over the span of the 20th and 21st centuries. Third, I consider the ways in which jazz and advertising have interacted not only to promote individual commodities, but to contribute to the continued intellectual and emotional entrenchment of the meta-concept of consumption in global capitalism. Undergirding these three trajectories, therefore, is the deeply vexed—and seldom discussed—issue of jazz's circulation in a capitalist society and the culture of consumption. While each chapter retains its own particular focus and comes to its own conclusions, these respective conclusions act to illuminate this central issue from different perspectives.

Mass Production, Mass Mediation, and the Emergence of the Consumer-Citizen

Before we narrow our focus to jazz, it is worth using the introductory space of this first chapter to situate our discussion in a broader discourse, to step back and consider the wider relationship between music, advertising, consumption, and capitalism. The term capitalism refers in essence to the investment of money (or capital) for the express purpose of making a profit (Fulcher 2004: 2). Historians generally agree that the practice of capitalism has existed for thousands of years, emerging alongside the advent of mercantilism in the earliest Mesopotamian city-states. As a pervasive social and economic system, however, capitalism did not take firm hold in Europe and North America until the industrial revolution in the 18th and 19th centuries. As the industrialized manufacturing process became increasingly streamlined, the overhead costs associated with manufacturing steadily decreased, and the industrial sector became increasingly profitable for capital investors. Industries steadily grew with investment, demanding an ever-larger labor force, until ultimately manufacturing jobs gradually eclipsed agrarian work as the dominant mode of labor for most individuals.

Capitalism in North America evolved dramatically with the advent of Taylorist management strategy and Fordist mass production in the early 20th century. Frederick Taylor's *The Principles of Scientific Management*, published in 1911, addressed one of the emergent concerns of the new industrial order: inefficient labor. While efficiently operated factories dramatically reduced manufacturing costs, the industrial technologies were expensive to operate, and inefficient labor became a frustrating and costly problem for capitalist factory owners. Among other things, Taylor called for more carefully regulated working days, and for the labor process to be divided into numerous small, easily repeatable tasks so as to minimize the time and skill required of each individual worker. Taylor's management advice was intended both to maximize efficiency during the working day, and to minimize the overnight "shut-down time," during which machines sat idle and unprofitable. Ford's assembly lines, which debuted in Detroit a mere two years after Taylor's book, were the first factories to actualize Taylor's ideas to the utmost. With Taylorist management wedded to an efficient, mechanized system of assembly, the Ford Motor Company was able to produce an unparalleled number of units of their first car, the Model T, at a cost that made the automobile affordable to an unprecedented percentage of the American populace (Lee 1993: 75).

The dramatic increase in the scale of production during the late 19th and early 20th centuries demanded a reciprocal increase in the scale of consumption so as to absorb the sudden proliferation of products on the market. In order to facilitate expanding consumption, manufacturers—once again following Henry Ford's lead—began to increase the wages for their laborers so that a factory employee would theoretically be able to purchase the product that he (or less often she) had helped to make. Ceaseless consumption thus became a crucial element of the capitalist system, a vitally important means of sustaining the economics of mass production. Higher wages alone were insufficient motivation, however, to persuade laborers to part with their earnings as readily and liberally as mass production required. Indeed, in his 1905 treatise, *The Protestant Ethic and the Spirit of Capitalism* (reprinted by Routledge, 2011), Max Weber recognized that human beings need compelling moral imperatives and cultural narratives—not merely economic ones—in order to be persuaded to buy into capitalist ideology.

This "spirit of capitalism," as Weber termed it, was largely provided by advertisers. Advertising was key in prompting the necessary switch from an agrarian ethic of ascetic thrift and self-sacrifice—an ethic that had predominated both in the North American and Western European working and middle classes, and among the myriad cultural and ethnic groups that emigrated to those regions through the 19th and 20th centuries—to an industrial one of self-fulfillment and instant gratification through ceaseless consumption. Advertisers were the story-tellers of modern capitalism, providing the all-important narrative underpinning to an otherwise abstract economic system. Advertising brought capitalism into the home by telling stories where the consumer was always the protagonist, and where consumption was the invariable solution to every social conundrum. These stories promoted consumption as a key component of early 20th century expressive culture.

Advertisers recognized their vital importance to promoting the new ideology of consumption early on. In the terminology of Louis Althusser's 1969 essay, "Ideology and Ideological State Apparatuses (Notes Towards and Investigation)," advertising acted to "interpellate" subjects within the ideology of consumption, an ideology that is central to "reproducing the conditions of [capitalist] production." In other words, advertisements "reminded" audiences that they were consumers, as if this were not a new social category that had developed fairly rapidly to sustain mass production (Althusser 1971: 127). The implication was that audiences had "always already" known that they were consumers but had either forgotten or somehow not noticed. In Althusser's view, advertising is one of many "Ideological State Apparatuses" (or ISAs) that perform a similar function in capitalism, including religion, the law, the polity, trade unions, the family, culture (including music, art, etc.), and education (Althusser 1971: 143). Collectively, these ISAs restructure not only the mechanical infrastructure of production, but also the epistemology—the patterns of thought and knowledge—of individuals. All of these ISAs work together to inculcate capitalist ideology in individuals, to the extent that our thoughts, our imaginations, even the terms in which we constitute and identify ourselves as subjects, are conditioned by capitalism and consumption. As Althusser explains,

> [T]he reproduction of labor power requires not only a reproduction of its skills, but also, at the same time, a reproduction of its submission to the rules of the established order, i.e. a reproduction of submission to the ruling ideology for the workers, and a reproduction of the ability to manipulate the ruling ideology correctly for the agents of exploitation and repression, so that they, too, will provide for the domination of the ruling class "in words."
> (Althusser 1971: 132–33)

One of the primary consequences of the newly streamlined processes of mass production was a glut of virtually identical products—soap, medicinal tonics, breakfast cereals—sold under different brand names. Producers quickly realized that they could no longer distinguish their product from the pack by simply enumerating its merits. Instead, they began to experiment with psychological approaches, playing to the fears and anxieties that they perceived in the marketplace. These strategies occurred primarily along two somewhat contradictory trajectories: the assertion of individual personality and of community belonging. North American culture was increasingly characterized by sameness: nearly every American and Canadian (especially in urban locations) now had access to the same food products, the same fashions, the same magazines, the same radio programming. Even within those various categories, there was considerable redundancy, as different manufacturers produced a multiplicity of virtually identical commodities under different brand names. Advertisers therefore needed to distinguish their products by shifting the challenge of and the anxiety about homogeneity to consumers.

Throughout the early part of the 20th century, advertisements began to imply that individual distinction could be achieved by consuming certain brands over their cognates within the same commodity category. As Timothy Taylor writes, "Cultivating one's personality was a way to stand out from the crowd, the mass, and this could be accomplished through consumption, purchasing goods that could be used to define oneself" (Taylor 2003: 10). Consequently, much of the contemporary advertising discourse focused on the "personality" of products. Taylor points to William H. Ensign's comments in 1928:

> National Advertisers find that radio . . . carries their names or the names of their products into millions of homes in a way which is not only conducive to good will building—but which stamps those names with a personality that makes them mean more than just something to be bought.
>
> (Quoted in Taylor 2003: 11)

Consumers could thus acquire a "magnetic personality" (Taylor 2003: 10) through the consumption of goods. In this way, as Althusser suggests, consumers began to define themselves—to constitute their subjectivities and personal aspirations—according to capitalist consumptive ideology, particularly vis-à-vis the nascent process of *brand identification*.

This kind of personality-driven strategy was first used in print advertising, particularly by soap manufacturers such as Pears and Pond's. From the 1880s through the 1930s, Pears became known for purchasing famous contemporary British high artworks to use in their print ads for their soap and other beauty products targeted at women (McClintock 1997: 281). Pond's, meanwhile, ran a long series of print ads using images of well known, American, upper class "society women" in advertisements for their Cold Cream facial moisturizer.

From 1924 until the early 1950s, prominent wealthy socialites and philanthropists such as Cordelia Biddle Robertson, Gloria Vanderbilt, and Anne Bairstow Cumming Bell Manners, the Duchess of Rutland featured in Pond's advertisements. Pond's advertising agency of record, the J. Walter Thompson Company, recognized that the endorsement of such socialites would enable the company to connect their product with the reputations, images, and personalities of these women, all of whom were regularly profiled in newspaper social columns as fashion and style tastemakers ("The Power of Refined Beauty"). Both Pears and Pond's, therefore, sought to lend their products a degree of uniqueness within a market flooded with virtually identical competitors by connecting their products with people and objects that projected an aura of distinction.

This kind of distinct brand identity, then, is contingent upon both the distinction of the people or objects with whom the brand is associated and, concomitantly, on the recognition of their distinction by the public at large. In this way, brand identity is founded upon what Robert J. Foster calls the "economy of qualities" (Foster 2007: 713). In Foster's view, brand identity is built through a combination of the value attributed to a brand by both the producer and the consumer. Without the images of the artists and the socialites, and without the recognition and valorization of those images by the communities of women that constituted the soap and beauty product market, neither soap manufacturer could have developed their brand distinction.

One of the most successful early personifications of a product in the medium of radio occurred with the Clicquot Club Eskimos, a musical radio program sponsored by Clicquot Club Ginger Ale that began in 1923, featuring a "banjo orchestra" led by banjo player Harry Reser (Taylor 2003: 8). According to a contemporary publication released by broadcaster NBC, "it was obvious that ginger, pep, sparkle and snap were qualities that form the very essence of the product [and so] manifestly peppy musical numbers of lively tempo were in order. The banjo, an instrument of brightness and animation, was deemed most suitable in typifying the snap of Clicquot Club personality" (quoted in Smulyan 1994: 106).

FIGURE 1.1   Clicquot Club Ginger Ale bottle, ca. 1914

Evidently, the Clicquot Club process of brand-personality development differed from the Pears/Pond's model. Unlike Pears and Pond's, Clicquot Club was not invested in the idea of prestige; on the contrary, the ginger ale brand was represented as being fun and universally accessible. Harry Reser's group featured several banjo players, a barking husky dog, and regularly appeared in "Eskimo" parkas and mukluks—in other words, a novelty group that was both recognizable and fun, while at the same time visually and sonically (by way of the barking husky) associated with Clicquot's "Eskimo" mascot (Smulyan 1994: 107). The radio show therefore helped listeners build a relationship with a Clicquot brand, as if it were a friend with a "peppy, sparkly, snappy, and animated" personality—the kind of friend with whom you might want to associate if you believed yourself to have those same qualities, or perhaps aspired to have them.

The inverse of personality advertising could be seen in ads that played to consumers' fears of standing out for the wrong reasons. Paradoxically, the consumer's impulse to be an "individual" and to cultivate a personality that would "stand out from the crowd" was contingent upon the judgment of her/his peers (Rubin 1992: 23). Hence, social anxiety was the counterpart to the desire for personal magnetism and distinction. This tension was in particular evidence in print ads targeted at women in nationally-circulated magazines such as *Vogue, Vanity Fair, McCall's*, and *Ladies' Home Journal*—this last magazine being the most widely-circulated periodical in the United States during the first half of the 20th century.[3]

One such ad for Woodbury's face powder from 1920 featured threatening ad copy: "Under Searching Eyes—Do You Ever Wince Inwardly? You want to shrink into the background. . . . You lose your confidence, your gaiety. Your very personality is dimmed just when you are most anxious to appear at your best" (Scanlon 1995: 208). A similar ad from 1922 declares: "Stranger's eyes, keen and critical. Can you meet them proudly—confidently—without fear?" These ads make it clear that, just as purchasing goods could endow the purchaser with "pep" and "sparkle," fear, anxiety, and self-consciousness could also all be assuaged through consumption.

Advertisers also promoted the idea that one could purchase membership in a community. This idea—which is an intriguing contradiction of the "personal magnetism" notion—was apparent in advertisements directed towards a universalized, "average" consumer. Advertisements in the *Ladies' Home Journal*, for instance, were often directed towards the "average woman" or the "American woman." The *Journal* thus invited women to join a national imagined community of consumption; every woman in the English-speaking world who wished to signify her membership (and who was able to subscribe to the magazine) could do so simply by purchasing a certain brand of soap, or canned vegetables, or household cleaner.

Membership in a particular consumption community, of course, is not about the shared act of consumption itself, on the contrary, it inevitably subtends something else: shared prestige, sophistication, distinction, or a modern outlook, for instance. *Journal* advertisements for Woodbury's face powder, for example, claimed that the product was preferred by "Philadelphia debutantes," at "the Ritz Carlton," at "the Lake Placid Club," and by "Three Hundred and Fifty-Two Stars at Hollywood" (Scanlon 1995: 211). Women who used Woodbury's therefore not only had skin that was "noticeably lovely" (Scanlon 1995: 208); they were also in an elite social group. In a contradictory, but nevertheless powerful way, women could be individually distinct, while at the same time part of an elite community that shared the same individual distinction.

Of course, community construction must necessarily exclude far more people than it includes. Jennifer Scanlon notes that the "average American woman" who was the target of *Ladies' Home Journal* and its advertisements was white, American-born, and middle-class (Scanlon 1995: 2). With rare exceptions non-white faces and nonwhite issues virtually never appeared anywhere in the *Journal*'s pages. On those occasions where they did appear, it was almost invariably to exclude them from the community, to mark them as different or "other." Scanlon cites only one advertisement from the 1922 Woodbury's campaign that featured an African American person; that person, however, was a servant waiting on the Euro-American "Debutantes of the South" who preferred to use Woodbury's face powder.

Because these kinds of advertisements were mass-mediated and targeted a mass audience, the sheer number of people both included within and excluded from the imagined communities of consumption was vast. The men and women who were left out, therefore, were not merely excluded from the elite groups who used the same face powder, listened to the same gramophone records, or drove the same automobile. As the mass media defined both the character and the limits of the mass audience through the lens of advertising, it also mapped the borders of the mainstream—a version of America (and of much of the English-speaking world more generally) that elided those who were nonwhite and nonmiddle class. At the same time, it offered those marginalized groups potential *entrée* into the mainstream by way of consumption. If mainstream communities of consumption were organized around the spectacularized commodity predilections of the torchbearers and tastemakers of the mass-mediated mainstream—"Hollywood actors," "Philadelphia debutantes," Gloria Vanderbilt, or Anne Bairstow Cumming Bell Manners—membership in these communities was ostensibly open to anyone who could afford to consume according to the preferred, refined habits. Hence, what the mainstream, whitewashed spectacle took away from disenfranchised groups with one hand, the free market—that supposed democratic leveler—seemed to offer with the other.

In this way, consumption has become a crucial component of self-expression, but also broader democratic freedom, and a defining element of social citizenship in capitalist democracies. In talking about citizenship in capitalist democracy, political scientists often distinguish between social and political citizenship. Whereas political citizenship is defined according to the rights granted citizens by the constitution and is upheld by government institutions, social citizenship is premised on "equal respect" at the sociocultural level. According to T.H. Marshall's 1949 essay, "Citizenship and Social Class," social citizenship goes beyond the government-mandated guarantee of economic security to include the right to "share in the full social heritage and to live the life of a civilized being according to the standards prevailing in the society" (quoted in Park 2005: 4).

Social citizenship is predicated on recognition: in order to be treated as an equal, in order to assume "full social heritage," one must be recognized as an equal. As many scholars have suggested, while political citizenship in 21st-century North America and Western Europe is somewhat more inclusive than it has been in the past, the naturalized constituency of social citizenship remains limited to Euro-American, middle class, heterosexual men. For the hundreds of millions of "political" citizens who fall outside of this extremely narrow bracket of naturalized social citizenship, it is necessary to actively demonstrate that they belong. Tautologically, this demonstration of belonging (ideally) leads to recognition of social citizenship, and finally entry into the category.

Because it is predicated purely on recognition, conspicuous consumption has become one of the primary means through which "nonnatural" (*i.e.*, nonEuro-American, nonmale, non*bourgeois*) constituents have achieved social citizenship. In this context, conspicuous consumption constitutes a performance of social citizenship that can be recognized by stakeholders within the field of social citizens. In this way, like Pierre Bourdieu's concept of cultural capital, social citizenship is "founded on a dialectic of knowledge [or in this case, accumulated commodities] . . . and recognition" (Bourdieu 1993: 7). Conspicuous consumption therefore has a potential political valence. With this in mind, advertising, too, can be politically powerful: if consumption can be a politicized act of self-expression, as the gatekeepers to consumptive behavior, advertisers are empowered to extend social citizenship by targeting communities that fall outside of the "naturalized" limits of social citizenship. Advertising can potentially mark an official recognition of the citizenship capital of consumers, and a conduit into the heart of the field of social citizenship in a capitalist regime: mass-mediated advertising.

On the other hand, this kind of consecration is predicated on what Lisa Sun-Hee Park calls a "'politics of worthiness' that views only those people who can prove their marketability and social worth as entitled to visibility, rights or services from society" (Park 2005: 134). In other words, if social citizenship—and, contiguously, appeal to marketers—is premised on capital accumulation, then only a small number of individuals qualify as "worthy." In theory, the "worthy" individuals are meant to act as model citizens, providing exemplars for the rest, and paving the way for economic success, cultural uplift, and full social citizenship. In other words, the concept is founded on the adage, "a rising tide floats all boats." In practice, however, the process is not nearly so tidy: a lot of boats will spring leaks along the way, and the vast majority of people will have been swimming from the outset.

Consumptive citizenship as a means of universal cultural uplift is fundamentally paradoxical in two further ways. First, because capitalism is predicated on the obsolescence of commodities, consumption is a tenuous way to achieve social citizenship. When fashion is the basis of a societal position, the terms for citizenship change with every season. Hence, citizenship achieved through consumption cannot be bought and paid for only once; it has to be renewed annually, if not seasonally. If consumers were suddenly satisfied with the commodities they had acquired, they would stop (or at least, severely curtail) their consumption. Without ceaseless mass consumption, there could be no ceaseless mass production—the very machinery of the capitalist system. As Adorno and Horkheimer have argued, in spite of the promise of capitalism to enable human satisfaction (together with universal social citizenship) through consumption, consumer *dissatisfaction* is therefore a critical structural element of the reproduction of the conditions of capitalist production. The fulfillment of capitalism's promise would therefore simultaneously mark capitalism's demise.

Second, it is an ontological impossibility within a capitalist system for everyone to be equally wealthy. While the moral narrative of capitalism and consumption—part of Weber's "spirit of capitalism"—is premised on the eventual possibility of limitless resources that can be accessed and shared based on a combination of merit and philanthropy, the immediate reality of global capitalist economics is that resources are structurally limited. Therefore, one person can only be rich if another person is poor. In this way, individual subjectivity under capitalism is founded to a significant degree on a kind of Hegelian dialectic: much as the master and the slave cannot fathom themselves as subjects without the other, so too is the subjectivity of a rich person constituted by seeing her or his own reflection in a hard-scrabble poor other. Hence, previously socially maligned and marginalized individuals who have achieved relative social citizenship by way of capital accumulation and conspicuous consumption can find themselves in a precarious position on what Paul Gilroy calls the "wobbly ladder" of citizenship (Gilroy 2010: 25). While they may feel impelled to participate in the general project of cultural uplift, they may also look down the ladder and see their desperate, former selves. Seeing the specter of their past in the other, they may be just as inclined to strategize to stay on their own rung—to "distinguish their own place" (de Certeau 1984: 25)—as they are to help out the others on the rungs below.

Hence, while capital accumulation and conspicuous consumption are not politically and ethically bankrupt, their usefulness as political tactics directed towards the uplift of an entire network of communities is surely deeply conflicted, precisely because both are primarily individualistic. While Gilroy's critique of conspicuous consumption is directed primarily at automobile ownership, it is applicable to the consumption of just about any commodity:

> The outcome [of politicized consumerism] represents a diminution of citizenship, as it is associated with a privatisation that confiscates the possibility

of collective experience, synchronised suffering, and acting in concert. In these circumstances, the [commodity] becomes the instrument of segregation and privatization, not an aid to their overcoming.

(Gilroy 2010: 22)

In Gilroy's estimation, consumption is a primarily private, individual act. Despite the potential sociability of consumptive acts—from shopping to dining out—buying a car (or a soft drink) by oneself for oneself does not constitute a community-minded action. If anything, consumption represents social scrabbling: performative position-taking on a "wobbly" sociocultural ladder.

In sum, consumption is the economic engine of global capitalism. Because consumption is primarily a localized, individual behavior, however, capitalism itself hinges on a critical mass of individuals choosing to embrace the social role of "consumer." Advertisers have historically played a critical role in this process, persuading individuals to take on this role—and, more broadly, to buy into capitalist ideology—by helping to construct mass-mediated cultural narratives wherein the consumer is the hero or heroine, and the act of consumption is simultaneously the quest and the happy ending. These narratives have implicated virtually every public and private element of social and cultural life, from intimate anxieties about one's own body, to public discourses about community and citizenship. Throughout the century-long history of mass-mediated advertising, advertisers have put numerous cultural resources to the task of "interpellating" consumers. Of these various resources, music has been one of the most important and most effective.

Music in Advertising: An Overview

Music is such an important resource for advertisers precisely because it is so important to each and every one of us. It is almost axiomatic to say that music is a crucial element of the social construction of identities and communities. Our musical tastes reveal a great deal about our social position and our cultural orientation. Conversely, we use music as a way to broadcast our identities to the world at large: through the band t-shirts that we wear, the music venues that we frequent, or the sounds that we purposefully allow to escape our earbuds or our automobiles, we use music to assert our individuality. At the same time as we represent ourselves to the world, we use music to carve out a niche in that world that we might share with others, seeking out like-minded individuals who subscribe to similar socialized identity categories in order to build communities of musical and cultural affinity. We use music to give form and meaning to our world, and to make ourselves comprehensible to the other subjects with whom we share it. As a communicative phenomenon that targets the most fundamental aspects of our individual and communal identities—our most intimate anxieties and desires—advertising naturally relies heavily on music to address us in a way that we will find to be meaningful. While this may seem obvious, it is worthwhile considering exactly how and why music has become so critical, both in terms of its specific use in advertising and its more general use in the construction and perpetuation of consumer culture.

In the first place, it is important to recognize that music has not been a recent addition to advertising; indeed, for much of the history of commercial exchange, long before the development of modern psychoanalytic marketing strategy, advertising *was* music. In her overview of the history of musical advertising in the *New Grove Online*, Robynn J. Stillwell suggests that vendors of all stripes have been using music as part of their street cries since at least the 13th century, and probably much, much earlier (Stillwell). During the 19th century, a sort of proto-jingle began to emerge in European and North American cities: companies such as the English Beecham's Pills published sheet music collections of "popular songs, folksongs, numbers from operettas and other light classical selections, and excerpts from Handel and Mendelssohn oratorios, all interspersed with advertising copy and music specifically intended to promote [their] products" (Stillwell). In American frontier towns, traveling salesmen organized medicine shows—essentially touring minstrel shows designed to draw a crowd in order eventually to make a marketing pitch (Stillwell).

While the relationship between music and advertising would change dramatically with the development of mass communication (first with the radio in the early part of the 20th century, and later with television), 19th century medicine shows served as models for advertising in the new media, especially in the United States where radio and (later) television was financed by the sale of air time to advertisers.[4]

Like the medicine show, the purpose of corporate-funded radio and television programming was essentially to draw an audience in order to sell them a product, or to lead them to develop an affinity for a particular brand. Unlike the medicine shows, however, these programs did not culminate with a sales pitch, especially in the early days of radio and television. Advertising was most often "indirect:" rather than an explicit marketing messages, audiences might hear a couple of oblique references to the brand or product name—perhaps in the title of the program, or in the name of a featured artist, such as B.A. Rolfe and his Lucky Strike Orchestra, featured on NBC's "Lucky Strike Radio Hour" in the 1920s. P.H. Pumphrey, the manager of the radio department of advertising agency Fuller, Smith & Ross, Inc. during the 1920s, who suggested that this strategy of indirection was designed to minimize the intrusiveness of the message stated:

> When the listener hears that "The Lucky Strike Dance Orchestra now plays Baby's Birthday Party," or that "Erno Rapee and his General Electric Orchestra will bring us the finale from Beethoven's Fifth Symphony," the commercial name registers, but except to the most captious, does not appear an intrusion.
>
> (Taylor 2003: 6)

This strategy was seen to work on two levels. First, like the medicine shows, radio programs used music to attract audiences to hear some kind of sales pitch. Second, by sponsoring music programs that consumers welcomed in their homes and enjoyed listening to, companies sought to build goodwill among their potential clientèle in hopes that consumers would purchase their product out of gratitude (Taylor 2003: 5).

Advertisers' special delicacy regarding the perceived intrusiveness of their message speaks to what Lauren Berlant has described as the durability of the Victorian ideal of the sanctity of the private, domestic space: "[The] categories [of public and private space] are considered by many scholars to be archaic formations, legacies of a Victorian fantasy that the world can be divided into a controllable space (the private-affective) and an uncontrollable one (the public-instrumental)" (Berlant 1998: 283). Listeners, of course, can control radio programming only insofar as they can select a broadcast frequency (of which there were very few in the early days of the medium) or choose to turn the radio off. Therefore, the radio itself represented a radical intrusion of public space and discourse into the domestic sphere, posing a real threat to the supposed sanctity and—above all—controllability of private space.

Moreover, the public/private division is gendered in a number of complex ways: It is predicated on a division of labor, first of all, wherein public space is the locus of masculine labor, while private, domestic space is the locus of the feminine. Concomitantly, the binary between the public as uncontrollable and the private as controlled is similarly gendered: whereas a man (and his labor) is subject to other forces in the public sphere—the employer, the state, etc.—at home, he is in charge in the normative model. As Berlant explains, "Domestic privacy can feel like a controllable space, a world of potential unconflictedness (even for five minutes a day): a world built for 'you' [i.e., man]" (Berlant 1998: 285). Program sponsorship, then, was a means for advertisers to dovetail their public messaging with something that would be welcome within the domestic sphere—most often music. In this way, advertisers sought to soften their impact, minimizing the sense that their messages were intrusive within the home or disruptive to domestic patriarchal control.

At the same time, this strategy of indirectly inserting advertisements into supposedly musical programs marks a fairly early and subtly effective example of mass media's role in reifying the ideology of consumption. By casually introducing listeners to corporate brands, these broadcasts made corporate brands a regular part of household routines and rituals, gently initiating North American radio listeners into consumer culture. This exemplifies why Louis Althusser calls radio's status an "ideological state apparatus" (1971)—that is, as an institution that "contributes to . . . the reproduction of the relations of production, i.e. of capitalist relations of exploitation" (Althusser 1971: 154).

Because of the central role of music in this early advertising strategy, the question of musical style became exceedingly important; musical style was often perceived to be contiguous to moral content. According to Taylor, the style question came down to a choice between classical and jazz, and by extension, the moral implications of each genre. For the most part, prior to the late 1920s, advertising agencies like J. Walter Thompson were often hesitant to use jazz music, lest that music's lowbrow associations cast the commodity or brand in a negative light. Where they did bow to lowbrow popular taste and employ jazz—often in connection with "vice" products like tobacco—advertisers did take additional measures to counter the perceived short attention spans and other intellectual deficiencies of a jazz audience, keeping ad copy punchy and comprehensible, and supplementing radio advertisements or sponsored programming with a clear, direct print campaign (Taylor 2003: 14).

Timothy Taylor reminds us that, during the 1920s, the categories of "jazz" and "classical" held rather different meanings. "Classical," he suggests, essentially referred to light classics and excerpts of well known classical works (such as Pumphrey's example of Beethoven's 5th). "Jazz," meanwhile, meant "highly arranged quasi-classical dance tunes performed by Euro-American musicians, many with classical musical training and backgrounds" (Taylor 2003: 12), as represented by the music of Paul Whiteman (and his many counterparts, such as the Casa Loma Orchestra and the Guy Lombardo Orchestra).

While Taylor's point is an important consideration, I contend that he is remiss in categorizing Whiteman's music as the subject of a mere misapplication of the term "jazz." While his music no doubt sounded very different from our modern conception, it nonetheless marked a key element of 1920s jazz discourse. As Gerald Early has shown (1998), Whiteman's orchestra was enormously popular at the time, debuted a number of significant "symphonic jazz" works (including George Gershwin's "Rhapsody in Blue"), and was cited as an influence and inspiration by many contemporaries, including Duke Ellington (Early 1998: 421; Gennari 2006: 45). Nonetheless, the radio programmers' preference for Euro-American-dominated "symphonic jazz" groups like Whiteman's over the so-called "hot" bands that consisted of predominantly African American musicians like Louis Armstrong, Freddie Keppard, and Fats Waller affirms that race was a corollary of musical morality: while programmers were willing to "lower their standards" so far as to allow lowbrow Euro-American jazz bands on the radio, the thought of programming African American groups—even in a medium where their race was invisible—was unconscionable.

As audiences became more acclimatized to radio (and hence to the implicit omnipresence of advertising in their homes) advertisers grew bolder in their methods. Toward the end of the 1920s, advertisers began to interpolate brief, direct messages within longer programs (Taylor 2003: 15). This gave rise to the further evolution of the jingle, which now became "a short, catchy musical composition set with advertising copy" (Stillwell). Advertisers hoped that audiences would recall the jingle even after the ad was over, and that this recollection would prompt them to purchase the advertised product (Karmen 2005: 9). To that end, many early jingles were in fact simply advertising copy set to contemporaneous popular tunes. "Have You Tried Wheaties?", generally accepted to be the first jingle heard on radio, was set to the tune of "Jazz Baby," a song by M.K. Jerome and Blanche Merrill ("Thoroughly Modern Millie").

"Have You Tried Wheaties" was thus also the first jingle to be composed in the jazz idiom (or at least a pastiche of the jazz idiom), which rapidly became the generic *lingua franca* for jingle composition (Huron 1989: 562). As professional jingle-writing firms proliferated over the next 30 years, many composers were drawn from Tin Pan Alley. Indeed, Frank Loesser, the composer of the musical *Guys and Dolls*, established his own jingle-writing firm, Frank Productions, Inc., in 1957, and promptly hired such legendary Broadway composers as Hoagy Carmichael ("Skylark," "Stardust"), Vernon Duke ("April in Paris"), and Harold Rome ("Fanny") (Samuel 2001: 112).

Other advertisers also sought to capitalize on both the general popular cache of the jazz style, and the familiarity of particular jazz-inflected tunes. Car manufacturer DeSoto, a division of Chrysler, paid thousands of dollars for the rights to Cole Porter's "It's De-Lovely" ("It's De-lightful, It's De-lovely, It's DeSoto!") in the 1950s (Samuel 2001: 113). Similarly, Ford Automotive sought to license Frederick Loewe and Alan Jay Lerner's "On the Street Where You Live," but was deterred by expensive ASCAP licensing fees (Devine Papers, "Ford Theatre"). Even Louis Armstrong performed in a spot for Schaefer Beer during the same period ("Schaefer is the one beer to have if you're having more than one!"). Evidently, whether or not advertising executives like those at J. Walter Thompson had overcome their distaste for jazz music, they had certainly recognized its enduring popular appeal.

With the advent of television, jingles proliferated even further. Television audiences grew rapidly: by 1951, 10–15 million Americans were watching television (Samuel 2001: xv); by 1960, over 90 per cent of American homes included at least one television (Samuel 2001: xiv). From an advertiser's perspective, television functioned essentially as what Lawrence Samuel calls "a surrogate salesman invited into the viewer's living rooms, an electronic display room filled with the cornucopia of the good life." As television spread, the major national networks' dependence on advertisements and programming sponsorship—their sole sources of income—to fund their daily programming schedules continued to grow (Huron 1989: 558). Hence, according to many media analysts, television programming developed from entertainment designed to generate widespread goodwill among consumers into targeted media vehicles that would allow advertisers to address a specific desired market segment.

While television audiences had long since become familiar with indirect advertising, this sudden invasion of direct advertisements into their homes during the 1950s caused many people to become increasingly jaded about the constant push to consume. The expansion of television further forced the radical realignment of the normative division of the public and private spheres that had begun with radio. Suddenly, advertisers had constant access to the domestic—becoming a visible, tangible presence in the quotidian life of the North American home, talking face-to-face to wives and children in the normative, feminized domestic space, often without the husbands and fathers around to supervise.

It is no coincidence that the discipline of media studies began to develop in the 1950s, at the same time as the influx of direct advertising. Books such as Vance Packard's widely read and highly influential *The Hidden Persuaders* (1957) targeted the use of manipulative psychological techniques in advertising, including subliminal messaging, and indexed Americans' growing distrust of mass media. Similarly, market analysts such as Sidney Levy (1959) and Irving White (1959) both began to theorize the psychological dimension of advertising. Drawing on Marx's notion of commodity fetishism, Levy and White proposed that consumers purchased items not necessarily because they needed the items themselves, but because they aspired to a lifestyle that those particular items represented. As Levy noted, "[goods can be thought of as] essentially psychological things which are symbolic of personal attributes and goals of social patterns and strivings" (quoted in Oliver *et al.* 1993: 33).

White elaborated on this observation in terms of the practice of advertising, suggesting that since consumers fetishize commodities—purchasing according to brand identity and personality, instead of basic "use value"—advertisers were attentive to "the total source of meanings, the whole interaction between the consumer and the product" (quoted in Oliver *et al.* 1993: 34).

Parallel to (and in many ways, generating) this growing skepticism, many advertisers developed increasingly subtle approaches to psychological advertising as a means instead to elicit an immediate emotional—rather than a reasoned—response from consumers. Noted advertising and marketing analyst Ernest Dichter was among the first to apply Freudian psychoanalytic techniques to the field in the 1940s and 1950s. In an argument that somewhat ironically aligned with Marx, Dichter proposed that commodities have "souls": virtually ineffable meanings that address consumers at a subconscious level.

The job of advertisements was not merely to list the functional "use values" of the commodity, but to tap into the deeper relationship between consumers and the commodity's soul. To that end, Dichter famously encouraged Procter & Gamble to conceive of and market soap not merely as a physical cleaning agent, but as a means of purging sin (Schwarzkopf and Gries 2010: 4). At the same time, televised advertising time slots grew increasingly short through the 1950s and into the 1960s, eventually leading to what Sut Jhally calls "the 'vignette approach'—in which narrative and 'reason-why' advertising are subsumed under a rapid succession of lifestyle images, meticulously timed with music, that directly sell feeling and emotion rather than products" (Jhally 2003: 333).

Because music is such a potent cultural signifier, it enables advertisers rapidly to communicate a great deal of cultural meaning while at the same time carrying a tremendous amount of emotional impact. As Nicholas Cook explains,

> It is not just the messages of the commercials that are subliminal. In a sense, the music is too. That is to say, viewers rarely hear the music as such; they are rarely aware of it as an entity in itself. Music transfers its own attributes to the story line and to the product, it creates coherence, making connections that are not there in the words or pictures; it even engenders meanings of its own. But it does all this, so to speak, silently.
>
> (Cook 1994: 38)

At the same time, it is crucial to remember that the collection of "tropes of meaning"—the emotional and cultural significances—subtended by a given genre exist apart from the advertisement. While a given advertising message will activate particular tropes of meaning over others, depending on the desired brand or product identity and personality, the advertisement itself does not generally create those tropes per se. An advertisement will participate in reifying and sustaining existing tropes of meaning, but the advertising activation of musical significations is contingent on the broader cultural circulation of the music and its meanings, much in the same way that the Pears and Pond's print ads depended on external, existing images and culture values and ideas for their brand identities. Therefore, because music operates in the quasi-subliminal way that Cook suggests, it has an essentially interpellative function in advertisements. A television viewer generally "already knows" what a musical genre means; thus, when that genre is articulated to a brand or product in an advertisement, the viewer's a priori knowledge of the genre extends to the commodity. To a considerable extent, it is through her or his cultural knowledge of musical signification that a viewer "always already" understands that Clicquot Club Ginger Ale has "pep" and "sparkle," or (as we shall see in the subsequent chapters) that the Chrysler Sebring is sophisticated and luxurious, and that Pepsi Jazz is youthful and sexy.

The psychological impact of music—especially musical genre—was a consideration for advertisers as early as the 1920s. In most of these cases, however, advertisers were trying to use sounds that consumers liked in order to identify the musical tastes of their target audience and select music that would appeal to them—in other words, drawing on the community-building aspect of psychological advertising discussed in the previous section. This is an instance of what David Huron identifies as the demographic appeal of musical styles: "Musical styles," he writes, "have long been identified with various social and demographic groups. Musical style might therefore assist in targeting a specific market" (Huron 1989: 566).

By the late 1950s and 1960s, however, advertisers had moved from trying to use sounds that their targeted consumers would *like* to conceiving sounds as representative of what consumers would *like to be*. This reframes music's ability to represent different demographics: not only do particular styles appeal to particular socioeconomic or cultural or ethnic groups, they also appeal to individuals who, for whatever reason, would like to be associated with those groups. As such, the signification of musical style combines the two trajectories of psychological advertising—the personal and the communal. By framing an advertisement in a particular musical (or indeed, sartorial, vernacular, artistic, etc.) style, advertisers work to connect their product with the cultural meanings embedded within that style, and with the communities linked to it. "By knowing the tastes of a desired clientele, a store [or an advertisement] can position itself as within—or as a 'logical' extension of—an already existing taste culture" (Sterne 1997: 35).

During the 1960s, for example, Thomas Frank has argued that what most people would have "liked to be" was countercultural. Frank traces the symbolic apotheosis of this idea to the widespread popularity of Norman Mailer's 1954 essay, "The White Negro: Superficial Reflections on the Hipster," and of the poetry and prose of the Beat movement. Mailer (as well as authors associated with the Beat movement, like Jack Kerouac) used the African American jazz musician (albeit, in a grotesquely essentialized form) as a countercultural model for a way of living that rejected the stultifying, numbing strictures of postindustrial American society. Mailer's essay outlines his concept of "the hipster"—an idealized, revolutionary man, who rejected the stultifying norms and mores of Eisenhower's America in favor of an incendiary mixture of nihilism, hedonism, and radical individualism. Mailer's construct is modeled after a violently essentialized conception of the African American, as represented in particular by the African American jazz musician. He articulates this conception as follows:

> Knowing in the cells of his existence that life was war, nothing but war, the Negro (all exceptions admitted) could rarely afford the sophisticated inhibitions of civilization, and so he kept for his survival the art of the primitive, he lived in the enormous present, he subsisted for his Saturday night kicks, relinquishing the pleasures of the mind for the more obligatory pleasures of the body, and in his music he gave voice to the character and quality of his existence, to his rage and the infinite variations of joy, lust, languor, growl, cramp, pinch, scream and despair of his orgasm. For jazz is orgasm.
>
> (Quoted in Monson 1995: 403)

By constructing this character as the hero of his hip revolution, Mailer brutally reduces the African American to a kind of ignoble savage who, in his mindless, rapacious, phallic potency and vitality, violently revolts against what Mailer views to be a stagnant, stultifying Euro-American *status quo*. While Mailer demonstrates a palpable delight in the grotesqueness of his construction, it is broadly indicative of what bell hooks and others have described as the dialectic of attraction and revulsion that underlies this sort of obscenely over-determined view of the African American man: "Within white supremacist capitalist patriarchy, rebel black masculinity has been idolized and punished, romanticized yet vilified" (hooks 1992: 96).

Frank argues that the popularity of the kind of dissidence that Mailer and his Beat colleagues represented had a curiously dialectical relationship with advertising: advertisers were inspired by the youthful, rebellious spirit of the age and, at the same time, the youthful spirit of the age was reflected back at audiences and reinforced through counterculture-themed advertisements. Music critic and counterculture maven Ralph Gleason listed a number of ads and branding strategies that he found particularly distasteful in a 1968 retrospective article entitled "So Revolution is Commercial": "an automaker proselytized for the 'Dodge Rebellious', AT&T used the slogan 'The Times, They Are A-Changin'', and Columbia Records ran ads featuring the line 'If you won't listen to your parents, The Man, or the Establishment, why should you listen to us?'" (quoted in Frank 1997a: 16).

Frank makes the point, however, that the advertisers' use of countercultural ideas should not be viewed as simple co-optation:

> To begin to take co-optation seriously is instantly to discard one of the basic shibboleths of sixties historiography. As it turns out, many in American business . . . imagined the counterculture not as an enemy to be undermined or a threat to consumer culture but as a hopeful sign, a symbolic ally in their own struggles against the mountains of dead-weight procedure and hierarchy that had accumulated over the years.
>
> (Frank 1997a: 9)

In the present day, this approach—now referred to in the industry as "affinity advertising" (Taylor 2007b: 246)—is all-pervasive, and hinges on the signification of musical style. As Steve Karmen (2005), Timothy Taylor (2000), Carrie McClaren (1998), and many other observers have argued, this strategy has almost entirely eclipsed the jingle. McClaren quotes Richard Lyon of Lyon Music, a New York-based company specializing in preparing music for advertisements: "Audiences today are too intelligent and sophisticated for [jingles] . . . People easily identify jingles as advertising and tune them out. Music in ads these days shouldn't dare sing the praises of the product, or even mention it" (McClaren 1998: 10). Lyon may be exaggerating the situation to some extent: the jingle is not entirely obsolete, but it has largely been relegated to lower-budget advertising, particularly on radio, that does not circulate nearly as widely through the mass market.

In place of the jingle, commercial composers like Lyon strive to compose music that signifies not the product itself, but the lifestyle of which it is an important part. McClaren elaborates:

> People react intuitively, and commercials turn that to an advantage. Jingles aimed to elicit brand-name recall, but ads now work by 'borrowing interest'—transferring value from the music to the product. . . . [Musical styles] work as a shorthand for consumer lifestyles, from rock-and-roll rebellion to sophisticated jazz to obscure, weirdo noise.
>
> (McClaren 1998: 10)

With the obsolescence of the jingle, advertisers have increasingly begun to license existing music that they feel effectively expresses their desired message. Of course, as we have seen with the cases of DeSoto and Ford, advertisers have been licensing music since at least the 1950s and borrowing (or stealing) popular melodies for much, much longer. The modern approach to licensing, however, is far more psychologically sophisticated. Whereas earlier licensing strategies sought chiefly to capitalize on the contemporary popularity of a song, current advertisers depend heavily on genre signification to build a brand identity and appeal to target demographic and psychographic markets. Kendall Marsh, an advertising music director with the firm Mental Music Productions, affirms:

> The baby boomer generation grew up with this music. Ad execs are in love with it, so they want to see their products associated with it . . . You don't have to say anything else. You're associating yourself with a product which has a resonance with this tune. You're buying into a lifestyle.
>
> (Quoted in Taylor 2007b: 238–39)

This state of affairs represents the ultimate realization of the 1959 theories of Levy and White. Jean Baudrillard's idea of the object value system, as articulated in "Toward a Critique of the Political Economy of the Sign" 1976 offers a useful lens through which to consider modern advertising. As we have seen, in the early days of mass-mediated advertising, ads combined statements about the utility of a product—its use value, in Marx's terminology. In modern consumer society, however, the use value of a given object (that is, its practical function, such as a pen's ability to write, or the ability of a pair of socks to keep one's feet warm) has been fully eclipsed by what Baudrillard calls its sign-value (that is, the ability of an object to confer some value—be it individual prestige, a sense of belonging, sexiness, hipness, *etc.*—upon its owner).

Thus, while the use value of a Pepsi soft drink product might be to quench a consumer's thirst (albeit ineffectively), its real importance lies in its cultural role; that is, its ability to communicate the youthful vitality of the consumer, and to highlight the consumer's membership in a community of other similarly youthful, vital Pepsi drinkers. Because musical style is such a potent signifier of demographic—because it carries so much cultural significance pertaining to age, ethnicity, class, and other target categories—music plays a key role in advertising the sign-value of a given product.

Studying Music and Advertising: Reviewing the Field

The tremendous importance of studying the usage of music in advertising has been acknowledged by major scholars in a variety of fields; despite this, there has been surprisingly little ethno/musicological scholarship on music and advertising. The two musicologists who have worked on advertising—David Huron and Nicholas Cook—have both approached the subject from the perspective of musical semiotics. David Huron's 1989 article, "Music in Advertising: An Analytic Paradigm," was the first to focus on the subject. Huron's comments on musical style are especially instructive in terms of my own work:

> [A]n observer can learn about social meanings in music simply by examining the advertising strategy. Radio and television advertisements are the most overt records joining life-style, social class, and material aspirations to musical style. They are, consequently, useful tools for unraveling musical meaning in a social and cultural context.
>
> (Huron 1989: 567)

Musicologist Nicholas Cook builds on David Huron's semiotic/hermeneutic perspective in his article, "Music and Meaning in the Commercials" (1994). Echoing Huron, Cook has suggested that, "as one of the most highly compressed (and highly resourced) forms of multi-media production, television commercials constitute an exceptionally fertile arena for investigating the negotiation of musical meaning" (Cook 1994: 30). Of special importance is his notion of "stripped down" musical composition or editing; that is, "music [that] embodies the features necessary for the recognition of genre, but otherwise has little or no distinctive musical content" (Cook 1994: 36). Cook's suggestion that a genre can be distilled to a collection of signifiers within a syntactically inchoate musical soundtrack offers a useful model for close musical analysis in an advertising context.

While one might have expected David Huron's and Nicholas Cook's compelling articles from the late-20th century to generate a burgeoning interest in the subject through the 21st century, I have been able to locate only seven other studies published since 1994 that deal directly with the topic. Two of these are historically focused, and largely uncritical: Robynn J. Stillwell has contributed a brief (but useful) historical overview, "Music and Advertising," in the *Grove Music Online*, and Richard A. Peterson gestures towards the role of corporate sponsorship in his comments on country music radio programming in his book, *Creating Country Music: Fabricating Authenticity* (1997).

The core of the published music-advertising scholarly corpus, however, consists of a book and four articles by Timothy Taylor—*The Sounds of Capitalism: Advertising, Music, and the Conquest of Culture* (University of Chicago Press, 2012), "World Music in Television Ads" (2000), "Music and Advertising in Early Radio" (2003), "The Changing Shape of the Culture Industry; or, How Did Electronica Music Get into Television Commercials?" (2007b), and "The Commodification of Music at the Dawn of the Era of 'Mechanical Music'" (2007a)—and Bethany Klein's 2009 monograph, *As Heard on TV: Popular Music in Advertising*, along with Kara Attrep's 2008 PhD thesis, "The Sonic Inscription of Identity: Music, Race, and Nostalgia in Advertising." Klein's work focuses on the advertising practice of music licensing, examining that practice in terms of the fraught cultural and aesthetic issues that arise from the collision of artistic practice and commodification.

Attrep's study is much broader, engaging with three case studies that consider music and advertising from a number of different vantage points: the interpellation of African American consumers by alcohol advertisers, corporatized multiculturalism, and nostalgia. Taylor's work, meanwhile, is extremely ambitious in the breadth of its scope, covering everything from exoticism in advertising, to corporate sponsorship of radio programming, to music licensing, to the sale of sheet music at the turn of the 20th century.

It is worth noting that there has been some work published on music and advertising from a variety of other fields—namely jazz studies, marketing/advertising studies, and practical methods for music composition—but, for a variety of reasons, this work is of limited usefulness. While there are no jazz studies publications dedicated specifically to the subject, Krin Gabbard (1995), David Ake (2002), and Alan Stanbridge (2008) have made passing references to jazz in advertising within the context of their work on other subjects. As a result of the tangential nature of their engagement with the subject, however, their insights are somewhat underdeveloped. In each case, they merely recognize the usage of jazz in advertising as a strikingly contradictory phenomenon—what Stanbridge calls a "paradoxical discursive position" (Stanbridge 2008: 1)—indicative of either jazz's newfound elite status (Gabbard and Ake) or of a "crass" commercialism that has exploited that status (Stanbridge 2008: 4).

However, none of these scholars has worked to interrogate the historical roots or contemporary effects of the phenomenon. The most thorough discussion of jazz advertising to date is Tony Whyton's monograph, *Jazz Icons: Heroes, Myths and the Jazz Tradition* (2010). During a chapter on the promotional strategy of the Impulse! label, Whyton explicitly calls for more detailed study of jazz from the perspective of advertising and—more broadly—consumption:

> [Acts] of consumption should be regarded as an integral part of the historicizing process in jazz. Advertising is not only a crucial aid to consumption; it also provides cultural theorists with numerous possibilities for analysis, as the medium has important links to art, politics and education. From

> a jazz perspective, advertising and marketing strategies are important in
> examining the sense of societal value instilled in the music.
>
> (Whyton 2010: 83)

There is also a small body of literature that deals directly with music in
advertising from advertising and marketing studies—a field that tends to strad-
dle theoretical and practical concerns more demonstrably, perhaps, than either
ethno/musicology or cultural studies. Marketer/scholars have focused on music
for both its value as a bearer of nonverbal meaning and as a tool to amplify or
enhance verbal messages. This field was essentially inaugurated by Gerald Gorn's
seminal study, "The Effects of Music in Advertising on Choice Behavior: A Classical Conditioning Approach" (1982). Since Gorn's 1982 study, however, there
have been only three other music-focused publications by advertising/marketing
scholars: Gordon C. Bruner II's "Music, Mood, and Marketing" (1990), Linda
Scott's article, "Understanding Jingles and Needledrop: A Rhetorical Approach
to Music in Advertising" (1990), and Kineta Hung's "Narrative Music in Congruent and Incongruent TV Advertising" (2000).

Despite seemingly universal acknowledgment of the value of this field of
research, since Hung's 2000 article, the *Journal of Marketing*, the *Journal of Advertising*, and the *Journal of Consumer Research*—three of the première journals dealing
with marketing and advertising—have published precisely zero articles focusing
on music in advertising. Indeed, lamentation of the paucity of published scholarship on music and advertising is a veritable literary trope among music and
advertising scholars. As Hung herself writes, "[D]espite the potential importance
of [this field], research in this area is scant and there is practically no research
that has examined how music creates meanings in advertising" (Hung 2000: 25).

Moreover, the extant scholarship on music in advertising within marketing
and advertising studies is for the most part deeply flawed, undermined by an
embryonic understanding (or, indeed, misunderstanding) of musical semiotics.
As Linda Scott explained in 1990:

> Those studies that have been done are riddled with inconclusive find-
> ings. In most cases, this research incorporates little work from other fields
> toward understanding the complexity of music as a cultural form. Conse-
> quently, the research is plagued by simplistic presuppositions about 'how
> music works'. These assumptions, which tend to characterize music as a
> nonsemantic affective stimulus, form the basis of an implicit theory of
> music that is carried through methodology to procedure.
>
> (Scott 1990: 223)

In other words, music was treated until fairly recently as essentially a jumble
of purely affective sounds, free of cultural baggage and semiotic content—in
essence, a "mood-altering drug" (Scott 1990: 226). Its function was simply to

put the consumer in an optimal frame of mind to spend. Gerald Gorn's study, for instance, sought to establish a connection between the usage of "liked music" in an advertisement and the favorable reception of the advertisement's message. Gorn neglected to consider any other factors, however, such as why the music was "liked," or what meanings implicit in the music might have been transferred to the product to favorable effect.

Similarly, the aim of Gordon C. Bruner's research was to establish a "taxonomy" of musical affect—to map a correlation between musical elements (such as volume, tempo, ascending vs. descending melodies, *legato* vs. *staccato* notes, "firm" rhythms vs. "smooth-flowing" rhythms) and the emotions and moods those elements generated in listeners. His ultimate goal was to use this taxonomy in conjunction with then-nascent compositional technologies (such as "computerization" and synthesizers) to enable advertisers themselves to compose advertising music that would instantly put listeners in a spending frenzy (Bruner 1990: 101)—a kind of marketing *diabolus in musica*. Like Gorn, Bruner's approach is undercut by a neglect of the specificities of musical style and genre. His presumption seems to be that a musical gesture carries the same meaning, regardless of the stylistic/generic context—as if a descending, *staccato* melody in Mozart would be received in the same way and have the same effect as a similarly contoured melody in *Men Without Hats*). This perspective entirely overlooks the historical and cultural situatedness of music.

Kineta Hung's 2000 article is rather more theoretically sound than these earlier studies but, like most advertising scholarship, nevertheless suffers from similar musical oversights. While her argument that an incongruity between musical style and the message of an advertisement can provide surprising rhetorical "twist" (Hung 2000: 26) that might entice consumers, she does not take the crucial step of defining "incongruity," or scrutinizing how exactly musical meaning might be incongruous with verbal meaning. Like Gorn and Bruner, Hung presumes that music means concretely, universally, and univocally—a presumption that ethnomusicologists long ago recognized as absurd.

Collectively, this work provides an important framework for my own study. Where my work differs from the extant scholarship—and makes a valuable contribution to the discussion—is in its focus on a single genre, namely jazz. Whereas Taylor's and Attrep's more diverse projects focus on the use of music in general, and Klein's work deals specifically with music licensing, my focus on jazz allows me to trace the activation and transformation of a more limited number of sociocultural meanings and themes—what I call "tropes of meaning"—associated with a genre as it is deployed in different contexts for a range of purposes.

Moreover, the history of this particular genre makes it an especially rich resource to examine some of the core paradoxes of advertising and the North American culture of consumption. As a music that is uniquely situated on the cusp of the categories of "art" and "popular," jazz offers a unique opportunity to access the fraught terrain of the art–commerce discourses. Furthermore, jazz is an unquestionably African American cultural practice with an indelible historical linkage to black modernism and black nationalism—a cultural *locus* that for Amiri Baraka reveals jazz's "original separateness"—and its position "outside the mainstream of American culture" (Baraka 1995: 181). Hence, its appearance in mass-mediated; "mainstream" advertising represents an exceptional lens through which to examine both the interpellation of African American consumers into the so-called American mainstream capitalist culture of consumption, and conversely, the mainstream American consumption of African American culture.

Theoretical Framework

I take as my theoretical point of departure two crucial challenges posed by jazz studies literature. First, the epigraph to this introduction: "Most jazz isn't really about jazz, at least not in terms of how it is actually consumed" (Gabbard 1996: 1). George E. Lewis has recently elaborated on Gabbard's seminal observation, proposing that jazz should be viewed "not as a set of musicologically codifiable (however vaguely so) characteristics such as 'swing,'" but rather as a "social location within which sound and musical practice take on additional meanings" (Lewis 2008: xlv).

To the consumer of the music and to the individual charged with representing jazz to that consumer, jazz is "about"—jazz means—highbrow sophistication, folk authenticity, and lowbrow lasciviousness. It is about politics, nationalism and counterculture. It is about class, gender, and race. Perhaps, above all, it is about improvisation—both musical and social. Naturally, these meanings have changed over the course of the 20th century, both in terms of their particular significance and in terms of their centrality in jazz discourses. Nevertheless, all of these meanings have become increasingly central tropes through the discursive and musical history of jazz, to the point that, in our own day, jazz is always about all of these things at the same time. In order to understand the significance of jazz in advertising—indeed, in order to understand the significance of jazz in the popular consciousness during the 21st century—it is therefore utterly crucial for us to consider the discursive histories of these tropes of meaning.

That being said, I do not seek to unravel the narratives that are tied to the tropes per se; the act of unraveling implies that there are discrete narrative threads to follow, with distinct beginnings and endings. These tropes of meaning, these things that "jazz is about," are not fixed chronologically or geographically: although their significance and their relation to jazz has changed over time, art, authenticity, gender, sex, nationalism, class and race were nonetheless key concepts in New Orleans in 1905, in Paris in 1930, in New York in 1950, and in Toronto in 2010. Nor are the tropes conceptually bounded: it would be impossible to talk about jazz as art (or jazz as "not art") without talking about other tropes. All of these tropes (along with their many variations) are immanent in every jazz utterance—every note, every referential image, every critical commentary, even every mention of the word—held in a kind of transhistorical tension, continually inflecting, affirming, and negating each other.

Every jazz utterance is thus an instantiation of a kind of meta-jazz conceptual complex. As a means of accessing this conceptual complex I consider the tropes at the level of discourse, examining the wildly diverse spoken, written, and musical utterances that have contributed to and/or developed out of these meanings, with a view to providing historical context for how the tropes have come to circulate—and indeed, how they have been reified, reproduced, and transformed—in the sphere of advertising.

In the second place, I seek to develop Tony Whyton's aforementioned assertion: "From a jazz perspective, advertising and marketing strategies are important in examining the sense of societal value instilled in the music" (Whyton 2010: 83). In this regard, five key media studies-oriented cultural theoretical premises direct my work. First—and most fundamentally—I build on Stuart Hall's concept of articulation. Hall defined the concept in this way in a 1986 interview with Lawrence Grossberg:

> An articulation is . . . the form of the connection that can make a unity of two different elements, under certain conditions. It is a linkage which is not necessary, determined, absolute and essential for all time. You have to ask, under what circumstances can a connection be forged or made?
>
> (Grossberg 1986: 53)

In Hall's view, the role of the theorist is to scrutinize articulations, examining the premises upon which an articulation is predicated, and considering the consequences of the linkage for the articulated elements. It is this theoretical model that I have adopted in my consideration of the articulation of jazz to a variety of commodities by means of advertising and marketing.

Second, I build on Guy Debord's concept of the spectacle. Debord uses the term polemically (and somewhat hyperbolically) to refer to society, culture, biology, and ecology—in essence, every element of life—under capitalism:

> Understood on its own terms, the spectacle proclaims the predominance of appearances and asserts that all human life, which is to say all social life, is mere appearance. But any critique capable of apprehending the spectacle's essential character must expose it as a visible negation of life—and as a negation of life that has invented a visual form for itself.
>
> (Debord 1995: 14)

While I object to Debord's dire characterization of "the spectacle" as a "visible negation of life" (a point upon which I shall elaborate in the coming paragraphs, and at greater length in the concluding chapter), Debord's ideas are extremely useful in terms of his emphasis on "the predominance of appearances." I use this notion in thinking through the ways that advertisers and marketers link commodities to various cultural values, mores, and virtues such as luxury (Chapter 3), individual agency (Chapter 4), cultural/ethnic diversity (Chapters 4 and 5), and community (Chapter 5). In particular, I draw upon the following excerpt from Debord's "thesis 17":

> The present stage, in which social life is completely taken over by the accumulated products of the economy, entails a generalized shift from having to appearing: all effective 'having' must now derive both its immediate prestige and its ultimate raison d'être from appearances.
>
> (Debord 1995: 16)

With this in mind, I consider each of the tropes of meaning mentioned above as "spectacularizations," designed to achieve various marketing and advertising goals.

Third, Louis Althusser's concept of "interpellation" is central to my understanding and analysis of advertising strategy. As outlined earlier in this chapter, in Althusser's view advertisements work to draw viewers into the culture of consumption by "reminding" them that they are consumers, as if this were not a constructed social category that developed sustain mass production under capitalism. The implication is that audiences have "always already" known that they were consumers, but have either forgotten or somehow not noticed. By responding to advertising interpellations—by embracing (or "remembering") their role as consumers—audiences/consumers willingly subject themselves to the fundamental capitalist ideology of consumption. As Althusser explains:

> The individual is interpellated as a (free) subject in order that he shall submit freely to the commandments of the Subject, i.e. in order that he shall (freely) accept his subjection, i.e. in order that he shall make the gestures and actions of his subjection "all by himself." There are no subjects except by and for their subjection. That is why they "work all by themselves."
>
> (Althusser 1971: 182)

This concept is especially crucial both to my overview of advertising history, and to my discussion of targeted marketing directed towards specified ethnic and gendered communities.

At the same time, I acknowledge Slavoj Žižek's critique of Althusser:

> Althusser speaks only of the process of ideological interpellation through which the symbolic machine of ideology is 'internalized' into the ideological experience of Meaning and Truth: but we can learn from Pascal that this 'internalization', by structural necessity, never fully succeeds, that there is always a residue, a leftover, a stain of traumatic irrationality and

senselessness ticking to it, and that this leftover, far from hindering the full submission of the subject to the ideological command, is the very condition of it: it is precisely this non-integrated surplus of senseless traumatism which confers on the Law its unconditional authority: in other words, which—in so far as it escapes ideological sense—sustains what we might call the ideological jouis-sense, enjoyment-in-sense (enjoy-meant), proper to ideology.

(Žižek 1989: 43)

Indeed, Žižek offers a valuable way of maneuvering around the Marxist notion of "false consciousness" that is the crux of both Debord and Althusser, as well as the Frankfurt School model of the culture industry-proletariat antagonism. According to Žižek, ideology and "false consciousness" are not simply stealth weapons—or, in Althusser's terminology, Ideological State Apparatuses—used by a malevolent culture industry to maintain its own hegemony, while concomitantly conditioning an unwitting and powerless proletariat to construct its own oppression. On the contrary, subjects willingly accept ideology as a fantasy that is more palatable than reality (or, in Žižek's Lacanian conception, the Real of our desire): "The function of ideology is not to offer us a point of escape from our reality but to offer us the social reality itself as an escape from some traumatic, real kernel" (Žižek 1989: 45). This crucial acknowledgment of the potential agency of consumers stands as the fourth key element in this book's theoretical scaffolding.

Finally, if we are to understand consumers as relatively free agents (operating within certain ideological and systemic constraints), then it follows that we can consider consumer behavior as essentially performative. Indeed, building on Žižek, we can think of the capitalist ideology of consumption itself as offering a crucial intellectual and expressive space for actors within the capitalist system to deal with the particular traumas of capitalism. Spending behavior and material acquisition become critical ways for consumers to engage with (or to assuage, or to obscure) broader sociocultural tensions around class, race, gender, and sexuality.

This notion essentially originated with Thorstein Veblen's 1899 study, (reprinted by Oxford University Press, 2007), *The Theory of the Leisure Class*, wherein the American economist and sociologist coined the term "conspicuous consumption" to theorize the consumption patterns of the bourgeois classes. Veblen was the first to identify what might anachronistically be called the performative character of consumption: he recognized that the consumptive choices of the traditional middle and upper-middle classes served as a means of consolidating their own class position while at the same time performing their aspirations of class advancement. In Veblen's view, then, conspicuous consumption was chiefly imitative: it offered a means of purchasing and performing membership within a community by imitating the consumer choices of established members of that community. Much contemporary consumption theory builds on Veblen's important assertion.

Many recent consumption theorists have focused on the relationship between consumption and citizenship in capitalism. According to theorists such as Gary Cross (2000), Lizabeth Cohen (2003), and Charles McGovern (2006), consumerism offered a tangible means for citizens in capitalist societies to understand and express the politics and ethics of liberal, capitalist democracy—particularly in the second half of the 20th century, when those principles were threatened by foreign totalitarianism and communism. "Freedom of choice" in the consumer marketplace served as the most visible of all of the pillars of Western democracy. Of course, freedom of choice was and is no more universally accessible than were any of the other foundational democratic rights, like freedom of speech, freedom of worship, freedom from want, and freedom from fear; the freedom to consume was similarly delimited by social stratification and the identity politics of race, class, gender, and sexuality. Hence, capitalist ideology offers consumption as the preferred expressive medium through which virtually every element of our identities: our individual desires and aspirations, our sense of cultural and community belonging, and our official social status as citizens is represented. Every relationship, from the smallest and most intimate to the largest and most public, is mediated by capitalism and expressed through consumption.

It is one of the basic premises of ethnomusicology that music is impacted by and implicated in broader sociocultural forces. The mere fact that capitalism and its attendant ideologies have shaped jazz music and discourse is by no means unique to that genre. On the other hand, because of the specificity of jazz's historical context, jazz's relationship with capitalist economics and ideology *is* unique. The theoretical framework outlined above will help us think through and discuss the precise character of that relationship, as it is articulated in advertising.

Methodology

Jazz Sells engages with three main, detailed case studies that pertain to different aspects of jazz's articulation to commodities. The first study (Chapter 3) deals with an example of the use of jazz in an advertising campaign: Chrysler Canada's 2003 advertising campaign featuring Canadian jazz singer and pianist, Diana Krall. The second study (Chapter 4), the 2006 campaign for Pepsi Jazz, explores the use of jazz as a brand. The third and final case study (Chapter 5) is TD Bank's sponsorship of the Canadian jazz festivals. Along the way, I touch on a wide variety of other, related subjects—Volkswagen's 1999 television campaign, featuring music by Charles Mingus (Chapter 2), the *Dinah Shore Chevy Show* (Chapter 3) a jazz-based TV campaign for the 1960 Plymouth Valiant (Chapter 3), the Honda Jazz (Chapter 3), and Coca-Cola's sponsorship relationship with Jazz at Lincoln Center (Chapter 4).

Given the diachronic nature of this project, my research methodology has necessarily involved a significant engagement with published and archived documents, including histories, analyses and interviews. Alongside a thorough engagement with extant jazz historical and historiographical literature, I undertook archival research at the John W. Hartman Center for Sales, Advertising & Marketing History at Duke University. This archive includes the collected papers of the J. Walter Thompson Company, one of the oldest and largest advertising agencies in the United States, and a company that has been (or continues to be) the agency of record for iconic multinational brands such as Kraft Foods, Ford Motor Company, Johnson & Johnson, and Kellogg's. While not directly applicable to the specific campaigns that are my focus, the collection is remarkably comprehensive, and represents a rare and invaluable look into the quotidian operations and concerns of what is generally a very secretive industry. For this reason, it enabled me to develop an important contextual frame for contemporary advertising and marketing.

In addition to this traditional archive, Internet resources such as the Hartman Center's online collections (the "Ad*Access" print collection and the "AdViews" television collection), "Ads of the World" (adsoftheworld.com), and YouTube were extremely valuable, especially in the earlier phases of my research as I tried to locate advertising campaigns for jazz-branded projects.

In adopting an ethnographic approach to my research, I follow the methods of ethnomusicologist Timothy Taylor and sociologist Bethany Klein. Like these scholars, I move away from the conventional model of media studies—as represented by scholars like Stuart Hall and Sut Jhally—that tends to treat advertisements as texts to be "read." Unlike conventional media studies, I seek to treat advertising both as text and as *praxis*, while situating both in thick context.

My ethnographic methods changed slightly for each of my case studies. Because my research questions circle around how advertisers seek to create meaning for commodities through jazz, the ethnographic portion of my research for the first two primary case studies consisted primarily in qualitative methodologies along two interwoven trajectories: the conceptualization and production of advertising/sponsorship campaigns. I conducted interviews with 12 individuals involved in these two aspects of the two campaigns: the marketing and branding executives from Chrysler Canada and Pepsi who were involved in generating the advertising concepts and liaising with the advertising agencies; the ad agency copy writers and art directors (from Batten, Barton, Durstien & Osborn and Doyle Dane Bernbach, respectively) who actually formulated the concepts and wrote the scripts; the creative directors and producers from the agencies who oversaw the development and execution of the campaigns; the film directors hired by the agencies to run the shoots; and the commercial music firms contracted to produce the soundtracks (David Fleury Music and Expansion Team, respectively).

Researching TD Canada Trust's involvement with Canadian jazz festivals naturally required a somewhat different tack. My study of the festivals introduces a third trajectory: reception. Whereas television viewing tends to be a solitary or small group experience, festival attendance is by definition a shared mass experience: a large group of people comes together to share an experience in a physical space. For this reason, I assumed several different roles in order to access the different aspects of festival production and reception: I attended festivals and engaged other audience members in conversation; I interviewed musicians (both participants and nonparticipants) before, during, and after the festivals; and in the months leading up to and following the festivals themselves, I interviewed festival staff from Toronto and Halifax, as well as several individuals from TD Bank. Unfortunately, because the large TD-sponsored festivals run simultaneously, it would have been impossible to spend more than one full day at every festival. Instead, I chose to spend four or five days at the three biggest festivals (in terms of budget, attendance, and programming): Vancouver, Toronto, and Montreal. This allowed me to see more events at more venues at each festival, and meet with a larger and more diverse number of musicians and audience members.

In this way, I considered both the advertisements and the festival sponsorships as ineffable species of a commodity chain (Wallerstein 1986; Quoted in Marcus 1995), examining every element of the process of the creation and execution of these advertising and sponsorship campaigns. According to George Marcus, this kind of research demands a multi-sited ethnographic strategy:

> [A]ny ethnography of a cultural formation in the world system is also an ethnography of the system, and therefore cannot be understood only in terms of the conventional single-site mise-en-scene of ethnographic research, assuming indeed it is the cultural formation, produced in different locales, rather than the conditions of particular sets of subject that is the object of study.
>
> (Marcus 1995: 99)

Indeed, my research methods were highly variegated, determined in large part by the "diffuse time-space" (Marcus 1995: 96) that characterized my subject, as well as by the availability, needs, and expectations of my research collaborators. Where possible, I met with people face-to-face: I met with musicians, advertisers, marketers, bank executives, and commercial composers in and around Toronto, and I conducted formal and informal interviews of audience members and musicians at the various festival sites as I travelled through Toronto, Montreal, Vancouver, and Halifax.

The vast majority of my interviews, however, were done over the phone. Most of the advertisers and marketers with whom I spoke were scattered all across North America—including San Francisco, Los Angeles, New York City, Purchase NY, and Windsor, On—and it was impossible to meet with them in person. While the advertisers with whom I spoke were extremely generous with their time and insight, I learned quickly that very few were willing to meet with me in person, or to talk to me on the phone for more than an hour. In several cases, one hour on the telephone was the most their schedules would permit; in other cases, even if I had traveled to their city, I would not have been permitted to physically enter the workplace because I am an industry outsider. There is so much money at stake in the business of advertising that an information leak could easily cost an agency not only multi-million dollar contracts, but also the trust of current and potential future clients. Consequently, the industry is largely closed to outsiders.[5]

On the other hand, a given advertisement generally has a very short media life. It is exceedingly rare for a spot to remain on air for longer than a couple of months; hence, the campaigns that were my focus—dating from 2003 and 2006—were ancient history from an industry perspective. As a result, the advertisers with whom I spoke were at liberty to be very open about their experiences. This would not have been the case if I had been studying more recent campaigns.

Evidently, this is not a traditional ethnomusicological study: my field is not linked to a fixed locus, or even to a fixed point in time. Rather, my field moves in time and space to "follow the thing" (Marcus 1995: 106). In this way, following Tim Cooley, Katherine Meizel, and Nasir Syed, I conceptualize my field as a "virtual" space. As these authors suggest, "Virtuality is only as real as any other cultural production: it has only the meaning with which people imbue it" (Cooley, Meizel, and Syed 2008: 91); however, a virtual field demands a highly diverse and flexible collection of methodologies.

As I have mentioned, "following the thing" in my research necessitated crossing the boundaries between nation states. While the "thing"—jazz—is an African American phenomenon, its circulation is hardly constrained by the state-enforced American borders. Hence, although two of my three primary case studies are based in Canada and an additional secondary case study (Honda Jazz) is located primarily in the European Union and Australia, I consider jazz as a chiefly American national phenomenon that circulates within a transnational network of cultural and capital exchanges. I suggest, therefore, that jazz must be considered within an American cultural and historical context, regardless of the particular national *milieu.*

With that in mind, jazz's tropes of meaning—like the sound of the music itself—permeate national boundaries. At the same time, of course, the "virtual space" that defines my field does not entirely transcend the geographical and cultural divisions and distinctions between nation states. Therefore, jazz and its attendant tropes of meaning must also be considered within the myriad national and cultural contexts through which it moves. Race relations in Canada—where cultural diversity has long been a political and cultural touchstone, especially since the 1980s—are different from those in the United States. Moreover, U.S. jazz in Canada or the U.K. must also be considered through the lens of the cultural relationship between the two countries. To that end, throughout the book, I highlight the malleability of the music and its meanings in international contexts, particularly in Chapters 3 and 5.

Chapter Outline

Jazz Sells is arranged into six chapters, including this introduction and a conclusion. Chapter 2 introduces several of the key questions and themes that structure the rest of the book, investigating the seemingly contradictory ways in which jazz has become implicated in commerce and consumer culture. I argue that the relationship between jazz and consumer culture has most often been understood as fundamentally oppositional. As I discussed in my literature review, a number of scholars have argued that the use of jazz in advertising constitutes an example of co-optation, a quintessential commodification of dissident counterculture by the culture industry; indeed, this argument is convincing and, in many respects, accurate. I propose, however, that greater attentiveness to the shifting discourses of jazz and commerce yields a more nuanced perspective that demands a reconsideration of the relationship between the two as something other than simple Manichean opposition. To that end, in Chapter 2, I examine the terms of this dichotomy by interrogating the presumed hierarchical relationship between them: rather than considering the effect of an oppressive and pervasive hegemonic system of commercial exchange on a subaltern music, I discuss the active engagement of two representative artists within that system: Charles Mingus and his widow Sue Mingus. Following a detailed consideration of Charles Mingus's own vexed relationship with the North American culture industries, I focus on a 1999 Volkswagen campaign that drew on Mingus's well established countercultural capital.

Chapters 3, 4 and 5 focus on my three case studies. In Chapter 3, I deal with the complex relationship between jazz and cars in North America. I situate the relationship historically, discussing the discursive alignment between jazz and cars in the 1920s. I suggest that this alignment was founded upon the role of Fordist mass production in the parallel proliferation of both jazz and cars in the American mainstream: while cars rolled off of Ford and GM assembly lines and into newly-paved driveways across the country, jazz made its way into American homes through the emergent technologies of radio and the recording industry. I focus particularly on American journalism, and on F. Scott Fitzgerald's *The Great Gatsby*: a novel that deals with the anxiety of the perceived decline of American ethnic purity and the pursuant degeneration of American morality.

From the 1920s, I jump ahead to the 1950s, a period that marked the coincidence of the so-called "Golden Age" of car culture with the waning years of what is often known as the "golden age" of jazz: the "Big Band Era." In this section, I examine the various ways in which the automobile began to symbolize both social status in particular and—more broadly—American social norms and American citizenship. I consider the ways in which jazz played a part in this process by looking closely at the Chevrolet-sponsored Dinah Shore Chevy Show and a jazz-themed 1959 advertising campaign for the 1960 Plymouth Valiant.

Next, I broaden my scope to consider the jazz-automobile relationship in a more global context, discussing the European and Australian campaigns for the

Honda Jazz, a small hatchback that was launched in the EU, Australia, Africa, and Asia in 2001. In the third and final section of the chapter, I look to my first case study: Chrysler Canada's spot for the 2003 Sebring featuring Diana Krall, entitled *The Look of Love*, developed by ad agency BBDO. I examine several interrelated discursive valences that emerged from my interviews with a number of the individuals involved in the creation and execution of the spot: the rationale for the perceived brand fit between Krall and her music with the Chrysler Sebring; the way in which that perceived fit is predicated on Krall's sophistication and sexuality; and concomitantly, how the advertisement inadvertently reiterates the troubling historical marginalization of women in jazz.

In Chapter 4, I turn to Pepsi Jazz, exploring how the relationship between the brand, the campaign, jazz music, and jazz discourses come together to create meaning—for the product, for consumers, and for jazz music. I focus on key tropes of meaning at play in the 60-second spot: diversity, agency, and sexuality.

First, I propose that the spectacularization of ethnic and cultural diversity in the Pepsi Jazz spot reflects PepsiCo's overarching corporate emphasis on diversity in its marketing and advertising, while at the same time playing with discourses of jazz as a collaborative, syncretic, and democratic music. I draw on Albert Murray's influential collection of essays, "The Omni-Americans: Some Alternatives to the Folklore of White Supremacy," proposing that Pepsi positions "Jazz" as an omni-American soft drink.

Second, I address the significance of individual agency in the advertisement. I use Michel de Certeau's essay, "Walking In The City," to examine how the advertisement's narrative and soundtrack work together to construct the heroine's individual agency in the ad, and to explore how her agency becomes crucial to the demographic targeting of the "Pepsi Jazz" campaign.

Finally, I problematize the use of "indulgence" as a marketing theme, and argue that the undoubtedly well intentioned intersection of indulgence, agency, and diversity in the Jazz ad is predicated upon some uncomfortable jazz discourses of race, sex, and social deviance.

In Chapter 5, I examine the rationale for and implications of TD Bank's sponsorship of the major Canadian jazz festivals. I begin by discussing the practice of sponsorship itself as an advertising strategy, and offer a very brief survey of the history of this unique species of marketing from the early days of radio, through the early days of television, up to the present day. After outlining the history of Canadian jazz festivals up to the inception of the TD title sponsorship arrangement, I explore the articulation of banking to jazz, first from the perspective of the festivals, and then from the vantage point of TD Bank. I examine the Bank's intertwined motivations for taking on the jazz festival sponsorship: their "comfort" brand positioning, their engagement with local communities, their promotion of cultural diversity, and their support of artistic excellence.

Next, I look at some of the tensions that have developed through TD's sponsorship, and theorize the jazz-banking articulation—and the practice of arts sponsorship in general—vis-à-vis Milton Friedman's notion of capitalist amorality. Finally, I consider the web of relationships that develops between sponsors and audiences in jazz festivals about the character of "false consciousness:" following Žižek, I contend that the utopianism that emerges in corporately-sponsored jazz festivals reveals "false consciousness" to be a voluntary condition, one that potentially allows us to gloss real social traumas, thereby inviting us to abdicate the social responsibilities entailed in democratic citizenship and entrust them to corporations.

In the concluding chapter, I draw some of these many different thematic threads together by highlighting the idea of improvisation. I suggest that the core narrative of most jazz-based advertising uses improvisation to knit together crucial skeins of the fabric of consumer capitalism—freedom of expression and freedom of choice. By framing material acquisition in the sound and language of jazz performance, the moral of the jazz advertising story reaffirms that consumption itself can be a kind of expressive improvisation: consumer capitalism invites us to select freely and creatively from an infinitely variable panoply of commodity choices in order to express the innermost reality of our identity, just as a mythic jazz musician might draw liberally upon an unfathomably varied aesthetic palette to express some otherwise-inexpressible truth about himself and his community. What's more, it is an expressive modality that seems to override the tawdry, mundane questions of commerce and economics, instead ostensibly accessing real, authentic cultural truth.

Needless to say, this improvisation-consumption analogy is deeply problematic and ignores the nuance and complexity of both improvisation and consumption; nevertheless, it is this kind of analogy that provides the kind of narrative and meaning that (as Weber suggests) human beings require to embrace consumption as a viable kind of self-expression, and thereby to sustain the all-important spirit of capitalism.

Notes

1. Unfortunately, this product was rebranded by the Little Potato Company in the spring of 2014. I will leave it to some other intrepid researcher to determine whether dropping the "jazz" has impacted the microwavable potato experience.
2. http://thingscalledjazzthatarenotjazz.tumblr.com/
3. Media scholar Jennifer Scanlon has explored the role of *Ladies' Home Journal* in the emergence of feminized consumer culture during the 1920s in her excellent book, *Inarticulate Longings: The Ladies' Home Journal, Gender, and the Promises of Consumer Culture* (Scanlon, 1995).
4. In much of the rest of the world, radio and television broadcast frequencies were more commonly controlled by the state, at least until recently.
5. Anthropologist Sherry Ortner's 2010 article, "Access: Reflections on Studying Up in Hollywood" (*Ethnography* 11: 211–33), details her experience contending with similar accessibility challenges in her research on the American motion picture industry.

Bibliography

Adorno, Theodor and Max Horkheimer. "The Culture Industry: Enlightenment as Mass Deception," *The Cultural Studies Reader* ed. Simon During. New York: Routledge, 2007. 29–43.

Ake, David. *Jazz Cultures.* Los Angeles: University of California Press, 2002.

Althusser, Louis. "Ideology and Ideological State Apparatuses (Notes towards an Investigation)," *Lenin and Philosophy and Other Essays.* New York: Monthly Review Press, 1971.

Attrep, Kara. "The Sonic Inscription of Identity: Music, Race, and Nostalgia in Advertising." Unpublished PhD Dissertation. Santa Barbara, CA: University of California, Santa Barbara, 2008.

Baraka, Amiri. *Blues People: Negro Music in White America.* Edinburgh: Payback Press, 1995.

Baudrillard, Jean, Carl R. Lovitt, Denise Klopsch. "Toward a Critique of the Political Economy of the Sign," *SubStance*, 5 (1976): 111–16.

Berlant, Lauren. "Intimacy: A Special Issue," *Critical Inquiry* 24 (Winter 1998): 281–88.

Bourdieu, Pierre. "The Field of Cultural Production, or: The Economic World Reversed," *The Field of Cultural Production: Essays on Art and Literature.* ed. Randal Johnson. New York: Columbia University Press, 1993.

Bruner II, Gordon C. "Music, Mood, and Marketing," *The Journal of Marketing* 54 (Oct. 1990): 94–104.

de Certeau, Michel. *The Practice of Everyday Life*, trans. Steven Rendall. Los Angeles: University of California Press, 1984.

Cohen, Lizabeth. *A Consumer's Republic: The Politics of Mass Consumption in Postwar America.* New York: Alfred A. Knopf, 2003.

Cook, Nicholas. "Music and Meaning in the Commercials," *Popular Music* 13 (1994): 27–40.

Cooley, Timothy, Katherine Meizel, and Nasir Syed. "Virtual Fieldwork," *Shadows in the Field: New Perspectives for Fieldwork in Ethnomusicology*, 2nd edition, ed. Timothy Cooley and Gregory Barz. New York: Oxford University Press, 2008.

Cross, Gary. *An All-Consuming Century: Why Commercialism Won in Modern America.* New York: Columbia University Press, 2000.

Debord, Guy. *The Society of the Spectacle*, trans. Donald Nicholson-Smith. New York: Zone Books, 1995.

Early, Gerald. "Pulp and Circumstance: The Story of Jazz in High Places", *The Jazz Cadence of American Culture*, ed. Robert O'Meally. New York: Columbia University Press, 1998. 393–430.

Finch, Russell. *things called jazz that are not jazz* (Accessed February 23, 2014) http://thingscalledjazzthatarenotjazz.tumblr.com

Foster, Robert J. "The Work of the New Economy: Consumers, Brands, and Value Creation," *Cultural Anthropology* 22 (Nov. 2007): 707–31.

Frank, Thomas. *The Conquest of Cool: Business Culture, Counterculture, and the Rise of Hip Consumerism.* Chicago: University of Chicago Press, 1997.

Fulcher, James. *Capitalism: A Very Short Introduction.* New York: Oxford University Press, 2004.

Gabbard, Krin. "Introduction: The Jazz Canon and Its Consequences," *Jazz Among the Discourses*, ed. Krin Gabbard. Durham: Duke University Press, 1995.

———. *Jammin' at the Margins: Jazz and the American Cinema.* Chicago: University of Chicago Press, 1996.

Gennari, John. *Blowin' Hot and Cool: Jazz and Its Critics.* Chicago: University of Chicago Press, 2006.

Gilroy, Paul. *Darker than Blue: On the Moral Economies of Black Atlantic Culture.* Cambridge, MA: Harvard University Press, 2010.

Gorn, Gerald. "The Effects of Music in Advertising on Choice Behavior: A Classical Conditioning Approach," *Journal of Marketing* 46 (Winter 1982): 94–101.

Grossberg, Lawrence. "On Postmodernism and Articulation: An Interview with Stuart Hall," *Journal of Communication Inquiry* 10 (June 1986): 45–60.

hooks, bell. *Black Looks: Race and Representation.* Boston, MA: South End Press, 1992.

Hung, Kineta. "Narrative Music in Congruent and Incongruent TV Advertising," *Journal of Advertising* 29 (Spring 2000): 25–34.

Huron, David. "Music in Advertising: An Analytic Paradigm," *The Musical Quarterly* 73 (1989): 557–74.

Jhally, Sut. "Image-Based Culture: Advertising and Popular Culture," *Gender, Race and Class in Media: A Text-Reader,* ed. Gail Dines and Jean M. Humez. Thousand Oaks, CA: Sage, 2003. 327–36.

Karmen, Steve. *Who Killed the Jingle?: How a Unique American Art Form Disappeared.* Milwaukee, WI: Hal Leonard, 2005.

Klein, Bethany. *As Heard on TV: Popular Music in Advertising.* Burlington, VT: Ashgate Publishing Company, 2009.

Lee, Martyn J. *Consumer Culture Reborn: The Cultural Politics of Consumption.* New York: Routledge, 1993.

Levy, Sidney J. "Symbols for Sale," *Harvard Business Review* (July–August 1959): 117–24.

Lewis, George E. *A Power Stronger Than Itself: The AACM and American Experimental Music.* Chicago: University of Chicago Press, 2008.

Marcus, George. "Ethnography in/of the World System: The Emergence of Multi-Sited Ethnography," *Annual Review of Anthropology* 24 (1995): 95–117.

McClaren, Carrie. "Licensed to Sell: Why the Jingle is Dead and Commercial Pop Rules," *Stay Free!* No. 15 (Fall, 1998). 28 November 2008 www.stayfreemagazine.org/archives/index.html.

McClintock, Anne. "Soap and Commodity Spectacle," *Representation: Cultural Representations and Signifying Practices.* Thousand Oaks, CA: Sage Publications, 1997. 280–82.

McGovern, Charles. *Sold American: Consumption and Citizenship, 1890–1945.* Chapel Hill, NC: University of North Carolina Press, 2006.

Monson, Ingrid. "The Problem with White Hipness: Race, Gender, and Cultural Conceptions in Jazz Historical Discourse", *JAMS* 48 (Autumn 1995): 396–422.

Oliver, Richard L., Thomas S. Robertson, Deborah J. Mitchell. "Imaging and Analyzing in Response to New Product Advertising," *Journal of Advertising* 22 (Dec. 1993): 35–50.

Ortner, Sherry. "Access: Reflections on studying up in Hollywood," *Ethnography* 11 (2010): 211–233.

Packard, Vance. *The Hidden Persuaders.* New York, NY: Simon & Schuster, 1957.

Park, Lisa Sun-Hee. *Consuming Citizenship: Children of Asian Immigrant Entrepreneurs.* Stanford, CA: Stanford University Press, 2005.

Peterson, Richard A. *Creating Country Music: Fabricating Authenticity.* Chicago, Il: University of Chicago Press, 1997.

"The Power of Refined Beauty: Photographing Society Women for Pond's, 1920s–1950," *Duke University Libraries* (Accessed 27 August 2010) http://library.duke.edu/exhibits/ponds/index.html.

Rubin, Joan Shelley. *The Making of Middlebrow Culture.* Chapel Hill, NC: The University of North Carolina Press, 1992.

Samuel, Lawrence R. *Brought To You By: Postwar Television Advertising and the American Dream.* Austin, TX: University of Texas Press, 2001.

Scanlon, Jennifer. *Inarticulate Longings: The Ladies' Home Journal, Gender, and the Promises of Consumer Culture.* New York: Routledge, 1995.

Schwarzkopf, Stefan. "Ernest Dichter, Motivational Research and the 'Century of the Consumer,'" *Ernest Dichter and Motivation Research: New Perspectives on the Making of Post-War Consumer Culture.* ed. Stefan Schwarzkopf and Rainer Gries. Hampshire, UK: Palgrave MacMillan, 2010: 3–38.

Scott, Linda M. "Understanding Jingles and Needledrop: A Rhetorical Approach to Music in Advertising," *The Journal of Consumer Research* 17 (Sept. 1990): 223–36.

Smulyan, Susan. 1994. *Selling Radio: The Commercialization of Radio Broadcasting, 1920–1934.* Washington, D.C.: Smithsonian Institution.

Stanbridge, Alan. "From the Margins to the Mainstream: Jazz, Social Relations, and Discourses of Value," *Critical Studies in Improvisation* 4.1 (2008).

Sterne, Jonathan. "Sounds like the Mall of America: Programmed Music and the Architectonics of Space," *Ethnomusicology* 41 (Winter, 1997): 22–50.

Stillwell, Robynn J. "Advertising, music in," *Grove Music Online.* ed. L. Macy (November 20, 2008) www.grovemusic.com.

Taylor, Frederick Winslow. *The Principles of Scientific Management* New York, NY: Harper and Brothers 1911.

Taylor, Timothy D. "World Music in Television Ads," *American Music* 18 (Summer 2000): 162–92.

———. "Music and Advertising in Early Radio," *ECHO: A Music-Centered Journal* 5 (Fall 2003): 1–28.

———a. "The Commodification of Music at the Dawn of the Era of 'Mechanical Music,'" *Ethnomusicology* 51 (Spring/Summer 2007): 281–305.

———b. "The Changing Shape of the Culture Industry; or, How Did Electronica Music Get into Television Commercials?," *Television & New Media* 8 (August 2007): 235–58.

———. *The Sounds of Capitalism: Advertising, Music, and the Conquest of Culture.* Chicago, IL: University of Chicago Press, 2012.

"Thoroughly Modern Millie," *Encyclopedia of Popular Music,* ed. Colin Larkin. Oxford University Press (Accessed October 28, 2008) www.encpopmusic4.com.

Veblen, Thorstein. *The Theory of the Leisure Class.* New York: Oxford University Press, 2007.

Weber, Max. *The Protestant Ethic and the Spirit of Capitalism.* New York, NY: Routledge, 2001.

White, Irving S. "The Functions of Advertising in Our Culture," *Journal of Marketing* (July 1959): 8–14.

Whyton, Tony. *Jazz Icons: Heroes, Myths and the Jazz Tradition.* New York: Cambridge University Press, 2010.

Žižek, Slavoj. *The Sublime Object of Ideology.* New York: Verso, 1989.

2

PIMPS, REBELS, AND VOLKSWAGENS*

For most of its history, the relationship between jazz and commerce has frequently been characterized as fundamentally oppositional. This stance can be seen in Stanley Crouch's acerbic criticisms of Miles Davis for his "pernicious effect on the music scene since he went rapaciously commercial" (Porter 2002: 302); in Amiri Baraka's furious characterization of the mainstream Euro-American (and middle class African American) commercial aesthetic of "social blandness" that threatened to efface jazz's African American cultural roots (Baraka 1995: 181); and in the assertions of jazz historians such as Grover Sales (1984), Lewis Porter (1997), and Mark Gridley (2006) that jazz does not belong to the category of popular music, and as such is not beholden to the vicissitudes of the marketplace. While a number of musicologists and sociologists have published compelling work in the last 15 years debunking this binary,[1] the notion of an opposition between music (and jazz in particular) and commerce has proved remarkably durable, both in jazz musicians' own understanding of their relationship to the culture industries and in the way that relationship is represented in the popular media.

In some respects, Charles Mingus, the bassist, composer, bandleader, and sometime author was the equal of Crouch, Baraka, Sales, Porter, Gridley and other historians in his adamant views that the encroachment of commercial concerns had an enormously deleterious impact on artistic production. Along with Baraka, Mingus was vociferously critical of the destructive impact that Euro-American-controlled culture industries had on the music of African Americans. Over the course of his career, Mingus became famous for his anti-commercial rants—both in person and in print. In 1953, for instance, Mingus publicly railed against Euro-American promoters who marketed musicians whom he deemed to be artistically

*Portions of this chapter first appeared in *Black Music Research Journal* 34: 2 (Fall 2014). Published by The Center for Black Music Research at Columbia college Chicago. Copyright 2014 by the Board of Trustees of the University of Illinois.

deficient: "impresarios bill these circus artists as jazzmen because 'jazz' has become a commodity to sell, like apples or, more accurately, corn" (quoted in Saul 2001: 398).

Since its arrival in North America in the years immediately following World War II—and particularly since it hired innovative ad agency Doyle Dane Bernbach in the late 1950s—Volkswagen has positioned itself as a brand apart. With now-legendary print ads like "Think Small" and "Lemon," the German carmaker purported to eschew American mass consumption and crass commercialism: rather than designing new cars that stayed at the cutting edge of automotive *fashion*, DDB's ads claimed that Volkswagen was solely interested in manufacturing products that were simple and reliable, even if that meant that they did not sell as many cars as their big American industry rivals. Using a combination of humor and irony, DDB's ads engaged potential drivers who were savvy, intellectual, and who had developed a critical distaste for the fashion trends of a bloated American automotive industry. As Thomas Frank has noted, "[B]y far the most powerful feature of the Volkswagen ads . . . is their awareness of and deep sympathy with the mass society critique" (Frank 1997: 64).[2]

In the late 1990s, Volkswagen was seeking to reconnect with what had become its primary North American demographic: young drivers. In 1997, working with Boston-based advertising agency Arnold Worldwide, the company launched a new campaign based around the slogan "Drivers Wanted." In a 2000 interview with *ADWEEK* magazine, Arnold's chief creative officer Ron Lawner described the character of the brand that the campaign was aiming to develop in humanizing, humorous terms that recall the DDB campaigns of the 1950s and 1960s, as if the Volkswagen brand were an individual Volkswagen driver: "[A]pproachable, honest, with a sense of humor; the kind of people you like to be around. . . . They are passionate, they have a lust for living and a lust for driving . . . but don't take themselves too seriously." Based on the extended version of the slogan, the ideal Volkswagen driver is also clearly someone who takes charge, who is in control, and who refuses to bend to social or institutional pressure—on the road or in life: "On the road of life, there are passengers and there are drivers. *Drivers wanted.*"

In 1999, Arnold produced a series of television ads on the "Drivers Wanted" theme that developed this brand personality. In fact, as *ADWEEK* writer Eleftheria Parpis explained, the advertisements in the series were not intended to sell cars based on specific technical attributes per se, but rather to attract consumers by introducing them to the new, distinctive, appealing brand identity. Hence, Ron Lawner's profile of the ideal Volkswagen driver is key to understanding any of the 1999 advertisements. Seven of these spots were named Best Spot of the Month by *ADWEEK*, one of the American advertising industry's most prominent periodicals, making it one of the most successful and influential television campaigns in the last several decades.

Among the first of the "magnificent seven" ads (as *ADWEEK* called them) was a spot for the Jetta released in March of 1999 called "Great Escape." As was true of nearly every spot in the campaign, the real star of "Great Escape" is the soundtrack: in this case, the music of Charles Mingus. The ad features a heavily edited rendition of Mingus's classic composition, "II B.S." taken from his 1963 album, *Mingus Mingus Mingus Mingus Mingus*.[3]

As Nicholas Cook has observed, "Musical styles and genres offer unsurpassed opportunities for communicating complex social or attitudinal messages practically instantaneously. One or two notes in a distinctive musical style are sufficient to target a specific social and demographic group, and to associate a whole nexus of social and cultural values with the product" (Cook 1994: 35). In a car ad where the car itself is secondary in importance to the personality of the brand, "II B.S." and its attendant "nexus of social and cultural values" becomes the mortar that holds the psychographic layers of the Jetta advertisement together.

This chapter explores the unexpected relationship between three seemingly tangentially related subjects: the music and discourse of Charles Mingus, particularly during the late 1950s and early 1960s; anti-commercial music and art criticism from the 1920s through the 1960s in the United States; and Arnold's advertising campaign for Volkswagen in 1999. I propose that "II B.S." generates meaning in the VW Jetta spot by drawing out three primary, integrated discursive themes: rebellion against institutional oppression, individual agency and self-determination, and a specifically masculinist authenticity. I suggest that it is through the interplay of these themes over the course of the spot that the consumer comes to understand the character of the Volkswagen brand that Ron Lawner described. These same themes are also central to the critical discourse of Charles Mingus in terms of his prose, his music, and his activism. Since "II B.S." is unquestionably embedded in Mingus's own biography and his ideas about the politics and economics of music-making, I argue that the Jetta ad depends on Mingus himself—almost as if he were an unseen character in the spot.

Finally, I assert that it is also important to understand that although Mingus is unquestionably a colossal figure in jazz history, he certainly did not stand apart from the broader flows of American socio-cultural, aesthetic, and economic discourse. In this sense, Mingus is both a participant in and a representative of the interrelated aesthetic and sociopolitical debates that held sway in the jazz field throughout the 20th century. These ideas and events framed his own music and discourse, and in turn, through Mingus, jazz history and discourse knit together the disparate elements of the Volkswagen psychographic profile. In short, then, this chapter explores how 20th-century aesthetic debates about jazz, masculine authenticity, individual agency, and the culture industries coalesce through the music and discourse of Charles Mingus during the late 1950s and early 1960s in order to sell Volkswagen Jettas in 1999.

"You've Taken My Blues and Gone": Jazz, Commerce, and the Culture Industries 1920–1960

Throughout the 1920s and 1930s, jazz was the subject of numerous critical attacks from many sectors of the American press.[4] Newspapers and magazines such as the New Orleans Picayune, Musical America, The New Republic and Ladies' Home Journal directed their assault at jazz's perceived lowbrow lasciviousness and the pursuant danger of miscegenation. In an article printed in the Ladies' Home Journal in December 1921 titled "Unspeakable Jazz Must Go!" Journal contributor John McMahon interviewed Fenton T. Bott, Director of Dance Reform in the American National Association Masters of Dancing. In Bott's view, "Don Juan never had such a potent instrument of downfall as the ultra-dance supplies to every evil-purposed male to-day. The road to hell is too often paved with jazz steps" (McMahon [1921] 2002: 163). Imbricated with Bott's fears of the threat jazz posed to sexual propriety was his moral outrage against the music's perceived status as mere crass commercialism.

For commentators like Bott, jazz had no intrinsic aesthetic value; its sole social value lay in its status as a commodity for commercial exchange. Bott therefore focuses his fury at American music publishers for putting profit ahead of their moral duty:

> Now, at the 1920 convention of our association we appealed to the music publishers to eliminate jazz music. A representative of the publishers came before us and replied that personally he was against the indecent stuff, being himself a church elder or deacon, but the publishers had to give the public what they wanted and they also had to reckon with stockholders calling for dividends. That's a fine argument!
>
> (Quoted in McMahon [1921] 2002: 162)

Other critics connected jazz directly to the trappings of commercial mass production—especially the automobile. In Harcourt Farmer's June 1920 *Musical America* article, "The Marche Funèbre of 'Jazz'," the author explicitly links jazz to the Ford Company:

> If we recall that the persons immediately interested in the survival of Jazz unmusic are the sellers of it, we are spared a deal of conjecture as to the reason of its continued existence even so far as this. But Jazz, like cheese and Fords, has to be pushed, else would there be no gorgeous dividends to split up.
>
> (Farmer [1920] 2002: 144)

Farmer extends the metaphor through the article, referring to jazz musicians as "jazz mechanics" and their performance process as "building jazz tunes" (Farmer [1920] 2002: 146). Like Bott, Farmer proposes that jazz is the offspring of the processes of industrial mass-production, and therefore does not even qualify as music. Hence, the only comprehensible rationale for producing this "unmusic" was money: "they rightly decided that the more ugly and noisy their stuff was the more it would sell. And it has sold. More Jazz sold last month than Beethoven" (Farmer [1920] 2002: 146). Writing in The New Republic in 1921, Clive Bell draws a recursive connection between the notion of jazz as a mass-produced commodity to the concept of the mass audience, which (in Marx's view) was itself a product of the processes of mass production and mass mediation:

> What, I believe, has turned so many intelligent and sensitive people against Jazz is the encouragement it has given to thousands of the stupid and vulgar to fancy that they can understand art and to hundreds of the conceited to imagine that they can create it.
>
> (Bell [1921] 2002: 156)

Bell contemptuously dismisses both jazz and its audience simply because he views both as products of mass culture: jazz is a Fordist faux-artwork, mass produced by "hundreds of the conceited [creators]" for dissemination among a shapeless, nameless, changeless mass of consumers who ignorantly and unreflectively consume whatever pap they might be fed—the "thousands of the stupid and vulgar".

This dismissal of mass culture was at the heart of Theodor Adorno's 1936 critique, "On Jazz".[5] Adorno writes,

> Jazz is a commodity in the strict sense: its suitability for use permeates its production in terms none other than its marketability, in the most extreme contradiction to the immediacy of its use not merely in addition to but also within the work process itself. It is subordinate to the laws and also to the arbitrary nature of the market, as well as the distribution of its competition or even its followers.
>
> (Adorno 2002: 473)

Like the American critics, Adorno argues that jazz has no value outside its status as a commodity and no social function other than its marketability. Indeed, he regards jazz as all the more insidious precisely because it purports to be countercultural. In actuality, this patina of rebellion merely serves to disguise its commodity status:

> Through its intentions, whether that of appealing to an elevated 'style' individual taste, or even individual spontaneity, jazz wants to improve its marketability and veil its own commodity character which, in keeping with one of the fundamental contradictions of the system, would jeopardize its own success if it were to appear on the market undisguised.
>
> (Adorno 2002: 473)

Adorno also echoes (and in some respects clarifies) the perceived relationship between jazz, commerce, and the supposed loosening of sexual mores among American youth—especially young women:

> The pace of the gait itself—language bears witness to this—has an immediate reference to coitus; the rhythm of the gait is similar to the rhythm

of sexual intercourse; and if the new dances have demystified the erotic magic of the old ones, they have also—and therein at least they are more advanced than one might expect—replaced it with the drastic innuendo of sexual consummation.

(Adorno 2002: 486)

It is worth noting that Adorno's writing does not evince the same moral hysteria that characterizes much of the contemporary American criticism; nevertheless, by connecting jazz, sex, commerce, and social decay (and implicitly, race), Adorno reiterates the commonplace American ideological viewpoint, merely within a different moral framework.

In virtually all of this commentary, there is a persistent—if usually implicit—relationship between "crass commercialism" and moral decay, almost invariably personified by the figure of the sexualized (Euro-American) female body. All of the authors (among many others) take it as axiomatic, first, that anyone involved with the performance, production, or distribution of jazz music is principally, if not exclusively, concerned with commercial gain; second, that jazz music and dance inherently inspire a level of uncontrolled libidinous excess that is morally abhorrent, especially where young listeners are involved;[6] and third, that the singular lust for financial gain blinded jazz advocates to the general decline of American moral standards in which their music was supposedly implicated. While jazz's purported "crass commercialism" was not seen to be directly, necessarily responsible for sexual exploitation, young women were the chief victims of profiteering "jazz mechanics," purposefully oblivious to the "break down [of] respect for womanhood" that the corrupted music had wrought.

Of course, there is a real irony in the fact that so much of this anti-jazz, anti-commercial spleen was vented in magazines like *Ladies' Home Journal.* As we saw in the previous chapter, mass-circulated magazines like the *Journal* were key Althusserian ideological state apparatuses in the early 20th century; along with commercial radio, these magazines were critical to the development of the sociocultural category of the consumer. Few institutions were commodities in a "stricter sense" (to paraphrase Adorno) than magazines.

This seeming contradiction between the strictly commercial operation of magazines and the anti-commercial rhetoric that many magazines published in an effort to discredit jazz music speaks to the precise character of the consumptive subject as it was taking shape. The consumer as constituted in mass media was by no means simply mindlessly, voraciously appetitive. On the contrary, consumers were expected to behave within fairly narrow moral constraints that were, in turn, closely aligned with normative gender and race codes. Beauty products like the Woodybury's face powder or Pears' soap discussed in the introductory chapter were acceptable consumer choices under this regime because they were linked to an appropriate model of Euro-American, bourgeois femininity; jazz was an unacceptable commodity because it was seen to threaten this feminine model.

Thus, even though jazz, cosmetics, and the magazines themselves were all equally commodified, only jazz was labeled "crassly commercial," and it earned this label because of its perceived moral transgressions rather than for anything relating to its economics. For the critics of jazz writing in these mass-mediated magazines, then, the Weberian moral spirit of consumer capitalism clearly trumped the amoral, commercial reality of consumer capitalism.

Nevertheless, given that jazz's most vehement critics focused their rhetoric on what they argued was a causal relationship between jazz's perceived crass commercialism and the moral turpitude of American youth, it is unsurprising that commerce would have been a similarly central theme in the commentary of the music's most ardent defenders. In his 1942 book, *The Real Jazz*, French jazz writer Hugues Panassié became one of a number of key commentators who positioned jazz as an anti-commodity that, far from being a crassly commercial driver of American moral and aesthetic decadence, was in fact a victim of a monolithic culture industry, hungry for profit at any cost. Panassié was especially vitriolic in his lamentation that African American jazz musicians "must submit to the corruption of an outrageous commercialism, as well as to the conventional musical notions of the white man and the current theories about necessary progress" (DeVeaux 1991: 536). He wrote with romantic passion and flair about informal jam sessions, spaces where he thought musicians were at liberty to make "the real jazz" without interference from the commercial realm:

> This is the music they are not permitted to play in the large commercial orchestras which they have been forced to join to earn their living. The jam session overflows and [allows] the musicians [to] play out of a love of music . . . simply because the music makes them feel intensely alive.
> (DeVeaux 1989: 11–12)

John Hammond, the well-known and highly-regarded record producer, critic, concert promoter, and social activist was more willing than Panassié to acknowledge that jazz musicians operated in a music industry governed by commercial exchange: for instance, he avidly campaigned for more competitive wages for African American musicians through the 1930s, working assiduously on behalf of the Count Basie Orchestra in particular. Nevertheless, Hammond's notion of jazz music aligned with that of his French contemporary in that both argued that jazz represented an authentic African American folk art, and that its folk status was contingent upon the music's transcendence of crude commercial concerns. This discourse anchored "From Spirituals to Swing," a 1938 concert at Carnegie Hall organized by Hammond and sponsored by *New Masses*. The concert opened with a recording of West African music, followed by performances of gospel, blues, boogie-woogie, New Orleans jazz, and concluding with an extended set by the Count Basie band. John Gennari summarizes the historiographical and political impact of the concert:

Hammond programmed a concert that represented black jazz as an authentic urban art, organically connected to localized, regional black folk cultures untainted by commercialism. In the parlance of 1930s Left populist rhetoric, Hammond's black face of jazz was the face of "the people."

(Gennari 2006: 47)

Meanwhile, jazz was a curiously complicated subject for African American commentators. African American newspapers like *The Chicago Defender*, *The Pittsburgh Courier*, and *The New York Amsterdam News* frequently reviewed jazz recordings and performances, promoting African American artists both locally and nationally.[7] A common theme in editorial writing on music, however, was once again the vexed relationship between jazz and capitalism. In a 1934 *Chicago Defender* profile of Noble Sissle, the jazz bandleader denies the possibility that jazz might be the highest expression of the African American cultural sensibility in part because of its commercial popularity and commodity status:

I know . . . that the musical libraries of the world are waiting for the symphonies, the overtures, the etudes and the grand operas that must eventually come from our group. Only we can write them—only we have a right to write. The world will accept our spirituals and our classic gems with the same open arms as they have our jazz. Young musicians must not stop at jazz—at the popular standard. I know. I play jazz. The price is too great. It always has been.

(Quoted in Stewart 1934: 12)

Like many of his contemporaries, he leans on Eurocentric standards in his conception of artistic achievement—"the symphonies, the overtures, the etudes, and the grand operas." While he acknowledges that jazz can be tremendously exciting for audiences, he suggests that its potential to enter the supposedly timeless pantheon of human musical achievement is limited by its contingency on the immediacy of commerce. In other words, in Sissle's view, until the quality of jazz music could be justified by something other than its commercial popularity and measured by something other than dollars and cents, it would never be more than a fad—a passing phase.

It is important to understand, however, that Sissle's perspective is not merely an elitist rejection of popular taste; rather, it is rooted in a much deeper distrust of the monetaristic logic of value under capitalism—an economic system that, in its American incarnation, emerged largely through the ruthless exploitation of African slave labor. As Sissle explains to his *Defender* interviewer, Ollie Stewart,

Spirituals, the songs that only the American Negro can sing and have a right to sing, are the heritage left by our forefathers, who with their life blood trickling from their lashed backs, purchased their right to freedom and at the same time the right to be the real folk songsters of America. Everyone else in this land of plenty received gold for their work—we received only misery—always paying, eternally paying. But now is the harvest time.

(Quoted in Stewart 1934: 12)

Sissle evocatively represents slave labor as a violently skewed kind of economic exchange: in an economic system ostensibly predicated on the exchange of labor for payment where "everyone else in this land of plenty received gold for their work," African American slaves were forced to do both the laboring and the paying. For them, there was no "exchange" per se; there was merely extraction.

Meanwhile, the repugnant injustice of slavery undergirded and enabled the smooth operation of capitalist exchange at higher, more visible levels. The agrarian economy in the American south was profitable precisely because slave owners were able to squeeze maximal labor out of their work force for negligible cost. Hence, if African Americans had historically been forcibly denied access to the supposed benefits of capitalism, and if capitalist logic entails a monetarist conception of value, for Sissle it becomes incumbent on African Americans to look for alternative, anti-capitalist ontologies of value that do not hinge on money. The musical "harvest time" to which he refers, then, is understood to be a cultural apotheosis, not an economic one. The commercial success of jazz music precludes it from being this apotheosis not because of any disdain for popular taste, but because its success reinforces the unacceptable (in Sissle's estimation) capitalist equation between money and value.

Similarly, the prominent African American writers and critics who were collectively associated with the Harlem Renaissance movement remained conspicuously ambivalent in their stance on jazz. According to Nathan Irvin Huggins, although many Harlem intellectuals frequented the New York jazz clubs through the 1920s and 1930s, surprisingly few of them wrote about it in any detail (Huggins 2007: 11). During his years as editor of the NAACP journal, *The Crisis*, W.E.B. Du Bois penned numerous articles about African American music, but pointedly ignored jazz (as well as blues) music, suggesting only that it should be generally disregarded until such time as it had developed into a "serious" form of art ("William Edward Burghardt Du Bois").

Those few Harlem intellectuals who did address jazz—notably Alain Locke and Langston Hughes—often reiterated the same kind of folk idealism that predominated in the writing of Hammond and Panassié, albeit with a markedly different ethic and intent. According to Hughes—the author of a regular column in *The Chicago Defender*, between 1942 and 1962 where jazz was a regular focus— the music's very existence spoke to the enormous innate creativity of lower-class African Americans:

[The] low-down folks . . . do not particularly care whether they are like white folks or anybody else. Their joy runs, bang! into ecstasy. Their religion soars to a shout. Work maybe a little today, rest a little tomorrow. Play a while. Sing a while. . . . These common people are not afraid of spirituals . . . and jazz is their child. They furnish a wealth of colorful, distinctive material for any artist because they still hold their own individuality in the face of American standardizations.

(Hughes 1926: 693)

In Hughes's view, jazz developed through the pleasure and play of a people who had been largely excluded from American capitalism; indeed, the music was precisely *enabled* by their exclusion. While middle class urban Euro-Americans were subject to the standardization and rationalization of American life, marginalized lower-class African Americans were left to choose to "work a little today, rest a little tomorrow, play a while, sing a while." Hence, for Hughes—as for Hammond and Panassié—jazz was a folk art: an art whose development was permitted by the physical and conceptual distance of its creators from American industrialization and commercialization.[8]

When the commercial system began to intrude upon the traditional lifestyles of these purportedly simple folk and their music, the effects were seen to be decidedly negative. In his 1936 book, *The Negro and His Music*, Alain Locke suggests that the process of commercialization was highly damaging: "The common enemy is the ever-present danger of commercialization which, until quite recently, has borne with ever-increasing blight upon the healthy growth of this music" (Locke 1968: 82). In Locke's view, it was the aesthetic and moral duty of jazz musicians to resist commercialization in all its forms.

Resonances of Locke's views on commercialization can be found in both the poetry and prose of Langston Hughes. In his 1940 poem, "Note on Commercial Theater," for instance, Hughes accuses a host of Euro-American-dominated culture industry institutions of co-opting African American music (the blues and spirituals in particular), and rendering it both culturally and politically anemic: "You've taken my blues and gone—/You sing 'em on Broadway/And you sing 'em in Hollywood Bowl/And you mixed 'em up with symphonies/And you fixed 'em/So they don't sound like me./Yep, you done taken my blues and gone."[9] In Hughes's view, by "mixing" African American music up with Euro-American pop and classical music and by performing it in commercial venues intended for Euro-American music, the unnamed Euro-American culture industry doyens ("You") effectively cut the blues and spirituals (and by extension, jazz) loose from their specifically African American folk-cultural origins (Hughes 1970: 190).

Intriguingly, the anxiety that Hughes and many of the other Harlem intellectuals shared with regard to the appropriation of African American cultural forms by Euro-American-controlled commercial interests is reminiscent in one respect of the fears expressed in Euro-American-run newspapers and magazines earlier in the 1920s. In both cases, commentators were concerned about the implications of racial mixing; however, there was a crucial distinction in the character of this

discourse in Harlem. Significantly, apart from the occasional colloquial personi-
fication of African American culture and African heritage through the casual use
of the female pronoun (Locke and DuBois, for instance, periodically refer to the
African American community or to the evanescent African homeland as "her"
or "she"), Harlem commentators never deployed the metaphors of miscegenation
and sexual exploitation—ideas that framed so much of the rhetoric of the early
Euro-American-authored jazz jeremiads—in their discussions of the ongoing
appropriation.

This telling rhetorical move suggests that, for the most part, the Harlem intellectuals were concerned with the biological coincidence of skin color (a consuming fixation for so many of their Euro-American counterparts) only insofar
as race aligned with socioeconomic power. They were not interested in using
sexuality as a metaphor because their goal was not to stir up fear and hatred; their
central motivation seems rather have been to incite their readers to think critically about socioeconomic inequity.

Sex and gender, however, did play key roles in the Harlem anti-commercial
discourse. Women—especially middle class African American women—were
regularly impugned for supposedly being uncritically voracious consumers of
mainstream entertainment manufactured by the Euro-American-run culture
industries. According to many of the Harlem commentators, it was women's
misdirected consumption patterns and preferences that kept compelling worthy
African American artists and African American art on the fringes of popular
acclaim and economic success. Langston Hughes's article, "The Negro Artist and
the Racial Mountain" (printed in *The Nation* in 1926), presents an instructive
example.

While the chief critical thrust of the article is directed at the African American bourgeoisie for being unsupportive of "authentic" African American art (for
Hughes, "authentic" art is that which is explicitly connected to the unapologeti-
cally Africanate cultural practices of the African American lower and working
classes, especially those who lived in or had recently moved away from the
American South), these "high class Negroes" as he calls them are signified principally by two female characters. The first is a mother who "often says, 'Don't
be like niggers' when the children are bad." The second, a "prominent Negro
clubwoman in Philadelphia," bears the brunt of Hughes's vitriol. He condemns
her for buying an expensive ticket to hear a Euro-American operatic singer
perform "Andalusian popular songs," but disdaining to attend a performance
of Negro folk songs by "a great black artist." Later, he is more expansive in his
critique:

> Yet the Philadelphia clubwoman is ashamed to say that her race created it
> and she does not like me to write about it. The old subconscious "white is
> best" runs through her mind. Years of study under white teachers, a life-
> time of white books, pictures, and papers, and white manners, morals, and

Puritan standards made her dislike the spirituals. And now she turns up her nose at jazz and all its manifestations—likewise almost everything else distinctly racial. She doesn't care for the Winold Reiss portraits of Negroes because they are "too Negro." She does not want a true picture of herself from anybody. She wants the artist to flatter her, to make the white world believe that all Negroes are as smug and as near white in soul as she wants to be.

(Hughes 1926: 693)

Hence, for Hughes and others,[10] women stand as the primary figures for a domesticated, deracinated, bourgeois inauthenticity that threatens to undercut the masculinized authentic African American artist.

Similarly revealing is the gendered tenor of the criticism targeted at those African American artists who were seen to have betrayed their commitment to authentic African American art. While no African American musicians were subject to this critique (at least, not during the 1920s and 1930s), a number of commercially successful African American poets were called out for producing work the popularity of which was a result of its being too precious, too effeminate, and too "white."

Literature scholar Jane Kuenz offers Countee Cullen as a particularly salient example of this phenomenon. Celebrated by early leaders of the Harlem Renaissance and New Negro movements like Locke and W.E.B. DuBois for his creative genius and deft literary craftsmanship, as his commercial popularity grew through the late 1920s and into the 1930s, Cullen had been largely rejected by the Harlem constituents for being (in the words of critic Saunders Redding) "effete and bloodless," "lisping," and entirely lacking in "virility: a schoolroom poet whose vision of life is interestingly distorted by too much of the vicarious. . . . [His] gifts are delicate, better suited to bon mots, epigrams, and the delightfully personal love lyrics for which a large circle admire him" (quoted in Kuenz 2007: 510). In Redding's criticism, we once again find the triple alignment of gender, commercialism, and authenticity that held sway in so much aesthetic discourse of the time.

Of course, this triple alignment was by no means isolated in 1920s Harlem. It continued to be a pervasive frame for aesthetic commentary with respect to virtually all artistic media in virtually every corner of the English-speaking world through the 1950s and 1960s and beyond. Writing in 1936 in his essay, "Bookshop Memories," George Orwell expressed his scorn for the predictable mediocrity of the mainstream British novel by reminding his readers of its feminine audience: "what one might call the average novel—the ordinary, good-bad, Galsworthy-and-water stuff which is the norm of the English novel—seems to exist only for women" (Orwell [1936] 2008: 11).

In his notorious review of James Gould Cozzens's 1957 novel, *By Love Possessed* (entitled "By Cozzens Possessed: A Review of Reviews"), the eminent literature critic Dwight MacDonald proceeded his evisceration of Cozzens's narrative and prose by casually dismissing his audience as dim-witted, bleating "matrons" who formulate their opinions in their totality by reading equally dim-witted "middlebrow" literary critics: "How do those matrons cope with it, I wonder. Perhaps their very innocence in literary matters is a help—an Australian aboriginal would probably find *Riders of the Purple Sage* as hard to read as *Golden Bowl*" (MacDonald 1958: 36).

In a *Down Beat* magazine article called "Here's the Lowdown on 'Two Kinds of Women'," printed in 1941, critic Marvin Freedman declared, "I *am* giving my theory on what's throttling our music, and, since the apple does not fall far from the tree, the theory is simple: Women control the public taste, and women do not like jazz!" (Freedman [1941] 1999: 119). Hence, the critical antagonism to the feminized consumers of culture industry-produced artistic commodities has been limited neither by time, by artistic mode, nor by geography.[11] The discourse was as prevalent in the 1940s and 1950s as it had been in the 1920s and 1930s.

Sociologists and cultural theorists such as bell hooks,[12] Hazel Carby,[13] and Kobena Mercer[14] have argued that this kind of misogyny was central to the emerging rhetoric of Black Power during the early 1960s. As hooks argues in her seminal study, *Ain't I a Woman: Black Women and Feminism*,

> While the 60s Black Power movement was a reaction against racism, it was also a movement that allowed black men to overtly announce their support of patriarchy. Militant black men were publicly attacking the white male patriarchs for their racism but they were also establishing a bond of solidarity with them based on their shared acceptance of and commitment to patriarchy.
>
> (hooks 1981: 98)

Presaging Mercer's and Carby's work in the 1990s, hooks observes that, in many cases, the corollary of African American male empowerment during the Black Power movement was the subjugation of African American women.

Amiri Baraka's work has been a particular lightning rod for feminist critiques of the Black Power movement. While Baraka was only one of a number of leaders of the movement who advocated for the restoration of patriarchal authority as a first step towards an empowered African American nation (or an African American community equitably integrated into the fabric of American citizenship), he was among the most visible, prolific, and unequivocally strident commentators to take up that cause. In this way, the ideological scaffolding of Baraka's aesthetic criticism was entirely distinct from that of his anti-middlebrow contemporaries like Dwight MacDonald. Whereas MacDonald was a self-avowed guardian of "highbrow" taste in the face of encroaching "midcult"[15] "artisans," critics, and consumers, Baraka fought passionately—and often violently—against the appropriation of African American cultural practices by the Euro-American-controlled culture industries.

Despite this vast ideological gulf between them, Baraka and MacDonald do share two notable rhetorical tropes: their loathing of an "inauthentic" consumerist middle class, and their concomitant disdain for women. Baraka targets much of his most heated criticism at the African American middle class: a group whom he accused of betraying their heritage because they recognized that it was socially and economically disadvantageous to act African American in a society that largely repudiated blackness. Writing in his 1963 critical history of jazz and blues music, *Blues People: Negro Music in White America*, Baraka averred,

> The middle-class black man, whether he wanted to be a writer, or a painter, or a doctor, developed an emotional allegiance to the middle-class (middle-brow) culture of America that obscured, or actually made hideous, any influences or psychological awareness that seemed to come from outside what was generally acceptable to a middle-class white man, especially if those influences were identifiable as coming from the most despised group in the country. The black middle class wanted no subculture, nothing that could connect them with the poor black man or the slave.
>
> (Baraka [1963] 1995: 131)

Hence, whereas for MacDonald the middle class continued to consume the "masscult" and "midcult" products of profiteering culture industries because (in his view) they were too witless to know better, in Baraka's estimation the African American middle classes willfully favored industrial cultural commodities because they wished to ingratiate themselves to the dominant race and to distance themselves from the lower classes. Thus, when Baraka asserts that swing music, for instance, "submerged all the most impressive acquisitions from Afro-American musical tradition beneath a mass of 'popular' commercialism," and that "swing sought to involve the African American culture in a platonic social blandness that would erase it forever, replacing it with the socio-cultural compromise of the 'jazzed-up' popular song," (Baraka 1995: 18) he is impugning both the Euro-American-controlled culture industries and their African American middle class consumers.

It is no coincidence that Baraka tends to use masculine referents for both African American and Euro-American artists and consumers. Responding to an interviewer's question about his views on interracial relationships, Baraka said: "[T]here are black men and white men, then there are women. . . . The battle is really between white men and black men whether we like to admit it that is the battlefield at this time" (hooks 1981: 97). Where MacDonald and the Euro-American highbrows largely positioned women as being the unwitting, primary consumers of the culture industries—and therefore, the group that was primarily culpable for the decline of American aesthetic tastes—like many Black Power leaders, Baraka positions women as being essentially incidental: passive spectators to the movement.

Baraka does not, however, deny that both African American and Euro-American women are profoundly implicated in the Black Power movement. On the contrary, throughout his poetry, dramaturgy, and prose of the 1960s, Baraka suggests that rather than being the principal consumers of commodities, women are *themselves* fundamentally commodities; in essence, women are a key form of currency for power transactions between African American and Euro-American men. In many of Baraka's more violent poems, he exhorts young African American men to rape Euro-American women. In his 1964 poem, "Black Dada Nihilismus," Baraka wrote, "Come up, black dada/nihilismus. Rape the white girls. Rape their fathers. Cut the mothers' throats."

Writing in his 1965 essay, "American Sexual Reference: Black Male," Baraka repeats this theme: "[T]he average ofay thinks of the black man as potentially raping every white lady in sight. Which is true, in the sense that the black man should want to rob the white man of everything he has" (Baraka 1966: 227). Here, as elsewhere, Baraka understands Euro-American women to be the most prized property of Euro-American men, and therefore the property most worthy of violent expropriation. Elsewhere in the 1965 essay, he further clarifies his meaning:

> In slavery times, theoretically, the slave master could make it with any black woman he could get to. The black man was powerless to do anything to prevent it; many times he was even powerless to keep his woman with him, or his children. . . . The reasons the black man was drawn to the white woman, I think, [reside in . . .] the wildly "protective" attitude white society has for The White Woman, as far as copulating with a black man is concerned. Also, because of this protective (defensive) odor the white man spread around the white woman, she became, in a sense, one of the most significant acquisitions of white society for a certain kind of black man.
>
> (Baraka 1966: 221–22)

According to the views that Baraka espoused in the 1960s, the rape of Euro-American women was an appropriately horrific response to the centuries of brutally violent oppression to which white Americans had subjected African Americans, including the industrial appropriation of African American cultural forms.

While women were not positioned as the principal consumer base that propped up morally and aesthetically vapid culture industries in Baraka's worldview, his critique of the culture industry consumers was nevertheless colored by a grotesquely gendered rhetoric wherein he substituted explicit homophobia for casual misogyny. As he writes in "American Sexual Reference: Black Male," "Most American white men are trained to be fags. For this reason it is no wonder their faces are weak and blank, left without the hurt that reality makes—anytime. That red flush, those silk blue faggot eyes" (Baraka 1966: 216). For Baraka, middle class Euro-American men are emasculated by their isolation from both physical labor and physical conflict. In his view, they are insulated from labor and conflict by a capitalist social-economic-military complex that displaces real labor to the socioeconomically disenfranchised, and puts military combat increasingly in the hands of war machines, the role of which is in part to continue to subjugate a global labor force so that they will continue to work to produce goods for the American middle class consumer. Because he is oblivious to these realities that propagate his power, the middle class Euro-American is similarly attracted to modes of leisure and entertainment that are similarly "unreal" and inauthentic, like swing music:

> White North American culture is committed to the idea of individualism, ego-satisfaction, and personal gain. "Free enterprise," an old white man with drooping eyes will tell you. And he will mean individualism, ego-satisfaction and personal gain—at the world's expense. It is unrealistic to think of the world as a place where some people should live in one manner, supported by the labor of the majority of the world's peoples. Not only is this thinking unrealistic, but by the exclusivity of its form (and E.X.C.L.U.S.I.V.E. is the word dead-loined white ladies cherish most) it also isolates the white man from the most common realities of the planet, so that most often his concerns seem stupid, fake and abstract, on one simple level.
>
> (Baraka 1966: 219–20)

Here, Baraka proposes that the myth of "free enterprise"—the occluded fact that American freedom is enabled by the subjugation of a significant number of disenfranchised Americans, together with huge swaths of the rest of the global population—produces an all-consuming "unreality" that renders most Euro-American social, cultural, and economic "concerns" "stupid, fake, and abstract."[16]

Baraka's language was unquestionably the most inflammatory of any of the theorists and critics I have surveyed, and there is undoubtedly considerable ideological distance between his work and that of Hugues Panassié, John Hammond, the writers associated with *The Ladies' Home Journal* and the 1920s Chicago newspapers, Alain Locke, Langston Hughes, George Orwell, and Dwight MacDonald. Nevertheless, we do see key common discursive threads: a pervasive distaste for the workings of a leviathan culture industry, a severe distrust of the bourgeoisie, and a profound contempt for the perceived ignorance of the culture industries' feminized consumer base. These threads form the discursive-rhetorical groundwork that undergirds American anti-commercial aesthetic commentary throughout the 20th century, and into the 21st century.

"You My Audience . . .:" Charles Mingus, Dissent, and Commodification

In his 1966 essay, "The Changing Same: R&B and New Black Music," Amiri Baraka identified African American bassist and composer Charles Mingus as one of the leaders of an activist, anti-commercial movement he saw taking shape within avant-garde jazz:

> In recent times musicians like Charles Mingus (dig "Fable of Faubus." etc.), Max Roach and some others have been outspoken artists on and off the stage, using their music as eloquent vehicles for a consciousness of self in America. The new musicians have been outspoken about the world through their music and off the stage as well. . . . Also, of course, the music is finally most musicians' strongest statement re: any placement of themselves socially. And the new music, as I have stated before about black music, is "radical" within the context of mainstream America. Just as the new music begins by being free. That is, freed of the popular song. Freed of American white cocktail droop, tinkle, etc. The strait jacket of American expression sans blackness . . . it wants to be freed of that temper, that scale. That life. It screams. It yearns. It pleads. It breaks out (the best of it).
> (Baraka 1968: 209)

Baraka clearly positions Mingus in opposition to mainstream (Euro-American) U.S. capitalism—what he elsewhere refers to as the American aesthetic of "social blandness" (Baraka 1995: 181). For Baraka, whereas the commercial mainstream represents a "strait jacket," typified by "popular song," and "American white cocktail droop, tinkle, etc." Mingus's music has a screaming, yearning, pleading "life."

Mingus's music is inextricable from his politics. From the mid-1950s, he was composing and recording music with explicitly politicized titles such as "Work Song" and "Haitian Fight Song" (later re-recorded as "II B.S.," the version used in the Volkswagen spot)—both written in 1955. The fullest musical exposition of his views on the American culture industries appears in his extended parodist work, "The Clown," recorded on the 1957 album of the same name, his first release with Ahmet Ertegun's Atlantic label. The piece features a narrative delivered by the actor Jean Shepherd (composed by Mingus), telling the story of a tragic, Pagliaccioesque clown, accompanied by a sequence of evocative musical episodes. Mingus made no attempt to disguise the semi-autobiographical nature of the piece, appearing in a Pagliaccio costume—complete with white garb and a made-up frown—on the record cover. He emphasizes the link musically as well: throughout the piece, the band intersperses a comical *leitmotif*—a kind of Johann

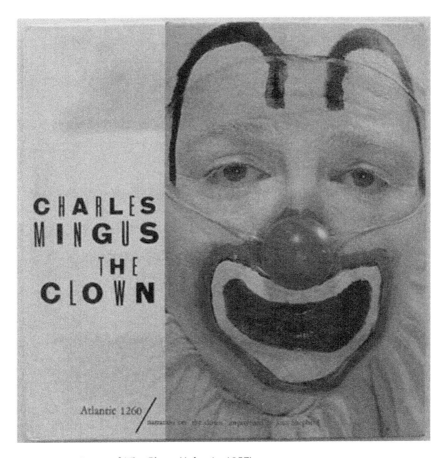

FIGURE 2.1 Cover of *The Clown* (Atlantic, 1957)

Strauss-pastiche circus melody—with free improvisation. Significantly, the episodes of improvisation always occur as accompaniment to Shepherd's narrative. Furthermore, the melodic content of the improvisations derives all its logic and coherence from the text—glissandi and dissonant crashes when the clown falls, plunger-mute effects to mimic the audience's laughter, sparse drone-oriented textures to evoke the clown's depression, and so forth.

Mingus's choice to accompany the clown with (relatively) freely improvised material is also meaningful: in 1957 when the piece was recorded (two years before Ornette Coleman's mythical arrival in New York at the Five Spot), free jazz was (and, to a certain extent, has continued to be) a highly modernist idiom in its experimental aesthetic and oppositional ethic. By accompanying the clown's tragic story with this deeply countercultural and anti-commercial music, Mingus fuses the clown's art with his own. The tragic story of the clown is therefore coterminous with what Mingus perceived to be the tragic impact of commercialism on jazz music.

Following a burst of the pastiche circus music from Mingus's band, Shepherd begins the narrative by describing the clown as a positive force who dreams only of sharing his positivity with the world:

> He was a real happy guy. He had all of these greens and all of these yellows and all of these oranges bubbling around inside of him. And he had just one thing he wanted in this world: he just wanted to make people laugh.

As the piece progresses, the clown becomes increasingly depressed by the realization that he is only able to make his audience laugh when something painful or grotesque accidentally happens:

> You know it's a funny thing. Something began to trouble this clown. You know, little things. Little things once in a while would happen that would make that crowd begin to move. But they were never the right things. Like for example, the time the seal got sick on the stage. All over the stage. The crowd just broke up. You know? Little things like that. And they weren't supposed to be in the act. And they weren't supposed to be funny. This began to trouble him. . . . All those greens and all those oranges and all those yellows, they just weren't as bright as they used to be.

The clown eventually comes to the conclusion that the only way he can successfully fulfill his dream of entertaining his audience is to harm himself for their amusement. The more violently he hurts himself, the more bookings he gets, and the more he gets paid. The climax comes during the clown's performance in Pittsburgh:

> About three quarters of the way through his act, a rope broke. Down came the backdrop, right on the back of the neck. And he went flat. And something broke. This was it. It hurt way down deep inside. He tried to get up. He looked out at the audience, and man, you should have seen that crowd. They was rolling in the aisles. . . . He really had 'em going. But this was it. This was the last one. . . . He knew now. Man, he really knew now. But it was too late.

The clown suffers indignity, pain, and eventually death in order to please his clientele. As his art—the joy that had originally provided him with so much personal pleasure and satisfaction—becomes commodified, sold for the pleasure of others, the clown loses control over his own humanity. He ultimately ceases to be a subject, becoming objectified for the pleasure of others to such an extent that his death is not even recognized. In the *denouement* of the story, the narrator remarks that, following the clown's death, his agent gets more calls than ever before. "Man, his agent was on the phone for twenty-four hours. The Palladium. MCA. William Morris. But it was too late. He really knew now. He really knew. . . . William Morris sends regrets." That the Hollywood talent agency William Morris—an essentially corporate entity (albeit one named for its late founder) that profits from the commodification and commercial exchange of human artistic labor—would be the only "person" to notice the clown's passing is a bitter irony.

Throughout his career, Mingus worked actively to change racist economics of the music industry that he critiques in "The Clown." He regularly fought for improved wages for himself and his collaborators. In a 1964 roundtable interview conducted by *Playboy* magazine, he contrasted his own perspective on money with that of free jazz pianist, Cecil Taylor:

> [Cecil Taylor] told me one time, "Charlie, I don't want to make any money. I don't expect to. I'm an artist." Who told people that artists aren't supposed to feed their families beans and greens? I mean, just because somebody didn't make money hundreds of years ago because he was an artist doesn't mean that a musician should not be able to make money today and still be an artist.
> ("The Playboy Panel" [1964] 1999: 273)

Mingus exhibited this point of view publicly in his dealings with Newport Jazz Festival organizer George Wein in 1960: in response to Wein's lowball offer of $700 for his band, Mingus refused to appear for anything less than $5000 (Gennari 2006: 181). When Wein refused, Mingus and Max Roach undertook to organize a counter-event in Newport, the Newport Rebel Festival. Scott Saul describes it as, "an *anti-festival* where the musicians seized the means of production: Mingus, Roach, and Eric Dolphy slept in tents along the beach, constructed the stage themselves, and solicited contributions from the audiences by walking around with can-in-hand" (Saul 2001: 400).

Indeed, according to Mingus's widow, Sue Mingus, the vast majority of the bassist's more notoriously violent outbursts were precipitated by disputes over money. I discussed this issue with Ms. Mingus in June of 2010 in a midtown Manhattan apartment that doubles as her home and the offices of Jazz Workshop Inc., the organization (run by Ms. Mingus) that oversees her late husband's musical and business affairs. During the interview, I asked Ms. Mingus about a story that had been related to me by Jed Eisenmen, one of the co-managers of the Village Vanguard, a jazz club in Greenwich Village that had often hosted Charles Mingus's groups from the 1950s on:

> ML: I was at the Vanguard the other night, and Jed, the manager . . . told me his favorite story about one time Charles, I guess, tore the door off the hinges and threw it at Max Gordon [the late owner of the club].

FIGURE 2.2 Charles and Sue Mingus (courtesy Sue Mingus)

SM: No, he didn't throw it at Max, he just threw it down the stairs. He didn't throw it at Max. He wrenched it off the door and threw it down the stairs. Yes, he did that. . . . But he wasn't. . . . Charles took action, maybe more violently than some, but if he wasn't getting paid. . . . It was over something where he wasn't paid. Normally he would either say that he would walk off with the cash register, or [laughs] . . .

ML: I guess you called it creative violence or something?

SM: Creative violence, yeah. Creative opposition, he would call it. Creative opposition.

(Sue Mingus 2010)

In her autobiography, *Tonight At Noon: A Love Story*, Sue Mingus describes other instances of "creative opposition" or "creative anger." including a visit Charles Mingus paid to executives at Columbia Records to discuss late royalty payments. He arrived at the meeting wearing a khaki suit and pith helmet and carrying a shotgun, and left the meeting with his royalty check (Sue Mingus 2002: 38). Mingus consistently responded to the inequitable working and wage conditions of the Euro-American-run music industry by finding creative ways to protest.

Fair wages were all the more important given the racial dynamics of the music industry at the time. As many contemporary African American and progressive Euro-American commentators observed, while the vast majority of jazz musicians were African American, virtually every power broker in the music industry—virtually every promoter, club owner, manager, publisher, critic, and record producer—was Euro-American. In his 1976 book, *Jazz Is*, the Jewish-American critic Nat Hentoff quotes African American trumpeter Rex Stewart's remarks on the issue: "Where the control is, the money is. Do you see any of us running any record companies, booking agencies, radio stations, music magazines?" (Hentoff 1976: 276). Mingus, too, was acutely aware of this imbalance. In the *Playboy* roundtable discussion, responding to accusations that his characterization of jazz as "Negro music" constituted reverse racism (so-called "Crow Jim"), Mingus declared,

> Until we own Bethlehem Steel and RCA Victor, plus Columbia Records and several other industries, the term Crow Jim has no meaning. And to use that term about those of us who say that this music is essentially Negro is inaccurate and unfeeling. Aren't you white men asking too much when you ask me to stop saying this is my music? Especially when you don't give me anything else?
> ("The Playboy Panel" [1964] 1999: 289)

Mingus's statement further underscores the significance of fair wages: the demand for a fair wage becomes a way for the African American musician to assert her or his ownership of the product *itself*, even as that product is disseminated through a Euro-American-run system of exchange over which the musician had little direct control. If, as Mingus asserts, jazz is "[his] music," he should be entitled to fair monetary compensation for his musical labor.

It is important to note that Mingus was not alone in these views. Speaking candidly to A.B. Spellman in the mid-1960s, avant-garde saxophonist Ornette Coleman said,

> [The] problem in this business is that you don't own your own product. . . . This has been my greatest problem—being shortchanged because I'm a Negro, not because I can't produce. Here I am being used as a Negro who can play jazz, and all the people I recorded for act as if they own me and my product. They have been guilty of making me believe I shouldn't have the profits from my product simply because they own the channels of production. . . . They act like I owe them something for letting me express myself with my music, like the artist is supposed to suffer and not to live in clean, comfortable situations.
> (Quoted in Kofsky 1998: 20)

Echoing Rex Stewart, Coleman concludes, "The insanity of living in America is that ownership is really strength. It's who owns who's strongest in America" (quoted in Kofsky 1998: 20).

Mingus also worked with great determination to change the terms of engagement between African American jazz musicians and the Euro-Americans who primarily controlled the production and dissemination of the music. In 1952, Mingus and drummer Max Roach founded one of the first record labels run by African American artists, Debut Records, together with an affiliated publishing company called Chazz-Mar, Inc. (Porter 2002: 112). While the two companies operated actively for only about five years, they did release music by a number of prominent artists—most notably the so-called "Greatest Jazz Concert Ever" featuring Charlie Parker, Dizzy Gillespie, Bud Powell, Mingus, and Roach, recorded live at Massey Hall in Toronto Canada in 1953. Following the dissolution of Debut and Chazz-Mar in 1957, Mingus founded a second publishing company, Jazz Workshop, Inc. (Porter 2002: 133) (a company that still exists in 2013, now owned and operated by Sue Mingus).

In 1960, emerging in part from the dispute with Newport Festival organizer George Wein, Mingus, Roach, and Count Basie's longtime drummer Jo Jones established the (very short-lived) Jazz Artists Guild, an organization mandated to "promote economic and artistic self-sufficiency" (Porter 2002: 135). In 1963, Mingus and Roach began working with the dancer Katherine Dunham, drummer Willie Jones, and saxophonist Buddy Collette to establish the School of Arts, Music, and Gymnastics, a Harlem-based community education initiative. While Mingus's school never opened, the concept presaged the Black Arts Repertory Theatre/School (BARTS) that Amiri Baraka and other artists active in the Black Arts Movement that would open in Harlem in 1965. Indeed, Mingus's abortive school and the short-lived BARTS project were both part of a larger trend towards artist-run collectives all across the United States that emerged at the height of the Black Power movement, focusing variously on recording (such as Nat Hentoff's Candid record label), publishing (*e.g.*, saxophonist Gigi Gryce's Melotone, Inc.), concertizing (*e.g.*, trumpeter Bill Dixon's Jazz Composers' Guild), and education, or in many cases, all of the above (*e.g.*, the still-thriving Association for the Advancement of Creative Music in Chicago, and the collectives associated with Sun Ra in Philadelphia, and Horace Tapscott in Los Angeles).[17] In all of these cases, musicians sought to move from critiquing the culture industries to actively changing them.

It is worth noting that Mingus's business ventures—along with those of Baraka, Gigi Gryce, Bill Dixon, Sun Ra, Horace Tapscott, the AACM, and many others—represent part of a larger movement in African American history towards socioeconomic self-determination that Manning Marable has called "Black Capitalism." For Marable, Black Capitalism includes three key tenets: "the accumulation of capital by individual Black entrepreneurs; strategies designed to maintain Black control over the Black consumer market in the U.S.; collective programs to improve the economic condition of all Blacks within the overall framework of U.S. capitalism" (Marable 2000: 139).

Mingus's own racialized engagement with capitalism certainly reflected Marable's theoretical framework: even when his entrepreneurship were primarily individualistic, his goals were unfailingly collectivist. In this way,

Debut Records, Chazz-Mar, the Jazz Artists Guild, and Jazz Workshop Inc. follow in a rich legacy of African American capitalist entrepreneurialism. As early as 1865, not long after the signing of the Emancipation Proclamation, African Americans established Freedman's Savings and Trust Company with a view to helping recently freed slaves in the southern states build their personal savings. Frederick Douglass served as the bank's last president before its insolvency in 1874 (Marable 2000: 139). In 1900, Booker T. Washington (with the support of steel tycoon and noted philanthropist Andrew Carnegie) established the National Negro Business League, an organization dedicated to "promoting the commercial and financial development of the Negro" (Marable 2000: 145). Washington explained his views on the importance of economics to the goals of racial uplift:

> Suppose there was a black man who had business for the railroads to the amount of $10,000 a year. So you suppose that, when that black man takes his family aboard the train, they are going to put him in a Jim Crow car and run the risk of losing that $10,000 a year? No, they will put on a Pullman palace car for him.
>
> (Quoted in Marable 2000: 145)

While Mingus's perspective was perhaps somewhat more nuanced (and perhaps somewhat less optimistic) than Washington's, he shared the NNBL's general viewpoint that Euro-Americans controlled American industry, and that carving a greater market share for African American-directed businesses could go a long way towards creating greater racial equality on a sociocultural level.

Mingus recognized, however, that capital was insufficient as a social corrective in and of itself. After all, it was not so much money itself as what that money represented—namely, prestige, power, and control—that was of value. The way that African American capitalist enterprises were represented in the media and (thereby) regarded by the mainstream public was crucial. With that in mind, more than almost any of his contemporaries, Charles Mingus became noted for the degree to which he controlled his own public discourse. Whether through his close friendships with prominent journalists and jazz critics such as Ralph Gleason and Nat Hentoff (on whose politically edgy Candid record label he released several albums, including the *Newport Rebels* recording that was made shortly after the 1960 "rebel festival"), through his frequent letters to major jazz periodicals like *Down Beat*, or through his collaborative and individual book projects, one was almost as likely to read Mingus as to hear him during the 1960s.

One of Mingus's most infamous rants against commercialism occurred in 1955 at the Five Spot, a club in New York. The rant was recorded, transcribed, and eventually published in 1960 in the collection *The Jazz Word* (reprinted in 1987) as an essay called "Mingus . . ." by Diane Dorr-Dorynek, a professional and romantic partner:

You, my audience, are all a bunch of poppaloppers. A bunch of tumbling weeds tumbling 'round, running from your subconscious . . . minds. Minds? Minds that won't let you stop to listen to a word of artistic or meaningful truth. You don't want to see your ugly selves, the untruths, the lies you give to life.

So you come to me, you sit in the front row, as noisy as can be. I listen to your millions of conversations, sometimes pulling them all up and putting them together and writing a symphony. But you never hear that symphony.

. . .

All of you sit there, digging yourselves and each other, looking around hoping to be seen and observed as hip. *You* become the object you came to see, and you think you're important and digging jazz when all the time all you're doing is digging a blind, deaf scene that has nothing to do with any kind of music at all.

(Quoted in Saul 2001: 400)

In this remarkable passage, Mingus inverts the performer-audience paradigm. Mingus, the supposed artist in the conventional paradigm, becomes the observer: he watches audience members performing their own hipness for each other and he responds to their performance with his music. In this new paradigm, however, Mingus loses control over the meaning of his art: because his pointedly satirical "symphony" is ignored by the audience—its collective target—he is reduced to an authenticating presence, a veneer of hipness that serves exclusively to reflect the audience's own hip performance back at them. Since his music has become commodified and circulated in the world of commercial exchange that was largely outside of his control, Mingus can no longer dictate the terms under which his music will be received and understood.

Mingus's manifesto/autobiography *Beneath the Underdog* is a testimony to his vexed relationship with the music industry. Throughout the book, he uses prostitution and pimping as a metaphor for the individual musician's relationship with the music industry. In his article "Outrageous Freedom: Charles Mingus and the Invention of the Jazz Workshop," Scott Saul explains, "Both prostitutes and musicians sold what had originally allowed them to escape 'from the usual tiddy, the hime, the gig'; both were service-workers in a pleasure industry that they did not control" (Saul 2001: 408).

Two key figures are central to the prostitution theme that unfolds through the book. Fats Navarro, the bebop trumpeter who died at the age of 26, serves as a cautionary image of the exploited musician who loses his dignity and ultimately his life through the machinations of the music industry. The Navarro character describes the bleak reality that African American musicians working in Euro-American-run culture industries must face: "Jazz is big business to the white man and you can't move without him. We just work-ants. He owns the

FIGURE 2.3 *Beneath the Underdog* (Alfred A. Knopf, 1971 [Vintage Books, 1991])

magazines, agencies, record companies and all the joints that sell jazz to the public. If you won't sell out and you try to fight they won't hire you and they give a bad picture of you with that false publicity" (Mingus 1991: 188). It is Navarro who presents Mingus with what he perceives to be the ultimate, stark choice all musicians must make: will he sell his genius and his art to the industry in order to make a living for himself and his family, or will he find some way to profit from the genius and artistry of others? Would he "play for money or be a pimp?" (Mingus 1991: 191). Navarro himself makes the choice to "play for money," and the choice costs him his dignity and finally his life.

The alternative to Navarro's exploited genius is Mingus's friend, the pimp Billy Bones. Bones stands as a clear contrast to Navarro: whereas "Fats" is an overweight junkie, Bones "carried himself at his full, proud height with great elegance." The description continues, emphasizing Bones's conspicuous wealth:

> On the street he wore expensive, proper clothes, appropriate for the San Francisco climate, and walked around in hundred-dollar Stetson shoes. He lived a kingly life, like a man on a continuous vacation with interruptions to see his florists or talk to his chef or instruct his brokers. . . . He could afford anything because he was the Black Prince of Pimps. . . .
>
> (Mingus 1991: 235)

Despite their very different social stations, Bones seemingly absorbs the same lessons through his affluence that Navarro did through his ruination. He passes that wisdom onto Mingus: "Now, Mingus, here's how to save yourself from depending on what rich punks think and critics say about jazz, true jazz, your work. By my reckoning a good jazz musician has got to turn to pimpdom in order to be free and to keep his soul straight" (Mingus 1991: 267). Only through exploiting others, Bones argues, can a musician earn a sufficient income to escape his own exploitation at the hands of the culture industries.

Indeed, Mingus deploys pimping as a metaphor to critique the faceless, soulless culture industries in particular, and capitalism in general. Throughout the book, pimping is compared favorably with corporate enterprise, as when Billy Bones's prostitute, Honey, says to Mingus's lover/prostitute, Donna, "You heard of Bethlehem Steel? Which you think is bigger business, pussy or steel?" When we recall Mingus's earlier, 1964 *Playboy* comments about Bethlehem Steel where that corporation served as a metonym for the racialized hegemony of American economics, Honey's comment allows Mingus (and invites his readers) to imagine a kind of inverted (albeit, violently patriarchal) vision of capitalism where African American capitalists control the most important and the most profitable natural resource: sex.

Moreover, all of the prostitutes who work for Mingus are Euro-American women, recalling the troubling sexual politics of Amiri Baraka, for whom the sexual exploitation of Euro-American women was a fair exchange for generations of Euro-American exploitation of African American labor and African American bodies. Indeed, via Billy Bones, Mingus concludes the sex industry is in fact *less* exploitative than supposedly legitimate industries like steel manufacturing or cultural production. Says Bones, "White man, you hate and fight and kill for riches, I get it from fucking. Who's better?" (Mingus 1991: 268). Clearly, Mingus glosses over the horrific sexual violence that is so often inextricable from the sex trade; nevertheless comparing pimping with other capitalist indus-trial endeavors, Mingus does raise important questions about the nature of labor exploitation and the role of African American people in the American capitalist economy.

In the end, however, Mingus rejects both the options of prostitution and pimping. The narrator reflects, "To be a pimp, one would have to lose all feel-ings, all sensitivity, all love. One would have to die! Kill himself! Kill all feeling for others in order to live with himself. Not to think. To keep going because you're already going. Mingus couldn't be this . . . a pimp" (Mingus 1991: 212). While he refuses to be dominated by the culture industries, he also recognizes that pimping would numb his artistic sensitivity. Toward the end of the book, he dismisses his two prostitutes, Lee Marie and Donna, returning their money and saying "I'm not a pimp! I don't want you to go, I don't want you to hustle. Give all this up. I'm a musician, this is my pad and don't come in here with your fucking commercial plans!" (Mingus 1991: 312).

Evidently, like those of so many of his contemporaries and predecessors, Min-gus's culture industry critique is framed in explicitly gendered terms. By using the sexualized female body (most often in the guise of the prostitute) in *Beneath the Underdog* as a metaphor for the economic exploitation of a musician at the hands of the culture industries, Mingus understands exploitation to be not sim-ply disempowering, but specifically *emasculating*. It castrates the masculinized musician, transforming him into a feminized, commoditized victim. Further-more, by having his character Billy Bones propose pimping as a way to escape exploitation, following Baraka, Mingus presents Euro-American women as a mode of currency through which African American men can gain restitution for the centuries of their own exploitation.

Even though Mingus himself does not directly advocate for pimping (hav-ing the character Bones make that suggestion in his stead), he certainly does not condemn it on moral or ethical grounds. All of Mingus's prostitutes work willingly, voluntarily submitting themselves for their admiration of Mingus's artistic genius and their desire for his sexual prowess. Mingus's entire pimping enterprise, therefore, is initiated and sustained by women, often over and above his own anxieties and wishes. When he does dismiss Donna and Lee Marie, it is because he worries that his work as a pimp has undermined his artistry. He never expresses any particular concern about his humanity—or theirs, for that matter. Indeed, in Mingus's fantastic account, it is the prostitutes—the women—not the artist/pimp who commodify and commercialize their own sexuality.

Once again, women are fundamentally responsible for propagating the com-mercial system, even when that system demands that they be exploited and dehu-manized. Mingus's perspective here recalls the way that Miles Davis (together with ghostwriter Quincy Troupe) deploys themes of pimping and prostitution in his 1989 book, *Miles: The Autobiography*. As Hazel Carby explains, "For the Davis of *Miles*, the issue of freedom relates to two clearly gendered spheres of existence.

He seeks freedom *from* a confinement associated with women, and freedom *to* escape to a world defined by the creativity of men" (Carby 1998: 138). In this way, commerce becomes a feminized domain that impinges on masculine artistic genius.

Indeed, *Beneath the Underdog* is only one example amongst a host of articles, interviews, song lyrics, and other written output in which Mingus frames his critique of the culture industries in terms of gender. In the version of his 1955 Five Spot rant published in the 1960 collection, *The Jazz Word*, for instance, Mingus adds two paragraphs directed at a (likely fictional) talkative, middle-aged woman in the audience—"the mother who brought a neighbor and talked three sets and two intermissions." The subjects of the officious housewife's conversation are almost entirely about the sexual and consumptive habits of her neighbors:

> [She] talked three sets and two intermissions about . . . how she's thinking of taking up teaching if Mary gets any more minks like that white one she just gave her sister Sal who's in and out on week days and leaves town on weekends with her Rolls Royce full of pretty teachers. And how it's difficult to keep the facts of life from her daughter Chi-Chi. The insurance man got fresh with me too . . . giggle giggle. Just a kiss . . . and oh! how cute he got he musta thought . . .?
>
> (Dorr-Dorynek 1987: 16)

Like in *Beneath the Underdog*, in the published version of the Five Spot rant, sex and commerce blend together in the feminized sphere of consumer capitalism—a sphere that simultaneously opposes and threatens masculinized artistic creative genius.

In spite of the deep antipathy towards a supposedly feminized commercial sphere that is clearly evident in these examples, Mingus was unquestionably heavily engaged in commercial exchange, not only an outspoken socioeconomic activist but also an entrepreneur with a paradoxically savvy approach to self-promotion. Scott Saul has convincingly argued that Mingus's anti-commercial rants were not only aesthetic statements; collectively, Saul proposes, Mingus's rants and other outrageous actions on stage—including physically throwing a football linebacker out of a club and destroying his bass on stage—become a kind of idiosyncratic tool to generate publicity. Referencing the audience response at the conclusion of the rant in the version composed by Mingus and Dorr-Dorynek, Saul writes,

> According to the Mingus legend, the audience heartily swallowed this brew of musical ambition and extra-musical honesty. In this account, "most of the audience [were] yelling, 'Bravo!' 'Tell 'em Charlie!' 'Someone has been needed to say that for years!' 'Most of us want to listen.'" Mingus's

speech was calculated to elicit just such a response—to box the audience on the ears and then to flatter them with the exceptional possibility that they were among "the few that do want to listen." . . . Tying the "musical soul" to the pursuit of emotional integrity, Mingus redefined his outrage as his greatest aesthetic selling-point.

(Saul 2001: 401)

Saul's point is amplified by the way that the Five Spot rant has circulated—as an article in a book. Hence, quite soon after the actual event in New York, the rant was reified, published, and sold. Moreover, as Saul has observed, Mingus had a hand in editing his own rant for publication in the first edition of *The Jazz Word*. Far from objecting to its circulation as a commodity, Mingus contributed to its commodification and mythologization.

Also in 1960, Mingus released the album, *Charles Mingus Presents Charles Mingus*.[18] The record takes the form of a staged live performance (in actuality, recorded in studio), with Mingus posing as master of ceremonies. While Mingus does not rant in his Master of Ceremonies monologues, per se, he nevertheless immediately baits his imaginary audience. In his introductory remarks prior to the first song of the "set," Mingus outlines the venue's performance policy:

Good evening ladies and gentlemen. We'd like to remind you that we don't applaud here at the Show Place . . ., so restrain your applause, and if you must applaud, wait 'til the end of the set, and it won't even matter then. The reason is that we are interrupted by your noise. In fact, don't even take any drinks or no cash register ringing, etcetera.

(Quoted in "Charles Mingus Presents Charles Mingus")

As in his Five Spot rant, Mingus here demands that he and his group be the exclusive focal point of the performance paradigm; the venue should be utterly silent except for the music. He even regards the audience's applause—presumably a marker of their appreciation of the music—as meaningless "noise" that would be best stifled. His instructions about drinks and the cash register (which he repeats in subsequent introductory remarks) are especially important: the constant clinking of glasses and ringing of the cash register are sure signs that the bar—the financial engine of any club—is doing brisk business.

In Mingus's imagined club, however, the commerce at the bar and its attendant sounds must take a back seat to the music. However, this album recapitulates the paradox of the Five Spot rant in that, from its very inception, it was conceived of as a product that would be mass-produced and sold. Like the rant published in *The Jazz Word*, Mingus's monologues on *Charles Mingus Presents Charles Mingus* become countercultural, anti-commercial commodities.[19] In sum, recognizing the popularity and salability of his rebellious behavior, Mingus employed it as part of his engagement with capitalism and the American culture industries.

Charles Mingus therefore occupied a number of discursive positions that are ostensibly contradictory, but fundamentally interrelated: he was an artist with an intense skepticism for commerce and commodification; he was a political activist who campaigned vigorously for equal access not only to wages for African American musicians, but also to the systems of industrial production and dissemination that determine those wages; he was (at least at certain times) a patriarchal ideologue who embraced and espoused both the dismissive chauvinism of early 20th-century cultural critics and the "black macho" tenets of 1960s Black Power; and he was a savvy and dogged entrepreneur who used the controversy he generated to improve his finances and to enhance his personal mythology. While his entrepreneurship in no way negates his other activities, those other discursive positions unquestionably enabled his entrepreneurial ambitions.

Mingus Sells Jettas: Improvisation and the Open Road

Of the so-called "magnificent seven" television spots produced by Arnold Worldwide for Volkswagen as part of the 1999 launch of the "Drivers Wanted" campaign, one largely eclipses the rest: the now-legendary 60-second spot for the Cabrio model entitled "Milky Way," featuring Nick Drake's "Pink Moon." Unlike most television spots, the Cabrio ad generated an overwhelming response in popular and academic media ranging from Rolling Stone, to news and entertainment website Salon.com, to over 750,000 YouTube hits, to an article by ethnomusicologist Timothy Taylor—media that reach a considerably broader, less specialized audience than the ad industry magazines that typically cover a new campaign.[20] Much of this response was due to the countercultural status of Drake, an English folk singer-songwriter who produced only three albums before dying of an overdose of the anti-depressant Tryptizol in 1974 (Wolk n.d.).

Beloved almost as much for his bohemian obscurity as for the tremulous beauty of his songs, Drake's popular re-emergence in the early 2000s was seen by many commentators to be tainted by the generative role of the Volkswagen ad. Aidin Vaziri's opening sentence in his *Rolling Stone* article was typical: "In what has to be one of pop music's cruelest ironies, cult folk hero Nick Drake, who overdosed on antidepressants twenty-six years ago after releasing three commercially disappointing albums, is on the verge of scoring his first ever chart hit thanks to a Volkswagen commercial" (Vaziri n.d.). Douglas Wolk's response for *salon.com* was similarly ambivalent, referring to Volkswagen's role in Drake's success as "a little depressing" (Wolk n.d.).

In the Cabrio ad, a group of young people glides wordlessly through a dreamy, moonlit landscape in their Cabrio convertible. When they arrive at their destination, a noisy house party, they exchange meaningful looks before pulling out of the driveway and back to the gleaming highway. Heedless of any social pressure to spend their evening in a conventional way, they reject the apparent predictability of the party for the freedom and mystery of the open road.

FIGURE 2.4   Nick Drake

The lack of dialogue is significant, and is a feature of all of the "magnificent seven" Volkswagen ads. Every one of the spots eschews wordy copy, allowing the narrative to unfold through the interplay of the images and the soundtrack. In every spot, the soundtrack is front and center. Nicholas Cook's comments on music and narrative structure in "Music and Meaning in the Commercials" (discussed in the previous chapter) are apt: "Music is the discourse that passes itself off as nature; it participates in the construction of meaning, but disguises its meanings as effects. Here is the source of its singular efficacy as a hidden persuader" (Cook 1994: 38).

Lost in the frenzy around "Milky Way" is another ad featuring the music of another countercultural icon: Charles Mingus's "II B.S." Released in March of 1999, several months before "Milky Way," the Volkswagen Jetta ad "Great Escape" is set in a nursing home—a site with an entirely different (and considerably more explicit) set of rigid social and institutional pressures and constraints from the "Milky Way" house party.

The spot opens in a cramped room. We see an elderly African American man wearing a black suit checking himself out in a mirror, accompanied by Mingus's solo double bass playing a bluesy pentatonic melody. He takes one last critical look, slides his fingers along the brim of his pork pie hat, then grabs his cane, checks his watch and ambles out the door. The scene shifts quickly, and we join him in the hallway. An industrial fire extinguisher and glowing red exit sign cue us that we are in some kind of institutional space. The man glances furtively from left to right before moving out into the hallway. Another quick cut, and we see a young woman—also African American—in pink nursing scrubs moving down the hall. The man gives her a nod and a tip of his hat, then casts a long look at her swaying hips as she walks by. She notices his gaze and glares at him, playfully scolding him for his presumption. Two elderly Euro-American men seated nearby, absorbed in conversation and ignoring the exchange, let us know that we are in some kind of geriatric facility. This is confirmed in the next frame, when after another abrupt shift we see an aerobics class in a large common area full of old people in mismatched sweat suits gingerly swaying their arms and rolling their shoulders. The camera cuts back to the man, who looks aghast at the scene, and makes a hasty move to escape the notice of the class instructor.

The scene changes again with the elderly man moving into a nursing station, where he attempts to slink passed a pink-clad, severe-spectacled, middle-aged white nurse with a telephone pinned between her ear and shoulder, supervising what seems to be a tray full of medication while also keeping a vigilant watch over the back entrance to the facility. The man moves towards the exit (marked "please use front entrance") as steadily as his cane and limping gait will permit. The nurse raises her eyebrows and notices him at the last moment, but by then he has already pushed open the door, letting sunshine stream into the antiseptic nursing station.

With one final abrupt scene shift, we are outside. The man squints as his eyes gradually adjust to the sun. A Volkswagen Jetta suddenly reverses into the picture, screeching to a stop in front of the door. The camera moves in on a younger African American man behind the wheel. The older man eases himself into the passenger seat. "Grandpop," says the younger man with a slight nod. "Hey, Booboo," comes the reply, "I'm glad you're on time." The camera zooms out, and the car peels out of the parking lot and heads for the open road. We follow the car for a while through a desert highway, watching the two men—grandfather and grandson—chatting and laughing. The grandfather rolls back the sunroof and tosses his head back in the ecstasy of his newly won freedom. The camera cuts to a highway sign, letting us know that the car is 134 miles from Las Vegas.

In the first place, the song plays a crucial role in structuring the narrative of the advertisement. The nursing home sequence is all set to the opening solo bass introduction—Mingus's own *rubato* improvised chorus over a 12 bar minor blues progression in G minor (albeit with some significant editing to keep the spot within the industry standard 60-second time limit, particularly in the last four-bar phrase). Each of the three four-bar phrases of the progression corresponds roughly to a setting in the nursing home. The brief scene in the grandfather's room is set to the first phrase, with the cadence back to the tonic sounding as the old man peeks out into the hallway. When the African American nurse appears, we hear the percussive sound of Mingus's fingers striking the ribbing of his bass that introduces the second phrase—a surprising musical moment that mirrors the abrupt camera cut and the nurse's sudden arrival. The remainder of the episode in the hallway (from the grandfather's exchange with the nurse to his evasion of the aerobics class) is heard against the second phrase—moving from the minor subdominant back to the minor tonic. The third phrase of the progression begins as the grandfather moves into the space near the nursing station. As he slips through the back door, there is a moment of silence. The instant where "Booboo" shows up in his Jetta, the drums enter with a swing groove and Mingus begins the memorable "II B.S." eight-bar ostinato bass line—edited down to four bars to stay within the prescribed time limit.[21]

In addition to its role in structuring the narrative, the soundtrack also acts to underscore the dramatic arc of the spot as it moves through increasing tension to resolution. The flexible pulse and phrasing of Mingus's solo echoes the grandfather's stealthy approach—perhaps even his halting limp—as he creeps through the halls past the nurse and the aerobics class. When he comes upon the nursing station, we suddenly hear a new sound: a Hammond organ playing a sequence of diminished seventh chords. Of course, there was no organ on the 1963 recording, nor on any other recording of "II B.S." or "Haitian Fight Song;"[22] the somewhat cartoonish addition of the Hammond was evidently the result of decisions made in the sound editing process, almost assuredly with the aim of further drawing out the feeling of tension and unease during the nursing station encounter. A later edit serves the same purpose: whereas the original recording of the solo concludes on a tonic G, the version in the advertisement ends on the penultimate pitch, a Neapolitan A♭ (accompanied by an A♭ diminished seventh chord on the added Hammond organ). This unresolved, dissonant dominant substitution is extended by three seconds of silence as the grandfather exits the nursing home and waits for his grandson. Only when the silver Jetta reverses into view do we hear the cadential payoff, as Mingus enters with the bass line in time, supported by drummer Danny Richmond's hi-hat cymbal. The bass ostinato builds momentum and the band digs into the groove alongside as the

Jetta turns out onto the highway, and we know that the grandfather has made good on his escape.

Of particular interest, however, and of greatest significance to this discussion, is the complex of ways in which Arnold Worldwide and Volkswagen's marketing team use Mingus's music to target the key characteristics of the consumer described in the psychographic profile. While Mingus's music is not necessarily literally humorous or light-hearted—at least not in the specific ways that Ron Lawner intended in his list—the "II B.S." soundtrack represents a nexus of discourses about jazz in general and Mingus's music[23] in particular that allows Arnold and Volkswagen to make the Jetta more appealing to their target demographic.

Just as the out of time bass solo helps to structure the pacing and narrative of the ad, so too does it anchor the discursive scaffolding that supports the ad's implicit psychographic message. The uneven pulse as Mingus glides lithely from melodic phrase to phrase emphasizes to the listener that the introductory bass solo is improvised—as clearly distinct from the riff-based composition that follows. The solo therefore not only mirrors the halting motion of the grandfather's escape; it also underscores the fact that his escape is similarly improvisatory. While the old man knows where the exit is, we can tell from his furtive movements and his palpable surprise when he encounters obstacles that his escape is essentially unplanned. It is only when he steps outside, the Jetta arrives, and his escape is sure that the soundtrack shifts to the more predictable, composed material of "II B.S." Even then, the composed material quickly gives way to Booker Ervin's improvised tenor saxophone solo, reminding us of the exhilarating uncertainty of the open road.[24]

The freely irregular pulse of the improvised bass solo and the unpredictability of the man's movements pose a vivid counterpoint to the hyper-rationalization of time that would most certainly be a defining element of his quotidian experience in the nursing home. Indeed, as he sneaks through the halls, each new scene that he finds reminds him (and the audience) of the strict schedule in the home: the African American nurse, no doubt on her regular rounds; the afternoon aerobics class; and most obviously, the wall clock, tray of daily medications, and scheduling bulletin board that he passes in the nursing station on his way out the door. Unlike Mingus's solo and the old man's escape, there is nothing remotely improvisatory about this representation of the nursing home's rigid routine.

There is clearly a tangible distinction between the way the old man wishes to structure (or more accurately, *not* structure) time, and the structure imposed on him by the nursing home routine. Significantly, according to historian E.P. Thompson, this kind of temporal dissonance is a common experience under the late-capitalist regime of industrialized labor. As Thompson explained in his seminal 1967 article, "Time, Work-discipline, and Industrial Capitalism:"

> Those who are employed experience a distinction between their employer's time and their "own" time. And the employer must use the time of his labor,

and see it is not wasted: not the task but the value of time when reduced to money is dominant. Time is now currency: it is not passed but spent.

(Thompson 1967: 61)

When time is essentially reducible to money, Thompson suggested, there is significantly greater pressure to track it and structure it in ever smaller and more rigid increments. In this way, while most viewers of the Volkswagen spot will not directly connect with the idea of living in a nursing home, the vast majority will certainly sympathize with the fracturing of temporal experience that is equally a part of nursing home life and life in the capitalist labor force. Indeed, temporal dissonance is a common thematic trope in advertising. Gail Stein, Communications Director at communications agency OMD, explained how this trope works, especially in advertisements directed at a predominantly female demographic:

We like to say, "Hey, take a moment." Because, you know, women are so busy, because they're moms, and they're going to work, and they're cooks and they're cleaners and so, we know that, like when we do focus groups with women, often what comes out is, "Geez, if I only had a few more moments to myself." So we often like to take that concept of the moment and spice it up a little bit.

(Stein 2010)

The experience of temporal dissonance is not unique to women, of course (although marketing research indicates that women tend to feel that they have a greater number of conflicting demands on their time) and so the nursing home scenario implicitly invites viewers to imagine their own improvisatory escape from their own routine; to dream of their own open road, with or without a particular destination, and of the Jetta that will take them there.

In this way, the message of the ad hinges on an intriguing paradox: the viewers are encouraged to enact their own escape from the industrial capitalist workaday world, but they are advised to do so by purchasing a Jetta—the industrial commodity *par excellence*. The central trick of the ad, then, is to transform the product of an arduous industrialized process into a mode of escape from that process—to somehow turn a commodity into an anti-commodity. Of course, Volkswagen has been pulling this trick since the brand's arrival in North America. Writing of DDB's iconic "Think Small" campaign for Volkswagen in the early 1960s, Thomas Frank explains, "The genius of the Volkswagen campaign . . . is that they took [the mass society critique] into account and made it part of their ads' discursive apparatus. They spoke to consumers as canny beings capable of seeing through the great heaps of puffery cranked out by Madison Avenue" (Frank 1997: 63).

Where DDB satirized the advertising industry to achieve the de-commodifying trick for Volkswagen in the early 1960s, in 1999, Arnold did it in large part by using countercultural musical icons like Mingus and Nick Drake. As we have now seen, while in reality Mingus had a decidedly vexed relationship with commercialism and the culture industries, for the most part he chose to represent himself as a paragon of anti-commercial artistry. By using his music in their ad, Arnold sought to hitch the Jetta to Mingus's larger than life *persona*, positioning the car as an anti-commercial commodity.

Naturally, there is no doubt that the majority of viewers would not be specifically aware of the rich detail of Mingus's long history of sociopolitical and economic activism, nor would they likely identify him as the composer of the soundtrack, nor would they necessarily even know the name Charles Mingus. Nevertheless, for that majority of viewers the jazz genre itself stands as an intuitive marker for anti-commercialism. In an interview printed in *SHOOT*, another advertising industry magazine, the spot's director Nick Lewin references the aura of "authenticity" that he saw in the actor who played the grandfather, Sunny Jim Jaines. In Lewin's estimation, Jaines's authenticity inheres in his direct connection to 1950s jazz greats. *SHOOT* author Jeremy Lehrer writes, "Lewin added that Jaines had spent some time hanging out with Thelonius Monk, which gave his portrayal authenticity. Lewin added that Jaines had oodles of character and knew plenty of other jazz greats. 'You couldn't mention a name he didn't actually know,' Lewin recalled" (Lehrer 1999: 10). While he may or may not have ever read Hugues Panassié, Alain Locke, Langston Hughes, or Amiri Baraka, when Lewin identifies Sunny Jim Jaines as "authentic" because of his long ago connection with Monk, he is signifying on a century of discourse that has concretized jazz as an anti-commercial art form, and he is confidently expecting that his audience will do the same.

In order to solidify the Jetta's anti-commercial credibility, however, Arnold's copywriters needed to show the viewers a more serious subtext—especially for the majority who would not readily map Mingus's anti-commercial pedigree onto the car. To develop that subtext, therefore, the ad purposefully (albeit subtly) recalls another escape from rigidly constraining systemic institutional pressures: the civil rights movement. Lewin takes credit for this additional layer, explaining that while the spot was mostly shot as the Arnold writers had scripted it, he and his directorial team added certain "aesthetic influences [. . .] such as still photographs from the '60s and the civil rights era" (Lehrer 1999: 10). Lewin's touches seem to have included 1960s-specific furniture in the old man's room, such as a plush orange sweepback armchair, a small, grey television, and a large turntable cabinet. There is only one black and white photograph in the room, framed atop the cabinet. While the picture is out of focus, given Lewin's comments and the blurry profile of the seated man in the picture, we might be vaguely reminded of an iconic photo of Martin Luther King Jr.

While Lewin's small additions act to draw it out, the civil rights theme would already have been embedded in the version of the script he received from Arnold. The narrative follows an elderly African American man escaping from an institution that seems to be controlled primarily by Euro-American people—the nurse at the nursing station and the aerobics instructor being the most obvious examples (it is worth noting that the smiling African American nurse seems to be considerably more sympathetic and does not cause nearly as much alarm as the second nurse or the aerobics class). The civil rights theme is anchored by the soundtrack, however. Even listeners who were not aware of Mingus's own political activism or of the original politicized title of the featured song ("Haitian Fight Song") would at the very least have connected "II B.S." to the period in question, especially in conjunction with the man's age and the vintage of his furniture.

The civil rights underscore brings an element of seriousness and pathos to an otherwise comical situation, and an element of heroism to an old man who might otherwise be merely ridiculous both in his lurching attempt at stealth and his obvious lechery. It also further universalizes the theme of escape: the ad is not simply about a geriatric man sneaking out of his nursing home; nor is it only about the broader story of weary, overworked Americans fleeing the rigidity of the capitalist working day. This "Great Escape" is about a ubiquitous utopian human drive to escape the perennial disappointment of the mundane and the *status quo* in search of transcendent joy and freedom.

The nursing home, then, represents several layers of meaning: it is what it appears to be, a rigidly anodyne geriatric residence; it is what North American viewers likely perceive it to be, an industrialized institution operating on a severely rationalized capitalist temporal regimen; concomitantly, it is the generalized stultifying consumerist, hyper-commercialized capitalist regime against which Volkswagen drivers ostensibly want to rebel; and, perhaps most remarkably, it stands indirectly for the Jim Crow-era American state against which the African American grandfather perhaps protested in his youth.

A linking theme between all of these potential components of the nursing home metaphor, however, is the metonymic relationship between women and institutional authority. All of the authoritative figures whom the old man must evade in his escape from the nursing home are women—the two nurses and the aerobics instructor. Of course, the women's authority is entirely destabilized by the comedic scenario and by the relative ease of the grandfather's escape. On the other hand, this nursing home is not just a nursing home, and therefore these nurses are not just nurses. Where, as Nick Lewin implies, the nursing home is meant to recall 1960s civil rights, then the act of undermining female authority recalls the reassertion of African American patriarchy that hooks, Carby, and Mercer have identified as a key ideological aspect of both the integrationist civil rights movement and the more politically radical Black Power movement.

More broadly, the spot plays with sexual stereotypes around emasculated African American men and dominating African American matriarchy that have endured from 19th-century minstrelsy through the 1950s Moynihan Report up to the present day. Where the nursing home represents the generalized consumerist, hyper-commercialized capitalist regime, the nurses stand for the discourse of a feminized consumer base that propagates that regime, in contradistinction to the liberated, masculine, creative, improvising Volkswagen driver. The nurses become Dwight MacDonald's "matrons," *Down Beat* columnist Marvin Freedman's "Two Kinds of Women," or the various women in Mingus's prose who threaten to dilute his artistic authenticity with their "commercial plans."

Thus, "The Great Escape" recapitulates the pervasive gendered element of the century-old anti-commercial discourse in order to help make its central point. By connecting the elderly hero with the masculinized jazz music and rhetoric that Charles Mingus represents, by contextualizing that heroism in a complex of overlapping discourses of anti-institutional, anti-establishment dissent, and by playfully undermining matriarchal authority, the Volkswagen spot successfully positions the Jetta as an anti-commodity through which drivers can escape all manner of social, political, and economic oppression, improvising their way along a free, open highway to whatever El Dorado—or Las Vegas—they can imagine.

Conclusion

It is worth noting that throughout his life, despite his misogynistic rhetoric, Charles Mingus worked closely with—and usually came to depend heavily on—a number of women. His first wife, Celia, managed both Debut Records and Chazz-Mar, Inc. more or less by herself, with artistic guidance from Mingus and Roach, but little to no administrative or logistical support (Porter 2002: 112). He commissioned his publicist and romantic partner Diane Dorr-Dorynek to write the liner notes to his celebrated 1959 record, *Mingus Ah Um*, his first release with Columbia records. It was also Dorr-Dorynek, of course, who published the essay "Mingus" that included the Five Spot rant in 1960.

His second wife, Sue, has overseen Mingus's professional affairs for the last 40 years as the director of Jazz Workshop, Inc. Since her husband's death in 1979, she has established three repertory bands to play his music, namely the Mingus Big Band, Mingus Dynasty, and the Mingus Orchestra, founded Revenge! Records to release pirated concert recordings that had previously been sold illegally, and published a number of books, including *Charles Mingus: More Than a Fake Book*, several editions of *Charles Mingus: More Than a Play Along* (all with Hal Leonard Publishers), and her own autobiography, *Tonight at Noon: A Love Story* (New York: Pantheon, 2002).

Recognizing that music licensing fees could go a long way to financing less profitable ventures like the repertory bands and other educational initiatives, Sue has also been using Jazz Workshop, Inc. and the official website, mingusmingusmingus.com, to market Mingus's music to advertisers. Her efforts have resulted in a number of notable television advertisements with Mingus soundtracks, including ads for fashion houses Dolce & Gabbana and Calvin Klein, furniture designer Hermann Miller, Canadian newspaper *The National Post*, and automakers Nissan and (of course) Volkswagen. While Mingus continually expressed a mixture of distrust and contempt for women in much of his written work, it is important to realize that while his apparent misogynistic rhetoric was certainly reflective of a broader stream of patriarchal discourse in jazz music, it did not necessarily extend to his personal life and relationships.

Similarly, despite numerous protestations to the contrary, it is also important to understand that Mingus was quintessentially entrepreneurial—albeit, an entrepreneur who engaged the culture industries with a fervently activist bent, often using the language of anti-commercialism. I asked Sue Mingus how she thought her late husband would respond to seeing his music being used to sell perfume and cars. Her thoughtful response confirms Mingus's vexed relationship with the culture industries, but also his fundamentally pragmatic outlook: "Oh, I think Charles was a realist. . . . If you can't pay the rent with what you're creating, you're in trouble." Later, discussing his socioeconomic activism, she said,

> Everyone faces this dichotomy. You know, on the pure side, your music is what it is: it's pure. And on the other hand, you have to fight . . . you have to, unfortunately, part of you has to be a businessman. I mean, there's just so much time you can waste doing that. Charles, there was a cut off point where he didn't bother, but he also fought fiercely for what he thought was his right as a musician, and what he deserved. But, I mean, that's not a contradiction. That's just pragmatism; that's real life, you know. That doesn't diminish your, you know, your awe and your appreciation . . . because you have to fight. I'm sure [all the great artists] fought for . . . what they deserved. I know they did. They didn't get enough for this score or that score and they wouldn't finish it.
>
> (Sue Mingus 2010)

For Sue, the fees recouped from licensing Mingus's music for advertisements more than makes up for any ethical or political concerns around helping to sustain a culture industry (advertising) and an ideology (consumption) that Mingus criticized so passionately during his lifetime. She is also fully convinced that her ever-pragmatic husband—the anti-commercial entrepreneur—would be entirely supportive of the idea, especially when he saw the artistic and educational initiatives enabled by advertising dollars.

There is, therefore an ironic synergy between Mingus's own entrepreneurship and the Volkswagen messaging. Just as Mingus deployed the 50-year-old discourse of jazz anti-commercialism as a rhetorical tool to help promote himself and his music in the 1960s—as well as to work to help seize greater market control for African American musicians—Arnold Worldwide uses Mingus's "II B.S." as a conduit to access the same anti-commercial discourse in order to rhetorically position the Jetta as an anti-commodity. In this way, drawing on Scott Saul's reading of the Five Spot rant, Arnold invites Volkswagen drivers to join an elite group of hip insiders, "[flattering] them with the exceptional possibility that they were among 'the few that do' get it" (Saul 2001: 401). These insiders are the kinds of "drivers wanted;" no poppaloppers need apply.

Notes

1. See for example Jason Toynbee, *Making Popular Music: Musicians, Creativity, and Institutions.* New York: Oxford University Press, 2000; Keith Negus, *Music Genres and Corporate Cultures.* New York: Routledge, 1999.
2. I address this era of Volkswagen's history in somewhat more detail in Chapter 3.

3. The tune was originally entitled "Haitian Fight Song," and first released on *The Clown* on Atlantic Records (1957), but was renamed for the 1963 album on the Impulse! imprint.

4. John Gennari (1991; 2006), Bernard Gendron (2002), and Kristin McGee (2009) have discussed these early critical responses to jazz music in greater detail. I draw heavily on their work in this section. I am also indebted to Karl Koenig and Robert Walser, whose respective books *Jazz in Print (1856–1929): An Anthology of Selected Early Readings in Jazz History* (2002) and *Keeping Time: Readings in Jazz History* (1999) together constitute a thorough, wide-ranging collection of the seminal critical writings on jazz music from the time period.

5. This article has been widely and justifiably disparaged in our own time, primarily for Adorno's fundamental ignorance about American jazz. Nevertheless, Adorno's article is a valuable document, in that it articulates the jazz-as-fetishized-commodity position thoroughly and with typical erudition (albeit, with a number of crucial factual errors and oversights), without resorting to the hysterical moralizing that characterized most American versions of this argument.

6. While they seldom identified race explicitly, all of these commentators were writing primarily about jazz music as a black art being performed for predominantly white audiences. Hence, their moral panic about jazz and female sexuality was structured by a pervasive terror of miscegenation.

7. Significantly, as Kristin A. McGee has pointed out, these newspapers frequently reviewed all-woman groups, particularly during the 1930s (McGee 2009: 50).

8. To some degree, Hughes also reiterates Panassié's primitivist discourse. In Hughes's concept, however, jazz's primitivism is tied to class rather than race. Sharon L. Jones has traced the bourgeois subjectivity of the Harlem Renaissance movement in *Rereading the Harlem Renaissance: Race, Class, and Gender in the Fiction of Jessie Fauset, Zora Neale Hurston, and Dorothy West* (Westport, CN: Greenwood Press, 2002).

9. Significantly, Charles Mingus and Hughes included this poem in their collaborative 1958 recording of Hughes's work, *Weary Blues* (MGM).

10. See also Wallace Thurman's work, including "Negro Artists and the Negro" in *New Republic* 52 (August 1927): 39.

11. See for example Joan Shelley Rubin, *The Making of Middlebrow Culture*. Chapel Hill, NC: The University of North Carolina Press, 1992.

12. bell hooks, *Ain't I A Woman: Black Women and Feminism*. Boston, MA: South End Press, 1981.

13. Hazel Carby, *Race Men*. Cambridge, MA: Harvard University Press, 1998.

14. Kobena Mercer, *Welcome to the Jungle: New Positions in Black Cultural Studies*. New York: Routledge, 1994.

15. MacDonald used the term "midcult" to refer to mass-produced artistic "commodities" that masqueraded as high culture—Cozzens's *By Love Possessed* being a prime example—thereby diluting high art, undermining the authority of the traditional highbrow gatekeepers, and generally initiating a precipitous artistic and moral decline. See for example, his classic essay "Masscult and Midcult," available in the collection *Masscult and Midcult: Essays Against the American Grain* (New York, NY: New York Review of Books, 2012).

16. It is worth noting—following Daniel Matlin's argument in his 2006 article, "'Lift up Yr Self!': Reinterpreting Amiri Baraka (LeRoi Jones), Black Power, and the Uplift Tradition" (*Journal of American History* 93, June 2006: 91–116)—that Baraka significantly toned down his "black macho" rhetoric in 1966, shortly after the publication of "American Sexual Reference: Black Male." This change in tone coincided with Baraka's move from Greenwich Village to Harlem, and concomitantly, a shift in his audience from a predominantly white bohemian to a predominantly black demographic. Matlin argues, therefore, that the disturbing violence of Baraka's pre-1966 rhetoric was calculated to elicit a polemical response from white audiences, whereas his gentler post-1966 language was geared towards fostering a black community through politicized art—albeit, a community still founded on robust patriarchal authority.

17. See Iain Anderson, *This is Our Music: Free Jazz, the Sixties, and American Culture.* Philadelphia: University of Pennsylvania Press, 2007.
18. The album was released on Candid Records, a label run by Mingus's friend Nat Hentoff—the famed jazz critic, historian, and civil rights activist—that specialized in politicized music. Candid had previously released "We Insist!, Max Roach's Freedom Now Suite," and would later press "Newport Rebels," the recording from the aforementioned Newport Rebel Festival in 1960.
19. It is important to note that Candid was a smaller label and had significantly diminished capacity for distribution and sales, as compared to Columbia—the label that released Mingus's other work during the late 1950s and early 1960s.
20. See Douglas Wolk, "Nick Drake's post-posthumous fame," *salon.com* (Accessed July 4, 2013) http://www.salon.com/2000/06/19/drake/; Aidin Vaziri, "Nick Drake's 'Pink Moon' is Rising," *rollingstone.com* (Accessed July 4, 2013) http://www.rollingstone.com/music/news/nick-drakes-pink-moon-is-rising-20000411>; Timothy Taylor, "The Changing Shape of the Culture Industry; or, How Did Electronica Music Get into Television Commercials?," *Television & New Media* (8 August 2007): 235–58.
21. Through the final 30 seconds of the spot, the bass line becomes a clear indicator of where the music team made cuts and splices to the original track. We never hear the cadential arpeggio from the original rendition, and the regular 8-bar ostinato appears in edited versions ranging from two to six bars as various spliced melodic phrases from the first 90 seconds of the 1963 recording spill into one another.
22. Mingus very seldom recorded with organists. See for example http://www.jazzdisco.org/charles-mingus/catalog/.
23. Mingus frequently objected to the word "jazz" as a restrictive genre descriptor, preferring the phrase "Mingus music" (Sue Mingus 2010).
24. The solo appears much sooner in the ad than in the original recording, a result of extensive editing to the 1963 track.

Bibliography

Adorno, Theodor. *"On Jazz." Essays on Music* ed. Richard Leppert. Berkeley CA: University of California Press, 2002. 470–95.

Anderson, Iain. *This is Our Music: Free Jazz, the Sixties, and American Culture.* Philadelphia, PA: The University of Pennsylvania Press, 2007.

Baraka, Amiri. "Black Dada Nihilismus," *The Dead Lecturer: Poems.* New York: Grove, 1964.

———. "American Sexual Reference: Black Male," *Home: Social Essays.* New York, NY: Morrow, 1966. 216–27.

———. "The Changing Same: R&B and the New Black Music," *Black Music.* New York, NY: Morrow, 1968. 180–211.

———. *Blues People: Negro Music in White America.* Edinburgh: Payback Press, 1995.

Bell, Clive. "Plus De Jazz," *The New Republic.* September 1921, in *Jazz in Print (1856–1929): An Anthology of Selected Early Readings in Jazz History,* ed. Karl Koenig. Hillsdale, NY: Pendragon Press, 2002. 154–57.

Carby, Hazel V. *Race Men.* Cambridge, MA: Harvard University Press, 1998.

Cook, Nicholas. "Music and meaning in the commercials." *Popular Music* 13 (1994): 27–40.

Davis, Miles and Quincy Troupe. *Miles: The Autobiography. New York,* NY: Simon and Schuster, 1989.

DeVeaux, Scott. "The Emergence of the Jazz Concert, 1935–1945," *American Music* 7 (Spring, 1989): 6–29.

———. "Constructing the Jazz Tradition: Jazz Historiography." *Black American Literature Forum* 25 (Fall 1991): 525–60.

Dorr-Dorynek, Diane. "Mingus," *The Jazz Word*, ed. Dom Cerulli, Burt Korall, Mort Nasatir. New York, NY: Da Capo Press, 1987. 14–18.

Farmer, Harcourt. "The Marche Funèbre of 'Jazz'," *Musical America* (June 19, 1920), in *Jazz in Print (1856–1929): An Anthology of Selected Early Readings in Jazz History*, ed. Karl Koenig. Hillsdale, NY: Pendragon Press, 2002. 144–46.

Frank, Thomas. *The Conquest of Cool: Business Culture, Counterculture, and the Rise of Hip Consumerism*. Chicago: University of Chicago Press, 1997a.

Freedman, Marvin. "Here's the Lowdown on 'Two Kinds of Women'," *Down Beat* (February 1, 1941), p. 9; in *Keeping Time: Readings in Jazz History*, ed. Robert Walser. New York, NY: Oxford University Press, 1999. 119.

Gendron, Bernard. *Between Montmartre and the Mudd Club: Popular Music and the Avant-Garde*. Chicago: University of Chicago Press, 2002.

Gennari, John. "Jazz Criticism: Its Development and Ideologies," *Black American Literature Forum* 25 (Fall 1991): 449–523.

Gennari, John. *Blowin' Hot and Cool: Jazz and Its Critics*. Chicago: University of Chicago Press, 2006.

Gridley, Mark. *Jazz Styles: History and Analysis*, 9th Edition. Upper Saddle River, NJ: Prentice Hall, 2006.

Hentoff, Nat. *Jazz Is*. New York: Random House, 1976.

hooks, bell. *Ain't I A Woman: Black Women and Feminism*. Cambridge, MA: South End Press, 1981.

Huggins, Nathan Irvin. *Harlem Renaissance*. New York: Oxford University Press, 2007.

Hughes, Langston. "The Negro Artist and the Racial Mountain," *The Nation* 23 (June 1926): 693–94.

———. *Selected Poems of Langston Hughes*. New York, NY: Vintage, 1970.

Jones, Sharon L. *Rereading the Harlem Renaissance: Race, Class, and Gender in the Fiction of Jesse Fauset, Zora Neale Hurston, and Dorothy West*. Westport, CN: Greenwood Press, 2002.

Koenig, Karl. *Jazz in Print (1856–1929): An Anthology of Selected Early Readings in Jazz History*. Hillsdale, NY: Pendragon Press, 2002.

Kofsky, Frank. *Black Music, White Business: Illuminating the History and Political Economy of Jazz*. New York: Pathfinder, 1998.

Kuenz, Jane. "Modernism, Mass Culture, and the Harlem Renaissance: The Case of Countee Cullen," *Modernism/Modernity* 14 (September 2007): 507–15.

Lehrer, Jeremy. "Formula for 'The Great Escape': Jetta and Jazz," *SHOOT* 40 (March 19, 1999): 10.

Locke, Alain. *The Negro and His Music*. Port Washington, N.Y.: Kennikat Press, 1968.

MacDonald, Dwight. "By Cozzens Possessed: A Review of Reviews," *Commentary* (March 1958): 36.

MacDonald, Dwight. *Masscult and Midcult: Essays Against the American Grain*. New York, NY: New York Review of Books, 2012.

Marable, Manning. *How Capitalism Underdeveloped Black America: Problems in Race, Political Economy, and Society*, Updated Edition. Cambridge, MA: South End Press, 2000.

Matlin, Daniel. "'Lift up Yr Self!': Reinterpreting Amiri Baraka (LeRoi Jones), Black Power, and the Uplift Tradition," *Journal of American History* 93 (June 2006): 91–116.

McGee, Kristin A. *Some Liked It Hot: Jazz Women in Film and Television, 1928–1959*. Middletown, CT: Wesleyan University Press, 2009.

McMahon, John R. "Unspeakable Jazz Must Go!," *Ladies' Home Journal*, December 1921, in *Jazz in Print (1856–1929): An Anthology of Selected Early Readings in Jazz History*, ed. Karl Koenig. Hillsdale, NY: Pendragon Press, 2002. 160–63.

Mercer, Kobena. *Welcome to the Jungle: New Positions in Black Cultural Studies*. New York, NY: Routledge, 1994.

Mingus, Charles, *Charles Mingus Presents Charles Mingus*. CD. Candid, CJM-8005/CJS-9005, 1960.

———. *Beneath the Underdog: His World as Composed by Mingus*. New York, NY: Vintage Books, 1991.

———. *Passions of a Man: The Complete Atlantic Recordings, 1956–61*. CD. Rhino: R2 72871, 1997.

Mingus, Sue Graham. *Tonight At Noon: A Love Story*. Toronto: Random House, 2002.

———. Interview with the author (June 21, 2010).

Negus, Keith. *Music Genres and Corporate Cultures*. New York, NY: Routledge, 1999.

Orwell, George. "Bookshop Memories," *Books v. Cigarettes*. Toronto: Penguin, 2008. 11.

Panassié, Hugues. *The Real Jazz*. New York, NY: Smith and Durrell, Inc., 1942.

Parpis, Eleftheria. "Best Campaign of 1999," *ADWEEK* (January 24, 2000).

"The Playboy Panel: Jazz—Today and Tomorrow." *Playboy*. February, 1964, in *Keeping Time: Readings in Jazz History*, ed. Robert Walser. New York: Oxford University Press, 1999, 261–93.

Porter, Eric. *What is this Thing Called Jazz: African American Musicians as Artists, Critics, and Activists*. Los Angeles: University of California Press, 2002.

Porter, Lewis. *Jazz: A Century of Change: Readings and New Essays*. New York: Schirmer Books, 1997.

Rubin, Joan Shelley. *The Making of Middlebrow Culture*. Chapel Hill, NC: The University of North Carolina Press, 1992.

Sales, Grover. *Jazz: America's Classical Music*. Englewood Cliffs, NJ: Prentice-Hall, 1984.

Saul, Scott. "Outrageous Freedom: Charles Mingus and the Invention of the Jazz Workshop." *American Quarterly* 53 (September 2001): 387–419.

Stein, Gail. Interview with the author (May 27, 2010).

Stewart, Ollie. "What Price Jazz?" *The Chicago Defender* (National Edition) (April 7, 1934): 12.

"Students in Arms Against Jazz," *The Literary Digest* (March 18 1922) *Jazz in Print (1856–1929): An Anthology of Selected Early Readings in Jazz History*, ed. Karl Koenig. Hillsdale, NY: Pendragon Press, 2002. 170–71.

Taylor, Timothy. "The Changing Shape of the Culture Industry; or, How Did Electronica Music Get into Television Commercials?", *Television & New Media* 8 (August 2007): 235–258.

Thompson, E.P. "Time, Work-discipline, and Industrial Capitalism," *Past and Present* 38 (December 1967): 56–97.

Thurman, Wallace. "Negro Artists and the Negro," *New Republic* 52 (August 1927): 39.

Toynbee, Jason. *Making Popualr Music: Musicians, Creativity, and Institutions*. New York, NY: Oxford University Press, 2000.

Vaziri, Aidin. "Nick Drake's 'Pink Moon' is Rising," *rollingstone.com* (Accessed July 4, 2013) http://www.rollingstone.com/music/news/nick-drakes-pink-moon-is-rising-20000411.

Walser, Robert. *Keeping Time: Readings in Jazz History*. New York, NY: Oxford University Press, 1999.

"William Edward Burghardt Du Bois." *Drop Me Off in Harlem: Exploring the Intersections* (Accessed April 3, 2010) http://artsedge.kennedycenter.org/exploring/harlem/faces/dubois_text.html.

Wolk, Douglas. "Nick Drake's post-posthumous fame," *salon.com* (Accessed July 4, 2013) http://www.salon.com/2000/06/19/drake/.

3

AUTOEROTICISM: SEX, CARS, AND JAZZ

Just about everybody has a dream car. For Fats Waller, it was his Lincoln sedan. Miles Davis favored Italian sports cars—Ferraris and Lamborghinis. For a great many Americans, the ultimate dream car has long been the Cadillac: At the height of her fame in 1926, Bessie Smith bought her husband a new Cadillac (Field 2002: 60); Coleman Hawkins drove Cadillacs throughout the 1930s (Daniels 2002: 174). When Elvis Presley achieved his first great success with Sun Records in 1955, he bought his first Cadillac. In 1956, he bought two more—a pink and black one for himself (to replace the first car, which was destroyed in a fire), and a second all-pink number for his mother, Gladys (who couldn't actually drive). In the early 1960s, Elvis hired George Barris, the Kustomizing King, to modify his latest Cadillac. Barris gold-plated almost every surface, from the headlight rims, to the hubcaps, to the accessories—including a television, telephone, record player, bar, ice cream maker, and electric shoe buffer. "I don't want anybody in Hollywood to have a better car than mine," Elvis declared. "A Cadillac puts the world on notice that I have arrived" (Widner 2002: 70).

Since its proliferation in the early decades of the 20th century, the automobile has been a potent signifier of social prestige. It stands alone among expensive consumer goods in its extreme visibility and audibility: Unlike a leather sofa, a wristwatch, a high-end dishwasher, or even a piece of jewelry, an automobile is designed for constant public display. Moreover, because the driver controls the actions of an automobile with his or her own body, the car and driver merge into a kind of cyborg hybrid—what Mimi Sheller and John Urry call the "car-driver."[1] Because of the blurred division between the automobile and its operator, drivers often identify in themselves characteristics that in fact belong to the car. When a car has chrome rims, an enhanced stereo subwoofer, or a

FIGURE 3.1   Cadillac with Elvis plate (Niels Gerhardt/Shutterstock.com)

powerful engine, the driver can imagine himself or herself to be equally glamorous, strong, or physically intimidating.

The automobile's symbolic potency is further enhanced by the contiguity between the physical and metaphorical work it performs. In both cases, the car's work is defined by mobility: physically, the car enables the driver to move much further and faster through space than he or she otherwise could; metaphorically, it greatly increases the driver's social mobility. As sociologist Grant McCracken has observed, the link between the car's physical and metaphorical work is manifest in the kinds of vernacular idioms we have used in North America to describe social advancement: "When Americans talked about 'getting ahead,' 'going somewhere,' 'traveling in the fast lane,' and 'heading straight for the top,' these were not cavalier remarks or empty metaphors. They were reflections of an important aspiration and reality in American life" (McCracken 2005: 70). Hence, not only did the automobile provide a new way of signifying social prestige during the early 20th century, but it also helped fundamentally to change the way that we think and talk about social status.

The spatial mobility afforded by the car takes on a different resonance when we consider it in terms of the particularly powerful symbolic meaning cars have in African American communities. According to recent statistics, even though African Americans constitute only about 12 percent of the total U.S. population, they represent roughly 30 percent of the automotive buying public, spending upwards of $45 billion annually on automobiles, automotive products, and related services (Gilroy 2001: 90).

For many African Americans, the automobile offered a literal antidote to the severely restricted mobility they had endured through generations of slavery, indentured servitude, and Jim Crow segregation. In a car, not only could African Americans suddenly travel vast distances, they could do so in private and on their own terms. In her critical autobiography, *Wounds of Passion: A Writing Life*, bell hooks reminisces about the sense of freedom she associated with the automobile:

> We can ride this car way out . . . Its leather seats, the real wood on the dashboard, the shiny metal so clear it's like glass—like a mirror it dares to move past race to take to the road and find ourselves—find the secret places within where there is no such thing as race.
>
> (hooks 1997: 47)

As such, African American car ownership is not only simple material consumption; it can also be a highly politicized act. The historical politics of car ownership—especially luxury car ownership—are particularly evident in a 1949 photo editorial in *Ebony* magazine entitled "Why Negroes Buy Cadillacs: The fact is that basically a Cadillac is an instrument of aggression, a solid and substantial symbol for many a Negro that he is as good as any white man. To be able to buy the most expensive car made in America is as graphic a demonstration of that equality as can be found" (quoted in Packer 2008: 189).

The love affair between Americans and the automobile, however, is also deeply vexed. This becomes particularly clear when we consider that relationship through the lens of jazz music. In the first section of this chapter, I discuss the discursive alignment between jazz and cars in the 1920s. This discourse circled around fear of the newfound freedom of American youth enabled by mass automobility. Hence, I suggest that the alignment of jazz and cars was founded upon the role of Fordist mass production in the parallel proliferation of both jazz and cars in the American mainstream: while cars rolled off Ford and GM assembly lines and into newly-paved driveways across the country, jazz made its way into American homes through the emergent technologies of radio and the recording industry. I focus particularly on American journalism, and on F. Scott Fitzgerald's *The Great Gatsby*, a novel that deals with the anxiety of the perceived decline of American ethnic purity and the pursuant degeneration of American morality. In the second section, I jump ahead to the 1950s. This period marked the coincidence of the so-called "Golden Age" of car culture with the waning years of what is often referred to as the "golden age" of jazz—the "Big Band Era." I examine the various ways in which the automobile began to symbolize both social status in particular, and—more broadly—American social norms and American citizenship. I consider the ways in which jazz played a part in this process by looking closely at the Chevrolet-sponsored *Dinah Shore Chevy Show*. I also examine the ways in which this program (and others like it) index the elision—if not the outright erasure—of African American membership in American consumer culture. In the third section, I consider the impact of an increasingly globalized market on the intersection between car culture, car advertising, and jazz music through the 1960s. I focus on a 1959 campaign for the 1960 compact Plymouth Valiant—a car that was designed in response to the explosion of interest in Volkswagen in the United States. I also look closely at the Honda Jazz, an economy hatchback launched in Europe, South Asia, Africa, and Australia in 2001. In the final section of the chapter, I look at another non-U.S. jazz-based campaign, a Canadian advertising spot for the 2003 Sebring featuring Diana Krall, entitled "The Look of Love," developed by ad agency BBDO.

Joyrides, Jazzy Tendencies, and the Decline of America

In F. Scott Fitzgerald's *The Great Gatsby* (1925; 2004), jazz and cars stand as twin symbols of the pleasures and dangers of the turn-of-the-century technological revolution. For Fitzgerald, both of these key American innovations were simultaneously representative of the pleasure, fun, and sexual freedom of "The Jazz Age" (a phrase Fitzgerald coined with his 1922 collection of short stories, *Tales of the Jazz Age*); at the same time, they also stood for the supposed artifice, excess, recklessness, and moral decay of the period.

In Gatsby's world, the automobile's primary purpose is to serve as a fashionable means of ferrying young, dilettante, bourgeois New Englanders from pleasure to pleasure (or vice to vice, as the case may be)—from the town to the house party to the seashore and back again. Of course, as pleasure follows pleasure—and drink follows drink follows drink—the pleasure-seeking pilots of the automobiles become increasingly reckless, heedless of the lethal danger they pose to themselves and others. Moments after leaving a particularly raucous party at Gatsby's mansion, the novel's narrator, Nick Carraway, encounters a spectacular car accident:

> Fifty feet from the door a dozen headlights illuminated a bizarre and tumultuous scene. In the ditch beside the road, right side up but violently shorn of one wheel, rested a new coupé which had left Gatsby's drive not two minutes before. The sharp jut of a wall accounted for the detachment of the wheel which was now getting considerable attention from half a dozen curious chauffeurs. . . . Then, very gradually, part by part, a pale dangling individual stepped out of the wreck, pawing tentatively at the ground with a large uncertain dancing shoe. Blinded by the glare of the headlights and confused by the incessant groaning of the horns the apparition stood swaying for a moment before he perceived the man in the duster. "Wha's matter?" he inquired calmly. "Did we run outa gas?"

> (Fitzgerald 1925; 2004: 53)

Jazz music is a key element of this reckless attitude, a central signifier of pleasure and danger. This is in evidence metonymically in the form of the dancing shoe with which the "dangling" driver of the wrecked car "paw[s] tentatively at the ground" following his accident, but it becomes clearer elsewhere in the novel. Carraway introduces one of Gatsby's parties with the remark, "There was music from my neighbor's house through the summer nights" (Fitzgerald 2004: 39). The music of choice to underpin all of Gatsby's parties was invariably jazz. The feature performance at the party preceding the "dangling" driver's accident is "Vladimir Tostoff's 'Jazz History of the World'" (likely a reference to Paul Whiteman, far and away the most celebrated jazz musician of the era). Even at the fateful gathering at the Plaza Hotel in New York City that precedes Daisy Buchanan's hit-and-run killing of Myrtle Wilson, the characters hear a "burst of jazz" echoing from a ballroom somewhere in the hotel, as they share whiskey and mint juleps (Fitzgerald 1925; 2004: 128). While jazz is not directly implicated in the hit-and-run, it acts as a musical accompaniment to the accident, and as an unsounded sonic signifier of the series of reckless behaviors that led to it—a kind of literary *idée fixe*. Here, as elsewhere, jazz, alcohol, and driving converge as symbols of the hedonistic, irresponsible, morally decadent, and ultimately dangerous lifestyle of the young Euro-American bourgeoisie during the jazz age.

The themes presented in *The Great Gatsby* were virtually ubiquitous in the American press in the 1920s. The symbolic parallel between jazz and cars seemed natural. As American Studies scholar Joel Dinerstein has suggested (2003), cars, trains, and the Fordist assembly line were collectively seen to have accelerated and mechanized the tempo of American life under industrial and post-industrial capitalism—both literally, in terms of increased speed of travel and labor, and figuratively, in terms of the distressing rate at which young people were maturing and exposed to theretofore adult pleasures and pursuant adult problems.

Similarly, jazz was often described less as a discrete, new style of music than as something that was done to music. The word frequently appeared used as a verb: word forms like "jazzing" or "jazzed" were commonplace, and usually referred to speeding music up. In a 1917 article entitled "The Appeal of Primitive Jazz," an unnamed author attempted to define the term: "Lafcadio Hearn, we are told, found the word in the Creole patois and idiom of New Orleans and reported that it meant 'speeding up things'. The Creoles had taken it from the Blacks, and 'applied it to music of a rudimentary syncopated type'." He went on to cite notable *vaudeville* performer, Walter Kingsley, a self-proclaimed expert on the new music:

> In the old plantation days, when the slaves were having one of their rare holidays and the fun languished, some West-Coast African would cry out, "Jaz her up," and this would be the cue for fast and furious fun. No doubt the witch-doctors and medicine-men on the Kongo used the same term at those jungle "parties" when the tomtoms throbbed and sturdy warriors

gave their pep an added kick with rich brews of Yohimbin bark—that precious product of the Kameruns. Curiously enough the phrase 'Jaz her up' is a common one to-day in vaudeville and on the circus lot. When a vaudeville act needs ginger the cry from the advisers in the wings is "put in jaz," meaning add low comedy, go to high speed and accelerate the comedy spark. . . . Jazz music is the delirium tremens of syncopation. It is strict rhythm without melody. To-day the jazz bands take popular tunes and rag them to death to make jazz. . . . It is an attempt to reproduce the marvelous syncopation of the African jungle.

("The Appeal of Primitive Jazz" 28)

Jazz, then, was not necessarily understood to be a kind of music in and of itself so much as it was a musical effect, something that musicians did to other music: "jazzing"—the speeding up and syncopating—of contemporary popular music.

Many European commentators attributed this perceived equation between jazz and speed to the pace of life in the United States. This notion grew out of a century-old European discourse—located particularly in France—wherein writers like Jean de Crèvecoeur and Alexis de Tocqueville positioned American youth, vitality, and vigor as an antidote to the supposedly tired, ossified, and stratified European society. Writing in *Letters from an American Farmer* (1782), de Crèvecoeur's description of the American—"this new man"—clearly premised his optimism for the new world on his pessimism about the old, contrasting the "ancient" with the "new:" "*He* is an American, who, leaving behind him all his ancient prejudices and manners, receives new ones from the new mode of life he has embraced, the new government he obeys, and the new rank he holds" (quoted in Levine 1996: 106).

Fifty years later, in *Democracy in America* (1835/1840), de Tocqueville argued that American political democracy and social equality[2] were made possible by the immigrant nation's physical and psychic distance from the lands, laws, and logics of Europe.

The emigrants who colonized the shores of America in the beginning of the seventeenth century somehow separated the democratic principle from all the principles that it had to contend with in the old communities of Europe, and transplanted it alone to the New World. It has there been able to spread in perfect freedom and peaceably to determine the character of the laws by influencing the manners of the country.

(de Tocqueville n.d.)

Both de Crèvecoeur and de Tocqueville paint a vivid picture of the "newness" of the United States—a "new" world populated by new people governed by a new social contract. Through the 19th century and into the 20th century, this abstract sense of American novelty crystallized for many Europeans in the innovative design of American cities, and especially in revolutionary manufacturing processes like the Fordist assembly line.

Until the early 1920s, however, this American mythology of the "new" did not have an aesthetic aspect to complement the abstraction of republican democracy and the practicality of Fordism. Indeed, de Tocqueville opined that the utilitarian character of American culture precluded the possibility of anything so introspective—and so impractical—as aesthetic cultivation: "Democratic nations . . . will habitually prefer the useful to the beautiful, and they will require that the beautiful should be useful" (de Tocqueville n.d.).

For many 20th century Europeans, however, jazz—with its rapid pace, frenetic melodies, and metronomic pulse—represented the aesthetic incarnation of the American character. In his 1936 memoir, *When the Cathedrals Were White*, Swiss modernist architect Le Corbusier attributed jazz's fast tempos and exhilarating rhythmic drive to the mechanized American soundscape: "The Negroes of the USA have breathed into jazz the song, the rhythm and the sound of machines. . . . New sounds . . . the grinding of the streetcars, the unchained madness of the subway, the pounding of machines in the factories . . . [f]rom this new uproar . . . they [African Americans] make music!" (quoted in Dinerstein 2003: 3–4). John Paul Sartre echoed Le Corbusier's analysis of American culture when he suggested, "Skyscrapers were the architecture of the future, just as the cinema was the art and jazz the music of the future" (quoted in McKay 2005: 17). For both of these writers, jazz expressed the essence of the American experience: noisy, industrial, fast, free, and new.

The homology between the rhythm and sound of jazz and the rhythm and soundscape of America was one of the chief reasons for both the music's popularity at home as well as abroad, and for its prominence in the American cultural imaginary. For Paul Whiteman and many of his American contemporaries, for example, jazz music and dance were aesthetic and kinesthetic responses to the acceleration and mechanization of American life. In his 1926 book, *Jazz*, Whiteman recalled, "The rhythm of machinery became the rhythm of American civilization, a clanging, banging, terrific rhythm, full of an energy that promised accomplishment" (quoted in Dinerstein 2003: 50).

Whiteman's optimism about the American machine aesthetic was not widely shared by his contemporaries, however. Most of the domestic writing on jazz and the acceleration of American life in the 1920s was far less celebratory in tone, and much of that writing focused on the automobile. Echoing the moral anxiety of John McMahon, Harcourt Farmer, and Clive Bell that we learned about in the previous chapter, numerous moralizing articles condemned the perceived link between jazz and "joyriding" or "hot-rodding"—the new vogue among young, urban, bourgeois Euro-Americans (like the Gatsby characters) for borrowing their parents' automobiles for all-night pleasure cruises. In a 1922 article in the Chicago Journal, "Students in Arms Against Jazz," an unnamed author describes the efforts of school superintendent Peter A. Mortenson to curb "jazzy tendencies" among his students:

> Jazzy tendencies among Chicago's high school pupils are to be suppressed by the pupils themselves, their leaders having decided on this course after an alarming state of affairs had been brought to their attention. Other methods having failed, we are told, an appeal to parents to save the high school girls and boys from the effects of jazz music, "shimmy" dances, "lovers' lane" automobile rides and immodest dress was circulated by Superintendent of Schools Peter A. Mortenson.
>
> ("Students in Arms Against Jazz" 170)

Mortenson's corrective manifesto focused on the confluence of jazz music, dancing, and joyriding as the agents of the precipitous moral decline among American youth. Among a series of pronouncements on the subject, Mortenson wrote,

- We believe the modern method of dancing has done much to break down respect for womanhood.
- We believe that jazz music has done much to corrupt dancing and to make it impossible for young people to learn the more refined forms of dancing, at the same time vitiating their taste for good music.
- We believe that the unrestricted use of the automobile is another demoralizing influence, and that parents who allow boys in their teens to take high school girls joy riding are doing much to break down the moral standards of the community.

("Students in Arms Against Jazz" 170)

An anonymous 1924 article in the Chicago Tribune, "Courting Danger in an Automobile," echoes Mortenson's concerns. Instead of calling on parents to intercede, however, this author appeals to the pastors of the nation. In his view, young people had fallen too far to be rescued by either parental intercession or state regulation. At this late stage in the decay of the American moral fabric, only "moral and religious inspiration" would be able to "counteract and counterbalance the social effects upon our youth of the jazzed and joyriding life of to-day" (quoted in Blanke 2007: 105). For Mortenson and the *Tribune* author, jazz, joyriding, and moral corruption were interrelated: jazz encouraged an indecent kind of dancing that called for sexualized movements and inappropriately intimate physical contact. These new kinds of music and dance fomented the hypersexualization of young people, and unsupervised joyriding gave young men the opportunity to victimize innocent young women—to indulge in their new "jazzy tendencies"—away from the watchful eyes of their concerned parents.

These articles linking jazz, cars, and moral decay were part of a broader, overarching concern in political, journalistic, and academic circles about the emergent dangers of youth automobility. Chief among these dangers, of course, was the lethal risk young drivers posed to themselves, their passengers, and other citizens with whom they shared the road. Pervasive fears over the startling number of accidents prompted the Safety and Traffic Engineering Department of the American Automobile Association to publish reports in 1937 and 1938 on the link between the age of drivers and the incidence of automobile accidents. The report's conclusions—that drivers aged 16 to 18 were nine times more likely to have an accident than drivers aged 45 to 50 (the statistically safest group)—fed the public and media hysteria around the subject (Blanke 2007: 47).

Broader sociological studies at the time focused on the impact of the automobile on changes in the lifestyle of American youth, with similarly dire conclusions. A 1921 report by the captain of the Los Angeles County Motorcycle Squad claimed, "Numerous complaints have been received of night riders who park their automobiles along country boulevards, douse their lights and indulge in orgies" (quoted in Flink 1990: 158). In Pasadena, the problem of "night riders" (a salacious variant of "joy riders") was even worse. According to a 1925 report by Pasadena's chief of police, "[T]he astounding number of 'coupe lovers' who park on dark streets in the Crown City necessitates the use of nearly all the police machines on patrol duty" (quoted in Flink 1990: 158).

The problem of "night riders," "joy riders," and "coupe lovers" was so widespread that Henry Ford himself supposedly attempted to intervene. According to automobile historian James Flink, there were persistent rumors in the 1920s that the famously morally conservative Ford shortened the seat in the Model T to an uncomfortable 38 inches, precisely to deter would-be "coupe lovers" from using his cars to indulge their indecent urges (Flink 1990: 160). At around the same time, Ford also spoke out against the evils of jazz dance, urging Americans to return to the more refined and less lascivious European steps of the 19th century—the waltz, quadrille, schottische, and square dance (Dinerstein 2003: 29). Ever the patriarchal moralist, Ford's attitudes represented a pervasive fear regarding the moral decadence of American young people.

To summarize: the proliferation of the automobile was critical to the widely documented sensation of sociocultural "acceleration" through the first decades of the 20th century, in part because cars allowed people—particularly young people—to travel further and faster than was previously imaginable. Because the emergence of jazz coincided with the proliferation of the automobile, that genre was popularly thought to be reflective of the same seismic sociocultural shifts that had led to (or were instigated by) the car. Furthermore, both jazz and automobiles developed and spread through new, industrialized processes that permitted greater manufacturing efficiency and greater quantity of product. In turn, as we saw in Chapter 2, this increased scope of production required new marketing strategies to ensure that all of the additional product sold. Hence, both the automotive and culture industries were key social and economic drivers of the expansion of consumer capitalism. In the final analysis, then, the contemporary conversations about the relationship between cars, youth, and jazz that we have discussed so far were equally about consumer capitalism.

American Dreams: Jazz, Cars, and Consumerism

According to the seminal 1929 sociological study by Robert and Helen Lynd, "Middletown: A Study in American Culture," the root of these problems was the freedom from parental guidance and restrictions that automobility afforded young Americans. The Lynds explained,

> The extensive use of this new tool by the young has enormously extended their mobility and the range of alternatives before them; joining a crowd motoring over to a dance in a town twenty miles away may be a matter of a moment's decision, with no one's permission asked.
>
> (Lynd 1929: 137)

The automobile permitted young Americans to travel further and further away from the protective gaze of their parents. This newfound independence allowed them to choose their own leisure activities, and with increasing frequency they were choosing jazz dances—complete with all of the moral risks those events and that music entailed.

The Lynds went on to acknowledge, however, that parents persisted in allowing their teenaged children to drive in spite of all of these attendant risks. The chief reason for this, they suggest, was status:

> [A]mong the high school set, ownership of a car by one's family has become an important criterion of social fitness: a boy almost never takes a girl to a dance except in a car; there are persistent rumors of the buying of a car by local families to help their children's social standing in high school.
>
> (Lynd 1929: 137)

Just as it would be for Bessie Smith, Fats Waller, Coleman Hawkins, Elvis, and others, the automobile stood as a central signifier of social status for the young people of the Lynds' "Middletown." This attitude is similarly in evidence in *The Great Gatsby*. Narrator Nick Carraway is awestruck after his first encounter with Jay Gatsby's Rolls Royce:

> He saw me looking with admiration at his car. "It's pretty, isn't it, old sport!" He jumped off to give me a better view. "Haven't you ever seen

it before?" I'd seen it. Everybody had seen it. It was a rich cream color, bright with nickel, swollen here and there in its monstrous length with triumphant hat-boxes and supper-boxes and tool-boxes, and terraced with a labyrinth of wind-shields that mirrored a dozen suns.

(Fitzgerald 2004: 64)

Like his Oxford education and his old-money English accent (both of which turn out to be invented), Gatsby's car communicates his wealth, class, and refined taste. Moreover, Carraway's (Fitzgerald's) almost phallic description of the car—"swollen here and there in its monstrous length"—seems intended to remind the reader that the Rolls Royce reflects not only Gatsby's wealth, but his masculine identity.

Through the 1930s and into the 1940s, advertisers increasingly began explicitly to gear car ads to appeal to the desire for social status. In 1940, De Soto (a division of the Chrysler Corporation, incorporated in 1928) released a series of print ads—developed by J. Stirling Getchell, Inc.—proclaiming the impression the upcoming 1940 De Soto would make on one's friends and neighbors. The ads show groups of people collectively watching an individual who owns one of the 1940 cars, and commenting in admiring tones on the aesthetic and technical features of the new vehicle.

One ad that appeared in the March 30, 1940 issue of *Life* featured the tagline, "You've Really Got Something There." The copy is revealing:

Part of what you pay for is the fun of being noticed—so why not enjoy it in your New Car . . . You wouldn't be human if you didn't get a "kick" out of having people admire your new car. Those envious looks and verbal "bouquets" are just part of the thrill you get when you drive a De Soto. Your friends are right, "You've got something there."

(Margaret Fishback Papers, "De Soto")

Significantly, while Jay Gatsby's cream Rolls Royce was exclusively available to individuals of considerable means, the 1940 De Soto was one of several models that brought fashionable styling to middle class Americans. According to the ads, the 1940 De Soto allows people from the middle classes to become objects of universal admiration and envy—status they could never achieve without the car.

The American passion for the automobile was never more in evidence, however, than during the decade and a half following World War II, the so-called "golden age" of car culture. After 15 or more years of depression and wartime thrift, the post-war economic boom of the late 1940s and early 1950s left many Americans with significantly more disposable income. Through the 1950s, as television became increasingly pervasive in the United States, automobile advertisers led the way in their attempts to exploit the new medium.

FIGURE 3.2 1940 De Soto advertisement (Hartman Center for Sales, Advertising, and Marketing History, Margaret Fishback Papers, Box OV12)

By 1955 and 1956, agencies were urging their clients to focus their efforts and their dollars on TV advertising. J. Walter Thompson (JWT), the agency of record for the Ford Motor Company, persuaded Ford to increase its TV advertising budget in large part by demonstrating the dramatic increase in television viewership over the first half of the decade. A JWT report from April 24,

1956 cited a number of convincing statistics. Entitled "Recommendations for Ford Division TV Advertising Expenditures for the Second Half of 1956 and for the Calendar Year 1957," the report claims that the number of American cities with access to television broadcasts had more than quadrupled since 1952—from 65 cities to 296—while the number of families who owned televisions had more than doubled over roughly the same period—from 10,500,000 in 1951 to more than 23 million in 1956 (Devine Papers, "Expenditure Recommendations").

The report also emphasizes the particular suitability of television for car advertising: "It is axiomatic in advertising to show the product in use whenever possible. In TV, an automobile can be shown in use and in action. Styling, performance, safety, special features, and hidden qualities are all susceptible to TV demonstration" (Devine Papers, "Expenditure Recommendations"). While print and radio were only capable of describing the dynamism of the latest automotive designs, television could show those cars in motion, engaging audiences in a whole new way. Additionally, the JWT report described the general make-up of a television audience. Unlike older visual media— magazines, newspapers, film shorts, *etc.*—television could engage an entire family all at once. Moreover, it was increasingly becoming a part of family routines across America. This was an important advantage for automobile advertisers because, as the report notes, "a product like an automobile which represents a large family investment and, therefore, is dependent upon family discussion before purchase rather than 'impulse' buying" (Devine Papers, "Expenditure Recommendations").

It is worth noting that nowhere in the JWT documentation is there any significant anxiety on the part of the agency regarding the potential intrusiveness of television advertising into the domestic intimacy of the family home—the kind of concern that led agency executives to proceed cautiously with their first forays into radio advertising in the 1920s. While not everyone was thrilled with the ubiquity of advertising in the 1950s (recall the anti-advertising polemics by Vance Packard, Sidney Levy, and Irving White that appeared at this time, discussed in the introductory chapter), agencies like JWT had become increasingly confident that the majority of their audience would be receptive to their messages—anytime, anywhere. Family leisure had grown increasingly contiguous to consumption, especially where leisure centered on the television.

Throughout the 1950s, the leader in automobile advertising on television was Chevrolet, a division of General Motors (Devine Papers, "Expenditure Recommendations"). The core of Chevrolet's television presence was *The Dinah Shore Show*. Beginning in 1951, Chevrolet sponsored the 15-minute, twice-weekly, music program on the NBC network. The show generally featured four or five performances by Shore, occasionally accompanied by a vocal ensemble—either The Notables or The Skylarks. In 1957, at NBC's urging, Chevrolet agreed to extend the program format to a single, hour-long, weekly broadcast on Sundays at 9 pm EST (Bratten 2002: 88). Re-named *The Dinah Shore Chevy Show*, the program now featured a mix of songs, skits, and interviews with special guests ranging from singers Frank Sinatra, Nat "King" Cole, and Ella Fitzgerald to baseball star Dizzy Dean. Throughout its decade-long run from 1951–61, Shore's repertoire was drawn principally from Broadway—show tunes by songwriters like Jimmy Van Heusen, Frank Loesser, George Gershwin, Irving Berlin, and others were staples on the program.

Shore's persona was key to the successes of both the program and the Chevrolet brand. The numerous commentaries on Shore (both in print and online) invariably focus on her warm, friendly demeanor, and describe her as down-to-earth, unaffected, and natural. She was presented as physically attractive without being overtly sexually provocative—an image that Chrysler marketers believed was key to appealing to the increasingly important demographic of Euro-American, suburban mothers. Shore's sexuality was certainly a factor in her appeal—she regularly appeared in strapless or off-shoulder dresses that drew the viewer's attention to her shoulders, neck, and chest. The camera, however, always remained focused on her face, never explicitly inviting a voyeuristic fetishization of her body. Thus, she was commonly perceived to be sexually demure, nonaggressive, and nonthreatening.

Shore's private life was also relatively stable (at least through the 1950s), and Chevrolet made much of Shore's image as a loving wife to film actor and director George Montgomery, and doting mother to their two children. Shore's biographer, Bruce Cassiday, writes, "[N]etwork publicists had decided to bear down heavily on the 'perfect marriage' image of the Montgomery's. It was a natural. They truly did not smoke or drink. They did not party. They lived their own lives away from the celebrity swirl" (Cassiday 1979: 131). Numerous profiles in periodicals such as *The Saturday Evening Post* and *Good Housekeeping* with headlines like "Husband, Kids Most Important to Dinah," and "Without George I'd be a Flop, says Dinah" regularly depicted Shore as a dedicated wife and mother whose own television career was incidental to her domestic life (Bratten 2002: 95–96).

In a sense, however, the reverse was true: the idyllic domestic scenes so abundantly documented in the media were critical to Shore's success with Chevrolet. These carefully managed public glimpses into her domestic life appealed to the entire American household—especially the all-important, long-ignored female demographic. Prior to the 1950s, men were the principal focus of car advertising: while advertisers (the vast majority of whom were male) recognized that cars were generally purchased with the whole family in mind (as JWT did in their work for Ford), men were invariably depicted behind the wheel—the decision-makers in the car, as in the family. Post-war shifts in American social geography had a virtually incalculable impact on the life of the middle class American family and the role of the car in it.

Throughout the middle part of the 20th century, Euro-American families increasingly moved from urban centres to suburban communities. Often referred to as "white flight," this phenomenon was fueled to a large extent by Euro-American anxiety around the dramatic racial demographic shifts in cities through

FIGURE 3.3 Dinah Shore with family (Grey Villet, The LIFE Picture Collection/Getty)

the period of the Great Migration. As huge numbers of African Americans moved to big cities to be closer to large employers (especially in manufacturing sectors like the automotive industry), nearly equal numbers of bourgeois Euro- (and some African-) Americans moved out of town. As Paul Gilroy (among others) has pointed out, white flight was entirely enabled by the proliferation of the automobile: automobility—rapid, convenient, and individuated transportation—allowed

Americans (at least, those with the financial means) to imagine the possibility of living a long distance from the workplace (Gilroy 2010: 34).

If the proliferation of the car had created the concept of commuting, so too did the emergence of the commute as an expected part of the working day spur the further proliferation of the car. Certainly, any middle class family that desired a suburban life likely required one car at minimum. Increasingly, however, advertisers and marketers for the major U.S. automakers worked to persuade consumers that they needed two—one car for men to get to work, and a second for women. On the one hand, a woman increasingly needed a car to take care of her basic domestic responsibilities in a suburban locale where shops and supermarkets were often not within a comfortable walking distance from home (Packer 2008: 39). On the other, the modern appliances that had become staples of many suburban homes—washing machines to take care of laundry, refrigerators and freezers that allowed shoppers to purchase and store larger quantities of food—afforded many middle class women more free time during the day. This helped foster a greater sense of independence, and a concomitant desire for greater mobility. Along with its rivals, General Motors had therefore been working assiduously especially since the early 1950s to develop advertising that would appeal to middle class, Euro-American, suburban women.

It was no coincidence, then, that Chevrolet had begun to sponsor the *Dinah Shore Show* in 1951. From the very beginning, Dinah Shore had been a key element of the Chevrolet marketing and advertising strategy. Significantly, however, just as Chevrolet worked to change its image to more effectively target women drivers, even before the Chevrolet sponsorship Dinah Shore had carefully constructed her own image, working to style herself as a Euro-American Everywoman in order to improve her own career prospects. This was no small undertaking for an ethnically Jewish singer from Winchester, Tennessee with a voice described by *Liberty* magazine as "bluesy and moanin' low" (quoted in Bratten 2002: 93).

Shore was born Frances Rose Shore to Russian Jewish immigrants Solomon and Anna Shore in 1916. In the early 1940s, she was best known for her recurring performances on the Armed Forces Radio Network, especially *Command Performance*, singing jazz and classic blues songs such as "My Man" (earlier a hit for Billie Holiday), Duke Ellington's "I Got It Bad (And That Ain't Good)," and the Harold Arlen/Johnny Mercer composition "Blues in the Night." Indeed, her stage name "Dinah" was taken from the title of the 1926 hit by African American blues singer Ethel Waters. Following a screen test for Warner Brothers in 1942, she was advised by the company make-up department that she couldn't expect to have a successful film or television career with her curly, dark hair, and her nose with its "noticeable hook" (Bratten 2002: 93). In other words, her features were too dark and too Jewish for either the big or small screens.

She responded quickly to the criticism, restyling and coloring her hair, undergoing cosmetic surgery to shorten her nose, and having her teeth filed and capped to fix a small gap (Bratten 2002: 94). In 1943, she met and married Hollywood

FIGURE 3.4 Dinah Shore in 1942 (Bob Landry, The LIFE Picture Collection/Getty)

star Montgomery (best known for various roles in a host of Western movies through the 1940s).[3] The couple had their first child, daughter Melissa, in 1948. Dinah further cultivated an interest in upper class, outdoor sports—especially golf. By the time she signed with NBC and Chevrolet in 1951, then, she had transformed herself from a Jewish girl with a robust voice and a bluesy sensibility to a California mom with bourgeois tastes. Tautologically, Dinah Shore, the quintessence of American bourgeois aesthetics and a key tastemaker from the

1950s through the 1980s, constructed her own identity in order to appeal to a mainstream audience whose tastes she purportedly directed and defined. If we can understand Dinah Shore herself as a kind of ideological state apparatus—an agent tasked with the promotion of the ideology of consumption—then her personal transformation speaks to the degree to which consumer ideology was (and is) impacted by other ideologies, especially around race, ethnicity, and gender.

Shore's constructed embodiment of the physical and social norms of the American mainstream was critical to her credibility as Chevrolet's pitchwoman. Like several U.S. automotive brands, Chevrolet sought to identify itself with the very spirit of America. The centerpiece of every broadcast was Shore's performance "See the U.S.A. In Your Chevrolet." Written by Leon Carr and Leo Corday in 1949 (Cross 2002: 114), the song closed every episode throughout the ten years of Chevrolet sponsorship. The lyrics exhorted viewers to use their Chevrolets to travel across the United States, linking Chevrolet ownership to American citizenship. The song opens:

> See the U.S.A. in your Chevrolet.
> America is asking you to call.

As the verse continues, potential Chevrolet drivers are reminded that the car is the best way to experience the highways and biways of "the greatest land of all." The opening lyric of the second verse maintains the nationalistic tone, but shifts from the general invocation of "America" to more specific references to iconic American landmarks. Drivers are "called" to America's heartland to pass through golden wheat fields, and to experience the majesty of the western Rockies.

Significantly, it is not Chevrolet dealers who are inviting Americans to buy Chevrolets to drive across the country; it is "America," the Rocky Mountains, and the agricultural heartland that are "asking you to call." It is as though the land itself is making the Chevrolet sales pitch. The song takes on all the more symbolic potency when it is performed by Shore—the wife and mother who had publicly proven her patriotism and all-American credentials through her many command performances on the armed forces radio network during World War II, her widely-publicized 1942 tour to entertain the American troops stationed in Europe, and her marriage to American serviceman (and film actor/director) George Montgomery. To her viewers (and through Chevrolet's marketing), Shore represented the archetypal American woman—selfless, a pillar of virtue, and a metonym for the American home.

Musically, the song is very much in the Tin Pan Alley vein, strongly reminiscent of the patriotic music of George M. Cohan ("Over There," "You're a Grand Old Flag," "Yankee Doodle Dandy") or Irving Berlin ("God Bless America," "Gee, I Wish I Was Back in the Army") with its anthemic melody and AABA form. Like many of Shore's performances especially from the 1950s on, in terms of genre classification, "See the USA in Your Chevrolet" sits somewhere in between jazz and Broadway. Shore delivers the melody on top of a dynamic orchestral accompaniment, overflowing with violin *obbligatos*. Her phrasing is fluid and relaxed, as she lets the lyric determine the melodic rhythm. The bridge of the song is performed by a vocal ensemble (presumably The Notables or The Skylarks) in a timbrally smooth, gently syncopated style that reflects 1930s and 1940s vocal groups—ensembles like The Pied Pipers, the group that performed with Tommy Dorsey's band, featuring a young Frank Sinatra. The melody in the bridge centres on a flattened 7th to 5th motive and cadences with a scoop from the flattened to the natural 3rd, both common motivic signifiers of the blues.

The generic ambiguity of "See the USA" mirrors Shore's ambivalent relationship with genre throughout her career. While she has occasionally been identified as a jazz singer, and she recorded numerous songs that have become jazz standards (especially prior to 1951), she in fact self-identified as an entertainer with eclectic tastes: "I'm not really a country singer, although I did make a couple albums and love its simple, straight-from-the-heart approach, but I have always sung a lot of jazz, show tunes, pop tunes, gospel and blues. My tastes are eclectic" (Daly, "Quotable Quotes"). Unlike more typical contemporary women jazz singers—Ella Fitzgerald, Billie Holiday, or Sarah Vaughan, for instance— Shore had no interest in improvisation. She delivered melodies clearly with little embellishment—a fact that is often represented as a rare virtue among singers at the time. In the brief biography posted online by the Museum of Broadcast Communications, for example, Henry B. Aldridge writes, "Even though by her own admission, Dinah Shore did not have a great voice, she put it to good advantage by enunciating lyrics clearly and singing the melody without distracting ornamentation. The result was the very definition of 'easy listening'" (Aldridge, "The Dinah Shore Show [Various]"). Her simple, unadorned approach to melody and her privileging of the lyrics made her performances broadly accessible and appealing—ideal for a primetime mass audience, a musical parallel of her Everywoman persona.

Crucially, both her persona and the musical character of the show were entirely blanched. Frances Rose Shore herself had been too Jewish for primetime and her music too "black." By contrast, Dinah Shore—the blond, bourgeois Californian wife and mother—was appealing to "mainstream" audiences because she was utterly deracinated: Her own inherited Jewish identity was all but erased, and the adopted African American identity of much of her 1940s music was elided within the predictably appealing schemes and sonorities of Tin Pan Alley-style tunes. While there were a handful of appearances by African Americans artists on her program—including notable African American jazz musicians Ella Fitzgerald (one of her most frequent guests with five appearances), tenor saxophonist Ben Webster, Nat King Cole, and Louis Armstrong ("The Dinah Shore Chevy Show," tv.com)—these artists represented managed ethnic incursions within a framework that was decidedly Euro-American.[4] Indeed, while there were other more regular appearances by jazz artists, nearly all of them were Euro-American: Baritone saxophonist Gerry Mulligan (with his mixed race quartet), pianists Red Norvo, Victor Feldman, George Shearing, and Big Tiny Little, trumpeter Al Hirt, clarinetist and bandleader Benny Goodman, and singers Mel Tormé, Louis Prima, and Frank Sinatra. Of course, virtually all variety shows of the era had the same racial dynamic, whether hosted by Milton Berle, Steve Allen, Peggy Lee, or Pat Boone (host of Chevrolet's other program on the rival ABC network, *The Pat Boone Chevy Showroom*, from 1957–1960).

From a musical perspective, the preponderance of Euro-American jazz musicians on the show was not only symptomatic of the racial politics of 1950s television broadcasting; it also constituted yet another fallacious representation of jazz music as a predominantly Euro-American cultural practice. While scholars such as Richard Sudhalter (1999) and Randall Sandke (2010) have convincingly shown that many Euro-American musicians played a crucial formative role in the development of jazz, no credible researcher would deny that the music was a syncretic African American cultural expression in which Euro-American musicians participated. At no point in American history were Euro-American musicians the sole (or even the primary) creative force behind the development of jazz music—except, that is, in rare, fictive instances like the world of television variety shows. Just as jazz audiences in the 1920s could accept Paul Whiteman as the "King of Jazz" in part because their access to African American music and musicians was limited by segregation laws and racist radio programming policies, so did the predominance of Euro-American jazz musicians in 1950s variety television show programming reinforce the audience's a priori belief that jazz was (or at least, had become) Euro-American music.

As jazz scholar Kristin A. McGee has observed, this racialized television paradigm was sustained by programming sponsors: "[T]he commercial interests of corporate sponsors and the consequential economic imperative of program ratings required that the networks attract mass audiences by representing popular culture through a . . . nonparticular, nonethnic identification" (McGee 2009: 203). Inevitably, however, sponsors' and networks' programming decisions were driven by the expectations—and the racial anxieties—of their audiences-cum-consumers. Hence, the race politics of sponsored television programming reflected the race politics of the "white flight" to the suburbs that had helped foment the proliferation of car advertising in the first place (and, it could be argued, the proliferation of television itself): the isolation and containment of race and ethnicity on television mirrored the isolation and containment of race on a national scale through Euro-American suburban migration.

Euro-American anxiety around racial containment impacted not only Dinah Shore's television program, but also her personal life in the late 1950s when, towards the end of her marriage to George Montgomery, rumors began to surface that she was in fact African American herself, merely "passing" for Euro-American, and the evidence lay in an African American child to whom she had given birth out of wedlock (Bratten 2002: 99). This gossip was entirely scurrilous and entirely false, and it likely grew out of the memory of her pre-1942 Semitic features and her pre-1950 musical performance choices (together with the somewhat more credible though still unsubstantiated rumors of a 1950s extramarital affair with Frank Sinatra). Nevertheless, the persistence of this scandal clearly shows the depth of Euro-American fears around racial containment, and represents yet another instance where—like in the 1920s and 1930s—jazz music became a site for Euro-Americans to play out fears and fantasies around the specter of miscegenation.

With all of this in mind, the timing of the end of Dinah Shore's relationship with Chevrolet becomes noteworthy. Shore biographer Bruce Cassiday suggests that the singer herself made the decision to leave the show in order to deal with an emergent family crisis—allegations that her husband, George Montgomery, had begun an affair with a co-star in his movie, *Samar*, while filming in the Philippines. The couple separated shortly after the end of Chevrolet's sponsorship in 1961 and divorced in 1962 (Cassiday 1979: 147). In actuality, however, the *Dinah Shore Show* continued without Chevrolet sponsorship until 1963 (Aldridge, "The Dinah Shore Show [Various]").

Although the official explanations of Chevrolet's decision not to renew their sponsorship made no mention of Shore's personal life, given how central Shore's idyllic home life had been to Chevrolet's marketing, it seems curious that the fracturing of her family would coincide with the termination of Chevrolet's sponsorship of her television show. If in fact Shore's separation did influence Chevrolet's decision to end their sponsorship, the whole affair speaks to the fragility of icons of feminine virtue. With the shattering of her happy home life, Shore was presumably no longer seen to be an effective spokeswoman for Chevrolet's target audience—suburban Euro-American families. Evidently feminine mobility was desirable only in the literal, physical sense that helped sell cars; the contiguous metaphorical, social sense of mobility—the kind that would make single motherhood socially acceptable, for instance—remained vexed.

The fallacious miscegenation scandal also reveals the impact of the anxiety of racial containment on fundamental marketing strategy in the auto industry. While *The Dinah Shore Chevy Show* represented a belated recognition by car marketers of the purchasing power of women, both the television show and Dinah Shore's own public image (both the official one represented in the press, and the unofficial one circulated by gossip and innuendo) demonstrate that African Americans continued to be largely excluded from the car-buying public. While, as we have seen, Dinah Shore would occasionally host African Americans as special guests, she rarely had more than three or four nonEuro-American guests over the course of her 52-episode seasons ("The Dinah Shore Chevy Show," tv.com). Hence, while Euro-American women began to be recognized as legitimate and valuable consumers of automobiles through the 1950s, African Americans continued to be widely ignored.

This kind of racism has a long history in automobile advertising. As Jeremy Packer (2008) has explained, African Americans were entirely excluded from automobile advertising in both visual media—television and print—for the majority of the 20th century. Even *Ebony*, with its enormous African American readership, and its editors and columnists who regularly celebrated the joys of car ownership, was entirely ignored by car advertisers until 1953—fully eight years after its inaugural issue. When the first car advertisements did appear, the models were uniformly Euro-American. It was not until 1966 that *Ebony* finally featured a car ad with African American models—and that advertisement was by Studebaker, mere months before that company declared bankruptcy.

Perhaps even more remarkable, Cadillac—the car whose virtues *Ebony* writers extolled more than any other—did not advertise in the magazine at all until 1972, 27 years after *Ebony*'s inception. Of course, this seems somewhat less surprising (if no less appalling) when we consider that, according to official company policy, Cadillac dealers were forbidden to sell to African American buyers until well into the 1940s. Previously, African American Cadillac owners had to purchase their cars used, or use a Euro-American buyer as an intermediary. The preponderance of Euro-American faces in sponsored television programming, then, was neither a simple coincidence nor an isolated instance: both were symptoms of a much deeper, systemic exclusion of African Americans from car culture—and concomitantly, from the American culture of consumption.

The exclusion of would-be African American car buyers becomes more problematic still when we take into account the racial makeup of the auto industry labor force. The advent of Fordist production in the first decades of the 20th century, and the attendant dramatic increase in the demand for unskilled labor drew countless African American men from the southern states northward to work in automotive plants. By 1966, nearly 130,000 African American men were working for the "Big Three" automakers (GM, Ford, and Chrysler) alone (Rose 1987: 53). George Lipsitz has noted that independent companies like Fisher—the Detroit-based company that manufactured most of the bodies for the Big Three for much of the 20th century—also employed a high percentage of African American workers (Lipsitz 1998: 161), so the total number of African Americans in the industry was likely much higher. Therefore, just as jazz—an African American cultural practice—is recast as predominantly Euro-American by the *Dinah Shore Chevy Show* producers' preference for Euro-American jazz musicians, the African American physical labor that manufactured so many American cars is elided by the Euro-American models in so many car ads, including those in *Ebony*. Hence, the use of jazz music in car ads and sponsored programming targeted exclusively at Euro-American audiences represented a rupture of both an African American cultural product and of African American labor from African American people. Moreover, it reiterated a radically racially delimited construction of the American "mainstream:" if jazz was America's national music and if the car had become a national cultural icon (and, further, if consumption had emerged as a national pastime), then the mass-mediated representation of the race of jazz musicians and car drivers clearly pointed to the racial definition of American national belonging.

Jazz Economies: Plymouth, Honda, and Globalization

The end of the *Dinah Shore Chevy Show* in 1961 also symbolically marked the final days of the "golden age" of American car culture. Faced with a recession in 1957 and 1958, American consumers began to lash out against the stylish but practically useless tailfins and "Jetaway" transmissions that had become the hallmarks of the American automotive design. In what came to be known as the "Buyer's Strike" of 1958, many Americans stopped purchasing new cars— or worse, started purchasing European-made models. Sales of American cars dropped nearly 8 million in 1955 to only 4.3 million in 1958, an enormous decrease of 46 percent (McCarthy 2007: 130). Meanwhile, sales of European cars soared, increasing over 1000 percent, from approximately 60,000 in 1954 to 614,000 in 1959. Smaller, plainer, more fuel efficient, and, above all, significantly less expensive than their American counterparts, the European cars were anathema to the principles of the "Forward Look" that had precipitated the "Golden Age" of car culture. As such, the proliferation of European cars seemed to suggest a paradigm shift in taste among American consumers.

The chief beneficiary of this shift was Volkswagen, the German automotive company that that had been founded in 1937 under the guidance of Adolph Hitler, as part of the rapid development of public infrastructure during the early years the Nazi regime. Indeed, given its tainted past, Volkswagen's American advertising campaign is widely regarded as one of the most successful rebranding endeavors in advertising history. As we saw in Chapter 2, upstart American ad agency Doyle Dane Bernbach (DDB) designed an ingenious campaign that capitalized on consumer frustration with the Detroit automakers, while drawing attention to Volkswagen's simplicity, attention to detail, and reliability using a bold sense of humor and irony.

At around the same time as DDB's Volkswagen campaign, the American companies launched their response to Volkswagen and the other European interlopers. Concluding that the decade-long supremacy of the tailfin had indeed come to an end, Chrysler, Ford, General Motors, and Plymouth (a division of Chrysler) all released new lines of small, "compact cars" (a term coined by George W. Romney, president of the American Motors Corporation). Among these, the Ford Falcon was the most popular (Ford sold 600,000 in 1960 alone), but the Dodge Dart, the Chevrolet Corvair, and the Plymouth Valiant also sold extremely well—so well, in fact, that by 1961, compacts accounted for 35 percent of American automobile manufacturing (McCarthy 2007: 145).

The compact was a particularly natural fit for Plymouth, Chrysler's low-priced brand. Speaking in an interview in *Automobile Topics* magazine in 1926—two

years before the launch of the brand—company founder Walter Chrysler discussed his vision for Plymouth:

> There is no question in my mind but what the people who prefer a low
> priced, quality automobile are desirous of having built into that car certain
> features that heretofore have not been made available to that field. The
> industry has not given sufficient attention to the man who drives a small,
> low priced car. It simply has gone on the assumption that the same measure
> of comforts that must be incorporated into every car of higher price, if it
> is to be successful, could not be built into the smaller cars.
>
> (Quoted in Curcio 2000: 392)

Chrysler's vision was still manifest in 1959 with the launch of the Valiant. Unlike
the other compacts on the market at the time, the Valiant represented a blend
of "Forward Look" styling with moderate size and price (Stevenson 2008: 217).

The 1959 television advertising campaign for the 1960 Plymouth Valiant
clearly demonstrates this attempt to walk the line between extravagant style and
conservative size and price. In so doing, the Valiant ads—a series of humorous
cartoons—play on some of the same themes as the Volkswagen campaign had.
One of these ads pokes fun at the huge, ostentatious, gas-guzzling "Forward
Look" American cars (which, of course, Plymouth itself had been manufacturing only two years earlier). The ad opens with a close-up of a Euro-American,
fedora-wearing driver who is introduced by the voice-over with the phrase,
"This is a motorist. He hates cars like this." At that moment, the scene shifts
to show the motorist sitting in a car that is clearly an exaggerated, humorous
reference to the Cadillacs of the earlier 1950s: exaggeratedly long and low, with
ribbon stretched around its circumference, angel wings on the rear doors, a
disturbingly life-like canary hood ornament, and the signature mile-high tailfins. Once we the viewers have had a chance to appreciate the grotesque car, a
gas pump materializes next to it, only to be rapidly emptied, accompanied by a
trombone glissando. With the gas pump emptied, the ad switches to live-action
film of a Plymouth Valiant in motion. The voice-over announces, "So he drives
Valiant," and goes on to list some of the car's many appealing features, emphasizing how its economical mileage is offset by a surprisingly spacious interior and
ample storage.

On the other hand, another of the Valiant ads took aim at Volkswagen's "think
small" ethos. Once again, we are introduced to the cartoon "motorist:" "This
is a motorist," intones the voice-over, "He hates cars like this." This time, the
motorist is pictured in an impossibly tiny car with his knees squished up against
his shoulders, and his head squeezed between the steering wheel and the ceiling.
When the car begins to move, it lurches and jumps. Again, the ad switches to
live-action footage of a driving Valiant, accompanied by voice-over copy extol-
ling its blend of economy and comfort. According to this Plymouth response, the

FIGURE 3.5 Plymouth Valiant ad, 1959 (courtesy Chrysler Group LLC)

FIGURE 3.6 Plymouth Valiant ad, 1959 (courtesy Chrysler Group LLC)

Beetle was in fact too small to be comfortable. Indeed, all of the American-made compacts were deliberately larger and slightly more expensive than the Beetle: the Valiant had a wheelbase of 106.5 inches (compared to the Beetle's 94.5 inches) and sold for around $2,000 (compared to $1,650 for the Beetle). In so doing, Plymouth and the other American automakers gambled (successfully, as it turned out) that in spite of the demise of the "Forward Look" vogue, Americans had retained a vestigial connection between the size and cost of a car and its prestige value.

The Valiant ads are especially interesting from a musical perspective. While jazz had long been the *lingua franca* of jingle writing (De Soto's 1955–57 campaign using Cole Porter's "It's Delightful" being a notable example), and while we have already seen that corporations like Chevrolet had sponsored jazz-oriented radio and television programming as part of their marketing, the Valiant ads are among the earliest television advertising spots that I have been able to find that use instrumental jazz *qua* jazz. The Valiant music is not simply jazz-inflected pop music in the jingle tradition: the close, dissonant voicings, homophonic textures, and usage of the flute for added orchestral color recall the influential arranging technique of Gil Evans, while the dry, *vibrato*-less sounds of the trumpet and alto saxophone suggest the influence of Miles Davis and Lee Konitz (or perhaps Paul Desmond), respectively. Evans, Davis, and Konitz, of course, were all involved with the seminal "Birth of the Cool" recordings (recorded in the late 1940s, but not released as a full album until 1954), which represented the height of jazz artistry and sophistication in the late 1950s.

FIGURE 3.7   Plymouth Valiant ad, 1959 (courtesy Chrysler Group LLC)

This becomes clearer still in a third advertisement, wherein jazz actually plays a structural role in the ad's narrative. Here we see a small jazz band—trumpet, saxophone, and bass—accompanying a Jack Kerouac-esque beat poet. The poet reads the copy:

> It has been inferred that the Chrysler corporation has the last word, and the last word is Valiant. The line, fine. Push button drive, va-voom, and an inclined engine like zoom. Gets a mapful of miles—and that's no jazz—on one tiny gallon of regular gas. And take a tip: go see the new Valiant. You'll flip!
>
> ("1960 Plymouth Valiant Commercials x6")

In each of these ads, the jazz soundtrack seems to remind us that, first of all, in spite of its size and unspectacular appearance, the Valiant is cool and sophisticated, ideal for a man like the "motorist" in the spots. Second of all, the music reminds us that the Valiant is an American car—and, by extrapolation, that the Volkswagen is not. Indeed, alongside frugality, the Plymouth's staunchly American identity had been an integral part of the brand from its inception. The very first Plymouth ad—appearing in the July 7, 1928 edition of the *Saturday Evening Post*—drew on profoundly nationalistic rhetoric to explain the origins of the brand name:

> We have named it the Plymouth because this new product of Chrysler engineering and craftsmanship so accurately typifies the endurance and strength, the rugged honesty, the enterprise, the determination of achievement and the freedom from old limitations of that Pilgrim band who were the first American colonists.
>
> (Curcio 2000: 393)

In the Valiant ads, jazz music replaces the invocation of the Pilgrims in asserting the Valiant's staunchly American identity and recalling the cultural richness that attends to that identity. In this way, the 1959 TV campaign foreshadowed the thematics of a 1967 print campaign, where the Valiant was dubbed "the imported American car." The Valiant, in other words, had all of the virtues of the Volkswagen—the economy, the reliability, the size and maneuverability— but with none of the stigma of buying "foreign."

The jazz soundtrack also has a gendered element: it shows that the Valiant is a man's car. As we have seen, masculine identification had become profoundly connected to the speed, sophistication, and the size of one's car (recall Nick Carraway's phallic description of Jay Gatsby's Rolls Royce). Since driving a car had become a kind of gender performance wherein the cyborg car-driver can become "large, gleaming, and formidable" (McCracken 2005: 77), by driving a compact car like the Valiant, a man risked having his masculinity called into question.

With this in mind, it becomes more meaningful that the jazz soundtrack for the Plymouth ads is instrumental. Whereas Dinah Shore's music was deliberately generically ambiguous so as to appeal to both men and women, the music in the Valiant spots is unequivocally jazz, with its history of masculine performance fully intact. This is the "hip" music of Norman Mailer's 1957 "White Negro" essay and Kerouac's 1957 book, *On the Road*—music marked by "joy, lust, languor, growl, cramp, pinch, scream and despair," to quote Mailer (quoted in Monson 1995: 403); or for Kerouac, "life, joy, kicks, darkness, music, . . . night" (Kerouac 1976: 180). Indeed, both of these 1950s Beat Generation writers are referenced by the Beat poet in the third spot.

By way of contrast, a pair of advertisements for the family-oriented Valiant Wagon draw the viewer's attention to practical, family matters such as the car's extra seating for children, and its additional trunk space to store household items such as "lumber, ladders, shrubbery, and camping equipment." These spots both show families driving together (in live action, not cartoon form); indeed, in one spot it is the woman who drives. For both ads, the soundtrack consists of a string orchestra performing a simple, attractive, consonant piece that recalls the "light classical" music of Ferde Grofé or Walter Schumann. The distinction could not be starker: the Valiant Wagon is a domestic, feminized car with music to match. The regular Valiant, on the other hand, is a man's car, driven by a single (albeit cartoon) man, and accompanied by masculine-coded instrumental jazz music.

At the same time, of course, the animated male characters in the ads are hardly overwhelming in their virility: none of the goofy driver with his blank smile, the lanky, scarf-clad poet, nor the short, pudgy, bespectacled jazz musicians suggest the kind of roiling sexual energy that Mailer and Kerouac describe. These men seem to be outsiders and intellectuals; we might anachronistically identify them as "nerds." Clearly, the J. Stirling Getchell team decided that prospective Valiant owners would likely have the same sense of irony and appreciation for self-deprecating humor that Doyle Dane Bernbach successfully recognized in future Volkswagen drivers. While the Valiant "motorist" is a man, he is seemingly one who understands and is amused by the phallic significance of the tailfin and the implied link between number of engine cylinders and sexual prowess. Even as the jazz soundtrack identifies the Valiant as a masculine space, the ads playfully destabilize the constitution of normative masculinity. Instead of being "large, gleaming, and formidable," the Valiant driver is self-deprecating, clever, and above all, hip.

If the Valiant advertisements have ambiguous messaging about gender, however, their relationship to jazz seems at least equally ambivalent. To a certain degree, the ads seem to be making light of the music. It is worth recalling that Plymouth was a lower-end brand. There are certainly tremendous marketing challenges to overcome in presenting a low-end product in a positive light; however, such brands do have the luxury of using humor in their advertising (like

Volkswagen did with their "Think Small" and "Lemon" ads), a strategy that would not be so readily available to a more expensive line. Whereas a Cadillac or a Lincoln is a serious car, a Plymouth Valiant can afford to be a fun one. To some degree, jazz becomes the thing that makes the Valiant fun in the ads by serving as the butt of the joke. The ads are, of course, cartoons: the characters have comically exaggerated features—especially the beat poet, whose long, lanky frame seems rather ridiculous juxtaposed with the short, round musicians. Significantly, the word "jazz" is used only once in the ads, and it is as a synonym for "lie:" "Gets a mapful of miles—and that's no jazz—from one tiny gallon of regular gas." So even though the music in the ads was doubtless influenced by the highly sophisticated, artistic, and masculinized work of Gil Evans and Miles Davis, that artistry is undercut to a considerable extent by the comedy.

The 1960 Valiant spots reveal a curious ambivalence at the heart of the web of meanings that jazz signifies: the potential jazz connotations of American nationalism, masculinity, hipster intellectualism, and artistic seriousness do not necessarily preclude the music from also being fun and humorous. Indeed, if we look outside of the U.S. context and the 1950s historical moment, the connotations of Americanism, masculinity, and artistic seriousness that were so critical to the thematic balance of the Valiant ads become increasingly diffuse—and in many cases, are eclipsed entirely. We can recognize this intuitively in many of the examples of jazz brand names mentioned in Chapter 1, particularly those where the articulation between jazz and the product in question is most tenuous—recall Potato Jazz and the "Jazz" species of apple.

An especially salient comparison with the Plymouth Valiant—and with the role of jazz on the *Dinah Shore Chevy Show*—is the Honda Jazz, an economy hatchback that first appeared in the European, British, and Australian markets in 2001. The Honda Jazz is, in many ways, the European heir to the Volkswagen,

FIGURE 3.8 Honda Jazz (courtesy Honda UK)

the Plymouth Valiant, and the other 1950s and 1960s compact cars. Small, fuel efficient, and reasonably affordable (a 2014 Jazz sells for £10,995 or about US$18,300), the Jazz is marketed chiefly to individuals and young families, especially those who live in bigger cities and have a heightened consciousness of easy maneuverability when faced with heavy traffic or a lack of parking. In these respects, it fits more or less the same market niche as did the first generation of compact cars in the United States in the middle of the 20th century.

Evidently the consumer market for automobiles has changed since the 1950s, particularly in terms of the global nature of competition amongst automakers. Prior to Volkswagen's arrival in the United States, automakers had focused primarily on their continental markets. Ford, General Motors, and Chrysler sold chiefly within Canada and the U.S. European consumers might choose between British Jaguars or Rolls Royces (among many other brands), French Citroëns and Renaults, or German Volkswagens and BMWs. In the emerging post-war markets in East Asia, drivers chose primarily between the Japanese brands, Nissan, Toyota, and eventually Honda (whose first cars rolled off the assembly line in 1968). Beginning in the 1930s, Ford and GM expanded their European operations, but they did so by purchasing indigenous manufacturers (GM bought Vauxhall in the UK and Opel in Germany, for instance) rather than by importing cars built—and branded—in the U.S. Hence, even while capital may have flowed back across the Atlantic, the brand identity of Ford- and GM-built cars for sale in Europe remained European.

Today, of course, the global interpenetration of formerly domestic markets and manufacturers has drastically changed the way that cars (and, indeed, all commodities) are bought and sold. Numerous iconic British automotive brands are now owned by nonBritish corporations, with Rolls Royce controlled by German manufacturer BMW, and Land Rover and Jaguar owned by Indian automaker Tata Motors. Corporate control of Chrysler, the smallest of the "Big Three" American automakers, has changed hands twice over the past two decades, from Daimler-Benz (the German manufacturer of the Mercedes Benz brand) to Italian-owned Fiat. This global corporate turmoil impacts the character of individual purchasing decisions as well. In Canada, for example, the top selling passenger car every year since 1998 has been the Honda Civic, a compact sedan built for the North American markets in the town of Alliston, Ontario for a company headquartered in Tokyo, Japan. Whereas it was striking to see someone driving a foreign-made car in 1959, in 2014 many drivers would have a difficult time saying which corporation owns their preferred brand, let alone where the car was actually built.

The global character of the industry presents unique challenges for marketers, who need to find ways to sell singular globally ubiquitous brands and models to a regionally and linguistically diverse consumer base. The Volkswagen Golf, for instance, was the top-selling vehicle in Europe in 2013, thanks in part to a combination of innovative advertising and decades of brand loyalty (Volkswagen has been by far the top-selling brand in Europe for several generations). In Canada, the Golf does not even rank in the top 10 in sales, despite a seeming national predilection for smaller hatchbacks. Meanwhile in the United States, a country where the three top selling vehicles are all pickup trucks, the Golf is not available for sale at all (Cato 2014). Corporations address this challenge structurally by opening marketing offices in each region, and empowering those offices to develop region-specific advertising campaigns and, if necessary, to change the name of a given model to better fit the market.

This was true for the Honda Jazz. Released in the summer of 2001, the vehicle was initially called the Fit. While it was released first in Japan and then in North America with this name, the marketing team in the European Union recommended a different name for that continent. "Fit," they suggested, was not a word that resonated with English-speaking consumers in Europe, nor was it a word that would be readily comprehensible to nonEnglish speakers. As Kate Saxton, Honda's manager of Public Relations Communications for the European Union explained to me, language poses a particular challenge in regions like Europe—as well as India and Africa—where consumer English fluency cannot always be taken for granted (Saxton 2014). After some discussion, the European office proposed the name "Jazz" chiefly because, in Saxton's words, "it works in many different languages and cultures [so] there's no risk of misunderstanding the meaning" (Saxton 2014). In Honda's estimation, the word jazz had essentially the same significance in the UK as it did in France, Spain, Italy, and Slovenia.

That significance had several aspects. According to internal documents from a meeting on March 9, 2001, the name Jazz was successful both because it was "Pan-European"—it held the same meaning in the multiplicity of European languages—and it sounded euphonious when paired with the name Honda. It was also thought to be appropriate for the diminutive size of the hatchback. Additionally, it connoted an aura of "style and sophistication" that was thought to appeal to the young, primarily urban demographic. At the same time, it needed to be "contemporary" and "fun" ("Honda Jazz—Naming"). Finally, it was seen to be a name with a chiefly "unisex" appeal, one that skewed "slightly . . . to a female target market, but not exclusively" (Saxton 2014).

Obviously, all of this sounds somewhat vague—and indeed, most of these descriptors could apply to the desired brand positioning and market niche for just about any economy car. Unfortunately, Kate Saxton advised me that everyone who had worked on the naming concept with the Honda Jazz in 2001 was now long gone from the company. However, a look at three of the recent advertisements for the car from different regions gives us a clearer sense of Honda's marketing goals and, most importantly, the role that the jazz concept plays in the pursuit of those goals.

In 2006, Honda EU contracted Hamburg-based agency, Scholz & Friends to produce a television ad for the German market. The agency developed a spot that has subsequently generated significant online notoriety (with upwards of 300,000 hits on YouTube) based on the iconic 1980s puzzle video game, Tetris.

As many readers will no doubt recall, in the game various oddly-shaped puzzle blocks dropped from the top of the screen. The player's aim was to use the game controller's directional keys to fit the blocks together before they piled too high. The player scored points by linking a solid row of blocks across the playing area.

The ad uses the original soundtrack that accompanied the gameplay in the 1989 Nintendo release of the game, an 8-bit version of a 19th-century Russian folk song called *Korobeiniki* that would be immediately familiar to viewers who remembered playing the game. The ad is also visually reminiscent of the game, showing a variety of cargo items—many of which are shaped to resemble the Tetris puzzle blocks—floating from the top of the picture into a waiting, open Jazz hatchback. As more and more parcels, pieces of furniture, garden tools, and other household objects flow into the car, a "score clock" in the top right corner of the screen tracks the growing volume of the cargo, finally stopping at 1323 liters—a surprisingly ample capacity for a car of its class.

An actor enters the picture to close the hatch just as a voice-over announces, "1323 Liter Spielraum. Der Honda Jazz." Like many German compound words, "Spielraum" doesn't have a direct English cognate. While it literally means "play room," it connotes both the sense of fun and pleasure associated with the word "play," as well as the secondary idea of mobility and flexibility—as in the English expression, "room to play with." In this way it acts as a pun, linking the simple pleasure of a childhood game with the act of packing the hatchback. In turn, we are reminded that the Jazz's ample cargo capacity permits a different kind of pleasure: it is much easier to take spontaneous, unplanned excursions on the open road when you have sufficient storage space to pack for virtually any eventuality.

Also in 2006, Honda Australia launched a campaign that played on another 1980s childhood icon, Thomas the Tank Engine. The spot "Village Green," created for Honda by the Melbourne office of ad agency Foote Cone Belding, features a bright yellow Jazz rolling through a pastoral small town that recalls Thomas the Tank Engine's fictional Island of Sodor. Like Thomas, "Jazz" is anthropomorphic, with wide eyes in place of headlights and a front bumper that doubles as a mouth. The soundtrack, too, is strikingly similar to the theme song from the 1980s television show. The tempo is identical at 180bpm; the bass line plays the I and V of every chord, establishing a jaunty "two" feel; the character and contour of the melody is very close to the 1980s original; even the closing harmonic cadence—a Neapolitan ♭IImaj⁷–I resolution—recalls the surprising parallel chromaticism of the *Thomas* theme.

Unlike the German "Tetris" ad, "Village Green" works to develop the Jazz's general character rather than honing in on a specific feature. This character emerges through the voice-over narration and a jocular conversation between other anthropomorphic cars, all performed by British actor Tony Robinson (best known for his role as Baldrick in the British comedy *Blackadder*) filling in for *Thomas*'s Ringo Starr (Macleod, "Honda Jazz Cars Ever So Nice"). We quickly learn that the Honda hatchback is personified as a cheerful, attractive young woman. While the name "Jazz"—used in the ad as if it were a proper name—is not specifically gendered, Robinson identifies the car using feminine pronouns both in the voice-over and in the dialogue between the cars. As the narrative of the ad progresses, "Jazz" drives along a country byway over a bridge and into a small village. She encounters four cars parked overlooking the village green, and greets them with a friendly "Morning!" as she glides past. As she moves on, three of the parked cars speak of her admiringly and tease a fourth car (identified in the voice-over narration as "Grumpy Car") who dissents from their opinion. "She always looks well," says one. "I hear she's even nice on the inside," adds another. "I bet she's expensive," offers the third, apprehensively. At that moment, a truck pulls in front of the cars, temporarily blocking them from view. On the side of the truck opposite the parked cars is a billboard advertisement for the Honda Jazz with its retail price prominently displayed: $15,990. The narrator accentuates how reasonable this price is, letting us know that the other cars "would have fainted with surprise at the price."

Both of these ads are clearly designed to appeal to the all-important "20-something" demographic targeted in Honda's 2001 planning process. Both the Tetris and *Thomas the Tank Engine* themes speak to potential buyers in their mid-20s: people who had been children in the decade in which the video game and TV show first appeared, and who are likely to remember both fondly. This age group is frequently the target for competitively-priced economy hatchbacks: they are likely just graduating from college or university, are perhaps starting their first full-time job, and are thinking about buying their first car. While they may have a smaller budget than an older demographic, they are also less likely to have families and children, and so are typically unconcerned about factors that would be a primary focus for older buyers: prestige and luxury in the first place, size and enhanced safety features in the second. At the same time, with their first substantial pay check in one hand and the keys to their new car in the other, they are eager for their first taste of the freedoms and pleasures of adulthood (even if they are not so keen to be reminded of the new challenges of that phase of life). Hence, automakers tend to characterize economy hatchbacks as small and economical both in terms of purchase price and fuel-efficiency, but also stylish and fun. In an intriguing historical coincidence, then, Honda is using jazz to sell cars to more or less the same demographic that was the focus of so much anxiety in the U.S. in the 1920s and 1930s. In that time period, cars and jazz were equally blamed for a dangerous physical, moral, and social mobility among young people that was leading America into an inexorable moral decline; in the 21st century, Honda uses jazz to celebrate youth mobility and sell cars to young people.

Evidently there is any number of musical genres—or other modes or artistic and cultural production—that could represent these qualities. Certainly, jazz *can* be universally evocative of youth, style, and play, but not without visual help; hence the articulation to more clearly "playful" themes of a childhood video game and television show in the German and Australian ads. In and of itself, the jazz genre—roughly a century old in 2006—could just as easily connote a sense of age, stolidity, or permanence that would undercut the youthful image that is so crucial to the marketability of the car. So what is it about jazz that would make it worth the risk? What could jazz offer that no other genre could?

The answer appears at the top of the "pros and cons" slide in the 2001 Honda naming presentation, written prominently in all-capital letters: "JAZZ = IMPROVISED MUSIC" ("Honda Jazz—Naming"). While improvisation is a feature of innumerable musical practices around the world—particularly in India, a key Honda Jazz market—no other genre stands as a clear, universally comprehensible cipher for improvisation in the way that jazz does. Although jazz improvisation per se is not likely to be specifically meaningful to most 25-year-old first-time car buyers in 2006, a more generalized notion of improvisation is powerfully relevant, especially at that particular moment in life.

Most recent college and university graduates are very conscious of their place on the cusp of an unknowable future. For many, this can be a moment of tremendous anxiety and insecurity, counterbalanced by a prevailing optimism and an overwhelming drive to experience all the pleasures (and dangers) that adult life has to offer. This kind of emotional precipice is ripe for exploitation by advertisers and marketers: it gives them an opportunity to gently prick consumers with the thorns of their own anxiety, and in the same gesture to propose a commercially available salve. In this way, the Honda ads essentially formulate a consumptive ideal of young adulthood, interpellating young people as adult consumers. They normalize consumer behavior as a crucial expressive aspect of burgeoning adulthood. They equate leisure with consumption—in this case, the countless consumptive leisure activities to which car ownership can grant access. And they seek to ensure that young viewers will grow from adolescent consumers who grew up spending their parents' money into adult consumers who will spend their own.

This is most visible in the 2008 follow-up to the "Village Green" spot, "Jazz Comes to Town," produced by a different Melbourne-based agency, DraftFCB. Created for the Australian launch of the 2008 redesign of the Jazz model, this new campaign borrowed from its *Thomas the Tank Engine*-themed predecessor by recapitulating its anthropomorphic cars and gentle sense of humor, but introduced a sleek stylization that distanced the newer ad from its 1980s source material. Whereas the animation in "Village Green" was characterized by a slightly jarring sense of movement, no doubt meant to remind viewers of *Thomas*'s stop motion sequences, "Jazz Comes to Town" featured a computer-generated smoothness more reminiscent of a contemporary Pixar film. The soundtrack was also updated, with a pop-infused song composed for the ad by London advertising music house Adelphoi Music in place of the jovial, juvenile sound of the 2006 spot.

Once again, the ad opens with Jazz (once again personified as a young woman) driving across a bridge into the city, only this time instead of a country village, she pulls into the thick of London rush hour traffic. She looks up at the towering buildings and exclaims, "Wow! Jazz, you've arrived!" She moves into a round-about, politely dismissing the helpful advice of a friendly London taxi—"Thanks, but I'll be fine!"—before deftly avoiding a collision in the adjacent lane. Next, she encounters a suavely flirtatious male SUV who compliments her on her "inner beauty" and offers to buy her a drink. She declines, saying "No thanks, I don't drink much," humorously dodging a potentially awkward social situation with a much older suitor, while also reminding viewers of her fuel economy.

She drives off alone and switches on her sound system, playing the Adelphoi-composed song: "I took a ride, saw the sights of the city [and] I've never had so much fun in my life." As darkness falls on the end of her first day in the city, Jazz says to herself, "I was made for this place." The music swells and then fades as she drives past a rooftop billboard advertising the price of the 2008 model—unchanged from 2006.

In all of the ads I have described—German and Australian—"Jazz" is linked with a pleasant demeanor, easy humor, and sense of optimism, which was no doubt intended to present an enticing character for young people (young women especially) about to move out into the world for the first time. In the Tetris ad, the car is presented as the ideal instrument to deal with the vicissitudes of 21st century modernity. "What kind of trip could possibly require a bicycle, an ottoman, a stereo speaker, and a caged budgie," the ad implicitly asks? "Life!" it answers emphatically. The Honda Jazz, therefore, affords the comfort and security that young people need to improvise spontaneously in response to unpredictable circumstances—whether they are behind the wheel, behind a desk at work, or in any other facet of their life.

In the more narrativistic structure of the Australian ads, meanwhile, the personified car makes decisions that are similarly improvised—spontaneous and unplanned—and free from the scrutiny of parents or teachers (recall her rejection of the paternal taxi in the 2008 ad), but every step that she takes is sure and unerringly confident. Far from being paralyzed by indecision, she treats the challenges she faces as a kind of game, responding to each with a playful spontaneity, and reveling in the new, unanticipated circumstances that every decision begets. In short, she reflects the kind of person that an anxious 25-year-old might wish to be. Concomitantly, the ad presents the car as one that that same 25-year-old would surely wish to drive. The brand name "Jazz" becomes a pivot point between what the car *is*, what the driver *does*, and what the young consumer might *wish to be*.

Curiously, despite the evident centrality of the jazz concept to the car's brand identity, and of prominence of the word "jazz" in all of the advertising and marketing messages about the car, jazz *music* is entirely absent. Indeed, this is true of nearly every advertisement for the car in every region in which it is sold. Clearly, in the estimation of Honda and its various international advertising agencies the sound of the music is largely irrelevant to the car's brand identity; the word itself is sufficient to communicate the message. Drivers, they apparently decided, would be most likely to make the desired connections between jazz and the car if jazz music were largely left out of the equation.

While no one still at Honda was qualified to confirm this supposition, it seems most likely that the decision to ignore jazz music—or indeed, any clear connection to jazz history or visual culture—reflected the real concern that the brand risked appearing too old if the music was emphasized too explicitly. A more overt use of jazz may have threatened other elements of Honda's desired demographic target as well. Fifty years after the *Dinah Shore Chevy Show* and on the other side of the Atlantic from Chevrolet's target market, Honda seemingly shared GM's 1960 conclusion that an overt use of masculinist, instrumental jazz music or iconic jazz imagery could potentially alienate a female demographic. In other words, Honda has tried to strike a balance invoking a vague notion of jazz improvisation, while evading the burdensome history of a discursively mascu-linist, century-old style of music.

Of course, this move has not worked out quite as smoothly as Honda might have liked. Indeed, despite Honda's careful efforts to target young consumers since the car's launch in 2001, the automaker has struggled against the Jazz's popular reputation as an "old lady car"—the kiss of death for any commodity positioned to appeal to young people. In online discussion forums, one frequently finds comments that extol the Jazz's reliability, but deride its image. On the UK-based youth social networking website The Student Room, for instance, this theme was ubiquitous among respondents to a question from a commenter seeking advice on whether to buy a used Jazz. Wrote one contributor, "The only bad thing about the Honda Jazz is the old lady image. If you want a reliable car and aren't bothered about looking cool then I would recommend it." Another echoed, "It is often associated with an old lady image so it will be cheap to insure and there's not much chance that it's been abused by a boy racer before you." Added a third, "Dull as ditchwater, but reliable. Not a car for anyone interested in cars, but capa-ble enough of getting from A to B" ("Honda Jazz," *The Student Room*). Although the sound of jazz may have plainly stood for youth, adventure, excitement, and risk for F. Scott Fitzgerald's Nick Carraway, Jay Gatsby, and Daisy Buchanan in the 1920s—and to some extent even for viewers of *The Dinah Shore Chevy Show* and the Plymouth Valiant ads in the 1960s—in 2006 the music's meaning was decidedly more multifarious and ambivalent. This likely explains the absence of jazz from the advertising soundtracks: music from the 1950s or 1960s could only serve to make a car that potential consumers already perceive to be geri-atric seem even older.

By contrast, in the Volkswagen ad for the 1999 Jetta discussed in Chapter 2, the 1963 Mingus recording used in the soundtrack could more readily connote a sense of youthful vitality appropriate to the car because of the age of the main character in the ad. For the septuagenarian hero, "II B.S." would have been the sound of *his own* youth—an especially potent evocation at a moment when he was escaping from a nursing home site that represented the burdens and constraints of advancing age. Jazz music was therefore connected to the Jetta by way of the playfully engaging character of the old man. However, it is worth noting that it was ultimately his much younger grandson who drove the getaway car. In this way, the old man's youthful fantasy is linked to the embodied youth of his grandson. The car therefore appeals to both young people and those who aspire to recapture their own fleeting youthful vitality and vigor.

If the jazz brand is in fact partially culpable for the Honda's "dull as ditchwater" reputation, it is undoubtedly only one of many branding, marketing, and design factors that contribute to that image. That being said, the apparent failure of these various campaigns to achieve the sense of "style and sophistication" that Honda sought to develop for the brand can perhaps be attributed to the lack of any *explicit* connection to jazz *history*. While Tetris and *Thomas the Tank Engine* are certainly connected with youth, neither the video game nor the television show has any connection to jazz. Honda's marketers and contracted advertisers seem consistently to take it for granted that consumers will intuitively make the connection between jazz and the characteristics with which they hope to imbue the car: style, sophistication, fun, and improvisation. With no jazz soundtrack, and with no demonstrable connection to jazz history or visual culture, jazz is left as a signifier that floats perhaps too freely. Because the music can mean so many different things, because it occupies so many competing and contradictory cultural positions, jazz can mean more or less whatever viewers of the Honda ads want it to mean: it *can* be stylish and sophisticated, but it can also be merely old. Recall Robert Foster's concept of the "economy of qualities," outlined in Chapter 1: brand identity, according to Foster, is built through the shared investment of producers and consumers. If the consumer is granted too much creative leverage in the equation, however, the producer risks losing control of the identity and narrative of the brand. Honda needs "Jazz" drivers to *feel like* improvisers, but they can only be permitted *actually* to improvise to a point. Honda needs to offer a *spectacle* of improvisation (in the Debordian sense described in the introduction), not necessarily the real thing. On the other hand, the Volkswagen ad likely succeeds largely because it does tether jazz as a signifier to a particularly evocative character—the elderly African American man—thereby delimiting and directing the decoding possibilities (to use Stuart Hall's term) open to consumers. In order to be effective as a marketing tool, then, perhaps jazz requires some kind of anchor—or perhaps more accurately a bridge that clarifies the articulation between the music and the commodity.

"This is My Car:" Chrysler, Pop-Jazz, and Diana Krall

In the spring of 2001, Steve Denvir—a copywriter from the ad agency BBDO—and Mike Smith—an art director from the same agency, and Steve's longtime working partner—were chatting over lunch at the Pilot Tavern, a jazz club on

Cumberland Street in Toronto. Denvir recalls, "[Mike] and I used to work at the Pilot all the time. . . . Well we'd go because there's nobody on the phone, no accountant poking around bothering you, so we'd want to bang around stuff" (Denvir 2010). At the time, Denvir and Smith were the creative team assigned to one of BBDO's premiere clients, Chrysler Canada. The year before, Denvir and Smith had designed a new campaign for the company, focusing on pride of ownership. Says Smith,

> [Steve] and I were in the throes of producing this campaign based around pride of ownership. Because one of the things was that nobody would ever really, truly own up to driving a Chrysler. People were buying them, but it wasn't one of those things that you kind of threw the keys on the table and said, "Hey, look at this, this is what I just bought. It's a Chrysler." . . . Great cars, well-engineered, all of those kinds of things, but nothing to brag about. . . . So we created this campaign based around that, and it was basically around the line, "This is my car." So it would be about people talking about their cars, and they would say, "Well, this is very cool. This is my car."
>
> (Smith 2010)

The first "This Is My Car" television commercials featured Chrysler designers talking about how their automotive design reflected their personalities, and describing the aspects of the design of which they were especially proud, or which they thought were especially cool. One of the first ads, called "Authority," opens with what looks like an old reel-to-reel film of a kindergarten class in which one student is behaving particularly badly. As we follow the child's various crimes and punishments, we hear the anxious-sounding voice of his female teacher reading his report card comments: "Doesn't understand that rules are for everybody. Refuses to color inside the lines. . . . Does not respect authority." At the end of the report card, we hear a new, smooth male voice: "Hey, it's true. Everything I know I did learn in kindergarten." The image changes to show a smiling man with dark hair wearing a leather jacket leaning on a 2001 PT Cruiser. A caption above the car identifies the man, "Bryan Nesbitt, PT Cruiser Designer." The man's voice concludes, "This is my car."

The success of that campaign, according to Denvir, was grounded in its explicit identification of consumers of the Chrysler brand:

> [The client] wanted a campaign for Chrysler brand, and there are like six different cars in the Chrysler brand, all of which are targeted at different people. The problem is, how do you have one unifying thought that pulls all this together. So we're sitting over lunch at the Pilot: "What if we don't start from the product, we start from the consumer?"
>
> (Denvir 2010)

"This is my car" spoke to and for existing Chrysler owners, reminding them of the pride and excitement that they derive from their Chrysler vehicles; at the same time, it addressed potential new Chrysler owners, inviting them to join in a cool, insider club.

While these ads had been extremely successful for Chrysler (the PT Cruiser, in particular, was selling very well in Canada), Denvir and Smith were seeking to take the campaign in a new direction. This particular discussion at the Pilot was chiefly about selecting a celebrity spokesperson whom they could connect with the upcoming release of the 2002 Sebring convertible. As Smith remembered,

> To make a long story short, we had worked through a whole bunch of fictitious people, and I'm a great Diana Krall fan, which is where it actually came from. And, um, we talked about what could we do, what kind of person could we have for this, etcetera, and we thought, "Well, why not do something really seriously and kind of get this campaign really moving." So we needed somebody with credibility rather than a fictitious person, like a bookkeeper or a soccer mom, or something, because we had done that for minivans already. And while that's fine that that's believable, if we could actually give it some testimonial heft without actually being testimonial per se. And I said, "I know exactly what to do with this thing. Diana Krall is the person we need to use." So we chatted about it. Steve's a great music guy as well, so he got on board with that. And the thing developed instantly. It developed a life of its own.
>
> (Smith 2010)

Initially, the Sebring was to be the only car connected with Diana Krall, much like the PT Cruiser the only car linked to its co-designer Brian Nesbitt. When Denvir and Smith pitched the Krall ad to Chrysler's marketing team, Chrysler brand manager Pearl Davies and her colleagues became extremely excited about the possibility of making Krall the star of not only the Sebring ad, but of ads for several other cars included in the overarching "This Is My Car" campaign as well. Denvir explains,

> [T]he client so fell in love with . . . that they wanted to build the whole damn campaign around it. We said, "No, no! This is one element of 'This is my car'. This is a celebrity, here's this, it's all over." We battled about that, but we ended up paying a bunch of money for her.
>
> (Denvir 2010)

The ad for the Sebring—a print ad that appeared in Canadian magazines such as McLean's and Canadian Living—retained the narrative structure of the earlier "This Is My Car" commercials. In it, Krall was pictured seated on a piano bench next to a Sebring convertible. The tagline for the ad read simply, "This Is My Car."

The narrative became far more complicated for the other cars, however. If the Sebring ad identified that convertible as Diana Krall's car, what was her relationship to the other Chrysler models? After all, they could not all be her car. Steve Denvir explains, "[W]e had structured the one with Sebring around 'This is my car'. All of a sudden the 300M is in there, and she can't say 'This is my car'" (Denvir 2010). This was a particular challenge for the 300M television spot. Whereas print ads need to present a simple but compelling idea, television spots need to tell a story. Furthermore, the 300M spot somehow needed to showcase the title track from Krall's 2001 album, *The Look of Love*, which Chrysler Canada had agreed to license for use in the campaign. To make the challenge even greater, neither the BBDO creative team nor the Chrysler Canada marketing team had any say in the choice of the soundtrack. According to both Denvir and Smith, Krall's management, S.L. Feldman & Associates, selected (indeed, insisted upon) "The Look of Love" for them. Most of the parties involved in the creative process had no objection to the choice of song, with the exception of Denvir. "[B]y the end of it I fucking hated the song," he said. "I wasn't that big a fan of it in the first place" (Denvir 2010). Denvir summarized the daunting challenges he and Smith faced in developing the ad from a set of seemingly disparate concepts and requirements into a cohesive, 60-second story:

> But we had to try to turn this into a story. . . . It's a piece of film that's sixty seconds long, or in one case thirty seconds. Well, why is she there? Why is she there singing? Where the fuck's the car? How do you make something coherent out of this? . . . And they also wanted. . . . If I recall, they wanted to cut three different spots out of it. I had no idea how we'd do it.
> (Denvir 2010)

The story they developed was, as both Denvir and Smith admitted, rather loose and unclear. The 60-second spot (aired both on Canadian television and in cinemas) is set on a rainy night in a loft. The loft is sparingly furnished, with exposed yellow brickwork, a single window, hardwood floors that are bare except for a Turkish rug, a grand piano, and an antique brass clock that reveals the late hour—1:24 am. The spot opens with a shot of Krall walking slowly towards the window and looking out, accompanied by a dramatic dominant seventh chord with a flattened 9th, drawn from Claus Ogerman's lush string accompaniment by sound editor David Fleury.

As the song begins, the camera cuts to a new shot of Krall, seated at the grand piano and singing the lyric. The rest of the spot alternates between shots of Krall at the piano—sometimes singing, sometimes playing—and shots of a silver 300M driving through the industrial area along Lake Ontario just east of downtown Toronto in the pouring rain. The spot concludes with a brief shot of Krall looking out the window once again, a cut to a close-up shot of Krall singing the last words of the first section of the song—"takes my breath away"—and a final cut to a shot of the car pulling up next to a building.

As Krall sings the opening lyric of the song's B-section ("I can hardly wait to hold you, feel my arms around you, how long I have waited"), the camera pans up from the car to a figure silhouetted in the lone illuminated window in the building. A voice-over enters overtop of Krall's lyric, the only nonmusical sound in the spot: "Introducing the 300M Special from Chrysler." Following the voice-over, the scene fades, replaced by a plain black screen with the Chrysler logo. As the spot ends, the slogan, "This is my car" fades in.

The story, therefore, is as simple as it is subtle and indirect: Krall is alone in her loft, waiting for somebody. We the viewers never see the person for whom she is waiting, as he is invisible behind the windshield of his 300M, but given the lyrics to "The Look of Love," we are meant to assume that the 300M driver is Krall's lover. Hence, unlike the earlier ads in the "This is my car" campaign, in the 300M spot the car does not belong to the star; rather, as Denvir bluntly explained, the 300M belongs to "the guy who's banging Diana Krall, I guess" (Denvir 2010).

The simple story, of course, was not the point of the spot; nor was the story intended to compel the viewer to buy a 300M. The point of the spot and the thrust of its sales pitch was Diana Krall. In the first place, Krall's burgeoning fame in Canada was very appealing to both the creative team and the Chrysler marketers. As Mike Smith notes, Krall's "star-factor" was extremely important (Smith 2010). Since the 1997 release of her fourth CD, *Love Scenes*—an album that earned Krall's first Grammy nomination and her first "Gold" certification by the Recording Industry Association of America—Krall's career had been on a rapid upward trajectory. In 2000, her CD *When I Look In Your Eyes* received a Grammy nomination for "Album of the Year." *The Look of Love*, released in September of 2001, went platinum within only a few months of its release, far outselling its main rival on the market at that time, the vaunted re-release of Miles Davis's seminal recording, *Kind of Blue*.

The fact that Krall was becoming a recognizable celebrity would have been insufficient, of course, were it not for the qualities she purportedly represented. Krall was seen to be a particularly strong brand-fit for the Sebring and 300M, the two higher-end, more luxurious models in the Chrysler fleet. Steve Denvir suggests, "[Diana's] a great fit. She's stylish, she's sophisticated. We paired her up with the Sebring, which was the car that wanted to aspire to that" (Denvir 2010). It is important to recall that the purpose of the "This is my car" campaign was to instill pride in Chrysler owners. The creative and marketing teams recognized that their consumers did not necessarily regard Chryslers—even luxury models—as "stylish and sophisticated." Hence, by pairing cars that aspired to style and sophistication with an individual who was gradually becoming (in Canada, at least) a cultural paragon of those virtues, it was hoped that the Sebring and 300M would be able to acquire those virtues too.

As Pearl Davies explained in a 2002 interview with Canadian newspaper *The National Post*'s David Hayes, "[W]e talk about the refinement of the vehicles, the quality of the craftsmanship, and we can draw a parallel between her art and our vehicles" (Hayes 2002). This parallel was literally constructed in the 300M television advertisement through the alternating shots of Krall and the vehicle. The relationship between Krall and Chrysler is effectively summarized by Bill Sullivan, a former of executive Vice President of Rolex Watch USA, describing a similar advertising arrangement between Krall and his company: "The claim that's associated with the product is very subtle. It doesn't say, 'Hey, go out and buy a Rolex watch'. It just says, 'These people represent quality. Isn't it natural that the perpetual spirit of their activities relates to the perpetual spirit of the product?'" (Hayes 2002).

At the same time, the 300M spot was addressed to would-be consumers who were similarly stylish and sophisticated—or, more accurately, who aspired to be regarded as such. Davies confirmed, "the [demographic] position for the brand was upscale, elegant, and around finer things" (Davies 2010). In this way, Diana Krall was a good brand-fit because she represented a kind of ideal consumer: just the sort of "upscale" and "elegant" person who should want to drive a Sebring or 300M. If the Sebring was her car and the 300M was her lover's car, then consumers who identified with and/or aspired to emulate Krall would ideally look to those vehicles as being appropriate for their social station—or at least, as affordable alternatives to other cars that historically connoted that degree of opulence.

To a certain degree, Krall's music was (and continues to be) the linchpin of her style, sophistication, "upscale-ness," and elegance. Mike Smith explained,

> [Jazz is] cool and sophisticated. Shorthand for that. You know, it's not stuffy, as I say—it's not classical, so it's not stuffy. It's not raucous and rock and roll-y. So it sits in a kind of gap, and it's not elevator music, and it's not adult pop, which is another kind of thing. . . . It's a strange kind of little middle ground . . . of exclusivity.
>
> (Smith 2010)

The setting of the 300M was designed to draw out these elements of jazz's signification. For Pearl Davies, jazz is "elegant," "upscale," and "urban," and the setting needed to reflect those ideas (Davies 2010). At the same time, however, according to film director Rob Quartly, jazz has a sense of "mystery" and "intrigue" that was evoked by the various elements of the setting—especially the bare, aged brick, the rain, and the late hour. Mike Smith echoes, "Jazz is like a late-night thing, and it's kind of smoky and foggy and all of those kinds of things" (Smith 2010). Quartly explains that all of the aspects of the commercial interact to create a kind of signifying nexus:

> It matched. It was a cohesive visual element between the car travelling in the city and her performance. A loft, brick, industrial, city feeling abode fit with the car at night outside. All of those elements. . . . By making it rain, I was able to bring an element in from the exterior when she's playing

the piano and there's rain in the background, and the light [reflected off of] the rain is bouncing off of the floor or through that skylight that we built. It's all a way of making the mosaic fit like little jigsaw pieces.

(Quartly 2010)

Quartly suggested that the spot's narrative plays into this nexus as well. Where Denvir felt that the story was vague, an ultimately unsuccessful attempt to cope with a nearly impossible set of circumstances, Quartly characterized it as a masterful display of subtlety and nuance—a story that suggests instead of tells. I asked him why we never see the driver of the car in the ad. He answered,

To me it goes into a sort of blatant thing. Try to imagine how you would see him: is it a silhouette, does he have a hat on, does he have long hair, does he have short hair? You start asking all these questions, and you start thinking about it. Whereas I think it's nicer not to ask those questions.

(Quartly 2010)

Quartly articulated his rationale further in response to a different question: "If you want to be that kind of blatant, but I prefer not to. Especially if you talk jazz music it's way better to be more elusive" (Quartly 2010).

Evidently, this sense of mystery, elegance, sophistication, and bourgeois elitism is quite different from the qualities that Honda sought to mine from the jazz connection with its 2001 hatchback. There is nothing playful, youthful, or funny about the Chrysler ads. On the contrary, Chrysler looked to ostensibly the same musical genre to achieve virtually opposite branding ends, drawing on contrasting tropes of meaning. In the first place, the evanescent, elusive quality that Quartly and Smith identify emerges from the visual iconography of the music. In particular, the bare brick of the loft space in the film, and late night setting, even the rain and fog that are so important to Quartly's cinematography seem to signify on the iconic seedy, urban, basement jazz club.

According to historian Benjamin Cawthra, the mythologization of the smoky jazz club as a visual icon can be credited at least in part to legendary jazz photographer Herman Leonard. Leonard's photos taken at the Royal Roost in New York City in the early 1950s commonly featured the great musicians of the era—from Dizzy Gillespie and Dexter Gordon to Sarah Vaughan and Billie Holiday—performing on the bandstand, invariably wreathed in smoke. Leonard insisted that the smoky effect was in fact accidental, the unexpected result of an occasion when his camera flash malfunctioned while a secondary flash positioned behind and above the bandstand worked: "[I] unintentionally ended up with a backlighting effect, silhouetting a trumpeter with a cigarette in his hand. The flash highlighted the smoke dramatically and I really liked the effect" (quoted in Cawthra 2011: 110). Regardless, Leonard's photos further enshrined the link between jazz and tobacco. Cigarette smoke might otherwise have been demonstrative of the cramped, uncomfortable, and unhealthy working conditions jazz musicians commonly faced, but Leonard's lens transformed it into something beautiful, ethereal, and iconic—the wisp of smoke escaping a musician's lips almost a metaphor for the evanescence of the saxophonist's improvised bebop melodies to which Leonard would have borne witness that night.

Krall's music also lends the 300M a "classic" quality. Unlike a musician like Charles Mingus, Krall is not aesthetically invested in innovation or experimentation; rather her stated primary aesthetic goal is to reinterpret the standard jazz repertoire. She identifies with performers such as Nat "King" Cole, Carmen McRae, and Tony Bennett (with whom she has performed on a number of occasions)—singers whose heyday was the "golden age" of jazz in the 1950s (Reid 2002: 20). In this way, her music signifies a quality of seasoned age that plays against Krall's own relative youth (Krall was born in 1964). This tension between youth and age is of great value in the marketing of a luxury car—a commodity that depends on a similar mixture of pristine beauty and timeless opulence for its market value. In the case of Chrysler, a company that largely lacks the crucial history of opulence (as compared to Cadillac or Lincoln, for instance), Krall's music provides the timeless quality.

This can best be understood using Grant McCracken's concept of "patina." McCracken explains,

> Patina is, first of all, a physical property of material culture. It consists in the small signs of age that accumulate on the surface of objects. Furniture, plate, cutlery, buildings, portraiture, jewelry, clothing, and other objects of human manufacture undergo a gradual movement away from their original pristine condition. . . . In Western societies, this physical property is treated as a symbolic property. . . . What makes this message unusual is that it is not, strictly speaking, concerned with claiming status. This relatively simple, even banal, message is left to other, more mundane, aspects of status symbolism. Patina has a much more important symbolic burden, that of suggesting that existing status claims are legitimate. Its function is not to claim status but to authenticate it. Patina serves as a kind of visual proof of status.
> (McCracken 1988: 32)

In McCracken's view, the idea of patina emerges from the rigid English class system of the 16th century, a time when qualification for aristocratic status depended upon not just individual wealth, but on a family history of wealth dating back at least five generations (McCracken 1988: 33). Patina—the visible accumulation of age on valuable family possessions—served the role of "gatekeeper," distinguishing between time-honored aristocratic families and nouveau riche merchants. In the Chrysler context, Krall's "golden age" music lends a kind of audible patina to a brand that lacks it, and to a car that "aspires" (to use Denvir's word) to attain it.

Intriguingly, however, the advertisers with whom I spoke all suggested that the music is largely ancillary to Krall's image. In Mike Smith's view,

> Well, [jazz was] appropriate in that Diana Krall was appropriate, and the music is her, basically. So it wasn't a question of saying that, "hmm, these cars need jazz," it was a question of saying, "These cars need a bunch of the things that Diana Krall brings to them." It's a sophistication, it's a coolness— the jazz sound goes a long way towards carrying that. But she's completely different. And she was young, she's popular, certainly more accessible than if we had ended up with an old jazz standard, for instance, just as a piece of music. It needed to have the star-factor.
>
> (Smith 2010)

Steve Denvir echoed Smith's point, arguing that while there are certainly numerous musicians who might be musically similar, there were none at the time who had the other qualities that Krall offered.

> Sorry, you can take any number of jazz figures and, you know, they're not household names. Whereas she was getting to be one. The only other way to do something like that is to go really old school, like Tony Bennett or somebody, which doesn't hit the demographic because it's kind of old. Whereas she was new, she was fresh, just beginning to be pretty well known, so it was a perfect fit.
>
> (Denvir 2010)

Thus, although jazz music is an integral part of Krall's elegant, cool, and sophisticated image, for these advertisers it was ultimately secondary to that image, valuable only insofar as it was attached to Krall.

Critical to Krall's elegance and her status (according to Rolex's Sullivan) as a "person of quality" was her physical appearance and her well documented *haute couture* tastes. Davies suggested that these aspects of Krall's persona were important to the Chrysler brand as well:

> Well, she is a beautiful woman, and . . . I think she was always in her Jimmy Choo shoes and black dresses at that point in time, which just never hurts if you're going to associate with beautiful people. So that sex appeal is something you'd like to associate with.
>
> (Davies 2010)

Rob Quartly talked about the importance of Krall's look to the Chrysler brand in terms of cross-over marketing. I asked him about how wardrobe decisions were made for Krall prior to the shoot:

You know, I can't remember now—it's gotta be ten years ago. But I would definitely have said, "Hey, you know, she looks killer on that album cover. Why don't we feed off of that? Why don't we tie her look—which is her new look that's being launched—with the look of the commercial, launching her song with the car at the same time and fit to make it all cross-referenced?" . . . Things should cross over. There has to be a consistency from the look, feel, and practicality. If she was wearing something totally different on her album cover or any other visualization she had done from that album or that song, they're not getting as much bang for their buck, you know what I mean? They're buying her look, they're buying her feel. Anytime you work with a star, you're crazy to try to reinvent that star, because [it's his or her look that] you want.

(Quartly 2010)

To that end, Krall appears in the 300M spot in attire that is strongly reminiscent of (though not exactly identical to) the clothes she wears on the album cover: a black dress with a deep plunging neckline and a thigh-high slit, and strappy Jimmy Choo stilettos.

Krall's shoes (which were mentioned numerous times in the various interviews I conducted, complete with her preferred brand name) make a feature appearance in the spot. Quartly describes the genesis of that particular shot:

I mean, her Jimmy Choo shoes, or . . . I think she's wearing them on that album cover too. . . . I remember designing. . . . [Laughs.] I think Mike [Smith] and Steve [Denvir] got a big kick out of it, but I said, "Hey, you know what? I'm going to put the camera on the floor right in front of her shoes and we're going to crane up her legs."

(Quartly 2010)

The shoes themselves become an important component of the spot, signaling Krall's elegance and "quality" while simultaneously linking the 300M spot to her album cover, and concomitantly, her other artistic activities. Of course, the shoes also serve the more obviously practical purpose of accentuating the other stars of this shot, Krall's smooth and slender legs. When I watched the spot with Steve Denvir, he asked me to stop the player when we came to this particular shot so we could talk about it.

Stop it for a second. You can do [focus group] research on some of these things, and you'll get a second by second measure of interest. They have a little control thing, "Oh I like that, I don't like that, I don't like that." The shot of the leg really spiked it. Obviously a bunch of guys in the group.

(Denvir 2010)

Rob Quartly, too, used the word "sexy" to describe a number of other aspects of the advertisement as well. When I asked him to describe the pacing and movement of the ad, he said, "You know, I think you have to use the word 'sexy'" (Quartly 2010). "Sexy" came up again in response to a question about the decision to use a silver car and rain towers in the spot: "Silver cars at night? Wet? Sexy" (Quartly 2010). The wet car becomes all the more symbolically potent when we consider it in the context of the alternating shots between the car and Krall. As the scene shifts back and forth between the glistening, wet car and Krall's lithe body, the whole scenario becomes tinged with a sense of sexual tension and excitement. While Quartly is reluctant blatantly to spell out the relationship between Krall, the car, and the song (preferring that the ad's symbols and themes should remain elusive), he does admit that the car—carrying its invisible driver inexorably, tantalizingly closer to an anticipated tryst with Krall—might itself somehow represent "the look of love" (Quartly 2010).

We can extend the metaphor further by recalling John Urry's concept of the car-driver cyborg. Given that the 300M driver is never seen, he (presumably he is male) has no tangible existence apart from the car. His invisibility has two consequences: First, it interpellates male viewers, inviting them to imagine themselves in his place. Secondly, the invisible driver in the ad—and all of the vicarious drivers watching at home or at the cinema—virtually becomes the car, "gleaming, large, and formidable (McCracken 2005: 77). Krall's "look of love" is therefore decidedly prismatic: Krall's seductive gaze falls first on the invisible driver in the ad, second on the viewers projecting themselves into the role, and third on the car itself. And since the 300M is the only tangible target for Krall's "look of love," it is almost as if it is the car itself that becomes, metaphorically at least, Krall's lover.

Of course, Krall's image and sex appeal have been key elements of her persona throughout her career—especially since *Love Scenes* (1997). In the sole extant biography of Krall, *Diana Krall: The Language of Love*, Canadian poet and author Jamie Reid dwells frequently, at great length, and with a somewhat discomfiting level of specificity on Krall's dazzling beauty:

> On stage in the act of playing, Diana Krall is even more beautiful than in the glamorous photographs gracing her recent album covers. . . . In between musical phrases, her long-fingered hands sweep her long and silky blond hair back from her face. She is almost without make-up—with only a hint of pale lipstick on her full and sensuous lips. She looks for all the world as if she has just come on stage from washing her face, her transparent complexion youthful and dewy, fresh as an adolescent's. Her teeth are as white and straight as the keys on her Steinway grand.
>
> (Reid 2002: 11)

Descriptions like these—always in similarly sumptuous tones—pervade the book, becoming a veritable trope. By the same token, according to her website,

Krall has often been the subject of profiles in fashion magazines like *Allure, Hello, People,* and *GQ*. Krall's beauty and fashion sense have received at least as much attention in the media as her music, if not more.

While Krall's sex appeal has no doubt been a significant factor in her commercial success and popular acclaim, it has also contributed to her marginalization as a serious jazz artist. Speaking in an interview with Wayne Enstice and Janet Stockhouse for their 2004 collection, *Jazzwomen: Conversations with Twenty-One Musicians*, Krall says,

> Lately, I've had a problem (chuckles sardonically) because you're not supposed to be attractive. "You're only successful 'cause you're a white, blond, girl-next-door type'. 'Girl next door meets sex kitten'," was one quote in the paper. A put-down. I'm frustrated because my photographs in some instances are too glamorous for certain publications. I can't be a serious artist because of my looks; or I'm only successful because of my looks. Because of that, there's a prejudice against digging a little deeper.
>
> (Enstice and Stockhouse 2004: 188)

Jazz scholar Sherrie Tucker explains that this has been a common problem for women jazz musicians—particularly Euro-American women jazz musicians—throughout much of the music's history. On the one hand, Tucker suggests, "idealized" Euro-American women like Krall (and, for that matter, like Dinah Shore) are able to gain access to mass media with relative ease, especially as compared with nonEuro-American women. On the other hand, their pervasive "visibility in the entertainment industry" often seems to stir the contempt of the (mostly male) gatekeepers within the jazz genre. Because race, appearance, and sartorial sense (especially as a demonstration of both fashion savvy and bourgeois prestige) very often *do* eclipse exceptional musical skill when it comes to achieving media visibility, many critics, collectors, and even other musicians treat these traits as a priori evidence of a lack of musical substance (Tucker 2000: 10). Historically, Tucker suggests, women singers (a group that has constituted the vast majority of female jazz musicians) have been a particular target for critical scorn, in large part because their sexuality is understood to preclude the possibility of artistic excellence:

> In the gender division of jazz and swing labor, the normal configuration is for men to skillfully operate instruments and for women to perform privatized popular versions of femininity with their voices and bodies. As jokes and cartoons in Down Beat indicate, stereotypes about "girl singers" highlighted a shortage of musical knowledge and an entertaining excess of sex appeal.
>
> (Tucker 2000: 5)

While Krall has experienced tremendous commercial success in her career, she has regularly been criticized in the media for a perceived lack of artistic seriousness, resulting in a reluctance on the part of many critics to categorize her music (especially her most recent recordings, which tend to foreground her singing) as jazz at all. Mark Miller, the longtime jazz critic for the Canadian national daily newspaper *The Globe and Mail*, for instance, titled his 2001 review of *The Look of Love*, "Has Diana Krall Gone Pop?" (Reid 2002: 177). *Down Beat* critic John McDonough echoed Miller's skepticism in his review of the record: "It's a lovely album. But I don't think of it as a jazz album any more than I would consider Linda Ronstadt's trilogy of Nelson Riddle to be jazz albums. . . . I don't think being popular is necessarily to lower yourself. In rating it, I would certainly rate it four stars. But it's not a jazz album" (quoted in Reid 2002: 185).

Several of the advertisers with whom I spoke expressed similar viewpoints. Toronto-based advertiser Scott Thornley, while enormously respectful of Krall's talent, was reticent about characterizing her as a jazz artist per se: "She's a fantastic chanteuse. She's a part of a very rare and very wonderful—and wonderfully talented—group of females who are fantastic at doing standards, and every once in a while do one of their own songs, and the song is really good" (Thornley 2010). David Fleury was more explicit, suggesting that Krall plays "cocktail piano," not jazz:

> You know. . .I don't know, if you play Ornette Coleman or you play Diana Krall, my clients would say "Diana Krall is jazz, and that's really great jazz." And anybody who knows jazz would go, "Jesus. It's cocktail piano." You know? And it's really that difference. [The client says,] "No, when I said jazz I meant Diana Krall." "Oh, I'm sorry, I thought you meant *jazz*."
> (Fleury 2010)

Similarly, Rob Quartly distinguishes between "jazz"—by which he means the music of artists like Charles Mingus or Miles Davis—and "pop-jazz," a term that he applies to musicians like Nat "King" Cole, Michael Bublé, and Krall. For Quartly, "pure" jazz is characterized by an emotional depth that somehow transcends language, whereas "the pop form, like Diana Krall, . . . is a little bit more saccharine" (Quartly 2010). Alongside a perceived deficit of emotional sincerity is a perceived lack of aesthetic (and perhaps intellectual) rigor in Krall's music. This is evident in Fleury's contrast between Krall and Ornette Coleman, as well as in the contrast Thornley and Quartly make between Krall and Charles Mingus. In both cases, the male musician is an improviser and a composer—a creator of music—whereas Krall is merely an interpreter of existing songs.

Intriguingly, Krall herself uses similar criteria to distinguish between what is and is not jazz. She insists that she is a true jazz pianist, because "that's where I do the improvising" (quoted in Reid 2002: 187); however, she acknowledges that, because she refrains from vocal improvisation, she might not qualify as a jazz singer: "I look at myself more as a storyteller kind of singer rather than a jazz singer. . . . The lyric is really important for me. It has to be very strong and timeless" (quoted in Reid 2002: 187). In her interview with Enstice and Stock-house, she comments on this issue at some length:

> I wish I could have been there at that Great American Songbook at Donte's with Joe Pass and Jimmy [Rowles] and Carmen McRae. Those were the days when they were singing songs, and they weren't into worrying about whether you scat sang or not. You knew you were a jazz singer by the way you approached things. It wasn't about, you know, 'You're not a jazz singer unless you're singing 'Giant Steps'. I was teasing the band that I'm going to write lyrics to that. (Laughs.) And I'm not putting down people who do, but I'm a singer, whether I'm a jazz singer or not, and a piano player. I'm definitely a jazz piano player—I improvise, no question. I sing songs, but I'm not going to try to be a horn player with my vocal. I'm trying to be an interpreter of lyrics.
>
> (Enstice and Stockhouse 2004: 185)

In this statement, Krall takes a fascinatingly ambivalent position on the question of improvisation and jazz authenticity. She acknowledges that improvisation is widely regarded as a predicate for qualification as a jazz musician, and uses that predicate to assert her credentials as a jazz pianist. On the other hand, how-ever, she simultaneously questions the status of improvisation as the universal standard for jazz qualification, characterizing it as a modern trend to which such recognized jazz authorities as Joe Pass, Jimmy Rowles, and Carmen McRae did not subscribe. At the same time, in an ingenious rhetorical maneuver, by invoking Rowles (with whom she studied and had a close, personal relationship) and McRae (a singer to whom she is often compared), she asserts her own jazz pedigree. This invocation of her personal connections to major historical figures be regarded as another instance of the interplay of patina and fashion, wherein Krall's musical and social connections to jazz history constitute patina, while the technical wizardry required to improvise through "Giant Steps" can be seen (in her view, at least) as mere fleeting fashion.

Sherrie Tucker has written about the "problem" of improvisation for women jazz musicians:

> For jazzwomen, to improvise has often meant to trouble gender (con-sciously or not, intentionally or not, willingly or not). Women who see themselves as challenging musical structures are sometimes heard primar-ily as challenging people's expectations for what women sound like, what women do, what jazz musicians look like, what is the gender of jazz.
>
> (Tucker 2004: 250)

In Krall's case, however, her decision not to improvise presents the same set of challenges. If Krall does not improvise, can she be considered a jazz singer? If she can be considered a jazz singer in spite of her refusal to scat, what is it that qualifies her as such?

Integral to Krall's challenge is the fact of personal choice. In interviews, Krall regularly asserts her personal agency in making the decision to improvise on the piano but not with her voice: "But I choose not to scat sing. I choose to focus on the lyric" (Enstice and Stockhouse 2004: 186). Indeed, Krall takes sole responsibility—and asserts personal agency—for nearly every formative decision in her career. She rejects the Billie Holiday trope, the passive victim of coercion by a corporate promotional machine seeking to profit from her image. While she does welcome advice from those close to her (including her management, S.L. Feldman & Associates), Krall insists that she alone is ultimately in control of both her day-to-day operations, and of the overarching direction of her career: "Yeah, but the core of that machinery is myself. So that's what is the most important thing, that I am in control of my own life. It's not they, them, the machine, marketing, blahblahblah, that is pushing me. It's these people working together" (quoted in Reid 2002: 178).

She has been particularly active in cultivating her own image: For the most part, she personally chooses the photographs that will be used in her album artwork and various magazine spreads. No doubt she had some influence in the way she was represented in the 300M ad as well. The little black dresses and fancy shoes that comprised her 2002 look, then, were not simply the result of industrial image-making: they were also a matter of her personal taste. Steve Denvir experienced her passion for shopping first hand while Krall was in Toronto for the commercial shoot: "When she was here she spent twelve grand at fucking Holt Renfrew, I think. . . . But here's someone who knows clothes, and she has a personal shopper, and a dresser and all this shit, so it's a whole package" (Denvir 2010).

Krall herself hardly shies away from acknowledging her dedication to shopping and fashion. While she suggests that she is very comfortable in a nondescript "raincoat and sneakers," she is equally at home in more luxuriant attire: "You know, I'm starting to think now I love to dress up in great clothes. I love to be a girl" (quoted in Enstice and Stockhouse 2004: 189). Just as Krall chooses to eschew vocal improvising, she chooses to embrace her love of fine clothes and shopping.

Krall also chooses to present herself as a marketable commodity through a growing number of sponsorship arrangements with a variety of corporations; in addition to her relationships with Chrysler and Rolex, corporations such as CIBC (Wakeham 2010), Jaguar, Lexus, and the now defunct Eaton's (Hayes 2002: 48) have either sponsored her international tours, or have used her image in their advertising. While the various corporations generally initiated the relationship with Krall—usually for the same reasons that Chrysler sought to link her with their brand—she too has benefited tremendously from these arrangements in terms of promotion.

Pearl Davies was reluctant to comment about how specifically Krall and her management team had used the Chrysler marketing to their advantage, but she did cautiously acknowledge that Krall had gotten something out of the relationship, suggesting that the Chrysler ads may have helped her move from the relative isolation of the jazz market into the broader (and more lucrative) world of popular music: "I think she was very secure within the world of jazz, and at the time we were with her she was trying to break out of just that jazz crowd and get to more of a mainstream level of followers. I think they were able to break out of that traditional small world of jazz" (Davies 2010). Steve Denvir spoke about the issue more candidly:

> [Krall's] management team really knew how to play it up too. Because we went to talk about a second year, and just as we got into the thing we wanted to do, they [her managers] present them [the Chrysler people] with a gold record. The management team presents our client with a gold record because of their contribution to the sales of that. And it was incredible promotion for her. Fabulous. It's a trade off.
>
> (Denvir 2010)

The music video produced by Krall's record label, Verve (a division of MCA-Universal), for "The Look of Love" is revealing. The video follows two black-clad workers as they plaster billboards with images of Krall (in her omnipresent black dress) on abandoned buildings around an unidentified city. As if by magic, the images of Krall move, singing the song. In the video, then, Krall literally becomes an advertisement—albeit an advertisement for herself and her own album. Significantly, Krall's management was quite dissatisfied with this video. Denvir explains,

> They had been challenged in terms of an attempt to get a video for this track. They were talking about buying our footage. I don't think we got enough to hit a three-and-a-half minute thing. But they had a. . .. They had something that was just terrible. They were trying to fix it, but they never did get a video solution for it. . . . [At least] not a good one.
>
> (Denvir 2010)

No one involved in the Chrysler ad seems to be able to remember exactly why the Chrysler footage was not released for Krall's use, though Denvir suspects that budget limitations may have been to blame: "They try and do things on the cheap a lot, the record companies, if they can" (Denvir 2010). Regardless, it is fascinating to consider that Krall and her management sought to replace a music video that presented her as a billboard advertisement with a revised music video that had originated as a television advertisement.

Evidently, Krall has no qualms about explicit, ambitious commercial self-promotion—a trait she shares with Charles Mingus and numerous other musicians throughout the history of jazz music. In addition to benefiting her own career, however, Krall has also used these sponsorship and advertising arrangements to benefit the charities she supports—activities that recall the charitable initiatives that Charles and (especially) Sue Mingus have pursued through Jazz Workshop Inc. According to David Hayes, Krall donates roughly half of her income from corporate partnerships into charities such as the Leukemia/Bone-Marrow Transplantation Program at Vancouver General Hospital and the Leukemia Research Fund of Canada. Chrysler Canada donated two cars, in addition to making a financial contribution to Krall's charities. Hayes quotes Krall's manager, Steven Macklam: "We won't do a sponsorship only for money. There has to be a large charity component attached to it" (Hayes 2002). Krall thus exerts a considerable degree of control over her finances, as well as how she is represented in the media, both sonically and visually.

This reframes the sexual subtext of the 300M ad to some extent. If Krall actively controls (or at least strongly influences and directs) the way she is represented, it seems very likely that she and her managers would have had to approve of the spot. In this way, the sexualization of Krall's image is not simply a voyeuristic objectification that victimizes the singer; on the contrary, it seems to have been entirely consensual, part and parcel of a promotional enterprise, overseen by Krall herself, wherein she openly used her sex appeal (albeit in a conservative fashion) to advance her career.

Of course, like her choice to reject vocal improvisation, Krall's choice to use her sex appeal to her advantage once again puts her at odds with jazz convention, and puts her at risk of reifying herself as the kind of "girl singer" stereotype Sherrie Tucker describes. Given the sexual tension between Krall and the 300M cardriver that is the focus of the Chrysler narrative, Donna Haraway's metaphor of the feminist cyborg (first postulated in her 1985 essay, "A Cyborg Manifesto: Science, Technology and Socialist-Feminism in the Late Twentieth Century") offers a useful lens through which to consider Krall's conundrum. Haraway explains,

> From one perspective, a cyborg world is about the final imposition of a grid of control on the planet, about the final abstraction embodied in a Star War apocalypse waged in the name of defense, about the final appropriation of women's bodies in a masculinist orgy of war. From another perspective, a cyborg world might be about lived social and bodily realities in which people are not afraid of their joint kinship with animals and machines, not afraid of permanently partial identities and contradictory standpoints. The political struggle is to see from both perspectives at once because each reveals both dominations and possibilities unimaginable from the other vantage point. Single vision produces worse illusions than double vision or many-headed monsters. Cyborg unities are monstrous and illegitimate; in our present political circumstances, we could hardly hope for more potent myths for resistance and recoupling.
>
> (Haraway 2004: 13)

For Haraway, the cyborg itself—or, by extension, the possibility of a human-cyborg sexual coupling—is ambivalent. On the one hand, it represents the domination of feminine-coded flesh by masculine-coded technology. On the other hand, Haraway suggests that since the blending of flesh and metal once seemed the far-fetched purview of science fiction, the collapse of the human/machine binary demands that we reconsider other seemingly far-fetched couplings. In light of the emergent possibility of the cyborg, we must scrutinize all accepted, "common sense" binaries (Barthes 1957). For Krall, the matter is comparatively simple: Throughout her career at large, and in the 300M ad in particular, she demands that we question whether it is possible to be simultaneously regarded as elegant, sexual, feminine, and a jazz musician.

Conclusion

In this chapter, I have examined the relationship between cars and jazz through the 20th and 21st centuries. Although this might seem to be an unusual pairing, I suggest that the two elements have been inextricably linked in journalism, literature, and advertising since the early 1920s. My examination consisted primarily of a close consideration of sponsored television programming and advertising by automakers that have used jazz. Obviously, this history is selective, focusing on a necessarily limited number of case studies; nevertheless, it draws out some key themes in terms of the changing alignment between jazz and the automobile. It is worth summarizing them here.

In the first place, jazz seems always to have assumed the ancillary role in the relationship. As Steve Denvir puts it, "[I]f you're talking about jazz and advertising, nobody cares about jazz in advertising. I'm sure there are some people out there who are real fans, and, you know, who are going to do whatever. But jazz is a signifier. It says sophistication, it says stylish, and it's a real short hand" (Denvir 2010). Denvir's argument is particularly relevant to advertisements or programs that focus on celebrities who sing jazz. As we have seen with Dinah Shore and Diana Krall, advertisers are primarily concerned with the qualities of the "star"; on the surface, jazz matters insofar as it is one of those qualities. By contrast, when those qualities aren't crystallized in the persona of an individual, or at least to some tangible connection to jazz history (as has consistently been the case with the Honda Jazz marketing campaigns in Europe), they risk becoming diffuse and the identity connection between jazz and the commodity can become tenuous at best, confusing and contradictory at worst.

But of course, a singer or musician is inseparable from the cultural meaning that attends to her or his genre; hence, ancillary or not, the signification of jazz is still extremely relevant. In this chapter, we have seen how that signification has changed as social norms and mores have evolved over the course of the past century. Whereas F. Scott Fitzgerald could use jazz to signify speed, freedom, and danger, for Steve Denvir, Mike Smith, Rob Quartly, and Pearl Davies, jazz signifies a unique combination of cool elegance, refinement, sophistication, exclusivity, and mystery or elusiveness. In the 1920s, the link between jazz and the automobile made sense because both were suggestive of a way of life that had accelerated so much that it was virtually out of control; in the 2000s, jazz can align comfortably with the car because both represent elegant, sophisticated, refined, and above all expensive personal taste and style. No longer only hot and lusty, jazz can now also be cool, detached, and rich. Evidently, over the course of 80 years, the sound of jazz music changed, and its context and cultural position changed along with it.

At the same time, some of the tropes of meaning attached to jazz have been remarkably durable—particularly jazz's relationship to sex. For Fitzgerald, the moralizing Chicago journalists, and the Chrysler advertisers, if the automobile serves as a means of transporting oneself from pleasure to pleasure, jazz serves as a sonic (or visual) evocation of pleasure—be it wildly hedonistic, transformatively liberating, or coolly seductive. Despite the 80 years intervening years and concomitant musical and cultural changes, jazz evoked sexuality as potently in 2002 as it did in 1922.

If jazz means sex, however, it must also stand as a node where sexuality, race, and gender converge. It thus offers a unique lens through which to access the vexed interrelationship between these elements. In the context of car advertising, jazz allows us to see how and why different individuals and groups are included within and excluded from car culture—a key element of citizenship, capitalism, and the cultures and communities of consumption.

Notes

1. *See* Mimi Sheller and John Urry (2000), "The City and the Car," *International Journal of Urban and Regional Research* 24: 737–57.
2. Writing in 1835, 28 years before the 1863 Emancipation Proclamation, de Tocqueville treats slavery as a troubling aberration from the genuine American dedication to universal human equality, rather than a fundamental paradox.
3. Interestingly, Montgomery too disguised his own ethnic heritage to advance his career. Born George Montgomery Letz to Ukranian immigrants in Brady, Montana, the actor dropped the surname Letz when he signed with production house 20th Century Fox in 1940, using his decidedly British middle name as his surname instead. Hence, Dinah Shore and George Montgomery, all-American couple, were both in fact of Eastern European descent.
4. By way of comparison, it is worth noting that while Shore's producers did occasionally include performers of other non-white ethnicities, they were commonly relegated to occasional special ethnic episodes. Valentine's Day, 1960 featured an all-Italian cast, while nearly all of the performers on Christmas Day of the same year were Japanese, including Yukiji Asaoka, the Yamakawa Sisters, Kabuki Dancers, Komo Zura, Tony Toyoda, Mitsumi Maki, Tony Charmoli and the Three Ohmori Brothers ("The Dinah Shore Chevy Show," tv.com).

Bibliography

"1960 Plymouth Valiant Commercials x6," *YouTube* (Accessed November 5, 2008) http://www.youtube.com/watch?v=hodncVpNVjk&feature=related.

Aldridge, Henry B. "The Dinah Shore Show [Various]," *Museum of Broadcast Communications* (Accessed December 27, 2010) http://www.museum.tv/eotvsection.php?entrycode=dinahshores.

"The Appeal of Primitive Jazz," *The Literary Digest* 55 (August 25, 1917): 28–29.

Barthes, Roland. *Mythologies*. Paris: Editions du Seuil, 1957.

Blanke, David. *Hell on Wheels: The Promise and Peril of America's Car Culture*. Lawrence, KS: University Press of Kansas, 2007.

Bratten, Lola Clare. "Nothing Could be Finah: *The Dinah Shore Chevy Show*," *Small Screens, Big Ideas: Television in the 1950s*, Ed. Janet Thurmim. New York, NY: IB Tauris, 2002. 88–104.

Cassiday, Bruce. *Dinah! A Biography*. Toronto: Franklin Watts, 1979.

Cato, Jeremy. "When it comes to car buying, we are not like Americans at all," *The Globe and Mail*. 20 February 2014 (Accessed March 1, 2014) http://www.theglobeandmail.com/globe-drive/news/canada-versus-the-united-states-a-tale-of-two-car-markets/article16976409/.

Cawthra, Benjamin. *Blue Notes in Black and White: Photography and Jazz*. Chicago, IL: University of Chicago Press, 2011.

Cross, Mary. *A Century of American Icons: 100 Products and Slogans from the 20th-Century Consumer Culture*. Westport, CN: Greenwood Press, 2002.

Curcio, Vincent. *Chrysler: The Life and Times of an Automotive Genius*. New York: Oxford University Press, 2000.

Daly, K. "Quotable Quotes," *Dinah Shore Fan club* (Accessed December 27, 2010) http://www.dinahshorefanclub.com/dsquote.htm.

Daniels, Douglas Henry. *Lester Leaps In: The Life and Times of Lester "Pres" Young*. Boston: Beacon Press, 2002.

Davies, Pearl. Interview with the author (October 7, 2010).

de Crèvecoeur, J. Hector St. John. *Letters from an American Farmer*, ed. W. P. Trent and Ludwig Lewisohn. New York, NY: Duffield, 1904.

Denvir, Steve. Interview with the author (June 7, 2010).

"The Dinah Shore Chevy Show," tv.com (Accessed December 23, 2010) http://www.tv.com/the-dinah-shore-chevy-show/show/8238/episode.html.

Dinerstein, Joel. *Swinging the Machine: Modernity, Technology, and African American Culture between the World Wars*. Boston: University of Massachusetts Press, 2003.

Enstice, Wayne and Janis Stockhouse. *Jazzwomen: Conversations with Twenty-One Musicians*. Indianapolis, IN: Indiana University Press, 2004.

Field, Patrick. "No Particular Place to Go," *Autopia: Cars and Culture*. London: Reaktion Books, 2002. 59–62.

Fitzgerald, F. Scott. *The Great Gatsby*. Toronto: Scribner, 2004.

Fleury, David. Interview with the author (May 14, 2010).

———. Personal communication with the author (January 5, 2011).

Flink, James. *The Automobile Age*. Cambridge, Mass: MIT Press, 1990.

Gilroy, Paul. "Driving While Black," *Car Cultures*. Ed. Daniel Miller. New York: Berg, 2001. 81–104.

———. *Darker than Blue: On the Moral Economies of Black Atlantic Culture*. Cambridge, MA: Harvard University Press, 2010.

Haraway, Donna. "A Manifesto for Cyborgs: Science, Technology, and Socialist Feminism in the 1980s," *The Donna Haraway Reader* ed. Donna Haraway. New York: Routledge, 2004.

Hayes, David. "The Boys in the brand: When Diana Krall is on state, nobody sees Sam Feldman and Steve Macklam. But when it comes to selling the acclaimed jazz artist, they're the two guys who really make the operation sing," *National Post*. Don Mills, ON: March 1, 2002. 46.

"Honda Jazz—Naming: A Presentation to Honda (EU) Product Planning," *Honda EU* (March 9, 2001).

"Honda Jazz," *The Student Room*. 26 September 2012 (Accessed February 15, 2014) http://www.thestudentroom.co.uk/showthread.php?t=2133658.

hooks, bell. *Wounds of Passion: A Writing Life*. New York, NY: MacMillan, 1997.

John F. Devine Papers. 1956 and Undated. Box 4–1956, Folder "Expenditure Recommendations for 1956–1957." John W. Hartman Center for Sales, Advertising, and Marketing History, Duke University.

Kerouac, Jack. *On the Road*. New York, NY: Penguin Books, 1976.

Levine, Lawrence. *The Opening of the American Mind: Canons, Culture, and History*. Boston: Beacon Press, 1996.

Lipsitz, George. *The Possessive Investment in Whiteness: How White People Profit From Identity Politics*. Philadelphia: Temple University Press, 1998.

Lynd, Robert Staughton and Helen Lynd. *Middletown: A Study in American Culture*. New York: Harcourt, Brace, 1929.

Macleod, Duncan. "Honda Jazz Cars Ever So Nice," *The Inspiration Room*. 22 April 2006 (Accessed January 11, 2014). http://theinspirationroom.com/daily/2006/honda-jazz/.

Margaret Fishback Papers. Box OV12, Folder, "De Soto". John W. Hartman Center for Sales, Advertising, and Marketing History, Duke University.

McCarthy, Tom. *Auto Mania: Cars, Consumers and the Environment*. New Haven, CN: Yale University Press, 2007.

McCracken, Grant. *Culture and Consumption: New Approaches to the Symbolic Character of Consumer Goods and Activities*. Indianapolis, IN: Indiana University Press, 1988.

———. "When Cars Could Fly: Raymond Loewy, John Kenneth Galbraith, and the 1954 Buick," *Culture and Consumption II: Markets, Meaning, and Brand Management*, ed. Grant McCracken. Indianapolis, IN: Indiana University Press, 2005.

McGee, Kristin A. *Some Liked It Hot: Jazz Women in Film and Television, 1928–1959*. Middletown, CT: Wesleyan University Press, 2009.

McKay, George. *Circular Breathing: The Cultural Politics of Jazz in Britain*. Durham, NC: Duke University Press, 2005.

Monson, Ingrid. "The Problem with White Hipness: Race, Gender, and Cultural Conceptions in Jazz Historical Discourse," *JAMS* 48 (Autumn, 1995): 396–422.

Packer, Jeremy. *Mobility without Mayhem: Safety, Cars, and Citizenship*. Durham, NC: Duke University Press, 2008.

Quartly, Rob. Interview with the author (September 2, 2010).

Reid, Jamie. *Diana Krall: The Language of Love*. Markham, ON: Quarry Music Books, 2002.

Rose, Dan. *Black American Street Life: South Philadelphia, 1969–1971*. Philadelphia: University of Pennsylvania Press, 1987.

Sandke, Randall. *Where the Dark and the Light Folks Meet: Race and the Mythology, Politics, and Business of Jazz*. Plymouth, UK: Scarecrow Press, 2010.

Saxton, Kate. Interview with the Author (February 3, 2014).

Sheller, Mimi and John Urry. "The City and the Car," *International Journal of Urban and Regional Research* 24 (December 2000): 737–57.

Smith, Mike. Interview with the author (July 19, 2010).

Stevenson, Heon. *American Automobile Advertising, 1930–1980: An Illustrated History*. Jefferson, NC: McFarland & Company, Inc. Publishers, 2008.

"Students in Arms Against Jazz," *The Literary Digest*, March 18 1922. *Jazz in Print (1856–1929): An Anthology of Selected Early Readings in Jazz History*, ed. Karl Koenig. Hillsdale, NY: Pendragon Press, 2002. 170–71.

Sudhalter, Richard. *White Musicians and their Contributions to Jazz, 1915–1945*. New York, NY: Oxford University Press, 1999.

Thornley, Scott. Interview with the author (November 16, 2010).

de Tocqueville, Alexis. *Democracy in America*, trans. Henry Reeve (Accessed February 19, 2014) http://xroads.virginia.edu/~HYPER/DETOC/.

Tucker, Sherrie. *Swing Shift: "All Girl" Bands of the 1940s*. Durham, NC: Duke University Press, 2000.

———. "Bordering on Community: Improvising Women Improvising Women-in-Jazz," *The Other Side of Nowhere*, eds. Ajay Heble and Daniel Fischlin. Middletown, CT: Wesleyan University Press, 2004.

Wakeham, Hugh. Interview with the author (October 27, 2010).

Widner, E.L. "Crossroads: The Automobile, Rock and Roll and Democracy," *Autopia: Cars and Culture*. London: Reaktion Books, 2002. 65–74.

4

THE NEW SOUND OF COLA

In July 2006, the Pepsi Corporation launched a new cola-based beverage, Pepsi Jazz. With the tagline, "Jazz, the new sound of cola," this diet soft drink was available in three unique flavors: Caramel Cream, Strawberries and Cream, and Black Cherry French Vanilla. The 60-second commercial,[1] "Sounds of the City," opens with a shot of a streetscape. There is no specific indication of the exact location; with the narrow roadway, heavy traffic (both vehicular and pedestrian), cacophony of honking horns, and green street signs, the scene strongly recalls the East Village in Manhattan, but it really could be in any big city in the United States. Barely a second into the film, a graphic fades in, superimposed over the street scene: "Diet Pepsi presents."[2] A moment later, a second graphic replaces the first: "*Diet Pepsi Jazz*." Behind the "Jazz" logo, a single figure slowly comes into focus amid the hubbub of the busy street. As she moves closer to the front of the scene, the clicking of her high heels comes to the fore, above the noise of the traffic.

Then the scene changes. Suddenly, the logo has disappeared and we are looking at the woman's shoes—white pumps. Her footsteps now dominate the soundscape. The scene shifts abruptly again to a close shot of the woman's hands holding a bottle of "Jazz." She opens the bottle, but instead of the telltale carbonated hiss as she loosens the cap, we hear a sizzling hi-hat cymbal. The camera moves up to reveal a light-skinned woman, likely in her mid-late 20s with a shock of dark, curly hair. As she brings the bottle to her lips, the click of her high heels on the pavement transforms into the click of a drumstick on the side of a snare. She takes the bottle away from her mouth and grins slightly, looking down at it. The city sounds fade, replaced by a typical swing rhythm on a hi-hat cymbal—*ching ch ch ching ch ch ching*.

Suddenly, the picture lurches again to a cab that has braked suddenly to avoid running into the woman. The cabbie honks his horn and gestures at the woman, laughing. To the woman's ears, however, the honk is transformed into a jazz horn section. As she continues to walk down the street, the scene cuts frenetically from one image to another. A dog barks at a mewling cat—only the dog's bark is a trumpet playing a minor triad, and the cat's retort is a quick descending blues scale on a piano. The camera shifts back to the woman for a fraction of a second, and we see her looking amusedly at the squabbling animals.

Then another quick cut, this time to a wailing baby in the arms of a weary-looking mother. The baby's cries, too, are transformed into a bluesy, moaning alto saxophone. We jump back to a shot of the woman—now focused on her calves and pumps as she walks on. The scene shifts again to a jackhammer, only instead of the relentless pounding of the machine pulverizing asphalt, we hear a snare drum roll. The angle changes, revealing the road worker who is operating the jackhammer as he yells instructions at one of the other workers. Instead of shouting, however, we hear him scatting another blues scale melody: "Scoo bad a m-bay ba doo m-ba dap beep bap. Squee be m-doo be do bow . . . bom." As the worker continues to shout/scat, the camera cuts back to the woman, smiling and staring at him. When he notices her watching him, his melody loses its momentum (m. 4 of the excerpt). With a backward glance and a coquettish flip of her hair, the woman continues on her way, while the road worker gives her a long look.

The scene shifts back to the woman again. She looks cool, confident, and content in her "jazz world" as she takes another sip of the drink. Now some nondiegetic sounds have begun to enter the soundscape and the groove begins to cohere. A double bass enters (with no visible source) and the drumbeat solidifies into a medium-tempo backbeat. She is unfazed by an old woman in a blue frock sitting at the side of the road who shouts at her—possibly because, to her ears, the shout sounds like a deep-voiced man scatting. She watches a traffic cop gesturing frantically and blowing his whistle, but hears a flute playing another blues scale lick. She notices a cyclist honking her horn at a car, but hears a saxophone.

A waiter on a nearby patio drops a tray, but instead of smashing glass and porcelain, she hears a drum fill with a cymbal crash. A businessman steps out of a cab onto the sidewalk in front of her. He shouts angrily into his cell phone and viciously slams the cab door, but she only hears a scat vocal—the same melody that the road worker had sung earlier. Nondiegetic horns enter playing a B♭ blues-scale melody (F-A♭-B♭-D♭-B♭) and the woman takes another sip from the bottle before exiting the scene into a café. A voice-over enters: "Indulge your senses with Jazz: zero calorie colas in Strawberries and Cream and Black Cherry French Vanilla." The "Jazz" graphic from the opening of the spot returns, this time with the product tagline, "the new sound of cola." As she exits, the horns and bass fade, leaving only drumstick clicks.

But now a new character enters the scene: a Euro-American man wearing a checked shirt and a bowler hat steps out of the café holding a bottle of "Jazz." The camera zooms close on his face as he takes a pull from the bottle. As he drinks, the stick clicks change into a new drum groove—a more intense house pattern on a tight snare. When the groove begins, the scene cuts to a close-up of his red Oxford shoes, which gradually start to tap along with the new beat once the liquid has made its way from his lips past his hips to his feet. The camera stays close to his shoes as he begins his own walk through the cityscape. Through Pepsi's remarkable elixir, taste and hearing are drawn into a synaesthetic sensory nexus, the core of which is jazz—not merely jazz the music, but rather some ineffable, evanescent conceptual complex that envelops all the senses and makes everything groovy.

This chapter ventures into a different kind of "Pepsi Jazz" nexus, exploring how the relationship between the brand, the campaign, jazz music, and jazz discourses come together to create meaning—for the product, for consumers, and for jazz music. In the first part of this chapter, I give a detailed overview of the development of the Pepsi Jazz brand and the cinema/television ad. This overview is based chiefly on my interviews with individuals involved with various aspects of the campaign: Diet Pepsi brand manager Lauren Scott; OMD (the media agency) Communications Director Gail Stein; DDB (the advertising agency, Doyle Dane Bernbach) producer Elizabeth Hodge, creative director Kathryn Harvey, and copywriter Howard Finkelstein; and Expansion Team (the music house) founder and director Alex Moulton and composer Genji Siraisi.[3]

The next two parts of the chapter focus on key tropes of meaning at play in the 60-second Pepsi Jazz spot. First, I address the issue of diversity. I suggest that the spectacularization of ethnic and cultural diversity in the Pepsi Jazz spot reflects PepsiCo's overarching corporate emphasis on diversity in their marketing and advertising, while at the same time playing with discourses of jazz as a collaborative, syncretic, and democratic music. I draw on Albert Murray's influential collection of essays, "The Omni-Americans: Some Alternatives to the Folklore of White Supremacy," proposing that Pepsi positions "Jazz" as an Omni-American soft drink.

The fourth part of the chapter addresses the significance of individual agency in the advertisement. I use Michel de Certeau's essay, "Walking in the City," and Michael Bull's study, *Sound Moves: iPod Culture and Urban Experience*, to examine how the advertisement's narrative and soundtrack work together to construct the heroine's individual agency in the ad, and to explore how her agency becomes crucial to the demographic targeting of the "Pepsi Jazz" campaign.

In the concluding part of the chapter, I problematize the use of "indulgence" as a marketing theme, and argue that the undoubtedly well intentioned intersection of indulgence, agency, and diversity in the Jazz ad is predicated upon the deeply vexed discursive confluence of jazz, race, sex, and social deviance.

Developing the New Sound of Cola

The summer is a crucial time for the soft drink industry. As the mercury rises, soft drink sales increase dramatically across North America. The largest soft drink producers—Coca-Cola and Pepsi—often try to make a particular splash

FIGURE 4.1   Cola Wars (Nenov Brothers Images/Shutterstock.com)

in the market during this vital period by releasing what are commonly called "flanker products." Flankers are ancillary brands with new flavor profiles that are launched to create buzz among consumers, with the hope that the new products will draw consumer attention to the parent brand (Harvey 2010). If a flanker is an overwhelming success, it might make its way into the parent brand's core stable of products; if not (as is more often the case) it will most likely be phased out at the end of the season.

This method of launching new beverages emerged partly in the wake of Coca-Cola's disastrous release of the reformulated "New Coke" in 1985. That year, in an attempt to compete with Pepsi (which had recently eclipsed Coke in terms of market share), Coca-Cola discontinued its iconic original formula, replacing it with a new brand and a new, sweeter recipe. After three months of enraged phone calls and letters from their rapidly eroding consumer base, Coca-Cola switched back to its original formula.[4] Since that time, flankers are gently introduced into the marketplace, and consumers are allowed to decide for themselves whether the product should survive (Stein 2010).

Pepsi Jazz was a 2006 flanker (Stein 2010), following in the illustrious footsteps of Pepsi Free, Crystal Pepsi, and Pepsi Vanilla. Conceived early in 2006, it was launched in July, and discontinued by early-mid 2007. The people at the media and advertising agencies who were involved with developing the Jazz campaign do not remember the product particularly fondly. Gail Stein affirmed, "Sales were not good." While she could not recall exactly what the problem was, she did suggest several possible reasons for the product's failure:

> [T]he R&D behind it may have been too expensive to make for the amount of cans that they were selling. It could have been that the stores didn't feel it would turn quickly enough and wanted our other Pepsi products. It could have been that consumers just don't like it—I don't recall.
>
> (Stein 2010)

Stein's final point jibes with the anecdotal recollections of the other advertisers, whose descriptions of the product ranged from the diplomatic "It was a little sweet for me" to the blunt "[S]ometimes a product speaks for itself. I tried it. I went out and bought it when it came out. I was definitely not planning on buying it again. No matter how many . . . ads you put out, you can't put lipstick on a pig, right?"[5]

Nevertheless, the product was intended to fulfill a marketing role, and indeed, from Lauren Scott's perspective, Jazz was a success. As the Diet Pepsi brand manager at the time of the launch, Scott insists that the product was quite well received by the public, but was eclipsed by the 2007 season's flanker, Pepsi Max:

> Well, I think a lot of times "products succeeding" is a relative term. From a consumer standpoint it actually did fairly well, and even from our bottlers, they were fairly pleased with the performance. But at Pepsi, we're very bad at sticking with things, and so it becomes the flavor du jour. So it actually was doing very well, and I think it had found its niche. The following year we actually launched the caramel flavor, but then it came, "well we need to launch something else," and then "where are we going to take it from," and so that's when you start to pick at some of your own products.
>
> (Scott 2010)

In Scott's view, the termination of the product had more to do with Pepsi's corporate practices than with Jazz's marketplace reception. Regardless of consumer's feelings about Jazz's unusual flavor profile or of Pepsi's occasional fickle approach to marketing, the beverage did typify a successful flanker: it ably performed its marketing duties, creating consumer buzz during the all-important summer season in 2006.

Of course, Pepsi Jazz was not solely a marketing ploy; it was intended to meet a perceived consumer need as well. Gail Stein summarizes:

> [T]he target was women . . . between the ages of 25 and 54—because that's the age when women drink diet drinks; when they're younger, they're

drinking sugar drinks. . . . We also knew that, just from the psychographic profile, that we wanted to reach women that are kind of busy throughout the day and are looking for a pick-me-up at some point during the day that's sinless. So, here was a diet soda that tasted like a dessert, and we said, "you know what, we think . . ." and again, through a lot of the research that we did—"we think that the target audience are these really busy, multi-tasking women that would love to know that there's this little treat that they can have at 3 o'clock in the afternoon.

(Stein 2010)

The dessert-themed flavors of the drink (Strawberries & Cream, Black Cherry French Vanilla, and later Caramel Cream) were central to the demographic and psychographic targeting. Stein suggests that the most frequent target for consumer complaints about diet soft drinks is the after taste. With the richer, sweeter Jazz flavors, Stein explains, "we were trying to provide an alternative to that beverage to those that feel there's an after taste, or, they don't quite like the taste" (Stein 2010). At the same time, the idea of offering busy women a sweet, "sinless" indulgence in the middle of the afternoon was central to Jazz brand positioning. Creative director Kathryn Harvey told me,

You know, they might have a Diet Pepsi every day, but you might want to, in addition to having a Diet Pepsi at 3 o'clock when you maybe have a little bit of doldrums, or when you get home from work at the end of the day and you still have to cook dinner for your kids, or, you know, have other activities, you might want to have a little bit of a pick-me-up, and you might want to have something with a lot more flavor than you might normally do.

(Harvey 2010)

This focus on mid-afternoon indulgence was evident in the early efforts to come up with a name for the new product. Before settling on Jazz, the Diet Pepsi branding team worked with a specialized naming agency to come up with a number of possibilities. Along with Jazz, the early favorites were "Splurge" and "Indulge." Lauren Scott remembers, "So obviously, Splurge, Indulge are definitely more transparent on what the product is, versus Jazz, which is a little bit more or a concept and a feeling. It definitely is a unique name for a product, it's not as transparent" (Scott 2010).

Scott could not recall who exactly proposed the "Jazz" brand name, but the element of ambiguity was certainly a point of appeal to the focus groups during the testing process. Several of the members of the advertising team admitted to being initially confused by the name, but suggested that its meaning became clearer as they thought about it more carefully. Genji Siraisi, the composer who scored the commercial, had a similar reaction: "I thought it was interesting. It's like any time you hear about a brand that isn't out yet, especially from a company that big, it seemed odd. Like, 'Really? They're going to do that?'" (Siraisi 2010). Copywriter Howard Finkelstein recalls,

> When they said it was called "Jazz" at first, I was like "Okay." I didn't really get it. You know, I said, "Oh. Maybe they just thought of a word that sounds good." And then as we worked on the creative development of different ideas, I just started kind of reading up on jazz. I was like, "Oh this name actually kind of works for this."
>
> (Finkelstein 2010)

It is worth noting that the Jazz campaign was not the first time that Pepsi had used jazz music in a campaign. Like virtually every other American corporation of its vintage, Pepsi has run numerous television and radio ads featuring jazz-based jingles. In 1940, Pepsi introduced "Pepsi Cola Hits the Spot," a swing-inflected jingle based on the English folk song "Do Ye Ken John Peel" (*The Pepsi Generations*) that would eventually become one of the most successful promotions in radio history. According to former Pepsi president, Roger Enrico, while the jingle began its life in 15-second spots on four radio stations, it quickly became so popular that radio stations began playing it in their regular rotations, largely in response to listener requests. By the time Pepsi switched to a new jingle—"Be Sociable"—for its first television campaign in 1953, the corporation had pressed 1500 copies of the record for distribution to jukeboxes, and sold 100,000 copies of the sheet music for a nickel per copy, the same price as a bottle of Pepsi (Enrico and Kornbluth 1986: 18). Neither "Be Sociable" nor its 1963 successor, the syntactically awkward "Now It's Pepsi—For Those Who Think Young"—based on the 1920s jazz standard "Makin' Whoopee" by Eddie Cantor—repeated the success of "Pepsi Cola Hits the Spot" in terms of radio play or sheet music sales (although "Now It's Pepsi" inaugurated the highly successful "think young" brand positioning that has dominated Pepsi marketing up to the present day). Nevertheless, both of these jingles were designed with the same intent: like De Soto's use of "It's Delightful" (discussed in Chapter 1), both sought to capitalize on the popular appeal of the jazz style at the time, and (in the case of "Pepsi Cola" and "Now It's Pepsi") on audience familiarity with an existing folk or popular melody.

As one might expect based on the copycat intensity of their rivalry, Coca-Cola had begun its own foray into jazz marketing two years earlier. In 2004, the New York cultural institution the Lincoln Center opened Frederick P. Rose Hall, a multistage concert facility to house the activities of the organization's newly established jazz wing, Jazz at Lincoln Center (J@LC), under the overall direction of trumpeter Wynton Marsalis. Housed at the Time Warner Center at Broadway and 60th overlooking Central Park, Frederick P. Rose Hall includes three venues:

the 1200-seat Rose Theater concert hall, the 450-seat Allen Room studio theater, and Dizzy's Club Coca-Cola, a jazz club and restaurant ("Hall Rentals"). Dizzy's itself is overseen by Todd Barkan, the former manager of the iconic (now-defunct) San Francisco jazz club, Keystone Korner. According to Barkan, Coca-Cola came on board with a "very substantial financial donation" several years prior to the opening of the club in exchange for naming rights. Like J@LC's other sponsors—including men's clothier Brooks Brothers, financial institution HSBC, and MasterCard, among others—Coca-Cola was attracted to the optimism and positive energy that surrounded J@LC in its earliest days (Barkan 2010). With its transformative mission to "entertain, enrich and expand a global community for Jazz through performance, education and advocacy" ("About"), and with its highly visible African American artistic and managing director, Wynton Marsalis, J@LC has maintained a very positive image amongst the general public (if not always amongst jazz musicians, critics, and scholars) that reflects well on its sponsors and other partners.

As part of the sponsorship arrangement, Coca-Cola also lends some "promotional consideration"—along with its brand name—to an annual fall festival hosted at Dizzy's (Barkan 2010). From 2005–2009, this took the form of the Diet Coke Women in Jazz Festival, a month-long concert series at the J@LC venue featuring all women performers. In 2010, the women's festival was supplanted by the somewhat more amorphous "Coca-Cola Generations in Jazz Festival" that alternates between young, emerging artists and older, established musicians (most of whom are men). The change in brand association with the festivals is worth remarking: once again, a diet beverage is linked to femininity, while the parent, nondiet brand is somewhat more flexible in its identity. Of course, as Sherrie Tucker has argued, so-called "women in jazz" festivals and events functionally exclude women from the mainstream of masculinized jazz history and discourse by isolating them and treating them as a kind of novelty (Tucker 2004). By linking a "light" soft drink to women jazz musicians while reserving the more iconic brand name for their male counterparts, Coca-Cola still further disdains and isolates an already marginalized group within jazz history. Doubtless, Coca-Cola's sponsorship intentions were purely market driven (a point I explore further in Chapter 5), and the slight against women musicians was entirely unintended. Clearly Coca-Cola's marketers assumed that a festival of female jazz musicians was likely to attract a predominantly female audience, and it therefore made sense to name the festival after the Coca-Cola product that is chiefly marketed to women. Nonetheless, this snapshot of the Coca-Cola sponsorship with J@LC reveals how deeply etched this gendered binarization of jazz truly is, and how readily (if not purposefully) advertisers and marketers recognize and exploit it, even if they are not likely conscious of the historiographical stakes. As Tracy McMullen writes of the festival, "Could there be a more masterful way to 'allow' women onto the jazz stage while simultaneously writing them off of it, or a better way to patently signify 'women-in-jazz' as the continued margin of jazz? J@LC certainly masters the antinomy, declaring women 'in jazz' while simultaneously writing that women border/lack/want jazz" (McMullen 2010: 144).

Pepsi's Lauren Scott insisted that, despite the rivalry, PepsiCo's jazz branding was entirely unrelated to Coca-Cola's. The truth of her claim is borne out by the fact that the Pepsi Jazz brand was entirely different from Coca-Cola's sponsorship activities with J@LC, and indeed, from PepsiCo's own jazzy jingles of the 1950s and 1960s. As we have seen, virtually all jingles written in the mid-20th century used some jazz elements—a swing rhythm, a backup jazz band, a Modernaires-style vocal ensemble. This was largely because jazz was perceived to be a safe, broadly appealing, and uncontroversial (if slightly dated) popular music form, as distinct from rock and roll, country and western, or rhythm and blues. Moreover, Pepsi's reasons for commissioning jingles in a jazz style were identical to the jingle-writing strategy of nearly every other corporation and ad agency. There was nothing unique about Pepsi's use of jazz music in the 1950s and 1960s, so it is clear that the company's use of jazz at that time was not evidence of any special or exceptional interest in the music.

Coca-Cola's J@LC sponsorship in the early 2000s was also very different from the logic behind the Pepsi Jazz brand. This may seem surprising, given the chronological proximity between the establishment of Coca-Cola's J@LC relationship and the launch of Pepsi Jazz, and given that Pepsi and Coke—the two dominant players in the soft drinks industry—are in perpetual competition with one another. Lauren Scott's claim is affirmed by the character of the Pepsi Jazz campaign, which, despite the shared musical theme, was entirely different in terms of its *use* of the music. Jazz music was largely a secondary concern for Coca-Cola: that company was primarily seeking to capitalize on the positive public profile of Wynton Marsalis and J@LC, which meant sponsoring the events that flowed from J@LC's artistic vision—events that happened to feature jazz. Pepsi, on the other hand, was interested in the cultural position of jazz itself, and cultivating a fit between a sweet, diet soft drink and the popular image of jazz.

This is evident in the use of the phrase "jazz moment" in the marketing of the product. While the phrase does not appear in the advertisement, per se, OMD's marketing recap on the campaign[6] suggests that the goal of each ad—and by extension, the goal of the beverage—is to "deliver 'lively and engaging' Jazz moments" (Jazz from Diet Pepsi—Multisensory Challenge). I asked Stein to explain what was special about a "Jazz moment":

> I know you're looking at it from the jazz perspective, but that was not the driving force here. . . . [And] that wasn't a musical jazz moment. That was the sinless, kind of cool thing in the middle of the afternoon. And we called it that because that just felt like a synergistic way of describing what

the product was trying to do. But again, yeah, music was part of it, but I just don't want to mislead you, it wasn't the driving force behind any of it.

(Stein 2010)

When I asked Stein to talk about how jazz functioned as a connotative cultural idea (as opposed to a musical idiom) in the concept of a "Jazz moment," her response was more affirmative:

> So then, when you say it that way, you know, when you think of the word, "jazz," too many, the connotation is music and New Orleans and American-developed music, but a lot of times, jazz could also mean, "Wow, what a jazzy thing to do, what a cool thing to do." So I think that was the whole implication there. You know, "It's a special moment. Jazz up your life. Drink Diet Pepsi Jazz, and, you know, it's a sinless delight." You know, that's kind of where we were going with that.
>
> (Stein 2010)[7]

Stein's suggestion that jazz is "special" and "cool" is somewhat vague; other advertisers, however, were more precise about what exactly jazz was intended to signify. According to Kathryn Harvey, one of the key factors for Pepsi in the name selection was jazz's ability to confer an air of elitism and sophistication on the product (in spite of its $2 per bottle price). Harvey explains,

> [A]s I remember, the reason why we chose that name is that it had a little bit of a whimsy, there was like, relative to a mass product (which of course, any Pepsi product is essentially a mass product), it had an element of sophistication to it, and it certainly connotes. . . . Jazz is not for everybody, but it's for the enthusiasts and those that kind of appreciate it. It's a fairly sophisticated kind of music genre, and it also speaks to a certain level of complexity, which had to do with the flavor of the product had different notes and more complexity to it than a typical diet soda or something more straightforward like "cherry" or a straight-up flavor profile.
>
> (Harvey 2010)

Harvey was not entirely comfortable with my suggestion that Pepsi Jazz was meant to stand as "the wine of diet colas," but acknowledged that the observation was not without merit: "Yeah, you got it. Well, probably not. . . . That's probably a little overstated, but yeah" (Harvey 2010).

Other elements of the campaign worked to enhance the sense of sophistication and elitism—or "specialness," to use Stein's word—that attended to the brand. It is standard practice in the food and beverage industry to send out complimentary packages to celebrities and other "influencers" (including, for instance, fashion designers and wealthy, trendy young people); the Pepsi Jazz package, however, was meant to be a cut above. In addition to two cans of the soft drink, each package also included two baccarat highball glasses, two silver Tiffany & Co. bar spoons, one bottle of vanilla-flavored Stolichnaya vodka, one bottle of Chambord, and a Pepsi Jazz cocktail recipe book ("Jazz signature cocktails" included "Bada Bing Cherry," "Cat's Meow," "Berry Jam Session," and "Billie Holiday"). The package itself was a burgundy box with the Jazz logo inscribed in gold leaf on the top, tied with a gold satin bow. The interior of the box was burgundy velvet (Scott 2006). Diet Pepsi also planned a series of promotional events for their "influencers" called "Jazz Hour at the W," hosted by Starwood's "W" luxury hotels in New York, San Francisco, Los Angeles, Chicago, Dallas, and New Orleans (Scott 2006). Obviously, this level of luxury did not necessarily trickle down to the everyday consumer in a tangible way; still, the product packaging was meant to infer a similar sense of opulence. Initially, Scott says, the company discussed the possibility of using glass bottles for the product—a striking way to separate Jazz from its competitors on the shelf. When glass proved too expensive for mass production,[8] Scott and her colleagues settled on a metallic gold wrapper that they felt was similarly striking, but considerably more cost-effective (Scott 2010).

In short, then, the Jazz brand name signifies the same kind of sophistication, elitism, and luxury that "Splurge" would have connoted, but in a far more subtle way. On the surface, there is very little that is ostensibly sophisticated, elite, or luxurious about a $2 diet soft drink. It is important to consider, however, that the soft drink itself was not meant to be perceived as luxurious (although, as Harvey pointed out, the idea of luxury is supposed to reflect the richness and "complexity" of the Jazz flavors). Instead, it is meant to underline the richness of the "jazz moment." While the beverage alone is not necessarily luxurious, its rich flavor and its rich connotative associations transform the moment in time in which it is consumed. When the busy, 25–54-year-old woman takes a moment for herself at 3 o'clock in the afternoon (preferably every day) to drink a Jazz, she is transforming that moment from something mundane into something sophisticated, luxurious, "special," and "indulgent"—a "jazz moment."

According to Scott, a jazz moment is also innovative, flexible, creative; like the 1960s Pepsi jingle, it is "for those who think young."

> But I think if we're trying to develop the reason why a word like jazz works is because . . . there's something grounded in it being very different, being innovative. To a certain extent being laid back but still being energized. A playfulness, something that's fun. So I think that that's why that name worked for the concept of this product.
>
> (Scott 2010)

Just as the consumers interpellated by the Jazz psychographic are understood to be "different, innovative, energetic, playful, and fun," so too is the beverage. Both

Jazz and its consumers are pathbreakers, but they do not take themselves too seriously. In this respect, Jazz reflects the overarching brand positioning of the Pepsi parent brand. Since the 1960s, Pepsi marketing has been addressed to the "Pepsi Generation." Like many other seminal moments in Pepsi's marketing history, the company's focus on youth emerged largely in response to Coca-Cola. In his (perhaps prematurely sanguine) 1986 book, *The Other Guy Blinked: How Pepsi Won the Cola Wars*, former Pepsi president Roger Enrico describes the rationale for the Pepsi targeting of American youth—or, more accurately—of youthful Americans:

> For twenty years . . . we've positioned Pepsi as the 'leading edge' soft drink and called our consumers the 'Pepsi Generation'. And, for twenty years, we've used this Pepsi Generation campaign to reach out not just to the young but to all people who look *forward*, who are curious about the *next* thing, who want *more* out of life. We like that message because we're forward-looking people ourselves, and, of course, because the leading edge is a very good place to be. If we're new and bold and challenging and a lot of fun, what's left for the other guy? The past. Nostalgia. Rock-ribbed American values. Small towns, parades, picnics. All good stuff—we use some of it ourselves—but deadly in the soft drink business if that's your dominant image. So if we maintain our leading-edge imagery, Coke gets boxed in. That's not awful for the short term—there are still lots of people in Coke's America. But their numbers aren't growing.
>
> (Enrico and Kornbluth 1986: 16)

Since the end of Enrico's tenure, of course, Coca-Cola has regained its dominant market share. Nonetheless, Pepsi's psychographic targeting has continued to focus "people who look forward, who are curious about the next thing, who want more out of life." Hence, while a "jazz moment" is something special—luxuriant and sophisticated—it is simultaneously something fun and novel. As Scott observed, it is "laid back but still being energized" (Scott 2010).

Both of these elements—sophistication and youthful vitality—were key factors in DDB's development of the 60-second spot. The female lead—the light-skinned woman—serves as an anchor for both ideas, acting as a kind of demographic and psychographic archetype. While the decision to make the lead actor a woman seems to have come from the DDB creative team (copywriter Howard Finkelstein and art director Bonnie Lutz), her character was fleshed out considerably by the film direction team hired by DDB to execute the spot, a Swedish film-making collective (now based in Venice, CA) called Traktor. Indeed, she is one of the principal subjects of the first brief that Traktor wrote for the ad—the document that the collective submitted in its initial application for the contract:

> She could be in her late 20's early 30's, probably on her way to work, or lunch, with someone. She should not be a vacuous model, but someone

with character and a likeable vibe, a warm character that we believe in and will remember.

She is girlfriend material, if you could keep up with the fun stuff she does rather early on Sundays!

She's not the kind that just hangs around town, her steps have a purpose and she discovers things on the fly.

(Traktor 2006)

Naturally, the actress who was cast for the role—Leah Elias—effectively fits this character description. Like Traktor's character and Pepsi's demographic/psychographic target, she is a woman, clearly on the lower end of the 25–54 age bracket. She is stylish and sophisticated in her white pumps and floral sundress, but her easy smile tells us that she knows how to enjoy herself—how to "get more out of life." Her quick, purposeful walk seems to imply that she is a busy woman with places to go; and yet, the bright sunshine, the busy traffic, and the ongoing roadwork collectively suggest that it could be mid-afternoon. Evidently, she has a few minutes to herself in the middle of a busy day, and she is determined to turn them into a "jazz moment." With her youth, her style, and her vitality, it is clear that she is not just any diet soda drinker; she is a quintessential Pepsi generation diet soda drinker.

It is also significant that her "jazz moment"—or rather, the series of little jazz vignettes that unfold over the course of the ad—is humorous. Humor had been a key aspect of the Jazz brand positioning: Expansion Team director Alex Moulton remembers, "I think 'quirky' came up in the conversation a lot. 'Light', 'fun', 'playful', 'quirky', those were words that got thrown around a lot. And they never wanted it to be like hard-edged or too cool or too dirty or too, you know" (Moulton 2010). Hence, it was only appropriate that the advertisement be funny. Indeed, Howard Finkelstein remembers working on—but eventually rejecting—different ideas for the campaign that had a more serious tone: "[O]riginally a lot of our ideas were traditional jazz. John Coltrane. Kind of looking at the history of jazz" (Finkelstein 2010). These ideas were rejected in part because they did not convey the playful mood attached to the product. By the same token, part of the impetus for hiring Traktor to direct the spot was its reputed quirky sense of humor (Moulton 2010). True to form, in its ad brief it stressed that the tone of the ad must be unexpected and "cheeky": "As we mentioned, it could also be cool to thwart expectations when the viewer thinks they have our scheme figured out . . . and [leave] the viewer with a smile. Easy does it. Cheeky wins it!" (Traktor 2006). Traktor put this particular idea into practice in the character of the old woman: according to Elizabeth Hodge, both the character of the old woman and surprising sound of her unexpectedly rich baritone voice were proposed by the directors (Hodge 2010). Importantly, while being a "cheeky" moment, the juxtaposition of the young, light-skinned woman with the old woman also draws further attention to Pepsi's youthful brand positioning.

Of course, it is the soundtrack to the ad that really carries the comedic content, and at the same time does the work of holding the narrative together. Because the soundtrack was so crucial, DDB used an unorthodox approach when it came time to hire a composer. Usually, an advertising agency will hire a film director and shoot a rough cut of the spot first, and then send that to the composer or music house to serve as a reference for the soundtrack. As composer Genji Siraisi told me, "The picture is almost always first" (Siraisi 2010). In this case, however, the relationship between the ad agency and the music house was much more collaborative. Early on, DDB and Traktor agreed to forgo making a rough cut, instead simply sending a script to the handful of music houses that were solicited to apply for the job. As a result, the soundtrack submissions varied considerably. According to several of the individuals involved in the project, Siraisi's track was the clear favorite chiefly because it effectively captured the spot's humorous tone, and successfully knitted all of the narrative elements together. Finkelstein said of Siraisi's track, "We definitely wanted something simple. Each scene when a new instrument started making a sound, we wanted it to be crystal clear to the viewer that the sound was kind of representing what was on screen. So I think some of the tracks we heard, they were too busy, too much going on" (Finkelstein 2010). Elizabeth Hodge echoes,

> [W]e liked the general vibe of it. We just thought it was fun and just kind of boppy, and kept you going, and it also seemed like it really was structured in a way that best utilized the particular moments of the different instruments that we wanted to bring in for the car horn and the dog and the construction worker or whatever. It just, you know, it flowed the best, it was fun to listen to, and it just incorporated the kind of conceit of the commercial—you know, the individual kind of call-out bits—best.
>
> (Hodge 2010)

Once it had settled on Siraisi's submission, Traktor proposed another unusual move. With a version of the soundtrack in hand, and drawing on its own considerable experience directing music videos,[9] Traktor elected to shoot the spot like it would a music video: it played the recording on set, and attempted to synchronize the action to the soundtrack, rather than the other way around. While this would ultimately result in a number of problems both on set and in the subsequent editing process,[10] it did mean that Siraisi's soundtrack was an integral part of the process of executing the spot, rather than an element that is added on at the end once all of the visual content is complete, as is standard practice in the industry. Finkelstein remembers being excited by this collaborative approach:

> They sort of built on each other. . . . You know, we kind of had things planned out, like a construction worker with a piledriver on the pavement

being quick drum hits. So we had like general stuff, and it was really col-
laborating with the music company as well. And then once we shot it and
we had sort of a rough track, just editing it together to make it work. It
went back and forth a lot of times. We would make some progress on the
visual part, and then we would send it to the music company and they
would kind of re-record a song to that. Things would change and slide. . . .
It was interesting. It was definitely a very collaborative commercial.

(Finkelstein 2010)

Nevertheless, in spite of—or perhaps because of—this collaborative approach,
if it is considered apart from the film, the soundtrack makes very little musical
sense. Indeed, the other soundtracks submitted by Siraisi's colleagues at expansion
team—DJ Mocean Worker and Tim Kvasnosky—are more coherent as stand-
alone pieces of music. Whereas Siraisi's soundtrack sounds like a haphazard series
of apparently unrelated sonic events with little clear sense of harmony or melodic
continuity, the submissions by Mocean Worker and Kvasnosky both maintain
solid grooves, and evince a stronger sense of motivic development and musical
structure. Placed in the context of the visual, however, these strengths become
weaknesses. Mocean Worker's and Kvasnosky's comparatively seamless incorporation of the ad's visual narrative elements into their respective soundtracks
disguises those elements, making them less surprising and striking, and thereby
making the entire narrative of the spot more tenuous. Siraisi's seemingly disjointed soundtrack, by contrast, conveys the narrative with crystal clarity. In
this way, the soundtrack and the visual are integrally related, lending each other
coherence, structure, and meaning. Without this close bond, the spot would
lose both its sense of cohesion and its sense of humor. On the other hand, this
also means that, in spite of the supposedly collaborative approach, the music is
necessarily ancillary to the visuals. To reiterate Siraisi's observation, "the picture
almost always comes first" (Siraisi 2010).

Still, despite its lack of specifically musical cohesion, Siraisi's track does a
remarkable job of gesturing towards the jazz idiom, even while sounding very
little like any conventional idea of a jazz tune. Recall Nicholas Cook's description
of advertising composition as "stripped down," first mentioned in Chapter 1:
"the music embodies the features necessary for the recognition of genre, but
otherwise has little or no distinctive musical content" (Cook 1994: 36). Cook's
definition jibes with Siraisi's explanation of his own compositional approach to
the soundtrack:

[T]he swing element is a clear indicator culturally of some kind of jazz. . . .
And then the upright bass was another thing that gave it . . . the walking
bass line was sort of like a clear "this is jazz" indicator. And then having
the other instruments in there even though they weren't necessarily playing. . . . I mean, I tried to make the licks feel kind of jazzy, but of course

they're very short; it's not like there's any kind of real melody until you get to the scat line. All of them are like "ba dap." "Bay da be da dap." In like no more than three or four notes. And they're all disjointed by many beats, so it's kind of hard to establish any kind of real melody or chord change, per se. I mean, there was the chord change based on the walking bass line—somebody gave an outline—but with those [melody] lines being sort of out of the blue, it made it a little difficult musically to give it too much form.

(Siraisi 2010)

In a sense, Siraisi's soundtrack to the Jazz spot references jazz music, but is not a coherent, complete jazz piece; rather, it is a mix of elements that signal jazz. Improvisation, for instance, is evidently one key signifier of the jazz genre, practice in jazz music. While the scat singing and instrumental obbligatos *suggest* solo improvisation, the process through which they were created was anything but improvisatory. Siraisi performed and recorded all of the parts himself, using a combination of live instruments, synthesizers, and recorded samples, a process that is wholly dissimilar from his work as a jazz drummer with acid jazz/fusion groups such as Groove Collective, for instance (Siraisi 2010). Therefore, while the Pepsi Jazz ad signifies the codes and values of the jazz genre, the practices that went into its creation suggest that the soundtrack references jazz music without necessarily qualifying as such. As Siraisi explains, "[It's] pretty rare that people actually ask for jazz. And you know, usually when they're asking for jazz, they of course don't really want, you know, what jazz lovers might consider jazz, but so be it" (Siraisi 2010).

This mode of implicating jazz music without specifically *being* jazz music (at least in a traditional sense of the genre) is crucial to another aspect of the Pepsi marketing scheme—"thinking young." I asked Alex Moulton why he thought Pepsi had eschewed a more traditional sound in the spot:

I think it was a trend thing. I think they wanted to find a way to take it and make it cool; make it current. Yeah. I can't remember. There may have been some discussion about that early on, about whether they wanted a traditional jazz piece. . . . [But] I think they decided early on that they wanted to have a remixed feel.

(Moulton 2010)

Elizabeth Hodge confirms Moulton's assessment: "[W]e were hoping for [a] sort of traditional jazz sound, but remixed in this kind of contemporary format" (Hodge 2010).[11] In other words, Pepsi and DDB wanted exactly what Honda wanted for its Jazz ads: a soundtrack that would signify jazz—and by extension, all of jazz's desirable connotations—without sounding traditional or old. "New" and "now" were key, and the "remixed feel" became a way of signifying on tradition while still "thinking young." Even though jazz's raw musical materials may be as old as America itself, through the DJ's musical alchemy, those materials can be innovated and updated to become vital and relevant in the present day.

In sum, Pepsi's attraction to the Jazz brand lay primarily in its ability to signify sophistication, elitism, and prestige, while simultaneously remaining innovative, youthful, and fun. Hence, Pepsi designed the concept, script, and soundtrack for the Jazz ad to amplify those concepts that spoke to the Pepsi generation demographic. At the same time, Pepsi glosses the characteristics of the genre that are less appropriate for the brand, especially its long history.

"Coming Together": Diversity and the Omni-American Cola

While sophistication, youthfulness, and innovation were the chief reasons for jazz's utility as a brand fit, I would argue that there were two other important aspects that were not mentioned explicitly in our conversations, but are nevertheless integral to the Pepsi Jazz brand: diversity and individual/consumer agency. I address the first of these aspects in this section.

According to several advertising and marketing texts, the representation of diversity has increasingly become a hallmark of advertising in the 21st century. Writing in *Diversity in Advertising: Broadening the Scope of Research Directions*, advertising scholars Wei-Na Lee, Jerome D. Williams, and Carrie La Ferle outline the rationale for this recent industry paradigm shift:

> The successful advertiser of the 21st century must understand the importance of diversity in American society. Within the United States, advertisers need to recognize the distribution of consumers across a number of characteristics, including gender, age, ethnicity, sexual orientations, and so on, if they hope to build relationships and maintain market share in today's every-growing diverse society. Diversity of people, products, and images is crucial in the 21st century for an advertiser's bottom line; it also helps to contribute to a more representative and inclusive society.
>
> (Lee *et al.* 2004: 4)

The rationale for representing diversity in advertising is twofold, and can be parsed in terms of economics and social ethics. In the first place, the dramatic growth of annual spending among immigrant and minority consumers has been a major impetus for the shift in advertising focus. According to 2002 statistics from the Selig Center for Economic Growth at the University of Georgia, African Americans rated the top minority consumers, spending roughly $646 billion that year, followed by Hispanic Americans at $581 billion and Asian Americans at $262 billion. Most impressively, these numbers have increased by over 100 percent between 1990 and 2002 (Lee *et al.* 2004: 5). In order for advertisers to access minority capital, they must be willing to interpellate minority consumers in a variety of ways, including visually representing minorities in their advertisements.

On the other hand (as many advertisers argue), representing diversity on television and in print allows advertisers to use the machinery of capitalism and consumption to help create a more just and equitable society. Lee, Williams, and La Ferle, for instance, propose that the representation of diversity in mass media—especially a ubiquitous form of mass media like advertising—can help to normalize diversity as a social principle by "rendering [previously marginalized groups] identifiable and intelligible in the mass media," thereby "bringing [such groups] into public being" (Lee *et al.* 2004: 14). In other words, advertisers who embrace diversity are not only selling commodities to so-called minority groups; they are selling the principle of diversity to America.

African American activists in the United States have long recognized the imbrication of capitalism and American citizenship, and the potential power of economic affluence and self-determination to overcome social inequity. As we saw in Chapter 2, the Black Capitalist ventures that emerged within months of the signing of the Emancipation Proclamation marked capital accumulation and industrial investment as key elements of the African American civil rights movement right from its earliest days. It was not until the height of the civil rights movement in the early 1960s, however, that the vision of Black Capitalists like Frederick Douglass and Booker T. Washington began to bear fruit.

Significantly, one of the first major national corporations to begin making inroads into the African American market was Pepsi. The cola company's initial motivation for this marketing recalibration was likely principally financial. In large part because of its extremely economical price point (both Pepsi and Coke cost a nickel, but Pepsi's 12-ounce bottles were twice the size of Coke's), Pepsi had become the beverage of choice for the vast majority of African Americans across the U.S. by 1950 (Gibson 1969: 240). Through the 1950s, however, Pepsi's sales in African American communities lagged. In 1961, the company commissioned statisticians Elmo Roper and Associates to find out why. According to Manning Marable, Roper and his group came back with some startling findings regarding African American soft drink consumption:

1. Blacks comprised only 11 percent of the U.S. population, but made up 17 percent of the soft-drink market. Blacks purchased 300 million cases of soft drinks annually. White per capita consumption of soft drinks was 120 bottles, vs. 163 bottles for Blacks.
2. Blacks were far more "flavor-conscious" than whites. Forty-nine percent of all grape soda and over 33 percent of all orange soda in the U.S. was bought by Blacks.
3. Between 1951 and 1961, Blacks' consumption of Pepsi had remained constant, while Pepsi consumption among whites had increased 300 percent. "This lack of sales growth among Blacks meant a loss of 60 million cases per year to Pepsi-Cola." (Marable 2000: 159)

In the aftermath of the Roper report, Pepsi came to recognize that African Americans represented an essential but neglected demographic for soft drink marketing, and the company moved quickly to address this revelation. Almost immediately, Pepsi appointed Harvey C. Russell to the position of Vice President of Special Markets, making him the highest-ranking African American executive in any international business (Gibson 1969: 239). The following year, Pepsi became one of the first major corporations to feature African American models in a series of print ads—run in the African American periodical *Ebony* and in African American-owned newspapers across the country (Marable 2000: 159). In 1963, Pepsi began to produce a series of audio documentaries—released on LP record—called *Adventures in Negro History*. These documentaries were overseen by notable African American intellectuals Dr. Broadus Butler, Professor of Social Studies in Wayne State University, and Dr. John Hope Franklin, Senior Professor of History in the University of Chicago (Gibson 1969: 231). Additionally, Pepsi started to sponsor African American-oriented community organizations and events, including the National Medical Association (a group whose membership included more than 5000 African American physicians) and the International Golf Tournament, one of the few golf events to welcome African American participants. According to D. Parkes Gibson, Pepsi's sponsorship helped the tournament grow into "one of the top social and sports events in the Negro national community" (Gibson 1969: 245).

In the present day, multicultural marketing has continued to be a Pepsi corporate priority. Indeed, Lauren Scott—an African American woman, and the brand manager in the Innovation department at Diet Pepsi during the Jazz campaign—currently serves as a senior brand manager in the Multicultural Department in Diet Pepsi marketing. She explains the role of her department as follows:

> [F]or the different brand teams, we figure out what are the media components that they should be doing to advertise to African American consumers, and we also do some ground-up programming, specifically to those target consumers. So if you think about the brand team usually markets to a subset of the general market—we're targeting African American and Hispanic consumers with specific programming.
>
> (Scott 2010)

Pepsi continues to develop specialized, differentiated marketing programs to target the tastes and consumption patterns of consumers in different ethnic markets—African American and Hispanic consumers (the largest nonEuropean ethnic groups in the United States) in particular.

Grassroots involvement in community initiatives remains a central plank of Pepsi's multicultural advertising. According to Scott, for instance, the multicultural department will run specialized programmes during Black History Month and Hispanic Heritage Month. She also mentioned the *Yo Sumo* programme—a project of the Hispanic division within multicultural department. Literally meaning "I Count,"[12] the project was inspired by the 2010 American census. Its stated goal is to encourage Latinos and Latinas to go beyond simply "being counted," and instead to make themselves "count" by sharing their stories on a now defunct Pepsi-run website, www.pepsiyosumo.com. Ultimately, those stories were woven into a documentary about Hispanic cultural and social contributions to America called *Latinos Living the American Dream*, directed by Latina actress Eva Longoria-Parker (*Pepsi Yo Sumo*). Throughout the last 50 years, Pepsi marketing has worked to make itself synonymous with cultural pride, racial uplift, and social justice by celebrating—and wherever possible, sponsoring—cultural and ethnic diversity in the United States.

While this was not one of the stated goals of the Jazz campaign, the 60-second spot certainly reflects Pepsi's overarching marketing prioritization of diversity. As Kathryn Harvey pointed out (echoing the 1961 findings of the Roper report), it was expected that an "intense-flavored" drink like Jazz would "probably have a high skew toward African Americans . . . and Latinos" (Harvey 2010). This was reflected in OMD's media purchasing decisions: a print ad was run in the African American women's fashion magazine, *Essence* (Scott 2006), and Gail Stein was fairly certain that the 30-second television spot would have been in rotation on the BET (Black Entertainment Television) network (Stein 2010).[13]

The emphasis on diversity is most apparent, however, in the casting for the cinema/television ad. In my discussion with Elizabeth Hodge, whose role as producer included overseeing the casting process, I asked whether there had been an ethnic skew in the casting call for particular roles. I was particularly interested to know whether DDB had actively sought to cast an African American man in the role of the police officer, because it had struck me as significant that an African American man would have been cast as one of the only clear figures of authority in the spot:

> We weren't [specifically casting for a black police officer], but we did specifically cast a mixed cast. You know, and that's something that's true of Pepsi on every product. We always go in and try to reflect diversity in the cast, and in this case we were fortunate enough that we had a big cast, and so that's a pleasure on any number of levels. But we were able to really just get a lot of different looks in there. But yeah, that's something that Pepsi always strives for, was getting diversity in the cast of whatever commercial it might be. . . . So it was less "we want a black cop" than "we want diversity in the spot, and do it however you want," you know. It could just as easily have been a white cop and a black businessman; it just didn't . . . you know, it just didn't happen to be that way.
>
> (Hodge 2010)

Even in advertising like the Pepsi Jazz spot where there is no stated "ethnic skew" for the product or the campaign, diversity remains a corporate priority.

The case of Leah Elias—the female lead—is of particular interest, primarily because I have been unable to identify her ethnicity. Before I learned the actress's name, I had assumed that she was African American. When I learned the actress's name several months into my research, I assumed that she must be Latina. I maintained that assumption until I began to undertake interviews to prepare for this chapter. My very first interviewee—Gail Stein—could not recall the actress's name, but was reasonably certain that she was African American. Lauren Scott, my second interviewee, told me that she was of mixed race: "She definitely was African American, but she had some other stuff in her too. But the fact that she was multiethnic was a plus." Elizabeth Hodge, a later interview, did not recall Elias's ethnicity specifically, remembering only that "she looked great," and that—as had been the case with the police officer role—her ethnicity had not been a factor in the casting decision.

From the perspective of the producers and consumers of the ad alike, Elias's ethnicity remains essentially a blank slate. With no clear-cut ethnic signifiers for them to interpret, viewers can project nearly any ethnicity onto Elias. Since virtually anyone can identify with her, conversely, she is able to interpellate consumers from a far wider array of market segments than would be possible if she were patently Hispanic, African American, or Euro-American. In this way, Elias's own ethnicity is, paradoxically, extraordinarily diverse. In this respect, she is analogous to the city in which the spot is set. Just as Elias could belong to and could interpellate individuals from any number of ethnic categories, so too could the city—New York, but not quite; San Francisco, but not quite; Chicago, but not quite—pass for any number of cities. Both Elias's ethnicity and the city's identity are floating signifiers, inviting the viewer, in a sense, recursively to interpellate herself or himself through the act of projecting her or his own personal and civic identity onto the actress and the setting.

Elias's ethnic ambiguity was, to some extent, the result of casting happenstance. Elizabeth Hodge insists that her teased and curly hair—one of the only physical features that code her as African American—was simply the style she was wearing at the time. In later photographs of the actress posted on the website of Model Team, a Hamburg-based modeling agency that seems to represent Elias in Europe, her hair is shoulder-length and wavy ("Leah Elias"). The geographic ambiguity of the city, however, was fully intentional. In actuality, the city set was located on a back lot at the Warner Bros. Studio in Los Angeles. According to Hodge, the set had been specifically built to look "New York but not quite:"

> LH: [T]he back lot at one of the studios in LA [is] like New York town. They have these kind of different back lot settings, and this is one that we use a lot.

ML: Oh, OK, so it was specifically meant to look like New York, like it was a studio set meant to look like New York.

LH: It was, yeah. I mean, the studio made it look like New York. I think we just wanted it to feel like a city; we didn't want it to be recognizably New York, but we just wanted it to feel like a city neighborhood where plausibly a taxi would be and a traffic cop would be, and people would be sitting out on the stoop, and . . . I think we always were thinking it was kind of maybe East Village vibe, you know.

(Hodge 2010)

Howard Finkelstein remembers helping to make specific decisions to disguise the set's New York look. For instance, the advertisers chose to eschew the typical New York City yellow taxis in the shoot in favor of yellow and blue cabs. His explanation echoes Hodge's comments: "Again, just to make it feel like it could be happening anywhere. We're not talking to east coast, big city people; we're talking to everybody" (Finkelstein 2010). By casting the ethnically ambiguous Elias, and by designing a city with no fixed locus, diversity became central to the Pepsi Jazz campaign. If a floating ethnic or civic signifier can represent anyone or anywhere, in a sense, it is representing everyone and everywhere, all at the same time.

Jazz music itself, of course, also serves as a signifier of diversity in the campaign. For Howard Finkelstein, one of the key components of the jazz brand fit was what he perceived to be the essential heterogeneity of jazz performance practice: "It's kind of different styles coming together in an unexpected way, or it could be different every time, or it's sort of loose and not kind of something you've seen before, and different notes playing together. You know, by the end, I was like "Jazz is a pretty cool name" (Finkelstein 2010). This notion was Finkelstein's first real "eureka moment" in his work on the campaign. To him, the idea of different elements "coming together in an unexpected way" became the linchpin of his understanding of the brand fit. As a result, "coming together" served as the foundation for several of the early concepts that he and Bonnie Lutz devised for the campaign:

You know, we had things that were more like just playing off what jazz is. You know, like the separate pieces playing off each other—interacting and each with their own distinct style and kind of trying to compare the flavors doing the same thing. I think we had an idea where we kind of personified the berries and the different ingredients that sort of would come together.

(Finkelstein 2010)

Finkelstein and Lutz's idea gains further traction when we consider it in the context of the history and discourses of the music. First of all, jazz's profoundly syncretic origins have been widely documented. Drawing influence from West African music, Creole contradanse, European classical music, military marches, Mexican brass band music, and numerous other sources, jazz's genesis reflects Finkelstein's phrase, "different styles coming together in an unexpected way." Second—and likely more relevant to Finkelstein's conception of the jazz brand fit—jazz performance practice has often been discursively positioned as being homologous to American democracy. This discourse can perhaps best be summarized by New Jersey congressman Frank Thompson Jr.'s program notes to the 1956 Newport Jazz Festival:[14]

> The way jazz works is exactly the way a democracy works. In democracy, we have complete freedom within a previously and mutually agreed upon framework of laws; in jazz, there is complete freedom within a previously and mutually agreed upon framework of tempo, key, and harmonic progression.
>
> (Quoted in Saul 2001: 392)

In Thompson's view jazz performance practice is an artistic realization of the ideals of American democracy. Much like in the American Republic, jazz musicians must come together to interact within a "previously and mutually agreed upon framework of laws," overcoming their differences—be they cultural, ethnic, or ideological—in order to work collectively to produce a successful performance. This metaphor was also central to the 1987 Congressional Resolution—tabled by Michigan Rep. John Conyers Jr.—that identified jazz as a "rare and valuable national American treasure." According to Conyers's resolution,

> [Jazz] makes evident to the world an outstanding artistic model of individual expression and democratic cooperation within the creative process, thus fulfilling ideals and aspirations of our republic. . . . [It] is a unifying force, bridging cultural, religious, ethnic, and age differences in our diverse society.
>
> (Conyers 1999: 333)

Like Thompson, Conyers links jazz to the democratic principle of individual freedom within a collective framework. Furthermore, he couches the idea of individual freedom in the discourse of multiculturalism, suggesting that the collective jazz framework invites participation from individuals across "diverse" "cultural, religious, [and] ethnic" backgrounds, thereby mirroring official American diversity.

At the same time, it is crucial to remember that jazz is an essentially African American cultural practice that has become an integral part of the American mainstream. As Dr. Billy Taylor has written, "As an important musical language, it has developed steadily from a single expression of the consciousness of *black* people into a *national* music that expresses American ideals and attitudes to Americans and to people from other cultures all around the world" (quoted in Billy Taylor 1999: 329). In other words, jazz is an American music, and its broad appeal has delivered American cultural ideals to musicians and listeners in every corner of the world. The cultural roots of this music, however, are African American.

Albert Murray was one of a number of cultural critics who have used this understanding of jazz history and practice as a metaphor to posit a radically integrationist vision of American civilization in which African American culture is not only a component, but a fundamental foundational constituent. In his essay, "The Omni-Americans," Murray argues, "American culture, even in its most rigidly segregated precincts, is patently and irrevocably composite. It is, regardless of all the hysterical protestations of those who would have it otherwise, incontestably mulatto" (Murray 1970: 22).[15]

Murray's idea of an Omni-American with a mulatto heart comes into play in a subtle but important way in the Pepsi Jazz. In fact, Finkelstein expressed some disappointment that his notion of jazz as being about people and sounds "coming together" was not more central in the narrative of the advertisement. Without this narrative element, he suggests that the ad (which he otherwise felt was very successful) failed to some extent to articulate the brand fit: "I don't think the viewer got why the drink was called jazz. It's kind of like not an obvious connection" (Finkelstein 2010).

Notwithstanding Finkelstein's disappointment, however, I would argue that the idea of "coming together" is the implicit crux of the ad's message, manifest mostly obviously in the soundtrack. In essence, the ad's sonic story follows previously disjunct musical elements coming together to develop into a coherent jazz tune. This is evident in the early draft of the script, written by Finkelstein and Lutz, that Siraisi and the other Expansion Team composers used to design their soundtrack submissions:

> She sips her Jazz, and we hear the sound of her steps change to a drum beat. We follow her down the street. She passes a cab. The cabbie is honking, only it sounds like a saxophone. A dog is barking at a cat. The dog sounds like a trumpet. The cat, a piano. She takes another sip. She's clearly into her Jazz. She passes by a woman at a bus stop holding a crying baby. We hear a horn solo. A car door closes. We hear a cymbal crash. A construction worker's jackhammer sounds like a bass. *The sounds have built into a jazz tune.*
> (Finkelstein and Lutz 2006)

Therefore, while the idea of "coming together" is perhaps not as evident in the visual aspect of the Pepsi Jazz ad as it might have been in some of Finkelstein and Lutz's earlier versions, it could hardly be more explicit in the musical narrative.

The voice-over at the end of the spot is of special significance in this regard: while the ad copy simply carries a message about the product—"Indulge your senses with Jazz," the quality of the narrator's voice carries a great deal of semiotic information about jazz music. Howard Finkelstein recalls that the Pepsi marketers were adamant about the vocal quality they were looking for in the voice actor:

> [We listened to CDs of] maybe like 40 different people reading the copy at the end. . . . We liked this guy who sounded a little younger, maybe smoother, kind of cool. And I believe the client told us that they wanted it to be more like a Louis Armstrong, Zatarain's[16] jazz-type voice. . . . And this guy's voice that we liked, it just seemed a lot cooler to us. But yeah, and that was . . . We probably went back and forth a little bit, but eventually we said "Okay. We'll go with you want."
>
> (Finkelstein 2010)

Thus, through all of the multicultural musical collaboration that happens in the commercial narrative, the voice-over—the quintessential "jazz-type voice"— represents a kind of jazz ur-voice. And that voice sounds distinctively African American.

In this way, the Jazz ad mirrors both the democratic and the Omni-American ideals: through the combination of visual, musical, and nonmusical acoustic components, it represents people from many walks of life, many occupations, many cultures, and many ethnicities, each with their own song to sing, coming together to make music and to tell a story.[17] If jazz is an omni-American music, then Pepsi Jazz is the omni-American cola.

"Jazz Up Your Life": Pepsi Jazz and Consumer Agency

In order for the performance to come together in a meaningful way in accordance with the democratic and omni-American discourses, however, each constituent part must stand on its own; each part must remain radically individual, even while it is contributing to the collective. Ralph Ellison eloquently articulated what he saw to be an intrinsic but vital contradiction between individual agency and collective action that lay at the heart of jazz performance practice:

> There is . . . a cruel contradiction implicit in the art form itself. For true jazz is an art of individual assertion within and against the group. Each true jazz moment . . . springs from a contest in which the artist challenges all the rest; each solo flight, or improvisation, represents (like the canvasses of a painter) a definition of his [sic] identity: as individual, as member of the collectivity and as a link in the chain of tradition. Thus because jazz finds its very life in improvisation upon traditional materials, the jazz man must lose his identity even as he finds it.
>
> (Quoted in Gilroy 1993: 79)

Like the citizen of the idealized American democracy, it is the "jazz man's"[18] prerogative—even his obligation—to remain radically individual, even while submitting himself to the vicissitudes of the "previously and mutually agreed upon framework of laws."

That being said, the heroine of the ad is no "jazz man"; indeed, the more closely we look at her character, the more complicated the ad's representation of the discourses of diversity and "coming together" becomes. While it is true that the disparate sounds in the ad are gradually merging to create a coherent piece, it is important to consider that the heroine is not implicated in that interaction. In fact, contrary to the democratic ideal, she is not operating within a "mutually agreed upon framework" at all: instead, through the power of Jazz (the cola, not the music), she is spontaneously *generating* the framework. Her "jazz world" (as Elizabeth Hodge called it) is utterly solipsistic. For the most part, she is the lone subject in her world.

The other characters in the spot remain almost entirely objectified, not even aware that they are participating in the musical framework that the heroine is generating. The old woman in the blue frock has no idea that, when she shouts at the heroine, she is scatting in a silky baritone voice, and is therefore the object of ridicule. When the road worker notices the heroine staring at him, he very likely assumes that her gaze somehow connotes sexual attraction—hence the distracted cadence to his melody. He has no idea that, in actuality, he is the butt of her own private jazz joke. Therefore, while the song that emerges at the end of the ad is the totality of a number of integral, composite parts, the song is ultimately hers alone—although it is the soft drink that allows her to create it.

Michael Bull's comments on 21st-century iPod culture provide a useful lens through which to consider this element of the advertisement. While none of the advertisers with whom I spoke mentioned it in particular, the story of the advertisement seems clearly to draw on the idea of the personal music device. Like the iPod users in Bull's 2007 ethnography, the light-skinned woman in the jazz ad moves through the city in a "pleasurable and privatised sound bubble" (Bull 2007: 5). For Bull, the great appeal of the iPod is its ability to give users a feeling (if an illusory one) of control over their sonic environment. One of his informants, a woman from New York named Janet (who, significantly, matches the Pepsi Jazz demographic), explains her reasons for valuing the iPod in terms that speak to the potency of Pepsi's "jazz moment" notion:

> Well, I think I've come to the conclusion that overall I feel pretty out of control in my life. Stores play music to get me to buy more. Work tells me what to do and when. Traffic decides how quickly I get from here to there. Even being in public places forces me to endure other people and their habits (the guy slurping his soup, the brat crying for a piece of candy). I didn't realize how much I yearn for control and probably peace and quiet. Strange, since I'm blasting music in my ears. I think I'm really

> tired of living on someone else's schedule. The iPod has given me some control back.
>
> (Bull 2007: 8)

Like the "typical" busy woman described by the Pepsi demographic and psychographic profiles, Janet feels out of control. Like the light-skinned woman's Pepsi Jazz, Janet's iPod restores her sense of control, and allows her to take time out for herself, even on a busy street—albeit a feeling and a moment that are mediated by commodities. In both cases, the commodity subsumes the external noise of the soundscape, either blocking it out, or in the Pepsi ad—"reconfiguring . . . the spaces that [she] moves through" (Bull 2007: 4).

The idea of "creating your own song" with Jazz was a central theme of the campaign. We can observe the idea in action again at the end of the ad when the man with the bowler hat enters the scene. Alex Moulton explains, "The guy walks out, and it's the same melodic line, but a different drum beat on it. . . . The intention was where we say, 'Everyone's got their own version of a remix'" (Moulton 2010). Howard Finkelstein remembers developing a concept with Lutz for an interactive website that would have been based on the same premise:

> I know we had an idea for online that people could watch the commercial and then reassign the instruments, so instead of the jackhammer being the drum, the jackhammer could be the bass and the baby could be trumpet and the car horn would be a saxophone. And then kind of hit play and see the commercial play out again, only with your new soundtrack.
>
> (Finkelstein 2010)

This website was never developed for a variety of reasons (although budgetary limitations were likely a deciding factor); nevertheless, the website concept speaks to the importance of the idea of celebrating one's "own version of a remix"—and concomitantly, one's own individual agency within the culture of consumption.

This idea brings us directly to the importance of the consumer's individual agency. In the Pepsi spot, the heroine is depicted as being completely in control of her environment, at least in terms of its soundscape—even if it is only fleeting, only for a moment, and only in her own mind. In this respect, the woman's solipsistic "jazz world" can be considered in terms of what Michel de Certeau calls a tactic:

> [A] tactic is a calculated action determined by the absence of a proper locus. . . . The space of a tactic is the space of the other. Thus it must play on and with a terrain imposed on it and organized by the law of a foreign power. . . . It operates in isolated actions, blow by blow. It takes advantage of 'opportunities' and depends on them, being without any base where it could stockpile its winnings, build up its own position, and plan raids.

> What it wins it cannot keep. This nowhere gives a tactic mobility, to be
> sure, but a mobility that must accept the chance offerings of the moment,
> and seize on the wing the possibilities that offer themselves at any given
> moment.
>
> (de Certeau 1984: 37)

The woman seems to be moving on a set path, possibly from work (if it is in
fact 3pm) to the café—a route that is determined to a considerable extent by the
layout of the city streets and the movements of the vehicular traffic; a terrain
"imposed on [her] and organized by the law of a foreign power." What happens
on her trip, however, could never be mapped. Each *vignette* in the ad can be seen
to represent a spontaneous, improvised choice—a momentary decision to bring
certain people but not others into her "jazz world," and a second instant choice as
to how she will envoice those people once they have entered her world. Indeed,
"improvisation" was a key word mentioned in the Jazz brand positioning—so
important that it figured into a first draft of the product slogan, *"Improvise with
Jazz"* (Scott 2006). By making these improvisatory choices—by performing an
"improvisation of walking privilege" (de Certeau 1984: 98)—she is asserting her
agency, and is making the urban space her own, if only fleetingly. The instant
she disengages from a *vignette*, she releases it from her "jazz world" subjectivity
and it reverts to the way it was before she assimilated it. She cannot keep the
material space that her jazz tactics have won—and the ephemeral nature of these
little victories is the essence of a tactic.

More importantly (both for a Certeauian analysis and for the advertising
pitch), she is claiming ownership of the moment in time in which she makes
her decision; and those "jazz moments" that she has taken for herself are things
that no one can take back from her. Indeed, as de Certeau suggests, "Tactics are
procedures that gain validity in relation to the pertinence they lend to time"
(de Certeau 1984: 38) Through her jazz tactics—her solipsistic reframing of the
urban soundscape within her "jazz world"—the woman transforms mundane
moments into special "lively and engaging jazz moments."

With this in mind, we can see that, along with innovation, youth, vitality, and
sophistication, the "jazz moment" is predicated on a spectacle of agency—on the
control of your individual experience of time. The jazz moment is one that you
claimed back for yourself from the capitalist-regulated work day, or from the trials
of parenthood, or from any of the other host of grown-up challenges and responsibilities that demand and devour *almost* every minute of every day. In Chapter 2
we read Gail Stein's comments about the meaning of the "moment" in advertising,
particularly ads that are directed chiefly at female consumers. Stein's remarks are
worth revisiting here in somewhat more detail:

> [W]e love doing stuff like that. We've done that for many other brands. This
> one was a "jazz moment," another is a "special moment." Another brand that

I worked on, Nivea, which is a skin lotion, we had "happy moments," because when you put on the skin lotion it made you feel happy. We in advertising love to do stuff like that, because we feel like we can. . . . Everybody has, as they go through the day, ups and downs. And if we, as an advertiser, can give a consumer a special moment, we love doing that. And we like to do this often specifically when we're talking to women. We like to say, "Hey, take a moment." Because, you know, women are so busy, because they're moms, and they're going to work, and they're cooks and they're cleaners and so, we know that, like when we do focus groups with women, often what comes out is, "Geez, if I only had a few more moments to myself." So we often like to take that concept of the moment and spice it up a little bit. So if it's a happy moment or a jazz moment or a something else moment, that's something where we really feel like we can talk directly to . . . especially a female consumer and have them understand the message very quickly.

(Stein 2010)

This part of the Pepsi Jazz message becomes particularly clear in the vignette where the heroine encounters the mother with the screaming baby. Safely ensconced in her jazz world, the heroine grins at the scene as she walks past, enjoying the baby's saxophone wails. The contrast between the haggard mother and the heroine could not more stark: whereas the heroine strides confidently, enjoying her private joke, the child's mother stands immobile, looking stern and a bit worn out. Without a Pepsi Jazz, her baby's screams presumably just sound like screams. This is the kind of woman, it seems, who might appear in Stein's focus group complaining about how little time she has to herself. This is a woman in dire need of a "jazz moment" of her own.

The juxtaposition of these two characters presents a woman watching the ad with a choice in terms of identification: which woman is she, the weary mother or the liberated jazz woman? Which woman would she rather be? If her goal is to become a jazz woman—a woman confident in her ability to assert her individual agency and to take charge of her life and her environment— Pepsi Jazz offers her an easy way to get there. Yet again, we are confronted with the core capitalist paradox. Pepsi Jazz asks us to accept consumption—the engine of 20th and 21st century capitalism—as a balm for the anxieties and traumas of capitalism, particularly the hyperrationalization of time.

Conclusion: Indulge Yourself with Jazz

At the same time it is crucial to remember that, in spite of the celebration of diversity, individual agency, and democratic values, the "jazz world" is a completely constructed space by virtue of the simple fact that it exists in a television commercial. As such, the heroine's improvisatory choices are not improvised at all. When she walks through the city, she is not performing a de Certeauian tactic; she is following the script. Indeed, according to Elizabeth Hodge, Leah Elias was cast for the role because of the 100 to 150 women who auditioned, she was the most capable of simultaneously performing all of the script's demands— walking, drinking, and acting at the same time (Hodge 2010). It is worth noting that during the casting call backs, Elias and the 30 to 40 other finalists for the role were asked to walk on a treadmill for several minutes, drinking the cola and responding to instructions shouted at them by the Traktor direction team (Finkelstein 2010). Certainly, the treadmill was an effective and quite creative approach to casting the role, and the music video approach to shooting the ad was quite innovative for 2006; on the other hand, it reminds us that the representation of the heroine's improvisatory "tactics"—her manifest agency—were crucial to Pepsi's branding strategy for Jazz.

Of course, no one associated with creating the advertisement would pretend that it was anything other than a construction. Advertisements are inherently constructed representations; it would be quite impossible for it to be anything else. In de Certeau's terms, therefore, the heroine's jazz tactic is not a tactic at all, but a *strategic appropriation of a tactic*. De Certeau's concept of strategy essentially represents the opposite of—or, at least, the hegemonic counterpart to—the tactic:

> I call a strategy the calculation (or manipulation) of power relationships that becomes possible as soon as a subject with will and power (a business, an army, a city, a scientific institution) can be isolated. It postulates a place that can be delimited as its own and serve as the base from which relations with an exteriority composed of targets or threats (customers or competitors, enemies, the country surrounding the city, objectives and objects of research, etc.) can be managed.
>
> (de Certeau 1984: 35)

Because PepsiCo is a multinational, multibillion-dollar corporation, it would be anathema for the company to practice any kind of genuine tactic; on the contrary, in a de Certeauian framework, Pepsi is a hegemonic entity that works strategically to design the rigid social map in which individuals must try to "make do." The Jazz ad represents this kind of tactical "making do" (in the form of Elias's character) in order to "manage" the relationship between the Pepsi brand and its consumers. In this way, the concepts depicted in the Pepsi Jazz advertisement are not real agency or real diversity; rather, the ad presents a *spectacle* of agency and diversity intended to interpellate consumers who desire both of those things.[19]

The chief purpose of the strategic appropriation and the concomitant spectacle, however, *is* to suggest that *real* agency and cultural diversity can be achieved (at least in part) by consuming Pepsi Jazz. While this claim seems patently absurd, it raises important questions about the political potential of capital accumulation and patterns of consumption. Just as Volkswagen did by connecting the Jetta with Charles Mingus's music in 1999, and Honda has endeavored to do with the

Jazz hatchback in recent years, in the 2006 ad Pepsi equates Jazz improvisation with consumer choice, and in turn implies that consumer choice is coterminous with the abstract liberal ideal of individual freedom.

A further dilemma presented by the Jazz campaign lies in the issue of sensual indulgence. As we have seen, "indulgence" was a central theme of the Jazz campaign, and an integral part of the invitation to women (and men) to take a "jazz moment." This is most clearly evident to the consumer in the slogan, "Indulge your senses with jazz," but the word was a key plank of the product concept and brand positioning from the outset. The original concept for the brand (as recorded in the Marketing Plan Review) places the idea of decadent sensual indulgence is front and centre: "Jazz is a new line of delicious colas by Diet Pepsi with a smooth, rich, luxurious taste that lets you indulge your taste for the decadent anytime, without worrying about the calories. Jazz ~ Indulge Your Senses" (Scott 2006).

The sensual indulgence theme was critical to other advertising in other media as well. Just as the cinema/television ad creates a synaesthetic nexus, the packages delivered to celebrities and influencers also appealed to multiple senses: The aforementioned soft, velvet lining of the case, the rich flavor of the beverage, and the opulent beauty of the burgundy color palette, silver Tiffany spoons, and gold-leaf inscription, were accompanied by a CD of remixed jazz music and a "scent card." The package thus included something for each of the five senses. Also noteworthy was the print ad that appeared in *People Magazine* on October 16, 2006.[20] This ad forged its place in advertising history by being the first-ever multisensory print advertisement. A four-page spread, the advertisement opened with an image of a hand opening a bottle of the beverage on the recto side of the first page. When the reader turned the page, she was treated to a sensory barrage: a three-dimensional pop-up image of the bottle, surrounded by music notes was accompanied by a 10-second audio clip from the soundtrack to the TV ad, embedded on an audio chip (the same technology that is occasionally used in greeting cards). Page four included a "scented area," a "scratch-n'-sniff" patch that bore the rich aroma of the Black Cherry French Vanilla flavor. Sensual indulgence was therefore not merely a word in the slogan: It was a fundamental idea that impacted every facet of the development of the brand and the advertising campaign.

Implicit in the sensual indulgence theme is an element of sexual fantasy. Significantly, in one of the earlier drafts of the script for the cinema/television spot, the slogan "Indulge your senses with Jazz" is replaced by "Turn your senses on to Jazz" (Finkelstein and Lutz 2006). While the semantic content of the two slogans is very similar, the phrase "turn your senses on" brings the sexual element more clearly to the forefront. The representation of the heroine in the ad is also sexual to some degree. Kathryn Harvey remembers, "And she was lovely, the woman who we cast, and she had a beautiful walk, and she had a really nice sense of movement, and she was sexy, but not kind of a sexpot, you know" (Harvey 2010).

This casting choice recalls the casting of Diana Krall for the Chrysler ads and of Dinah Shore's 1950s role with Chevrolet: Elias is sexy without being threatening, enabling her to appeal to both men and women. That being said, the camera certainly does dwell on Elias's body. We are frequently shown close-ups of her slender calves during the walking sequences, and when she is not drinking from it, she conveniently holds the Jazz bottle next to her chest. Hence, while her attire suggests that the character is sexually unthreatening—no "sexpot"—a selection of camera close-ups invite us to "indulge" in Elias's body. In this respect, we, the viewers, might be mimetically figured by the leering road worker, whose long look after the woman unquestionably bespeaks sexual desire. Hence, in the cinema/television spot, indulgence merges with agency and diversity to produce a sales pitch that is multi-layered and nuanced.

It is important to consider, however, that in jazz history and discourse, the intersection of diversity, agency, and indulgence is far from innocent; indeed, it is a deeply fraught place, particularly when it is approached from the perspective of consumers (especially Euro-American consumers) of the music. As we have seen in previous chapters, time and again in critical and journalistic discourse, jazz music, musicians, and audiences have been depicted as sexually hedonistic.

Furthermore, the perceived impetus for this hedonism within this discourse often seems to be a desire by Euro-Americans to break free from the perceived doldrums of mainstream society—in other words, a desire to assert one's individual agency—by engaging with and African American culture that was considered to be less civilized and therefore more socially and sexually liberated.

Obviously, the Pepsi Jazz ad is in no way recapitulating the kind of naked racism that is at play in earlier literary and media examples of this phenomenon, like Norman Mailer's "The White Negro" (discussed in Chapter 1). On the contrary, Pepsi and its affiliate advertising agencies (together with all of the individuals with whom I spoke) wholeheartedly embrace the vision of the political potential of representing diversity in advertising outlined by Lee, Williams, and La Ferle (Lee *et al.* 2004: 14). Lauren Scott, in particular, was emphatic about her personal determination to "push the multicultural agenda, because I feel it should be in all of our brands" (Scott 2010). Nevertheless, I would argue that, in taking advantage of jazz's viability as a signifier of diversity, agency, and self-indulgence, Pepsi Jazz's message is predicated upon (if not cognizant of) racist discourses that are deeply embedded in jazz and American history. Pepsi's jazz remix might eschew the music's history, but it cannot erase it.

Notes

1. The 60-second spot was only ever shown in cinemas. An abbreviated 30-second version appeared on television. In the 30-second spot, the cat, the cyclist, and the waiter are excised, and the police officer's role is reduced. I have chosen to focus primarily on the 60-second spot throughout for several reasons. First, and most obviously, the 30-second spot is entirely contained within the 60 seconds, no material was added for the

shorter version. Secondly, this chapter deals chiefly with the *production* of the advertisement, not its reception. Hence, even though the 30 would have been seen by many more viewers (having been aired on television and not just in cinemas), the advertisers with whom I spoke regard the 60 as the final, complete, version. As Alex Moulton told me, "You got to see the 60. The 30 is kind of half-work. The 60 is actually the real deal" (Moulton 2010). Evidently, Moulton's comments raise interesting questions about advertisers as artists and their advertisements as artistic artefacts that are worth considering (albeit, beyond the scope of this study).

2. DDB copywriter Howard Finkelstein suggests that the immediate appearance of the Diet Pepsi logo is a hallmark of mid-2000s advertising. Fearing that television recorders like DVR and TiVo would enable TV audiences to skip over commercial breaks with ease, advertisers began to insert the company logo into the first few seconds of spots to ensure that their messages made at least some impact on their audiences (Finkelstein 2010).

3. Unfortunately, I was unable to speak with Bonnie Lutz, who worked as the art director on the campaign, or with actors Leah Elias (the "heroine" of the cinema spot) and Aflamu Johnson (the police officer). Neither they nor their respective agents responded to my interview requests. This was one of the instances where George Marcus's exhortation to "follow the thing" was mediated by the "accessibility" challenges that Sherry Ortner has described in her discussion of ethnography in the media industries (see my introductory chapter).

4. Remarkably, not only did Coca-Cola recover completely from this egregious marketing miscalculation, but it also won a significant number of consumers back from Pepsi and resumed its dominant position in the industry. Coca-Cola's turnaround was so dramatic that some marketing conspiracy theorists have suggested that "New Coke" was designed to fail, and that the entire episode was calculated with the twin aims of monopolizing consumer attention and restoring some of the luster that had faded from its original brand and formula.

5. The individuals in question understandably requested that these comments remain anonymous.

6. The marketing recap was focused particularly on the print component of the campaign.

7. I discuss the tension in Stein's idea of a "sinless indulgence" in greater detail in the concluding section of this chapter.

8. Special edition glass bottles were manufactured for some of the packages handed out at the "Jazz Hour at the W" events (Scott 2006).

9. The collective has directed videos for a number of high profile artists, including The Flaming Lips ("The Yeah Yeah Yeah Song"), Basement Jaxx ("Where's Your Head At" and "Plug It In"), and Madonna ("Die Another Day") (www.traktor.com).

10. Siraisi recalls that at the film shoot, Leah Elias was unable to walk quickly enough to keep up with the soundtrack. As a result, the directors had to slow the track down to the point where she could walk. The slow track adversely affected several other elements, however: The businessman's scat singing, for instance, lost its comedic and narrative effect when it was sung slower. Collectively, these problems required Siraisi to undertake many unanticipated extra hours of editing and rewriting his track to fit the film—exactly the opposite of what Traktor had initially proposed (Siraisi 2010).

11. Intriguingly, Hodge cites the music of DJ Mocean Worker—whose submission for the spot was rejected—as having a formative impact on the early plans for the style of the soundtrack. Moulton suggests that the popular "Verve Remixed" albums—the second volume of which was released early in 2006—may have also been influential.

12. The project has been criticized in some Hispanic communities, in large part because of its name. "*Yo sumo,*" translated literally, means "I count (numbers)"; *yo cuento*, which can mean both "I count (numbers)" and "I count (as a person)," better expresses Pepsi's intention for the project (Yoerg).

13. It is worth considering that the flavor-related findings of the Roper report—accepted logic in the soft drink industry since the mid-1960s—have become a self-fulfilling

prophecy. Since 1961, targeted marking campaigns have meant that beverages with intense flavor profiles have had a higher brand presence, and have been more readily accessible in African American and Hispanic communities. No doubt these factors have contributed to the continued strong sales of such beverages in those communities.

14. It was Thompson who sponsored the Goodwill Ambassador legislation, initiating the so-called "Jazz Diplomacy" tours of Africa, the Middle East, and the Easter Bloc countries.

15. Coincidentally, Coca-Cola-sponosored Jazz @ Lincoln Center is doubtless the leading exponent of the "jazz as democracy" position today. Moreover, the late Albert Murray—along with Stanley Crouch and Wynton Marsalis—has been one of the central figures in the development of J@LC's ideological position.

16. Zatarain's is a brand of instant New Orleans-style dirty rice. Using the slogan "Jazz It Up with Zatarain's," and featuring taglines like "We've reduced the salt and kept all the jazz," their ads use music that is reminiscent of Louis Armstrong's "Hot Five" and "Hot Seven" bands, and a voice actor whose gravelly, jovial tone clearly recall's Armstrong's inimitable growl.

17. Of course, by Siraisi's own admission, it's not especially compelling music, but that's beside the point.

18. I use Ellison's masculinist rhetoric in part to remind the reader that jazz has more often than not been perceived to be a fundamentally phallocentric music. To wit, according to Kathryn Harvey, part of the reason that the name "Jazz" was chosen for the brand over "Splurge" and "Indulge" was that "Jazz" was thought to be a less "girly" name. While the beverage was targeted primarily towards women, Harvey explains, ". . . it's still a mainstream product, you know, it's sold in Walmart, which is the definition of mainstream. So nothing can afford to be so purely girly, you know, that a guy can't have it at his desk. . . . So I don't remember what the particulars of what the other [naming] options were on that, but you probably as a rule wouldn't have something that would exclude men."

19. Recall Debord's explanation of spectacle, cited in Chapter 1: "The present stage, in which social life is completely taken over by the accumulated products of the economy, entails a generalized shift from having to appearing: all effective 'having' must now derive both its immediate prestige and its ultimate raison d'être from appearances" (Debord 1995: 16).

20. According to Gail Stein, the ad was supposed to have run two weeks earlier. *People* offered to move it, however, because the cover story for October 2 issue focused on the dangers of fad dieting—hardly a suitable theme to be paired with a flashy (and expensive) advertisement for a diet cola (Stein).

Bibliography

Barkan, Todd. Interview with the author (June 20, 2010).

Bull, Michael. *Sound Moves: iPod Culture and Urban Experience*. New York: Routledge, 2007.

Conyers Jr., Rep. John. "A Rare National Treasure," *Keeping Time: Readings in Jazz History* ed. Robert Walser. New York: Oxford University Press, 1999. 332–33.

Cook, Nicholas. "Music and meaning in the commercials", *Popular Music* 13 (1994): 27–40.

Debord, Guy. *The Society of the Spectacle*, trans. Donald Nicholson-Smith. New York: Zone Books, 1995.

de Certeau, Michel. *The Practice of Everyday Life*, trans. Steven Rendall. Los Angeles: University of California Press, 1984.

Enrico, Roger and Jesse Kornbluth. *The Other Guy Blinked: How Pepsi Won the Cola Wars*. Toronto, ON: Bantam Books, 1986.

Finkelstein, Howard. Interview with the author (September 22, 2010).

————, and Bonnie Lutz. "Diet Pepsi Jazz, Sounds of the City," *DDB Television.* 2006.

Gibson, D. Parkes. *The $30 Billion Negro.* London, UK: The MacMillan Company, 1969.

Gilroy, Paul. *Black Atlantic: Modernity and Double Consciousness.* Cambridge, Mass.: Harvard University Press, 1993.

Harvey, Kathryn. Interview with the author (July 19, 2010).

Hodge, Elizabeth. Interview with the author (July 29, 2010).

Lee, Wei-Na, Jerome D. Williams, Carrie La Ferle. "Diversity in Advertising: A Summary and Research Agenda," *Diversity in Advertising: Broadening the Scope of Research Directions,* ed. Jerome D. Williams, Wei-Na Lee, Curtis P. Haugtvedt. Mahwah, NJ: Lawrence Erlbaum Associates, 2004.

Marable, Manning. *How Capitalism Underdeveloped Black America: Problems in Race, Political Economy, and Society, Updated Edition.* Cambridge, MA: South End Press, 2000.

Marcus, George. "Ethnography in/of the World System: The Emergence of Multi-Sited Ethnography," *Annual Review of Anthropology* 24 (1995): 95–117.

McMullen, Tracy. "Identity for Sale: Glenn Miller, Wynton Marsalis, and Cultural Replay in Music," *Big Ears: Listening for Gender in Jazz Studies.* Durham, NC: Duke University Press, 2010.

Moulton, Alex. Interview with the author (August 31, 2010).

Murray, Albert. *The Omni-Americans: Black Experience & American Culture; Some Alternatives to the Folklore of White Supremacy.* New York: Da Capo Press, 1970.

Ortner, Sherry. "Access: Reflections on studying up in Hollywood," *Ethnography* 11 (2010): 211–33.

The Pepsi Generations: The Fifty-Year Story of Pepsi-Cola in Canada, 1934–1984. Toronto: University of Toronto Back-In-Print Service, 1999.

Pepsi Yo Sumo (Accessed January 18, 2011) www.pepsiyosumo.com.

Saul, Scott. "Outrageous Freedom: Charles Mingus and the Invention of the Jazz Workshop," *American Quarterly* 53 (September 2001): 387–419.

Scott, Lauren. "Jazz Marketing Plan Review." 2006.

————. Interview with the author (June 14, 2010).

Siraisi, Genji. Interview with the author (September 17, 2010).

Stein, Gail. Interview with the author (May 27, 2010).

Taylor, Billy. "America's Classical Music," *Keeping Time: Readings in Jazz History* ed. Robert Walser. New York: Oxford University Press, 1999. 327–32.

Traktor. "Diet Pepsi—Jazz—'Sounds of the City'—Traktor Treatment." 2006.

Tucker, Sherrie. "Bordering on Community: Improvising Women Improvising Women-in-Jazz," *The Other Side of Nowhere,* eds. Ajay Heble and Daniel Fischlin. Middletown, CT: Wesleyan University Press, 2004.

Yoerg, Ana. "Pepsi's Hispanic Campaign Inspires Slew of Comments", *Acclaro: Translating Global Business* (Accessed January 16, 2011). http://www.acclaro.com/translation-localization-blog/pepsi-yo-sumo-marketing-campaign-22.

5

"THE BANK OF MUSIC"

Vancouver's Granville Street Bridge is not particularly inviting to pedestrians. While it does have sidewalks, its size—eight lanes across and 732 meters long, spanning the width of the False Creek inlet, connecting South Vancouver to the downtown core—is more conducive to wheels than to feet. A less tangible but no less visceral deterrent is the noise. For most of the year, the soundscape on the bridge is heavily dominated by traffic noise. Cars, trucks, and buses race past any intrepid pedestrian who seeks to traverse the span on foot, overwhelming the soundscape with their din. The only sonic counterpoint to the traffic on the bridge is the sound of the traffic on the water, as the boats bellow warnings at each other, claiming their path through False Creek. Even the wind seems to rush by, possibly late for an appointment somewhere on Robson Street.

On the Saturday that I crossed the bridge in late June 2010, however, there was another sound: a small jazz band, faint but firmly present in the midst of urban soundscape. The sound grew steadily louder as I approached the southern part of the bridge—the section directly over Granville Island. Looking down over the edge of the bridge, I watched a crowd beginning to gather around a white tent in the middle of a pier in the northwest corner of the island, surrounded by restaurants on three sides, with water on the fourth.

Coming to the end of the bridge, I circled back northward towards the causeway that runs underneath to Granville Market. Turning a corner, a green banner gradually came into view, fastened to a concrete arch over the causeway. Almost camouflaged by the verdant foliage, the banner welcomes visitors to the TD Vancouver International Jazz Festival, and identifies the music that wafted along False Creek as not just jazz, but TD jazz. While the drivers on the bridge might have missed it, the drifting sounds invited cyclists or pedestrians like myself who were within earshot to pass under the green banner and gather together in the market for the annual TD Jazz Festival.

FIGURE 5.1   Under the Granville Street Bridge

On this Saturday, and for several Saturdays before and after, a similar scene was playing out in six other cities across Canada, as similar green banners welcomed visitors to the TD Victoria International JazzFest, the TD Winnipeg International Jazz Festival, the TD Toronto Jazz Festival, the TD Ottawa International Jazz Festival, the Festival International de Jazz de Montreal, presented by TD in collaboration with Rio Tinto Alcan, and the TD Halifax Jazz Festival. Late June and early July are Jazz Festival Season in Canada. The season typically begins in Winnipeg during the second-last week in June, and ends in Halifax in the second week in July. During that four-week stretch, all of the 10–14 day festivals overlap. National and international jazz artists crisscross the country, moving from one festival to the next; local musicians and fans turn out by the tens of thousands to perform, support their favorite artists, and hopefully find something new; and nearly every major city in Canada is painted green with jazz.

Indeed, since 2004, green has become the color of jazz in Canada for the month-long festival season. Until 2003, du Maurier—a division of Imperial Tobacco—had held the title sponsorships of all of these festivals. In October 2003, however, du Maurier withdrew its sponsorship in accordance with the 1997 federal Tobacco Act, Bill C-71. The Toronto Dominion (TD) Bank stepped in to fill the sponsorship void, rescuing the festivals from the real threat of extinction, and has since become the title or presenting sponsor of every nearly major jazz festival in the country. At the same time, the bank has steadily increased its stable of festivals in smaller communities across Canada—ranging from the Fredericton Harvest Jazz and Blues Festival in New Brunswick, to the Prince Edward County Jazz Festival in Eastern Ontario, to the Salmon Arm Roots & Blues Festival in Southeastern British Columbia. Over the past seven years, then, according to its own internal sponsorship and marketing reviews, TD Bank has transformed itself into the "Bank of Music" ("Post-Analysis" 2010: 8) and at the same time positioned itself as both a major stakeholder in and a tremendous influence on Canadian jazz communities.

In this chapter, I build on Stanley Waterman's observation that "Arts festivals exhibit a constant tension between culture . . . and cultural politics (the inevitable outcome of the entanglement between culture and politics)" (Waterman 1998: 64). TD Vice President of Corporate Sponsorship Michele Martin effectively summarizes this tension as it is manifest in the TD-sponsored events: "[The festivals have been] great ways to get publicity and to give back to the community, as well as getting some marketing recognition" (Martin 2010). On the one hand, TD's sponsorship represents both a community-outreach endeavor, and (following the stated mission of the festivals) an effort to advocate for the role of jazz music in Canada. On the other hand, TD marketers are explicit about the function of this outreach and advocacy as a marketing tactic—a means of building its brand within the communities to which the bank is ostensibly "reaching out."

This chapter is based on my fieldwork at the 2010 Montreal, Vancouver, and Toronto jazz festivals, together with numerous interviews with audience members, musicians, festival representatives, and representatives from TD Bank. In the first section of the chapter, I discuss the practice of sponsorship itself as an advertising strategy, and offer a very brief survey of the history of this unique species of marketing from the early days of radio, through the early days of television, up to the present day. In the second section, I trace the history of jazz festivals in Canada, and outline the process through which TD took over the title sponsorship and began to position itself as Canada's "Bank of Music" ("Post-Analysis" 2010: 8). Third, I focus more specifically on the TD Bank itself, examining the Bank's intertwined motivations for taking on the jazz festival sponsorship: its "comfort" brand positioning, engaging with local communities, promoting diversity, and supporting artistic excellence. In the fourth section, I consider the character of the communities that come together for the jazz festival, positing the concept of *spectacular communitas* to explore the tension between marketing and community-building that shapes TD's sponsorship efforts. I draw on Slavoj Žižek's explanations of the notions of spectacle and ideology to argue that every jazz festival stakeholder—including festival organizers, audiences, and participants, as well as the sponsor—is complicit in affirming and perpetuating the capitalistic and consumptive ideologies and practices that undergird the spectacular jazz festival communities.

Buying Goodwill: Sponsorship as Advertising

Of all mass-mediated advertising—print, television, digital, and radio—corporate sponsorship is perhaps the most complex and contradictory. A television viewer always recognizes a commercial break, a newspaper reader can (almost) always readily distinguish between articles and advertisements, and an internet user can close a pop-up window. On the other hand, an audience member at a sponsored event might have a more difficult time separating content from advertising— in large part because the two are often inseparable. At the jazz festivals, for instance, every proscenium arch is branded with the name of the sponsor. Every published festival document—both internal (such as mail-outs, maps, programs, etc.) and external (such as newspaper profiles and reviews)—names the title sponsor. Every MC is contractually obliged to mention the sponsor's name in the introduction to every event. Even the festivals' own branding is carefully designed to reflect the branding of the sponsor—in this case, the ubiquitous green at the TD-sponsored jazz festivals reinforces the connection to the bank's color scheme. With the sponsor's branding so ubiquitous, it becomes virtually impossible to consume a festival event without simultaneously consuming a TD advertisement. Indeed, from this perspective, every festival event *is* in effect a TD advertisement.

In a certain way, all advertising is a form of sponsorship. As we saw in the introduction, for instance, "free" television and radio programming could never exist without the funds networks recoup from advertisers. Advertisers "sponsor" the content that broadcasters provide to viewers so that they can access the audience's time and attention with advertising messages—primarily in the form of commercial breaks and (more recently) product placement embedded within programming narrative. In traditional advertising, then, there is a recursive circle of consumption: while viewers/readers/users consume broadcasting content, advertisers purchase short timeslots within that content so that they can, in turn, consume the consumers. Because consumers generally recognize their position in the equation—because they generally understand the game—the viewer/reader/user's role in the paradigm is seldom passive. As Stuart Hall has explained, any message that an advertiser chooses to "encode" in an advertisement must be "decoded" by the consumer (Hall 1973). Savvy consumers, then, are able to interpret the advertisers' message however *they* so choose—either by purchasing the advertised commodity, by taking a jaundiced perspective on the content of the advertisement, or (thanks to recent technological innovations) by removing themselves from the equation entirely by closing the pop-up window, turning down the volume, or using PVR.

In that sense, the form of the relationship between TD Bank and jazz festival audiences is no different than the relationship between the bank and the viewers of its television advertisements. What is different, however, is how the relationship is framed. Unlike traditional advertising, sponsorship is advertising that appears on the surface to be something else. As we have seen with the other advertisements we have considered, traditional advertising might seek to activate certain ethical or political precepts to build a brand identity; nevertheless, an advertisement is always explicitly related to a particular commodity—be it a product, a service, or an overarching brand. In this way, the commercial goals of traditional advertising are almost always stated (albeit with varying degrees of clarity) within the text of the advertisement. Sponsorship, on the other hand, is far less explicit. Unlike traditional advertising, the stated purpose of sponsorship is not to sell a product, service, or brand; rather, the purpose is philanthropic support.

Hence, while consumers are often prepared to be highly critical of traditional advertising, we are generally conditioned to consider sponsors as objects of gratitude. This key difference is enabled by a fundamental distinction between advertising content and sponsored content: in short, a sponsored event is something that (a) is of value to a community of consumers for some reason, and (b) could not exist (at least, not according to the perception of the community) without the financial assistance of the sponsor. Of course, this distinction in content means that there is a trade-off at the heart of the practice of sponsorship: while advertisers themselves determine the content of traditional print, television, radio, and internet advertising, sponsors choose to attach their brand to content that is determined by someone else. The risk in this equation is that the content might be bad; but the potential reward is that the sponsor will—ideally—win the gratitude and goodwill of the community of consumers who benefit from or are otherwise emotionally invested in the sponsored event. The sponsor thus demonstrates both the fact that it is dedicated to the needs of the community, and the fact that it shares the values of the community.

There can be no doubt, however, that corporate sponsorship is ontologically a species of advertising. Indeed, it has a long history as an advertising strategy. As I explained in Chapter 1 (via Timothy Taylor), much early radio programming followed the sponsorship model, and was explicitly intended to "generate goodwill in the audience, whose members, it was hoped, would purchase the products advertised out of gratitude to the sponsor for providing the program" (Taylor 2003: 5). From the advent of radio through the 1940s, many of these programs were jazz-oriented. Among the first of these programs was the "Lucky Strike Radio Hour" (later renamed the "Lucky Strike Hit Parade"), featuring B.A. Rolfe's 40-piece "Lucky Strike Orchestra," sponsored by the North Carolina-based American Tobacco Company in support of its Lucky Strike brand (Eberly 1982: 114). This program became so popular so quickly that it precipitated a host of copycat shows, including the "Old Gold Hour," featuring Paul Whiteman's orchestra, the "Camel Pleasure Hour" (later renamed "Camel Caravan," featuring Benny Goodman's group), "Kay

Kyser's Kollege of Musical Knowledge" (also sponsored by American Tobacco Company), the Chesterfield Show (which would feature Paul Whiteman after he left Old Gold), the Raleigh-Kool Program, and the Phillip Morris Show (Eberly 1982: 115–17). In fact, by the 1930s, cigarette companies had become the leading sponsor of popular music on the radio (Eberly 1982: 114).[1]

With the advent of television in the 1950s, the sponsorship advertising strategy was transferred to the new medium. In some cases, sponsored radio programs were reformatted for television. "Lucky Strike Hit Parade," for instance, was reconstituted as "Your Hit Parade," the iconic pop music program. In other cases, corporations sponsored wholly new programs, such as "Ford Theater" and "Ford Star Jubilee" sponsored by the Ford Motor Company (Devine Papers, "Expenditure Recommendations"), and "Perry Como's Kraft Music Hall" (JWT Broadcast Business Affairs Records, "Kraft—Perry Como") sponsored by Kraft Foods, Inc.[2]

As television became ensconced in the North American home—and as advertisers began to develop increasingly sophisticated techniques to exploit the medium—the simple notion of sponsoring programming to gain the goodwill of the audience was rapidly eclipsed. Indeed, the Ford- and Kraft-sponsored programs were developed by the corporations themselves in communication with their advertising agency of record, J. Walter Thompson. As was the case with the *Dinah Shore Chevy Show* (discussed in Chapter 3), the scripts for "Ford Theater," "Ford Star Jubilee," and "Perry Como's Kraft Music Hall" were screened carefully by advertisers and company marketers prior to airing to ensure that they represented the brand to the company's satisfaction.

With television networks increasingly taking over control of programming decisions into the 1960s, corporations began to consider other avenues for spending their sponsorship dollars (in addition to focusing their energies on developing shorter advertising spots during commercial breaks, of course). Early on, jazz musicians and jazz music became a target for would-be sponsors. The most famous example is likely pianist Dave Brubeck's 1957 tour of Europe, Asia, and the Middle East, sponsored by Pan American airlines. Brubeck's resultant 1958 album, *Jazz Impressions of Eurasia*, commemorated the sponsorship with cover art featuring Brubeck (laughing, wearing an oddly-shaped turban) standing in front of a Pan American jet, juggling an armful of Pan American-branded luggage.

Also in 1958, founding Newport Jazz Festival director George Wein pursued his first fully sponsored initiative: a jazz festival in the town of French Lick, a small town in southern Indiana best known for its sulfur hot springs. Earlier that year, Wein recalled, Sheraton Hotels purchased a hotel and golf course in the town close to the springs. Seeking to promote the new establishment as a tourist destination, Sheraton CEO Al Banks approached Wein about running a festival on the hotel grounds. Despite initial reservations (mostly related to the powerful stench produced by sulfur springs), Wein agreed and the festival was a modest success (Wein 2003: 202).

FIGURE 5.2 Dave Brubeck, *Jazz Impressions of Eurasia* (Columbia, 1959; Sony BMG, 2008)

Based on that early experience, in later years Wein sought out sponsorships for the Newport festival, working with corporations such as American Airlines, Pan American, the Joseph Schlitz Brewing Company, and most notably KOOL cigarettes (a division of Brown & Williamson tobacco company). With KOOL, Wein established a nationwide network of "KOOL Jazz Festivals" beginning in 1975, including sites in Atlanta, Oaklant, Hampton, Cincinnati, Houston, San Diego, and Kansas City (Wein 2003: 439). Japanese electronics manufacturer JVC took over the sponsorship from KOOL in 1984, and over the course of the next two decades expanded the newly-minted JVC Jazz Festivals into 150 cities around the world (Wein 2003: 455).

By the mid-1980s, corporations of all stripes were beginning to seek out sponsorship relationships with artists from across a host of musical genres, and many artists reciprocated by actively soliciting sponsorships for international tours. This trend likely started in 1976, when New York-based entrepreneur Jay Coleman established *RockBill*, a glossy magazine that he distributed to corporations on behalf of musicians and concert promoters to solicit corporate sponsorships. Coleman's early successes included fragrance company Jovan's sponsorship of a 1981 tour by the Rolling Stones, and a 1984 Julio Iglesias tour, sponsored by Coca-Cola. International music magazine, *Rolling Stone*, entered the sponsorship field in 1986 by publishing a monthly newsletter called *Marketing Through Music*. According to an introductory letter printed in the inaugural issue, the newsletter's purpose was to "encourage marriages between music and nonmusic marketers" (quoted in Taylor 2012: 166). While *Marketing Through Music* lasted for only three years, it presaged the burgeoning of large-scale music sponsorship. As Tim Taylor notes, by the mid-1990s, corporations were spending hundreds of millions of dollars annually on music sponsorships involving dozens of high profile artists (Taylor 2012: 166).

In the modern sponsorship context of artist tours and music festivals, sponsors have significantly less input into the content of the programs and events they help to finance than they did in 1930s radio or 1950s television programming, when programs were designed by advertising agencies and vetted by corporate marketing departments. Nevertheless, the ways in which most corporations manage their sponsorships leaves little doubt as to the primacy of their commercial and marketing goals. At TD, for instance, oversight of the nine major jazz festival sponsorships (Halifax, Montreal, Ottawa, Toronto, Toronto Beaches, Winnipeg, Saskatoon, Vancouver, and Victoria) falls not under the auspices of their philanthropic division, but under the Global Branding and Corporate Marketing department. The bank supports numerous smaller festivals as well: relationships that are overseen by the philanthropy-oriented Community Relations department. Even there, though, Community Relations manager Alan Convery is explicit about TD's commercial rationale for sponsoring an event:

> I'm looking for, what are the branding opportunities, and what kind of media coverage are they currently getting in the marketplace for the festival, in terms of recognizing their existing sponsors, or previous sponsors. . . . [I'm] looking to see where the festival is. So if it's not a festival where I . . . have a branch presence, then there's no sense in really doing anything. . . . [A]nd also what opportunities are there for entertaining clients at the jazz festival.
>
> (Convery 2010)

Evidently, TD's sponsorship priorities are strictly marketing-oriented. Furthermore, the TD and jazz festival employees with whom I spoke all seemed to acknowledge that the bank has little emotional investment in "promoting the art of jazz"—the stated mission of Toronto Downtown Jazz Society, the not-for-profit organization that runs the TD Toronto Jazz Festival, and the *raison d'être* for all of the festivals in Canada ("Sharing the Vision" 2011: 9). It is important to

distinguish between TD's corporate priorities, and the individual priorities, interests, and goals of TD employees: while the *individuals* at TD whom I interviewed
clearly spoke to their interest in—and often burgeoning love of—jazz music, *cor-
porately* the bank's priorities and goals remain purely marketing-driven. When I
asked Michele Martin, Vice President of Corporate Marketing, why TD had chosen jazz in particular as a genre with which to associate its brand, she responded,

> You know, I think these happen to be jazz festivals, but when you actually
> attend you realize they're much more than that. The diversity of the music
> is unbelievable, so I think they happen to have the word jazz in them, but
> they're not just jazz specific, so I don't think the bank is just looking just
> at jazz as well.
>
> (Martin 2010)

Alan Convery—a man with a richly varied musical background (he played
accordion, French horn, and baritone growing up), and a member of the board
of directors of Toronto-based contemporary classical music presenter/promoter,
Soundstreams—echoed Martin's views. I asked him if, somewhere in TD's corporate structure, there was a group of individuals with a passion for jazz that had
spearheaded the acquisition of the jazz festival title sponsorships; to put it another
way, I wanted to know if there was an element of individual choice or emotional
investment involved in the sponsorship. Convery explained:

> I don't think that individual choice is probably the right thing. I think
> there was a lot of research done into why we chose jazz to be our "com-
> fortable" music to use. . . . [We were thinking about] "What medium
> could we own in the marketplace?" And so music was one of the things
> that they thought the bank could own.
>
> (Convery 2010)

The language that Convery used to refer to sponsorship is similarly revealing in
this regard. In fact, everyone with whom I spoke at TD Bank regularly referred to
sponsored events as "properties," and characterized the relationship between TD
and the festivals as "ownership." In other words, the major jazz festivals are "properties" that TD Bank "owns" for the duration of the sponsorship arrangement.

The marketing focus of sponsorship is crystallized in Hugh Wakeham's comments about the distinction between sponsorship and donation. Wakeham's
company, Wakeham & Associates Marketing (WAM), works to connect arts
"properties"[3] with potential sponsors. Wakeham explains,

> There are some people that specialize in fundraising, which is more get-
> ting donations and gifts from foundations and other corporations. That's

not what we do. We do marketing alliances. So we develop marketing platforms utilizing the assets that arts [organizations offer].

(Wakeham 2010)

A donation is seen to be a philanthropic gift, whereas a sponsorship, according to Wakeham, is a "marketing alliance." Of course, the distinction is somewhat hazy, as donors certainly benefit from the fruits of their donations. In the context of Canadian tax law, all donations to registered charities (the vast majority of not-for-profit arts organizations, including all of the jazz festivals in the country, belong to this category) receive a tax receipt, entitling donors to write off a portion of the donation against their income taxes ("Charitable Donation Tax Credit Rates").[4] The most magnanimous donors often receive special treatment from the organizations to which they donate, maybe in the form of seeing their name in a program or on a plaque, or VIP access to elite galas or events, or the organization might name a concert series or a performance facility in their honor. Nonetheless, a donation is most often an individual act that is instigated by an individual passion or desire; insofar as the donor gains from her or his donation, the benefits are primarily individual as well—frequently related to enhanced privilege and/or prestige. A sponsorship, on the other hand, is a corporate marketing act; both the motivations for the sponsorship and the benefits that accrue from it are exclusively commercial.

A Brief History of Jazz Festivals

Surprisingly, the world's first jazz festival seems to have been a small and woefully underdocumented event in Tallinn, the coastal capital city of Estonia, in 1948 (Starr 1994: 232). This short (and short-lived) event featured local bands playing a Soviet-sanctioned interpretation of American music. The first American festival was held six years later in Newport, Rhode Island in 1954. In Western Europe, the largest festival is the annual event in Montreux, Switzerland, which was established in 1967.

The first "festivals" in Canada were either single concerts—such as the 1953 performances in Montreal and Toronto by groups led by Dizzy Gillespie and Charlie Parker (Miller 1989)—or short, one-to-two day events, like those mounted annually by the Vancouver Jazz Society between 1958 and 1960 ("Jazz Festivals" 2011). The first jazz festival in Canada that resembled the modern conception of a music festival—a series of concerts by numerous artists over a number of days—was the "Toronto Jazz Festival," which ran for four days in 1959 at the Canadian National Exhibition Grand Stand ("Jazz Festivals" 2011).

Through the 1960s and 1970s, several short-lived attempts were made to start festivals, including a variety of events in Montreal and a re-incorporated Toronto Jazz Festival based at Casa Loma (an enormous and idiosyncratic castle

in the heart of the city) from 1963–66 ("Jazz Festivals" 2011). In 1974, a touring festival called the "Belvedere King Size Jazz Festival," played at sports fields
and ice hockey rinks in Toronto (Varsity Football Stadium at the University of
Toronto), Winnipeg (Winnipeg Arena), and Vancouver (Pacific Coliseum). The
most ambitious operation of its kind to that point, the "Belvedere King Size
Jazz Festival" was also one of the first with corporate title sponsorship ("Jazz
Festivals" 2011).

According to Toronto Jazz Festival CEO Pat Taylor's recollection, however,
none of these small, local jazz festivals in Canada had the necessary scope or
resources to bring in "marquee" international talent over an extended period,
and none survived for more than a few years (Taylor and Le Breton 2010). The
first festival to operate on a large scale was the Festival International de Jazz de
Montreal in the province of Quebec, founded in 1980. Now the largest and most
successful jazz festival in the world, according to festival co-founder and CEO
Alain Simard the festival was run essentially without grants or sponsorship for
the first two years of its existence, with funding coming through a combination
of ticket sales and the sale of regional and national broadcasting rights to the
Télé-Québec and the Canadian Broadcasting Corporation respectively (Simard,
"History" 2011).

In spite of their relatively limited resources, Simard and his fellow co-founders,
Vice President and Artistic Director André Ménard, and Vice President of Operations Denyse McCann, managed to bring in headline acts Ray Charles, the
Chick Corea-Gary Burton duo, Pat Metheny, Dave Brubeck, and Tom Waits[5]
for their first two nine-day events. In its third year, however, the festival secured
its first "presenting sponsor"—a tobacco brand called "Accord Ultra Douce."
With the added finances, the festival was able to expand dramatically, featuring
three distinct concert series and a panoply of marquee performers ranging from
transplanted Montrealer Maynard Ferguson, to Pat Metheny, to Buddy Rich, to
Ornette Coleman, to a young Wynton Marsalis, to Miles Davis.

In total, the 1982 festival featured more than 300 musicians, bringing it to the
level of older, internationally renowned festivals like Montreux and Newport in
terms of programming scope. From that point, the festival continued to expand,
while moving through a series of different presenting sponsors: Accord Ultra
Douce from 1982–83, furniture manufacturer Belvedere from 1984–86, mining
company Alcan in collaboration with brewer Labatt Blue from 1987–92, tobacco
company du Maurier in collaboration with Labatt from 1993–1999, and General Motors with a variety of collaborators (Labatt, Stella Artois, and Rio Tinto
Alcan) from 2000–2009 (Simard, "History" 2011).

In large part because of the massive success of the Montreal festival, jazz communities in other cities looked to imitate the Montreal model, and corporate
sponsors were generally quick to get on board. In Toronto, bassist Jim McHarg
attempted to incorporate yet another instantiation of a Toronto Jazz Festival
with corporate backing from the Molson brewery in 1979. This short series at

Harbourfront featured local Dixieland and "Trad" jazz bands ("Jazz Festivals"), but—as Pat Taylor remembers—was a fairly dismal failure, and was not repeated the following year (Taylor and Le Breton 2010). Molson supported other festivals in Toronto, including the Molson Toronto International Jazz Festival in 1984, and "Great Jazz on the Lake" in 1985 and 1986 ("Jazz Festivals" 2011), and du Maurier sponsored two iterations of a "du Maurier International Jazz Festival" in 1985–86, but none of these events came remotely close to duplicating the success of the Montreal festival (Taylor and Le Breton 2010).

Prior to 1987, Toronto Downtown Jazz CEO Pat Taylor had worked as the director of programming at Massey Hall and Roy Thompson Hall, two of the preeminent concert halls in Toronto. In 1986, not long after the failed du Maurier International Jazz Festival in the city, Taylor approached Imperial Tobacco (the parent company of the du Maurier brand) about the possibility of sponsoring a jazz series at Roy Thompson Hall. As Taylor recalls, du Maurier's response was positive but entirely unexpected: "du Maurier said, 'Well, how about we give you more money and you start a jazz festival?' So with the permission of the [RTH] board of directors, we started the jazz festival. It came out of Roy Thompson Hall and went right into the clubs and the parks and around town" (Taylor and Le Breton 2010). The first edition of the Toronto "du Maurier Downtown Jazz Festival" ran in 1987, with Taylor as CEO and Toronto saxophonist Jim Galloway as artistic director ("Jazz Festivals").

The tobacco brand's jazz-sponsorship activities were not restricted to Toronto. Within eight years (from 1985 to 1993), du Maurier had taken over title sponsorship of the Atlantic Jazz Festival (1986; now the Halifax Jazz Festival), the Vancouver Jazz Festival (1986), the Saskatchewan Jazz Festival in Saskatoon, the Ottawa International Jazz Festival, the Jazz City International Jazz Festival in Edmonton (1991), and finally the Montreal festival (1993). These festivals all existed in some form prior to du Maurier's entry onto the scene, but the tobacco sponsorship enabled each festival drastically to increase its activities, and significantly raise its profile locally, nationally, and internationally. Taylor remembers,

> Well, I think du Maurier brought them to recognition, brought them up a level. So these festivals were going on, but they were smaller community events. Once du Maurier came in, they were brilliant at marketing, they were generous with their funding, so everyone received a little bit more funding to bring in bigger name artists, to extend the length of their festival and so on, and awareness—and the marketing awareness. So I don't know how many festivals du Maurier ended up with across the country, but I would have to guess about 8 or 9.
>
> (Taylor and Le Breton 2010)

Evidently, du Maurier's virtual monopoly on jazz festival sponsorship in Canada (presaging TD's monopoly at present) was part of a concerted advertising and branding strategy, a strategy that was conditioned to a considerable extent by government tobacco control legislation. In 1988, in response to lobbying by a variety of anti-tobacco advocacy groups, the Canadian federal government passed the Tobacco Products Control Act, banning virtually all tobacco advertising. Tobacco companies were still allowed to sponsor events, however, and Imperial Tobacco was an industry leader in connecting the brands in its family with a wide variety of events and institutions according to the respective target markets of each brand.[6] Aileen Le Breton currently serves as the Marketing and Sponsorship Manager at Toronto Downtown Jazz; prior to assuming that position in 2004, however, she worked for a number of years with a public relations agency connected with Imperial Tobacco. She has a clear recollection of Imperial's branding strategy:

> Brand image. So . . . each brand had a kind of different profile and different lifestyle associated with it. So the Player's brand was a little more rugged—that's why they went to racing; du Maurier was a little more sophisticated as a brand—that's why they went to things like women's golf, jazz; their Matinée brand was really targeted to women, so that's why they went into fashion, hosting fashion and stuff like that. So the image, the jazz, the audience, went with the du Maurier image and the market.
>
> (Taylor and Le Breton 2010)

Like the Chrysler 300M (discussed in Chapter 3), du Maurier sought to capitalize on jazz's patina of sophistication to promote the brand.

Clearly, the link Imperial Tobacco's marketers made between the du Maurier brand and jazz music was hardly a radical, intuitive leap. While I was unable to access anyone who worked in Imperial's sponsorship and marketing department during the inception of the festival sponsorships in the mid-late 1980s,[7] it seems reasonable to surmise that the tobacco manufacturer's marketers would have been very aware of the long history of tobacco industry sponsorship of jazz music—from Old Gold and Chesterfield in the 1930s, to KOOL's work with George Wein during the 1970s. Of course, jazz's historical connection to the tobacco industry is not simply a matter of marketing alliances: cigarette smoke is also a key visual trope in the canon of iconic jazz images. As we saw in Chapter 3, the jazz-tobacco connection concretized as an icon in the bebop photography of Herman Leonard, especially his celebrated series from the Royal Roost.[8]

Beginning in the 1960s, of course, North American health professionals became increasingly outspoken about the dangers of tobacco smoke. In 1964, American Surgeon General Luther Terry released *Smoking and Health: Report of the Advisory Committee to the Surgeon General*, the first report to document comprehensively the relationship between cigarettes and a host of health problems, including chronic bronchitis, emphysema, heart disease, and lung cancer.

From that point on, NGO advocacy groups and state legislators alike began to work to systematically undermine the heavily romanticized popular image of cigarettes.

In Canada, one of the key legislative moments in this process was the 1997 Tobacco Act (Bill C-71). This federal legislation called for the immediate termination of all tobacco sponsorships, a move that was initially regarded as cataclysmic for a huge number of tobacco-sponsored events and organizations. Responding to pleas from these groups—as well as heavy lobbying from the tobacco industry—the government introduced an amendment to the Tobacco Act in 1998. According to the amendment, it would be illegal for tobacco companies to enter into new sponsorship relationships as of October 1, 2000, while existing relationships would need to be phased out by October 1, 2003.[9] For the huge number of events and organizations that had come to depend on tobacco sponsorship for their existence, the amendment meant a few years to find a replacement for the tobacco sponsorship dollars. Unfortunately, many failed to find new funding and vanished after the summer of 2003. As Taylor notes, "We lost many events in the city that were sponsored by tobacco companies: the fireworks shows by Benson and Hedges, Craven A sponsored fabulous [country music] festivals and fairs. All those disappeared" (Taylor and Le Breton 2010). The arts were not the only area that was affected by the tobacco legislation: several major sporting events also suffered, including the Players Formula 1 Grand Prix auto race in Montreal and the du Maurier Canadian Women's Open LPGA golf tournament—one of the four major tournaments on the LPGA circuit prior to 2003. While both of these events have since been reconstituted with new sponsors, both disappeared for several years, and the golf tournament in particular has never regained its international profile.

By 1999, the Montreal festival had become the largest jazz festival in the world, and moved smoothly from du Maurier into a new arrangement with General Motors in 2000. Within the other, smaller festivals, however, there was great apprehension. A 2003 article in the National Post quotes then-Vancouver International Jazz Festival executive director Robert Kerr, "[We've] been holding our breath over the course of the last few years wondering about the future of several of the festivals. The shadow of Bill C-71 has been looming large and there's been a great deal of speculation as to whether we'd survive . . ." (Wherry 2003).

Early in 2003, Pat Taylor and the Toronto Downtown Jazz Society—one of the organizations and festivals at particular risk of extinction in the wake of Bill C-71—approached Wakeham & Associates Marketing, contracting the company to help connect the festival with a new sponsor. Wakeham described the genesis of the relationship with the festivals:

> And my partner at the office at the time—or, one of our senior staff at the time—was Pat's partner—life-partner [Marilyn Michener]. So she was

very concerned about Pat's festival, and you know, we'd been talking about it a lot internally at the office. . . . So we talked to Pat and said "we want to help you find a replacement for Du Maurier," and the clock was ticking and they were worried that the festival would actually die if the funding from Du Maurier went away. So we went out there and started pounding the pavement.

(Wakeham 2010)

From the beginning of the search, Michener, Taylor, and Wakeham agreed to target banks in their search for a replacement sponsor for du Maurier. Taylor remembers:

We knew that tobacco sponsorship was ending and we had targeted banks as maybe the ones with the big purses at that time. Beer companies, again, had really cut back on their sponsorship—so beer companies were very popular in the '70s and '80s with big budgets to sponsor events such as ours, but we saw them pulling back as well. We approached two banks that were interested—CIBC and TD.

(Taylor and Le Breton 2010)

Wakeham recalls that TD rapidly emerged as an eager collaborator, while CIBC (the Canadian Imperial Bank of Commerce) was reluctant to make a commitment.[10] Through his research and his professional relationship with TD, Wakeham was aware that the bank was undergoing a recalibration of its sponsorship goals, and was looking to music properties as a largely untapped sponsorship possibility.[11] According to Wakeham,

We were sort of plugged in with TD about their different sponsorships and we had sold different things to them at different times, and we were aware that they were going through a re-strategizing thing . . . and they were trying to figure out how to consolidate their sponsorships in a way that would create more of an impact with consumers, and would allow TD to be known for something specifically, as opposed to the shotgun effect that spraying your money around across a whole bunch of different things, and not really be able to build that awareness of what their brand stands for and what interest they hold from a sponsorship perspective. So we knew they were going through that exercise, and as they were going through it, we knew that music was something that they were honing in on as something that they might be focusing on. So as soon as we heard that, we just kept them on our radar screen as they were going through that process. And ultimately, their research showed that music was the number one way of building a connection with the consumer, and shared appreciation for music was so important, and that by them inserting themselves into the relationship between the audience and the performer would allow some loyalty to swing over to their bank.

(Wakeham 2010)

D'Arcy McDonald, Vice President of Global Branding and Corporate Marketing confirmed Wakeham's suggestion, but emphasized that the TD discussions about music antedated the discussions with Michener, Taylor, and Wakeham about the festivals: "We definitely were [already] thinking music. We probably weren't thinking what parts of music at that point" (McDonald 2010). Nevertheless, while TD's music-oriented sponsorship platform—which was eventually formalized under the "TD Music"[12] brand—was not generated by the jazz festival sponsorship per se, the relationship with the jazz festivals certainly accelerated and legitimized the new platform. Vice President of Corporate Marketing Michele Martin confirms, "That really kicked it off. I think, you know, we really needed something . . . that was *that* visible to get music going as our strategy" (Martin 2010).

Initially, however, the bank was reluctant to get involved exclusively with the Toronto festival because it was seeking some guarantee of national exposure. The Toronto market alone, which is already saturated with the TD brand, was insufficient. McDonald remembers, "So we knew du Maurier was exiting. It was a fairly efficient way to get a national platform in nine major cities—east to west—quickly" (McDonald 2010). Thus, when Michener and Wakeham made the original pitch to the banks solely on behalf of the Toronto festival, the response was positive but reticent. As Wakeham explains,

When we sold the TD package it was . . . at the time, we were only representing Pat's festival, and a lot of the sponsors were saying, "Well, we love jazz, we love the Toronto festival, but we need to have a national platform that we can sort of activate across the country all at one time with one series of events." So we went to each of the festivals individually and said, "Would you mind if we represented you as part of this package," and nine of them said yes, so we got nine festivals to agree to let us sell them as one opportunity to TD and Lexus and others. And that ultimately was what allowed it to occur, because TD wanted it, but not if they had to have ten separate relationships.

(Wakeham 2010)

The various national festivals had all been informally aligned since their inception: because of their shared relationship with du Maurier, and because of their universal recognition of the challenges faced by touring musicians in a geographically vast but sparsely-populated country like Canada, the respective festival producers and artistic directors regularly worked together to book cross-country festival tours for artists, and generally to share their ideas, successes, failures, and "best practices."

In response to the TD negotiation, however, this alliance was formalized under the moniker "Jazz Festivals Canada." Initially, "Jazz Festivals Canada" was in practice little different from the existing relationship between the festivals. The JFC personnel consisted of the artistic directors and CEOs of the TD festivals; JFC meetings, therefore, were the same as the meetings this group had had under its previous, unofficial alliance. The chief purpose of this new body was symbolic: to demonstrate explicitly the national scope of the festivals to the bank. Over time, Jazz Festivals Canada has become practically more useful. It provides TD a single point of contact, allowing the bank to negotiate with all of the festivals at the same time, instead of making arrangements with each festival individually, like du Maurier had done between 1985 and 1993. The incorporation of JFC has benefited the festivals too, by all accounts, in that it also represents a single node where each festival can access the others. According to Taylor, this has facilitated tour negotiations, arrangements with other cross-country sponsors (like Lexus and Bell Canada), and applications for government grants (Taylor and Le Breton 2010). In 2003, however, the immediate priority was to impress TD with the festivals' nationwide profile.

When the arrangement with TD was announced publicly on October 30, 2003, Vancouver's Robert Kerr declared, "This is a great day for jazz in Canada" (Wherry 2003). Since that time, TD has steadily expanded its stake in Canadian jazz. From its comparatively modest beginnings as title sponsor of the original six festivals (Halifax, Ottawa, Toronto, Winnipeg, Vancouver, and Victoria) and a secondary sponsor in Saskatchewan, TD's sponsorship has expanded to include Montreal (where the bank was the presenting sponsor for the first time in 2010), a secondary sponsorship of the Calgary Folk Festival,[13] as well as a variety of sponsorship arrangements with literally hundreds of smaller festivals in communities like Fredericton (New Brunswick), Kingston, Huntsville, Orangeville (all in Ontario), Salmon Arm, and Kamloops (both in British Columbia).

In effect, TD's rapidly expanding roster of jazz festivals mirrors the bank's fairly rapid international corporate expansion. In the wake of the 2008–2010 financial crisis in the United States, TD purchased many smaller American banks and financial institutions that were struggling to stay solvent, including New Jersey-based Commerce Bancorp, Chrysler Financial, and New England-based Bank North[14] (Martin 2010). At present, TD is the second-largest bank in Canada (ranked just behind the Royal Bank of Canada) and the eighth largest in North America (Pasternak and Alexander 2011), with over 81,000 employees, 19 million customers, and CDN$620 billion in assets worldwide ("Corporate Profile").

In spite of the increasing corporate expansion throughout the United States, TD has not attempted to incorporate its jazz festival sponsorship strategy into its American marketing campaign, focusing instead on sports—primarily professional sports properties like the TD Garden in Boston (home of the Bruins and Celtics) that it inherited from its American acquisitions. In Canada, however, the bank's roster of jazz festivals has grown in direct response to its ever-expanding number of Canadian branches (currently counted at roughly 1100). Whenever a branch opens in a new region, a TD-sponsored jazz or other music festival[15] will soon follow. As McDonald explains, Convery's Community Relations department—the division that oversees smaller-scale sponsorships—will generally urge new branches in regions that are newer to TD to look for music festivals to sponsor as a means of engaging with and marketing to the local community: "if we have to do something in Kamloops because everyone's doing something and the bank has to be present—[Convery] would help steer them towards a music-related property" (McDonald 2010). TD's newly-acquired presenting sponsorship of the Montreal festival is another, larger-scale example of the same principle. Aileen Le Breton explained her understanding of TD's rationale for taking over the Montreal sponsorship from General Motors: "[T]here's not a lot of TD branches [in Montreal right now]. It's not a popular bank in Quebec. But titling the Montreal Jazz Festival is really putting the profile out there for them" (Taylor and Le Breton 2010).

TD therefore uses small and large jazz festivals (together with a handful of folk and blues festivals) as a means of marketing to communities of consumers in a way that extends well beyond the doors of the branch, helping it to solidify its foothold in new markets. Unlike a branch presence, TD's jazz festivals are not restricted in their marketing potential by the limits of the visibility of a single, physical location. Through the festivals, TD's marketing message can entirely permeate a community. In a sense, every mention of the festival in a newspaper is a TD "impression"—a tiny TD ad; every green-clad festival volunteer is a reminder of TD's presence in the community; every one of the artists that performs at the festivals (9,770 at the large festivals in 2010 alone) becomes a kind of TD brand apostle; and the music carries with it the TD trademark as it circulates among the nearly 4 million Canadians who attend the festivals[16] as they sit in the festival theaters, or stand on street corners near the tent, or walk across the Granville Street Bridge.

Comfort and Community: Jazz Festivals as Brand Fit

As we have seen, the relationship between TD and the jazz festivals developed not through any charitable compulsion to promote jazz music, but rather largely through a number of serendipitous coincidences: the festivals' loss of their title sponsor made all six festivals available, and following its 2000 merger with Canada Trust, TD Bank was looking for arts-based properties to sponsor. When the bank started to cast about for arts properties that they might sponsor, it was largely happenstance that the festivals were unattached.

The mere fact that jazz was "an unencumbered property" (in D'Arcy MacDonald's terms) would likely have been insufficient in and of itself, however. According to Hugh Wakeham, the fact that du Maurier's abrupt departure (abrupt only because the festivals were collectively unprepared for it, not because it was unexpected) had left the festivals facing the real specter of extinction was also appealing to TD. Wakeham had the clear impression during the early stages of the negotiations that TD rather relished the "white knight" role that the circumstances invited: "They saw it as a real opportunity, because there was a lot of fear that there wouldn't be a company that would take over the festivals from the tobacco company, and they were almost able to position themselves as the hero that saved the festivals" (Wakeham 2010).

We can begin to see, therefore, that while TD did not necessarily have a specific individual or corporate stake in jazz advocacy, the bank did recognize early on that jazz festivals could potentially be an excellent "brand fit"—that is, that the broad cultural values attached to the music in Canada and to the festival paradigm aligned well with the values that the bank aimed to project in its marketing and advertising. Banking, of course, does not have the same iconic historical connection to jazz music that tobacco did. Nevertheless, since 2003, the bank has worked to leverage the festival relationship to re-frame and amplify the various elements of its own branding—chiefly its educational and environmental outreach, its promotion for cultural diversity, and its support for art, especially noncommercial art. By drawing attention to these corporate values, the bank seeks to position itself as a good neighbor—a staunch member of the community that shares the values of its neighbors and works to protect them. TD Bank looks out for its community so that everyone can be that much more *comfortable*.

TD's putative ethics and values contrast sharply with the festivals' previous title sponsor. While the relationship with du Maurier had provided the festivals with a stable, profitable economic framework, being associated with a tobacco manufacturer had its drawbacks, particularly during the 1980s and 1990s, when the anti-tobacco lobby was emerging as an increasingly influential voice in both government and public discourse. Former Halifax Jazz Festival President Chris Elson explains:

> Well, du Maurier brought along a lot of stigma. . . . We [in Halifax] were at a time sponsored by du Maurier and a casino, and I would say quite openly as a joke, "Well, all we need now is for prostitution to be legalized, or weed, and then we can get the trifecta, or the perfect four vices." And in a way, that's probably truer to the music's sources than being associated with one of the world's top-20 banks, or whatever, right? But that definitely brought negatives along as well.
>
> (Elson 2010)

One particular challenge the festivals faced was in their limited ability to undertake youth-oriented initiatives. The Halifax festival, for instance, has long been connected to the Creative Music Workshop, a camp for young Nova

Scotians focusing on jazz and improvised music directed by Halifax-based percussionist Jerry Granelli; however, during the du Maurier years, the camp's funding was limited. Wakeham suggests:

> [A] lot of the educational elements that the festivals were doing were going unsponsored because of the du Maurier connection to the overall festival. As soon as du Maurier's name was taken away, suddenly the educational elements were all very attractive to sponsors and were selling well. It changed the whole perception of the property for buyers for sure.
>
> (Wakeham 2010)

Once the arrangement with TD came into effect, the festivals were suddenly able to commence a host of youth- and family-oriented initiatives that would have been socially (and in some cases, legally) unacceptable under du Maurier. Taylor explains,

> Not that we were hiding [under du Maurier], but we sure wanted to make sure that as an event sponsored by a tobacco company that we didn't have children around, you know? We were legal age—18 and up, that's all we targeted. Now we can target youth. Now we have educational programs.
>
> (Taylor and Le Breton 2010)

Today, every TD-sponsored festival has a significant educational component. With the exception of Toronto, every festival runs summer jazz camps and workshops for high school-aged students, and offers performance opportunities during the festival to young camp and workshop participants. Toronto, meanwhile, has a program called "Groove and Graffiti," wherein local graffiti artists conduct workshops in area high schools prior to the festival, and then feature some of the more promising students in live graffiti art demonstrations during the festival.

Other educational initiatives are more clearly related to the jazz tradition. Starting with the 2010 festival, Toronto Artistic Director Josh Grossman initiated a program called the "Big Band Slam," in which jazz bands from four Toronto high schools were invited to participate in a concert at the Rex Hotel Jazz and Blues Bar, Toronto's premier jazz club, during the festival. Grossman explains the value of these educational initiatives to the festivals, and to the ongoing viability of jazz in Canada:

> We're inviting young musicians to perform, and I think that's really important too. We're not just fostering where our next ticket purchaser is going to come from, but who's the next generation of jazz musician that's coming. And [it's important] that we foster that as much as possible as well.
>
> (Grossman 2010)

FIGURE 5.3   Groove and Graffiti, TD Toronto Jazz Festival (2010)

Educational initiatives at the other festivals are similar in form and scope, offering young, aspiring musicians chances to meet both international and local performers in workshop settings, and often to perform at the festivals themselves ("Post-Analysis" 2010: 38).

All of these programs are currently supported by the Community and Public Affairs department at TD (CAPA), the division that includes Alan Convery's Community Relations office. The Community Relations support speaks to TD's prioritization of "kids and education" in its sponsorship that McDonald described. Chris Elson recognized TD's priorities early on in the relationship: "They definitely want to draw towards the family values end of the spectrum from their point of view, rather than the more sort of single-oriented, nightlife, edgy kind of thing that we used to get a lot of support for from du Maurier" (Elson 2010). Alan Convery described some of the specific strategies and programs TD has used to recalibrate the jazz festivals as family-friendly events:

> [A]t all of the major festivals and at a number of the smaller festivals, in terms of reaching out to the greater public, we'll do things like Monster Murals[17] or tattoo transfers for Friends of the Environment foundation. Two aspects: one, to show our commitment to the environment, so we'll support the recycling program at the Jazz Festival kind of thing, and we'll be on site so the kids can put on smocks and help paint the mural kind of

thing. So we do that at a number of events. In three festivals last year . . . we actually tried a reading tent area . . . for parents to bring their kids over during the sections of the festival and meet children's authors and have a reading. Trying to do some kind of focus on TD's literacy aspect as well, and encourage kids to . . . join the summer reading club at your local library as well too. So we're trying to do some cross-promotion on the community giving side at the same time, as well as give the parents something else to do with their kids at the festival at the same time for a little while.

(Convery 2010)

As Convery's comments make clear, the TD sponsorship also inaugurated a new era of publicly demonstrable environmental consciousness on the part of the festivals. According to Halifax Jazz Festival board member Dustin LindenSmith, the festivals' own environmental awareness was nothing new:

The staff in our organization have always felt kind of passionate about that and have wanted to . . . It's just something that philosophically we just want to do—reduce our carbon footprint, not print as much paper, all that kind of stuff.

(LindenSmith 2010)

Chris Elson suggests that the festivals' "green" priorities were not lost on the bank, as they fit well with the bank's own emergent corporate "greening" in 2003: "I think, again, the fact that we had already made a green turn as an organization even before we got involved with them that fits their conception of how they're doing some social good" (Elson 2010).

Founded in 1990, TD Friends of the Environment Fund (TD FEF) is mandated to "protect the earth every day by funding local environmental projects and programs" ("Welcome"). Since that time, TD FEF has become the core—and the most visible aspect—of TD's green branding. From the beginning of its festival sponsorship, TD has actively encouraged the festivals to "go greener" by recommending amendments to their existing practices, or by funding green initiatives through the TD FEF. Michele Martin explains,

They all will tell you, I think, that they've always had the environmental message in mind, and I think just by nature they tend to be pretty green events. So the more they can do, the better, and we certainly encourage them to find new ways to do stuff that supports the green message. I think Montreal is actually a carbon neutral festival. And I'm not sure if the others are necessarily carbon neutral, but they all do different things to support the environment in their own way. Halifax has some great things going on. . . . You know, they don't sell water on site any longer. They have stations, so people are reusing their own cups. Things like that which are very forward-thinking, and really great for the environment.

(Martin 2010)

In addition to funding innovations like these, TD FEF maintains a visible presence in the form of large displays at every festival. Each festival features a Friends of the Environment tent, including face-painting, rub-on tattoos, and the aforementioned Monster Mural for children, together with information displays that list a variety of TD FEF-funded projects and offer tips as to how individual festival audience-members might reduce their personal carbon footprint. TD FEF also funds on-site recycling programs, distributes branded reusable bags, and provides large, supervised bicycle parking areas, available "free of charge for festival-goers" ("Post-Analysis" 2010: 14).

Going forward, according to the *2010 TD Music Festival Sponsorship Post-Analysis*, TD FEF aims to "Implement more innovative and 'green' branding opportunities to maximize TD's exposure and highlight its ongoing commitment to the environment (*i.e.*, recycled vinyl, vegetable-based ink, *etc.*)" ("Post-Analysis" 2010: 15). TD's environmentalism, then, will continue to be a key aspect of festival operations and branding for the foreseeable future. To that end, the Halifax festival in particular is seeking to align with other environmental organizations. In 2010, the festival received funding from the "Ecology Action Centre," a Nova Scotian environmental lobby group.

FIGURE 5.4 TD FEF booth in Gastown district, Vancouver (2010)

Sponsorship alliances like these would have been unlikely, if not impossible, under the du Maurier relationship. They encapsulate what has been a fairly remarkable branding transformation. The festivals themselves have changed very little in terms of content: from the 1980s until the present, they have all sought to present a variety of jazz groups—invariably alongside performers who perhaps do not fit quite as comfortably within the genre category—to diverse audiences, "promoting the art of jazz." In terms of branding, however, the festivals have transformed utterly—changing from adult-oriented events that represented the last bastion of public tobacco promotion into family-oriented community occasions that promote the TD Bank priorities of literacy, education, and environmental advocacy.

The notion of "comfort" was also central in developing a brand fit between the bank and the festivals. According to Barry Silverstein, this component of the TD brand was developed in 2001, following the 2000 merger with Canada Trust (Silverstein n.d.). Since that time, comfort has become the centerpiece of nearly every TD marketing initiative, as evinced by the brand's slogan, "Banking can be this comfortable." While this link between jazz festivals and banking may not have been immediately apparent to many of the jazz festival organizers, it was a key factor in the bank's decision. Michelle Martin explains the alignment in terms of music in general:

> I think, you know, we've always just sort of used "banking can be this comfortable" as a brand position, and, you know, when you're at a musical event, typically it's a very comfortable experience for you. . . . So just sort of aligning our brand with what we think a musical experience is like for most people was kind of the connection there. . . . [Y]ou're typically on your own terms. You're typically there for fun and enjoyment, and you've selected music that means something to you and that you enjoy, so . . .
>
> (Martin 2010)

In Martin's view, the comfort element has more to do with the festival context in general than with jazz festivals specifically. While the other TD employees with whom I spoke were clearer about the particular value of jazz in terms of TD's brand alignment, their comments resonate with Martin's understanding of the festival-oriented rationale. According to Alan Convery, during TD's brand audit, the bank conducted a survey of a variety of musical genres, ranking them according to "comfort." According to the results of the survey, jazz ranked first among comfortable musics. Convery explains,

> From what I understand—and this is only because I'm given this information back to me—is that when individuals rate music in the focus groups that were used initially to rate the type of music that was most easy-listening for them, or what they'd most want to attend. . . . And things like jazz festivals rated one of the highest things over things like symphony

orchestras or chamber music concerts. So going to a jazz festival where you can hear mostly free music—versus paid music—was how customers at the focus group actually rated how they felt first about music.

(Convery 2010)

D'Arcy McDonald suggests that the "comfort" survey was not terribly valuable, and played a minor role in the sponsorship decision in and of itself (McDonald 2010). Nevertheless, the values and priorities that were linked to jazz in the survey were and are integral to the perceived fit between jazz and the TD brand.

Convery's comments still center on the value of the festival context; he implies that "comfort" in the festival scenario is related to the fact that audiences do not have to pay to attend many of the events. The contrast that Convery draws between jazz and classical music "symphony orchestras or chamber music concerts" is also noteworthy, and seems to recapitulate the comments of Chrysler's Pearl Davies, and BBDO advertisers Steve Denvir and Mike Smith (see Chapter 3), who describe classical music as old and "stuffy" (Smith 2010). Convery himself is a classical music aficionado, and he has spearheaded sponsorship arrangements through the Community Relations office with symphony orchestras across the country. In the context of festival branding, however, he acknowledges that, according to the focus group studies TD undertook prior to agreeing to the festival sponsorship, classical music did not rate as highly as jazz: "[That music is] still really important, and people are still really interested in those pieces, but it wasn't the first choice, I don't think, of [most] individuals" (Convery 2010).

More than merely being popularly preferable to classical music, however, TD perceives jazz to be broadly appealing in large part because of the potential diversity of the genre. As D'Arcy McDonald suggests,

Music is more in line with our values, and jazz specifically because it's such a wide genre that we can appeal to a lot of people. So if you think about our brand, we service a mass audience, and our normal media commitment is 25–54 year olds, so it's the phone book, right? It's almost everybody. We have 11 million customers. How do you find something that's big enough that you can sort of see different segments represented in it. So that's why I think jazz gave us all of that.

(McDonald 2010)

McDonald elaborates, using the example of the Montreal festival:

And then as recently as last Montreal International Jazz Festival, which we now title sponsor, seeing . . . was it Sonny Rollins? Famous artists who have just sort of done their thing then come back to jazz to sort of do more. And they drew like a hundred thousand people on René Levesque. . . . But then there was bluegrass, and then there was country—forms of country—and then there's like new age jazz, which is, you know, you could appeal to [a] younger [audience], and the more classical jazz helped us do a more affluent, upscale segment and hospitality and entertainment type thing. So we could sort of mold and shape jazz to do what we wanted because it was so flexible as a property.

(McDonald 2010)

For McDonald, jazz represents a tremendously variegated (or perhaps, nebulous) palate that offers something for everybody—and, concomitantly, allows TD to appeal to every market segment at the same time.

My own observations at the festivals I attended in 2010 (and indeed, the numerous festivals in which I have participated as a performer or audience member throughout my life) confirmed McDonald's claim: ticketed events at all of the festivals tended to attract a predominantly white, well dressed, and presumably reasonably affluent audience. Every audience member with whom I spoke at these events was either a jazz connoisseur, or had come with a friend who knew the music. By contrast, the audiences at the large, free events were remarkably diverse in terms of gender, class, ethnicity, and musical experience. Most audience members with whom I spoke at the free concerts had never heard of the bands they had come to see, and several had never encountered jazz before.

Of course, in Toronto and Montreal in particular, the free events tended to be more idiomatically varied than the ticketed, concert hall performances, featuring as many hip hop, bluegrass, and country oriented acts as jazz ensembles. The maiden "jazz" voyages of novice listeners at the free events, therefore, often sound more familiar to them than they might have expected—precisely because many of these groups (like Ray Charles and Tom Waits at the 1982 Montreal festival) do not self-identify as jazz bands, at least not in the conventional sense. This musical variety does help the festivals appeal to both well schooled listeners and first-time attendees, even as it challenges the cohesiveness of the jazz genre.

TD works to solidify the somewhat abstract connection between jazz and its comfort branding through a handful of more tangible initiatives. As McDonald told me, "People need to understand what [the bank] stands for and how they relate to it. And I think music is a good way to say, 'TD? That fits. They're the approachable bank. They're the friendly folks. They're the comfortable place to do business'" (McDonald 2010). One of the principal means of projecting this image at the Montreal and Toronto Beaches jazz festivals in 2010—a concept that has since been deployed at more festivals—was the TD Comfort Zone.

The TD festival post-analysis describes the Comfort Zone as "an elegant oasis in the center of the festival footprint, encouraging festivalgoers to enjoy a reprieve from the activities in a comfortable environment, courtesy of TD" ("Post-Analysis" 2010: 10). On a sunny afternoon in Montreal in early July, the *Place Confort* was well used, and no doubt much appreciated by festivalgoers

FIGURE 5.5   TD *Place Confort* in Montreal (2010)

seeking a cold Heineken (the festival's beer sponsor, and the only beer available on the festival grounds), and a seat in the shade. This notion grew out of the "TD Comfort Zone" seating at the Rogers Centre (the major league baseball stadium) in Toronto, a private box on the ground along the third base line. The box includes a handful of TD's iconic green armchairs—chairs that are conspicuously more comfortable than the hard blue plastic seating in the upper levels—and is used to host TD guests, most often prize-winners, or representatives from charities that TD supports. Michele Martin discusses the logic behind the revamped Comfort Zones at the festivals:

> [W]e use [the festivals] as a platform to elevate our brand and to really connect with our customers across that. So we do things like, for example, at the Montreal International Jazz Festival we have a TD Comfort Place because up until this point, the TD retail brand has been "Banking can be this comfortable." And so we want to make sure that when we're at a property, we're always connecting back the way that we activate it with our brand principles. So those are the kinds of things that we do. . . . And in Montreal, for example, where we did the TD Comfort [Zone], that's exactly what we wanted to achieve for people. So if it wasn't comfortable already, TD is offering you this extra opportunity for that.
>
> (Martin 2010)

More than the Comfort Zones, though, the primary visual link between jazz festivals and TD's "comfort" branding are the green armchairs. The armchairs are ubiquitous in TD's own television, print, and online advertising, serving as a brand icon. Since the first TD-sponsored festivals in 2004, each festival has had at least one chair somewhere on the festival grounds. In Ottawa, there has always been a chair has on stage at the main performance tent at Confederation Park; Toronto's chair can be found in the main entrance to the main tent at Nathan Phillips Square; Montreal and Vancouver both have chairs in the principal "soft-seat" theaters—the Théâtre Maisonneuve and The Centre in Vancouver for Performing Arts, respectively. In Halifax the chair is on a pedestal in front of stage at the main venue on Spring Garden Road.

Ironically, in the early years of the TD-sponsorship, a rumor circulated among musicians and regular attendees that, in spite of the ubiquity of the green easy chairs, festival ushers had been instructed to ensure that no one actually sat in them. Indeed, Dustin LindenSmith suggests that the elevated position of the chair in Halifax has the twin effects of drawing audience attention to the chair, while preventing audience members from using it (LindenSmith 2010). D'Arcy McDonald confirms that, at first, the chairs were intended to be off-limits to the general public. In recent years, however, audience members are permitted (if not exactly encouraged) to avail themselves of the chairs:

> [The chairs] are our icon, so we try to treat it as such. So the first couple of years we tried to sort of put it in a pristine location and give it some visibility, sort of as a hero role. Then over time, as we sort of relaxed and realized it's actually more powerful if people can interact with it, we softened those rules for sure. But I think initially we wanted to just sort of tiptoe lightly and figure out how best to use it. But yeah, they appear on most stages at the jazz festivals, in most indoor venues, anyways. And people seem to like it. When they see it, they know what it is, which is cool.
>
> (McDonald 2010)

It seems likely that someone at TD recognized the irony in displaying an icon of comfort to an audience, but not allowing the audience to use the icon to get comfortable. By allowing members of the audience—members of the festival community—to sit in the chairs, TD marketers are telling the audience that not only has the bank enabled an important community event through its sponsorship, but that the bank is an equal, engaged player in the community. Says Michele Martin,

> At the end of the day, it's just a huge community event, and something that we like to do, to be a part of, to show our commitment to the community. . . . It's brand awareness, but also showing the community that we're committed, and we enjoy giving back and enjoy supporting events that

the community finds important, and just when you're talking to people in festivals, you're seeing how they're feeling about the experience, it's definitely an indication that it's a positive thing, and something that everybody appreciates.

(Martin 2010)

This demonstration of community engagement showed festival cities that the bank was there to support them—not just to profit from them—and that TD shared their values. Indeed, Stanley Waterman (via Alessandro Falassi) proposes that traditionally the "ultimate" purpose of any festival is to celebrate "overt values recognized by the community as essential to its ideology and world view, to its social identity, its historical continuity, and to its physical survival" (Waterman 1998: 57). Insofar as the jazz festivals represent shared community values, by sponsoring the jazz festivals, TD is concomitantly sponsoring the values of the community.

With that in mind, from TD's perspective, the "festival footprints"—*i.e.*, the bounded geographic area in which most festival events occur—are not only valuable for the hundreds of thousands of "impressions" made by festival pageantry (*i.e.*, the number of people that see the TD brand on festival signage); they also represented TD-sponsored spaces that foster a kind of branded community interaction. This is particularly true in cities where the festival takes over normally busy streets, closing the roads to car traffic—namely Montreal (where a significant swath of downtown Montreal is closed for the duration of the festival), Vancouver (albeit only on weekends in the downtown eastside Gastown neighborhood), and Toronto Beaches (the weekend-long festival that shuts down Queen Street East in the evenings). Closing commercial streets to vehicular traffic is an exceedingly expensive proposition, and would be completely untenable for the festivals without significant sponsorship support. In so doing, however, it allows pedestrians temporarily to claim ownership of the streets of their city, and to move about freely and safely without having their paths conditioned by the mortal danger posed by automobiles.

In her article, "The Placeless Festival: Identity and Place in the Post-Modern Festival," Nicola E. MacLeod suggests that festivals are often conceived of as opportunities for people to connect (or reconnect) with their environment, thereby acting as a salve to the fractured connections between the individual, community, and place:

Festivals are often thought of as celebrations of the specificities of social groups and communities. From a geographical perspective, they have been defined as "one of the many practices that humans evolve in the process of connecting with their places, making homes for themselves and carving out landscapes in their own likeness."

(MacLeod 2006: 228)

By sponsoring the festival, TD actively fosters community interaction by affording community members a subsidized—and branded—public commons in which to convene and interact.

Ideally, these spaces invite communities to come together, enabling diverse sounds, sights, people, and ways of being to come together underneath the rich, green TD banner. Seemingly to that end, many of the free events are outdoors and are located on multiple stages within a limited festival footprint. On festival weekends in Vancouver, for instance, the kilometer-long car-free stretch of Water Street in the downtown Gastown district (coincidentally, not far from the TD Bank building at West Hastings and Cambie)[18] features two stages erected at either end of the strip.

Shows on the two stages are scheduled to alternate, theoretically allowing the audience to travel from one stage to the other and see all the performances. Inevitably, though, for such a large event, both stages fall behind schedule, and by the third set the shows are overlapping. This means that there is a constant flow of people moving between the two stages. Naturally, however, as de Certeau would remind us, these people do not simply move east to west: people encounter one another in the middle of the road (with no threat from automotive traffic), move in and out of the shops and restaurants that line Water Street, change their minds midstream and head back towards the stage they just left, or stand for a while to watch an unsanctioned (but not unwelcome) busker, capitalizing on the crush of people in the street.

FIGURE 5.6 TD Stage in Gastown

FIGURE 5.7 Vancouver Sun Stage in Gastown

Moreover, the bands at opposite ends of Water Street are almost always vastly different. At one point in an afternoon during the 2010 festival, the Middle Eastern jazz fusion band Haram (featuring mostly local Vancouver musicians) coincided with a band led by New York-based, Canadian ex-pat drummer Owen Howard. While Haram's 'oud, saxophone, riqq, drums, dombek, bass, and ney played scorching, heavily improvised interpretations of classical Arabic and Persian music on the TD stage at the east end of the street, Howard tried valiantly to explain the concept of polyrhythm to his audience (to seemingly little effect) before launching into a Paul Motian composition with his group on the opposite end. Standing in the middle of the two stages on Water Street, one could hear both bands simultaneously, together with the constant patter of street performers and the chatter of delighted onlookers enjoying the sunny Saturday afternoon. In this messy, heterotopic zone, sounds and bodies collided with other sounds and other bodies, seemingly creating the kind of idealized intercultural festival space that Max Peter Baumann has described in his article, "Festivals, Musical Actors and Mental Constructs in the Process of Globalization:"

> Numerous "worldwide music festivals," . . . make possible the perception of different traditional constructs, directly and side-by-side. Both musicians as well as audience become sensitized to differentiated perceptions. Such differentiation contributes, in the end, toward the dismantling of

existing prejudices, whether these are conceived in terms of ethnicity, religion, politics, social status, economics, aesthetics or science.

(Baumann 2001: 23)

The diversity that TD marketers have identified as a hallmark of jazz music invites a reciprocally diverse audience, helping to create the possibility of an intercultural space that is "comfortable" for everyone in the community, regardless of ethnic (or musical) background.[19]

TD's dedication to the community—particularly in its heroic, "white knight" guise—becomes clearer still when we consider the vexed economic and social position of jazz music in general. As I discussed in Chapters 1 and 2, jazz has been discursively constructed as a music that exists outside of the mainstream—indeed, a music where any kind of affiliation with explicit commercial enterprise could be irreparably damaging, and would certainly undermine its authenticity. Many of the festival organizers were very much aware of—and in some cases, invested in—this discourse. Pat Taylor, for instance, suggested that as a jazz promoter, first and foremost, the sponsors' priorities (be it TD or du Maurier) were only his concern insofar as they helped him fulfill the Toronto Downtown Jazz mission of ensuring that the art form continued to survive and thrive: "We're jazz promoters, and all we know about is jazz" (Taylor and Le Breton 2010).

TD marketers insist that they go out of their way to make sure that commerce does not impinge on either the artistry or its appreciation. In the first place, after a few ill-fated attempts early on, TD does not try to sell any specific products or services through the festival. According to McDonald, "And so we've over the years tried product dangles with not a lot of success. . . . We would never sell this commitment based on selling more widgets" (McDonald 2010). Martin elaborates,

> I think the last thing TD wants to do is intrude on the fan and attendee experience, so we always keep that in mind. We don't really, as I mentioned, do a lot of discussion about specific products, because we feel that this is about building our brand worth more than anything, so I don't think you would find us doing something along those lines.
>
> (Martin 2010)

From the festivals' perspective, Aileen Le Breton confirms McDonald's and Martin's claims: "Their message has always been about [how] they're happy to be involved. They don't use it as a sales pitch" (Taylor and Le Breton 2010).

Second, TD's involvement with the artistic direction of the festival is deliberately limited. While it advises the festivals on financial and marketing matters, it stops well short of giving them any specific, explicit artistic suggestions. Alan Convery was emphatic about this point:

> [We are] totally arm's length to the artist—the talent-management component from our side. We don't want to interfere with that aspect at all. We're

certainly interested in who they have. Typically when you negotiate with sponsorship, they'll say "we are pursuing this particular kind of talent, and this is what we had last year" as an example of what was out there. Or, "This is what we had last year and he's told us he's coming back again this year." But we don't have anything in terms of looking at the talent.

(Convery 2010)

To that end, the artistic directors themselves do not often interact with the sponsors, especially in the larger festivals like Toronto, Vancouver, and Montreal where there are sufficient full-time staff. In his first year as Toronto artistic director in 2010, Josh Grossman asserted that he had nothing whatsoever to do with the sponsors: "Yeah, to be honest I had nothing . . . and I continue to have nothing to do with that. I mean, I've met a couple of the people once at the media launch, but other than that I have no connection with them at all, so . . . no interaction" (Grossman 2010).[20]

Third, TD's prioritization of the art form is evident in the structure of the festival events themselves. While virtually every performance venue at every festival has some TD iconography, the stage will often be cleared of any TD marketing material prior to a performance so as not to distract the audience's focus. I witnessed this twice in Vancouver, where sponsors' logos were projected onto the walls of the venues (an effective and environmentally friendly form of advertising). During a performance by Barry Guy on the opening night of the festival, the projections disappeared during the music, reappearing during the intermission and following the concert. Similarly, at guitarist Bill Frissell's performance at The Centre a few days later, the green easy chair that was normally on stage at the venue was removed shortly before the opening act (Nils Petter Molvaer) performed, returned during intermission, and then disappeared again during the set by Frissell's group. Projected advertising on the Centre walls also disappeared during the performances. McDonald suggests that these decisions were made out of respect to the artists:

Because most artists don't want anything branded on their stage. So we can get on their before the show, intermission, and after the show. So it's quite normal for us to put it on stage and then remove it when the show begins. We'd like for it to stay, but we know it's unrealistic.

(McDonald 2010)

McDonald insists that, in spite of the ubiquitous TD branding, the stage truly belongs to the artists—it is "their stage," not the bank's.

Indeed, as was the case with the relationship between Charles Mingus and Volkswagen, jazz's anti-commercial (or at least, extra-commercial) status is crucial to its brand fit for TD. Even though it is extremely important for the festivals to attract large audiences—both for the economic health of the festivals themselves and for the efficacy of the TD marketing project—it is equally important that those large audiences come away with the feeling that the artists that they heard were (in Pat Taylor's words) "all about the music" (Taylor and Le Breton 2010).

If the main purposes for the festival sponsorship are (among other things) to generate goodwill and to reinforce TD's status as a valued member of the community who works to protect the community's interests, it is vital that audiences sense the economic fragility of jazz music, and that they understand TD's role in ensuring its survival. Hence, gratitude is a pervasive theme at every event. In accordance with the sponsorship contract, every MC at every festival event I attended in Vancouver and Toronto thanked TD specifically for their "support for jazz" or "support for live music," and the bank was mentioned frequently in Montreal as well. Without TD, audiences are continually reminded, the jazz festivals could not exist. At the same time, however, TD works to ensure that audiences aren't made to feel that they are being manipulated—that their gratitude isn't being exploited too nakedly. If the festival were too obviously corporatized, the music would lose the fragile quality of anti-commercialism for which audiences feel so grateful. On the other hand, TD's corporate presence must be just visible enough that we know where to direct our gratitude.

Corporate Social Responsibility: Ethical Marketing, Marketing Ethics

There is, of course, a fundamental dissonance in TD's position: is it possible for the bank to be genuinely committed to benefiting artists and communities when the endgame of its sowing of corporate goodwill is to reap massive profit from it, expanding its already substantial $620 billion in global assets? We can examine this tension by considering it in the context of the concept of Corporate Social Responsibility (CSR). The question of a corporation's social role has yielded conflicting responses from business scholars, economists, and CEOs. For political powerbrokers like former UN Secretary General Kofi Annan and Davos World Economic Forum executive chair Klaus Schwab, 21st century corporations must become increasingly mindful of the global impact—both the direct social and ecological effects of their production processes, and their more abstract influence on the development of state social, environmental, and economic policy. For Annan and Schwab, it has become incumbent on corporate CEOs to take a leadership role in the development of ethical and sustainable processes and policies around the world (Adler 2011: 209). By contrast, iconic Chicago School economist Milton Friedman famously dismissed CSR as a marketing "cloak," a duplicitous usage of the rhetoric of environmentalism or social activism to frame corporate activities in order to gain a market advantage. For Friedman, "there is one and only one social responsibility of business—to use its resources and engage in activities designed to increase its profits so longs as it stays within the rules of the game, which is to say, engages in open and free competition, without deception or fraud" (Friedman 1962: 133).

The truth of the matter—and the reality of TD Bank's position—inevitably lies somewhere in between the Davos/Annan and Friedman perspectives. Before we consider the festival sponsorships per se, TD's Friends of the Environment Foundation offers an especially apt point of entry into the ontological tensions around CSR. Much environmentalist literature in recent years has focused on the concept of "greenwashing," defined by Greenpeace as "the cynical use of environmental themes to whitewash corporate misbehavior" ("Greenwashing" 2011). Richard Dahl offers a slightly different, more expansive definition of the term:

> In a United States where climate change legislation, concerns about foreign oil dependence, and mandatory curbside recycling are becoming the "new normal," companies across a variety of sectors are seeing the benefit of promoting their "greenness" in advertisements. Many lay vague and dubious claims to environmental stewardship. Others are more specific but still raise questions about what their claims really mean. The term for ads and labels that promise more environmental benefit than they deliver is "greenwashing."
>
> (Dahl 2010: A247)

According to the Greenpeace definition, TD Friends of the Environment is not an example of greenwashing per se;[21] the term is more applicable to corporations and organizations like DuPont, Chevron, Bechtel, the American Nuclear Society, the Society of Plastics Industry, and Shell Gas who were the lead sponsor of the New Orleans Jazz and Heritage Festival at a time when the gulf coast was still recovering from a calamitous 2010 oil spill ("Greenwashing" 2011).[22] Because its product—financial services—is primarily abstract, TD has no opportunity directly to cause the kind of ecological devastation wrought by the corporations on the Greenpeace list. Nevertheless, it is important to remember that TD both fosters and depends upon the twin capitalist ideologies of endless economic growth and endless consumption—ideologies that many environmentalists have persuasively argued are fundamentally ecologically unsustainable. Business ethics scholar Tomi Kallio writes,

> While economic growth might promote environmentally sound behavior to some extent, it creates, to an even greater extent, consumption and thus more ecological burden. In addition, whereas economic growth without a doubt creates some sort of wealth, albeit rather unevenly distributed in favor of the rich, the existence of man is not constituted by economy but ecology—natural capital instead of human-made capital. Once natural capital has been turned into human-made capital, it cannot, at least not explicitly, be returned to natural capital. You simply cannot buy back the lost rainforests or extinct species.
>
> (Kallio 2007: 170)

TD, obviously, is in no way directly culpable for the destruction of rainforests, the melting of the polar icecaps, or the extinction of endangered species; nevertheless, the bank is implicated in ideologies and practices that do contribute to—indeed, are to a considerable degree predicated upon—the exploitation of natural resources, and the ecological calamities that often result from that exploitation. Thus, while its environmental stance is by no means untenable, it is certainly vexed.

Indeed, TD's own branding purposefully highlights the potentially contradictory juxtaposition of environmentalism and capitalist economics. In the first place, TD's ubiquitous use of the color green represents a literal confluence of the bank's environmental platform and its overall branding iconography. In this way, the bank's environmental activism is simultaneously a branding and marketing exercise; when TD marketers or Community Relations employees activate new "greening" projects, they are extending the TD brand at the same time. This is evident in the color scheme of all of the TD-branded "green" elements at the festivals: green tents and banners at the TD Friends of the Environment booths, green pageantry at the bicycle parking lots, green reusable bags given away by TD FEF. Indeed, even the foliage underneath the Granville Street Bridge becomes a kind of natural TD ad. When these elements are viewed against the backdrop of the green general festival pageantry, the green-toned festival programs, and the green TD-sponsored stages, all of the greens blend together and a dialectic emerges: TD Bank represents environmentalism, and environmentalism represents TD Bank. The fact that the color green also represents money—the other crucial element of TD's brand identity—makes the symbolic confluence all the more potent, and all the more fraught.

The dissonance between TD's stated social responsibilities and its stated marketing priorities grows louder when we look more closely at festival programming. On the one hand, TD's marketers insist that the bank is emphatically committed to the festivals' shared mission to "promote the art of jazz." What they mean by "the art of jazz," however, is an open question. As we saw previously in this chapter, one of the primary aspects of jazz that appealed to TD from a marketing perspective was the music's breadth and diversity. In fact, while the bank has no specific input into programming decisions, according to the festival post-analysis, TD marketers have urged the festivals to further broaden their programming to appeal to a wider, more diverse audience ("Post-Analysis" 2010: 8). In 2010, this meant that hip-hop acts like The Roots (Toronto) and De La Soul (Halifax), as well as classic rock bands like The Moody Blues (Montreal) had headline, main-stage performances at the festivals.

These kinds of programming decisions obviously benefit both the festivals and the bank, particularly from an economic/marketing perspective. These shows garner considerable media and public attention for the festivals, and sell out quickly; in turn, between media coverage and audiences on site, this meant tens of thousands of additional "impressions" for TD. These performers also appeal to a younger demographic from the usual festival audience. Alongside the educational initiatives, this kind of programming is perceived to be important in terms of developing future festival audiences. Pat Taylor explains,

> [It is] important for audience development. The festival's too old. A survey maybe going on ten years ago now showed that our average age was 58 years of age. We're now 37 years of age. We said, "That's way too old for us." So a lot of that has changed just with the style of programming.
>
> (Taylor and Le Breton 2010)

For Taylor as for TD, the definition of jazz must change with the tastes of its prospective audience if it is to be economically sustainable. Of course, jazz has always been an unusually diffuse and densely syncretic genre, encompassing a wide and even contradictory range of sounds, styles, and other genre signifiers. The generic diversification of jazz has always been a particular hallmark of jazz festivals, however: the first Montreal jazz festival in 1980 featured Ray Charles; George Wein's KOOL Jazz Festivals that toured across the United States in the late 1970s featured a panoply of disco, R&B, and soul artists (Marable 2000: 161; Wein 2003: 441); the headline act for the 2010 New Orleans Jazz and Heritage Festival was American rock/nu-metal artist Kid Rock; and the iconic Montreux Jazz Festival regularly includes performances by artists such as Sting, Paul Simon, Alicia Keys, and Wyclef Jean ("History" 2011). Not all jazz festivals share this conflicted relationship to their titular genre: The Newport Jazz Festival and Vision Fest in the United States, the Guelph Jazz Festival and l'Off Festival de Jazz de Montreal in Canada, and many Scandinavian festivals are seldom subject to genre debates. Nevertheless, these are exceptional cases within an overall trend towards diversification.

Festival directors have historically defended their more tenuous programming decisions by rhetorically positioning artists like Aretha Franklin (featured in Toronto in 2011), Feist (featured in Montreal in 2013), or The Chieftains (featured in Vancouver in 2013) as heirs to the jazz tradition, or citing jazz influence in their music. George Wein, for instance, was regularly criticized for including so many R&B and Soul artists in his KOOL Jazz Festivals (although his programming for the original Newport Jazz Festival remained consistently conservative). He justified his decisions in his autobiography, writing, "Soul was the music of black America [in the 1970s], in a way that jazz had not been for many years. And the soul performers we presented were consummate artists; the talent that these people had was unique. . . . This was a world of music that could not be dismissed. Our position as the number one promoters of black music was a point of pride" (Wein 2003: 441). In 2010, Toronto festival artistic director Josh Grossman echoed Wein's position, proposing that in Toronto and the other Canadian jazz festivals, the nontraditional acts that are programmed tend to perform in genres that have some historical connection to jazz—hip-hop, hi-life, and blues, for instance, all share jazz's African and African American cultural heritage (Grossman 2010).

Nevertheless, the festivals' inclusion (partly in response to TD's encouragement) of such high-profile acts in order to diversify its audience runs counter to the festivals' missions to a certain extent. While all of the festivals continue to focus extensively on more conventional jazz groups, one must wonder whether programming popular nonjazz artists constitutes "promoting the art of jazz." While booking such artists may boost media coverage and public profile, it is questionable whether audiences from Sting (Umbria, 2012; Montreux 2013), Bruce Springsteen (New Orleans, 2014), or comedian Steve Martin's bluegrass outfit (Ottawa, 2014) also attend performances by groups that do in fact self-identify as jazz bands, thereby achieving the stated mandate. Grossman, Chris Elson, and others connected with the Canadian events admitted that while it is difficult to track in detail how many audience members at pop-oriented concerts (many of which are free and unticketed) also attend the ticketed, conventional jazz concerts, anecdotally there does not appear to be a significant correlation. Certainly, the huge crowds that turn out for Arcade Fire (New Orleans, 2014) *et al.* boost overall festival attendance, thereby "promoting the art of jazz" to sponsors and state funding bodies—for whom attendance numbers are of critical interest—but that is surely not the only kind of "promotion" implied in the festival mission.

The potential conflict with the festivals' musical mandate is heightened when we consider it in relation to TD's marketing perspective. During my interviews with bank marketers, it quickly became clear that TD does not completely share the festivals' interpretation of the mission statement. The bank's understanding of artistic promotion aligns neatly with its marketing priorities: the success of the mission can be evaluated primarily in terms of "impressions"—the number of eyes that notice the festival pageantry, and the number of feet that walk the festival grounds. As Pat Taylor often reminded me, whereas the festival people are "all about the music" (Taylor and Le Breton 2010), TD is mainly concerned about the marketing, including in the way that it thinks and speaks about the music. Michele Martin, for instance, acknowledged that the festival programming is not strictly devoted to jazz:

> You know, I think these happen to be jazz festivals, but when you actually attend you realize they're much more than that. The diversity of the music is unbelievable, so I think they happen to have the word jazz in them, but they're not just jazz specific, so I don't think the bank is just looking just at jazz as well.
>
> (Martin 2010)

For Martin, diversity—not jazz—is the priority. In his comments on the recent sponsorship arrangement with the Calgary Folk Festival, D'Arcy McDonald seconds Martin's suggestion, further acknowledging that the bank is not "just looking at jazz:"

> [The] folk festival's not too dissimilar from some forms of jazz when you actually get into it. . . . I mean folk by definition—and I'm not an expert by any means—it's fairly wide, right? So it's not just a rock concert. It's more than that. Over the course of the day, fifteen or twenty acts roll through the stage—how many types of music they touch would probably be fairly significant.
>
> (McDonald 2010)

While McDonald certainly does not go so far as to suggest that a folk music festival would be identical to a jazz festival, the breadth of both festivals means that, in the absence of a viable jazz festival in the market, the Calgary Folk Fest is a more than adequate jazz surrogate. Clearly, jazz music is incidental to the bank's marketing goals. Hence, despite the artistic rhetoric around jazz inheritance or influence, the primary motivation for genre diversification in the festival context does not seem to be musical; rather, the priority is clearly the fulfillment of marketing and branding goals. There is a significant distinction between the musical development of a genre and the corporate-driven reconstitution of musical generic identities to achieve marketing ends.

TD's approach to community engagement presents a further point of tension between its social and marketing goals. The bank's stated priority is to appeal indiscriminately to everyone in the community, cutting across age, ethnicity, and gender boundaries. Intriguingly, though, the festival coordinators with whom I spoke were equally emphatic that the festivals' traditional core demographic—middle-aged, middle- and high-income homeowners—was of immense interest to the bank from the first moments of the negotiation. According to Hugh Wakeham, the marketing and sponsorship group that negotiated the original sponsorship arrangement between the festivals and TD Bank in 2003, "I think . . . the demographic of the jazz attendee is really appealing. It's sophisticated, it's relatively affluent, educated attendee, which is really attractive to a bank" (Wakeham 2010). Halifax's Chris Elson is more specific about his sense of what precisely would appeal to the bank about the jazz festival core demographic:

> I know that they must have spent money on understanding the demographics of a jazz festival audience. And it's no accident that we've got the green chair up there, and various instruments for investment and so on, because people who come to this festival—although we get a good range of ages—the ticket buying people for the main evening shows and stuff, they're people with careers and jobs that are allowing them to start to buy mutual funds, and RSPs, and have a financial adviser and all that sort of stuff.
>
> (Elson 2010)

Significantly, the research methodology TD employs in its post-festival marketing analysis seems to support Elson's perception of the bank's priorities. During and after every festival every year, TD surveys both festival attendees and nonattendees. The purpose of the surveys is, in essence, to gauge the efficacy of the festivals as a marketing tool by asking respondents to identify the title sponsor, to explain whether or not they feel that the sponsorship is a good brand-fit for the bank, and to suggest whether the bank's support of the festivals has effectively built goodwill in the community. TD's target demographic for these surveys is quite specific: all respondents to the 2010 post-analysis survey were between the ages of 19–55, had "some college or university education," had a household income greater than $55,000, and had "sole/partial decision-making responsibility for household banking decisions" ("Post-Analysis" 16). D'Arcy McDonald explains that this demographic target constitutes the "typical Canadian:"

> I think they fit a social demographic sphere. So I think they'd be male/ female, 25–54, probably 50K plus in household income. That's the typical Canadian household. So you'd probably skew that a little bit, but that would be the "average" person we want to get to.
>
> (McDonald 2010)

Of course, this target is really quite broad. Nevertheless, it is revealing that TD's concept of the "typical Canadian"—and the festival's core demographic— is identified solely according to categories that relate to the banking industry, namely income, education, and agency in financial decision-making. While TD's prioritization of this demographic is entirely logical from a marketing perspective, it radically undercuts TD's claims to celebrating diversity and engaging with the entire local community. Actively interpellating only those members of the community who are of immediate marketing value and calling that narrow segment "typical" does not specifically preclude the possibility of diversity and community, but TD's research parameters certainly delimit the scope of both ideas.

Deepening the conflict in TD's position is its use of all of its festivals to engage specifically (or "activate," in the corporate parlance) high-end clientèle— corporate investors and high net-worth individuals. Indeed, as Alan Convery explains, the opportunity to entertain these groups and individuals is one of the first things he looks for when deciding whether or not to sponsor a festival:

> And other festivals have a designated VIP area, so what's the value-add that, as a sponsor, you can add to a particular client. So if I have a series of high-end clients at my bank branch, and I want to take them to this festival because they're interested in it, I can get them the front row seating or the VIP seating at the festival so they can actually do something. And is there

actually an opportunity for a small reception, or a VIP reception to bring
in someone—the acts—to meet people. So what kind of value-add can I
add as a sponsor—can I work with the festival to be able to do?

(Convery 2010)

Evidently, all individuals within the community are not treated exactly equally,
in spite of TD's protestations to the contrary. Hence, the bank is trying to have
it both ways—trying to demonstrate its dedication to the community at large,
while simultaneously treating the richest members differently.

All of these related points of conflict speak to an intuitive contradiction in
the notion of a multinational brand like TD demonstrating its support for and
participation in local communities by investing in a single, nation-wide property
(Jazz Festivals Canada) that runs events in local communities. As we have seen,
at no point was TD interested in investing solely in one festival: when the group
led by Marilyn Michener representing the Toronto festival first approached the
banks in 2003, they indicated that they would only be interested in a "national
platform that [they could] sort of activate across the country all at one time with
one series of events" (Wakeham 2010). In other words, TD was never interested in the "local" as a singular, isolated locus; rather, it was interested in a
nationwide network of "locals." The network is not defined by any relationship
between the people in each respective locus; rather, the linking factor is their
shared status as festival audiences and potential TD customers.

It is worth considering that many local jazz musicians tend to feel neglected
by the festivals—particularly in Toronto and Montreal. A number of my own
musical friends and colleagues in both local communities indicated to me that
they only infrequently participate in festival events. One Montreal-based composer and improvising pianist I spoke with during the 2010 festival told me that
she would be improvising at a number of nonfestival events at a local informal
avant-garde performance space, the now-defunct l'Envers, but had no plans to
attend the festival. Another young Montreal musician, a trumpeter and recent
graduate of the Master's program in jazz performance at McGill University, performed at one official afternoon event at the festival with a group of McGill
alumni; however, he had no specific plans to attend any other concerts at the
festival. A more senior musician in the community, a saxophonist who did attend
a handful of concerts, suggested this kind of lack of engagement with the festival
is common among the musical community in Montreal, at least in part because
(in his view) the festival employs so few local musicians. With the exception of
a small number of bassists and drummers who are hired to be side musicians for
touring artists, the saxophonist claimed, few Montrealers are offered spots in the
festival.

Musicians in Toronto, Ottawa, Halifax, St. John's. Saskatoon, and Halifax
have similar stories: local musicians across the country regularly feel that they
are eclipsed by international stars, especially at the official, "big ticket" events.

Of course, it is important to remember that TD has no direct input into festival bookings. Moreover, even if these kinds of stories are exceedingly common, they are not necessarily statistically accurate. According to the Toronto festival's records, for example, roughly 85 percent of performers are Canadian, and a significant number of those Canadians are locals ("About Us" 2011). At the festivals in smaller urban centers with smaller budgets like Winnipeg, Victoria, and Saskatoon, the percentage of Canadians and local musicians is even higher. One former festival artistic director pointed out that it is practically impossible to accommodate every local musician, so inevitably many will be left disappointed and frustrated. Indeed, as an active member of the local jazz scene himself, he left the AD position in part because he found the process of rejecting festival applications from his friends and collaborators to be exceedingly taxing, both personally and professionally. Nevertheless, the fact that so many musicians feel disinterested in—even alienated from—events that supposedly represent celebrations of their chosen art form in their home cities is surely noteworthy.

All of this serves to underline the vexed character of TD's relationship to the local community. Obviously, TD's purpose in sponsoring the festivals is not merely to benefit local communities; rather, the bank's chief rationale is to market itself and its products to consumers in those communities. Hence, the foundational element of the communities is neither jazz, nor diversity, nor environmentalism, nor any of the other sociocultural themes TD champions; the defining value of the festival community is consumption. Indeed, the bank's marketers are unequivocal about the fact that these ethical themes are first and foremost marketing goals, not activist social missions.

Throughout my interviews with TD's marketers, they explained TD's rationale by emphasizing the value of publicly *demonstrating* the bank's concern for the welfare and betterment of the community. In the festival Post-Analysis, for instance, one of several goals for the 2011 festivals is to ensure that the myriad TD-sponsored educational initiatives—such as the "Groove and Graffiti" project in Toronto, and various high school outreach programmes in other cities—get more media attention: "Place a focus/spotlight on TD Jazz Festival Workshops: Go beyond sponsorship message by making the story bigger, personal and more newsworthy, touching the local communities in which the workshops take place" ("Post-Analysis" 2010: 35). Similarly, branding for the TD Friends of the Environment Foundation is pervasive on the festival grounds, *advertising* TD's dedication to environmental sustainability, and to funding community-organized environmental activist work. They also describe diversity not in terms of breaking down cultural barriers and prejudices, but in terms of accessing and activating multiple market segments through the same platform. According to Michele Martin, the festival "really is a chance for us to reach out and touch several different areas of interest for us" (Martin 2010). By the same token, in their comments about the variety of programming at the festivals, both Martin and McDonald slip seamlessly between describing festival "audiences" and "fans" to describing demographic "segments"—using the two concepts almost interchangeably. Cities and communities are not merely cities and communities; they are markets. And people are not merely people; they are market segments and consumers.

Ultimately, because TD defines the community of festival audiences primarily as consumers, the bank can never truly be even the symbolic member of that community that it purports to be. By tacitly identifying the community as consumers, the bank concomitantly identifies itself as a producer, creating an ontological divide between one and the other—"us" and "them." All of the social themes that TD references, then, do not constitute goals in and of themselves, but marketing strategies—means by which the producer ("them") can access the consumer ("us"). To use Victor Turner's (1969) terminology, the shared community feeling that TD endeavors to create—wherein TD is an engaged, activist member of the community—is not *communitas*, but a *spectacle* of *communitas*.

Conclusion: Jazz Festivals and The Spectacle of Community

Despite the unreality—or following Baudrillard, hyperreality—of the sponsor-driven festival community, it is important to recognize that audiences almost universally respond warmly to the sponsors. Even with the visual ubiquity of the TD brand on the festival grounds and the number of times the bank is mentioned in MC monologues, whenever audiences are exhorted to thank the sponsor, they invariably respond with warm applause and cheers. My own observations are confirmed by TD's (much more comprehensive) marketing analysis. According to the festival post-analysis, the vast majority of survey respondents and interview participants indicated that the festival sponsorship "favorable impact . . . on TD's Overall Image" ("Post-Analysis" 2010: 20), while a significant number (roughly 47 percent) suggested that the festival analysis had prompted them at least to consider switching their banking to TD ("Post-Analysis" 2010: 20). Evidently, jazz festival audiences are, in the main, very positively disposed towards the sponsors in general, and TD in particular. According to an Economic Impact Study commissioned by the Toronto festival in 2009, 92 percent of festival attendees had a positive experience, and 95 percent intended to return the following year ("Economic Impact Study" 2011: 4). Moreover, 75 percent "try to support companies that sponsor the Toronto Jazz Festival" ("Economic Impact Study" 2011: 25). As Dustin LindenSmith told me, "My general feeling is that they've been pretty openly supportive without being restrictive. So the relationship is good, and there's a lot to cheer about" (LindenSmith 2010).

Admittedly, I was surprised by this conclusion. As Adorno might ask, are festival audiences dupes, victims of false consciousness? Have they been tricked by a duplicitous marketing scheme that masquerades as community outreach and musical advocacy? An avowed Marxist like Thomas Frank would suggest that the reason for the audience's "comfort" with TD's branding ubiquity—with its expanding corporate "ownership" of a cultural practice (and of an environmentally activist ethic), and with its easy commodification of culture and activism—can be explained by the fact that in the 21st century, our conceptions and our responses have been conditioned by that very ubiquity:

> Even while we are happily dazed by the mall's panoply of choice, exhorted to indulge our taste for breaking rules, and deluged with all manner of useful "information," our collective mental universe is being radically circumscribed, enclosed within the tightest parameters of all time. In the third millennium there is to be no myth but the business myth, no individuality but the thirty or so professionally-accepted psychographic market niches, no diversity but the happy heteroglossia of the sitcom, no rebellion but the preprogrammed search for new kicks. . . . [Big business] is putting itself beyond our power of imagining because it has become our imagination, it has become our power to envision, and describe, and theorize, and resist.
>
> (Frank 1997: 274)

Or are jazz festival audiences savvier than that? After all, consumption and commerce do not enter the jazz festival paradigm solely through sponsorship or through advertising: promoters, presenters, audiences, and musicians are all complicit. At festivals, for instance, audience members move through a quasi-utopian public commons (or a spectacle thereof) from stage to stage, reclaiming public space. When they get to the stage, they look up the band on iTunes. Or they buy a CD. Or they choose to do neither. When they move from stage to stage, they also move in and out of the many shops that dot the festival footprint. Indeed, in its Economic Impact Study, the Toronto Jazz Festival claims to have generated $3.6 million in "indirect" and "induced" spending—a figure that includes money spent by audience members at local businesses. Hence, consumption and commerce are not simply things that sponsors like TD *do* to festival audiences through their marketing; on the contrary, they are ideologies that undergird the entire festival, and the entire festival community.

Most scholarship on the idea of spectacle (most notably Guy Debord's work) operates from the presumption that a spectacle is ontologically inauthentic—an artificial projection of authenticity meant to dupe the proletariat into a state of false consciousness. Slavoj Žižek, however, contests this notion, bringing more nuance to the concept: for Žižek (via Lacan and Hegel), the spectacle is not merely an external phenomenon, but is rather a crucial step in the constitution of subjectivity. Like a kind of inversion of the myth of Narcissus, Žižek argues that we cannot recognize ourselves as subjects without being able to see our subjectivity reflected elsewhere; we need to be able to experience ourselves from outside of ourselves, a kind of "self-fissure" (to use Žižek's term) that is only possible *through* spectacularization:

> If the essence is not in itself split, if—in the movement of extreme alienation—it does not perceive itself as an alien Entity, then the very difference essence/appearance cannot establish itself. This self-fissure of the essence means that the essence is "subject" and not only "substance:" "substance" is the essence insofar as it reflects itself in the world of appearance, in phenomenal objectivity, and "subject" is the substance insofar as it is itself split and experiences itself as some alien, positively given Entity.
>
> (Žižek 1989: xiv)

Žižek's understanding of the subjective self-constitution demands that we can reconsider advertising spectacles not as unidirectional, univocal interpellations, but as a kind of mimesis through which subjects can (if they choose) constitute themselves and position themselves within communities.

Because of the series of ethical spectacularizations—namely, educational outreach, environmental activism, the promotion of diversity, and the protection of fragile, noncommercial artistic practice—that are deployed through the jazz festivals, consumption in these contexts provides us with an opportunity to constitute ourselves as jazz fans, and therefore (according to the TD brand positioning) as community-minded individuals. By attending TD-sponsored events or consuming products that spectacularize music, diversity, community, environmentalism, or any other cultural virtue, we are able to see ourselves—and, concomitantly, to be seen—as virtuous subjects. By using corporate spectacles to constitute ourselves as ethical subjects, however, in a way we allow the corporations to *do* ethics for us. By participating in a spectacle of ethics in a festival, we see ourselves sharing in and contributing to a purportedly ethical milieu. We become ethical without really having *done* anything per se.

This can be considered in terms of Marx's concept of commodity fetishism, particularly the central ideal of *displacement*. For Marx, one of the key tenets of capitalist ideology is the displacement in commercial exchange of the intersubjective "relations between men" to an emergent "relation between things." Žižek takes Marxist commodity fetishism a step further. He proposes that if commodities can act as fetishized human relations, they can similarly become surrogates for all kinds of human thought, emotion, and belief:

> It is similar to Tibetan prayer wheels: you write a prayer on a paper, put the rolled paper into a wheel, and turn it automatically, without thinking. . . . In this way, the wheel itself is praying for me, instead of me—or, more precisely, I myself am praying through the medium of the wheel. The beauty of it all is that in my psychological interiority I can think about whatever I want, I can yield to the most dirty and obscene fantasies, and it does not matter because—to use a good old Stalinist expression—whatever I am thinking, objectively I am praying.
>
> (Žižek 1989: 34)

Through the jazz festivals, TD offers attendees a network of corporate Tibetan prayer wheels, doing our ethics—our community engagement and our environmental activism—for us, and leaving us to worry about other things. If we are observed participating in an ethical spectacle, then we are perceived to be ethical; and if we are perceived to be ethical, then we are constituted, both for ourselves and for the world, as ethical subjects.

This kind of consumption is not unethical or apolitical per se: TD has endeavored to demonstrate its corporate commitment to community building, social justice, and the environment, and jazz has been a key part of those demonstrations. Hence, the spectacularization of ethics works in both directions: corporations strive to behave in a demonstrably ethical manner so that consumers who value such behavior will buy from them; on the other hand, consumers who wish to be regarded—or to constitute themselves as—ethical can direct their consumption towards corporations that are known for their ethical commitment. However, this kind of political activism through consumption is available only to those who can afford it. Hence any sort of politicized consumption risks contributing to the imbalances and injustices it seeks to undermine.

This is where we can, as Žižek does, reintroduce the notion of false consciousness. For Žižek, false consciousness is not a condition imposed from above; on the contrary, it is a condition to which we willingly subject ourselves so as to shield our eyes and our minds from the knowledge of the deep social and cultural trauma wrought by many of the things that we do or buy to make ourselves more comfortable or more secure in "our own place" (de Certeau 1984: 35). Žižek explains:

> Ideology is not a dreamlike illusion that we build to escape insupportable reality; in its basic dimension it is a fantasy-construction which serves as a support for our 'reality' itself: an 'illusion' which structures our effective, real social relations and thereby masks some insupportable, real, impossible kernel . . . The function of ideology is not to offer us a point of escape from our reality but to offer us the social reality itself as an escape from some traumatic, real kernel.
>
> (Žižek 1989: 45)

In other words, false consciousness is the condition of willingly (if perhaps unwittingly) embracing ideology because it is preferable to the traumatic "Real."

Indeed, this conception of ideology and false consciousness is rendered dramatically visible at the TD Vancouver Jazz Festival concert sites in the Gastown district. The district's Water Street location is mere steps away from Vancouver's notorious Downtown Eastside—the neighborhood that stretches eastwards along the coastline from the terminus of the festival footprint at Carrall Street. A 2008 demographic study of "single room occupancy hotel" tenants in the Downtown Eastside commissioned by the City of Vancouver found that 77 percent of residents have incomes of less than $15,000 per year, and 52 percent use illegal drugs (with 28 percent using drugs frequently). A similar study commissioned by the United Nations discovered that roughly 70 percent of Downtown Eastside residents report having Hepatitis C, while 30 percent have HIV/AIDS (Condon 2008).

Such statistics throw the visible affluence and spectacle of *communitas* at the TD festival into jarring relief. TD's celebration of cultural diversity becomes particularly uncomfortable in light of the disproportionately high number of immigrants (especially from mainland China) and Native Canadians living in dire circumstances in the neighborhood (Brethour 2009). While these people are rarely visible within the safe, comfortable confines of the festival footprint, they remain on the periphery, just beyond the ken of festival audiences. TD's comfort messaging is not therefore as inclusive as it might seem: while TD invites a rainbow of cultural and ethnic diversity, people of diverse class backgrounds are less welcome. Indeed, in the Vancouver context in particular, TD's comfort message is to some extent predicated on the *exclusion* of the lowest class residents of the Downtown Eastside.

With this in mind, TD's "comfort" brand positioning undergoes a significant inversion. TD is not only aligning itself with comfort as a signifier of convenience and ease of use. In a sense, the bank is advocating for the principle of comfort *itself*. TD is not just appealing to us to use its services; it is reminding us that it is *acceptable for us to be comfortable*, to have sufficient financial resources that we might want to consider taking out a GIC, or an RRSP, or a mortgage, or an Infinity Visa. Moreover, it is letting us know that we do not need to trouble ourselves unduly about global class, race, gender, and ecological injustice and trauma, because the bank is keeping an eye on those problems for us. By attending a TD festival we are reaffirmed in our belief in the sustainability of our lifestyle, and assuaged by the knowledge that somebody else is vigilantly looking out for global injustice and trauma. Paul Gilroy's comments in this respect are apt:

> When [commodities] speak on behalf of their owners and users, they speak instead of their owners and users. Even if they are gesturing their official refusal of racial discipline towards power, it will not prevent the whirlpool of consumerism from sucking them in.
>
> (Gilroy 2010: 60)

The discourse of corporate social responsibility as it is manifest in marketing practice invites consumers to abdicate their own personal sense of ethical responsibility and obligation. We are encouraged to continue to consume, soothed by the knowledge that our consumption—and the comfort we derive from the commodities we acquire—is supporting ethical corporations who have assumed our responsibilities and who are pursuing and activating social change and justice on our behalf. All we need to do is to keep shopping and trust that everything will turn out right.

Notes

1. I am indebted to Nan Enstad for pointing me towards the tobacco industry's involvement with jazz sponsorship in the 1920s and 1930s.
2. It is important to note that while corporate sponsored programming has long been the norm in Canada and the United States, pervasive corporate influence in media programming has been a more recent phenomenon in Europe, where television and radio have historically received considerably more state funding and direction.
3. In recent years, in response to the current climate of economic uncertainty, WAM has branched out into other sponsorship areas as well, including sports.
4. The portion varies depending on the amount of the donation, and from province to province.
5. While Ray Charles and Tom Waits have both clearly been influenced by jazz music, neither self-identifies as a jazz musician per se. The number of performers with similarly oblique connections to the jazz tradition (not to say "nonjazz artists") has increased steadily since the festivals' inception as they work to appeal to a younger, more diverse demographic.
6. The Tobacco Products Control Act also mandated that ancillary tobacco brands could not sponsor events; any sponsorship could include solely the name of the parent corporation. Imperial and other companies circumvented this part of the legislation by re-incorporating all of its brands as separate corporate entities—essentially creating a collection of confederated "shell companies" (Thompson).
7. Several individuals who were senior members of the marketing department at the time have since passed away. I was able to contact one individual who had worked in marketing for both Imperial and subsequently for the jazz festival after Imperial shut down its marketing operations. In light of the present political climate in Canada, however, where large-scale tobacco manufacturers have been frequently (and justifiably) vilified in scholarship and in the press, especially for their ethically dubious marketing practices, that individual politely declined to speak with me.
8. When I contacted the Herman Leonard estate to request permission to use one of Leonard's Royal Roost images, the estate's agent declined my request. As a policy, apparently, the estate does not grant licensing rights to anyone who wishes to use Leonard's iconic images in connection with discussions about cigarettes. Evidently, the cultural position of tobacco in North America has changed dramatically since Leonard took those photos in 1948.
9. As I mentioned previously, the "ban" on tobacco sponsorship did not prohibit tobacco companies from funding events, but it did ban their ability to feature corporate branding at the events.
10. Since that time, CIBC's marketing team has changed and, in recent years, Wakeham has worked with them on a variety of music- and jazz-related projects, including sponsorship of tours by Michael Bublé and Diana Krall. Wakeham suggests that in these projects, CIBC has been deliberately attempting to gain a foothold in TD's music-sponsorship monopoly, and ideally replicate the success of their rival: "it's funny because CIBC turned it down, and then . . . at a certain level, and then later on, CIBC became our client, and they kept saying 'What we want to do is something like what TD has done with jazz'. And we said, 'Well, it's interesting that you're saying that now, because we pitched you and you didn't want it at the time'. And the guy we were talking to was furious . . ." (Wakeham 2010).
11. In this way, music contrasted particularly for TD with professional sports—long a favored property for potential sponsors.
12. TD Music is not a department within TD. It is a brand that appears on music properties sponsored by either the marketing or the community relations departments.
13. The Calgary Folk Festival is somewhat anomalous in the TD stable of sponsorship properties. I discuss this in greater detail later in the text.

14. According to Michele Martin, when TD purchased Bank North, the company had only a very marginal sponsorship department. Bank North, on the other hand, had a sizeable department, principally due to Bank North's ownership of the Boston Garden sports complex. Following the acquisition, TD left Bank North's sponsorship department largely intact, appropriating it for its own sponsorship activities. Hence, most of TD's sponsorships are overseen by former Bank North employees (Martin herself being one example) working out of an office in Portland, Maine.
15. While the vast majority of TD festivals are jazz festivals, there are a growing number of nonjazz festivals in the stable, including the TD Irie Music Festival (a Toronto-based Caribbean music festival), TD Sunfest in London (a self-described "world music festival"), and the aforementioned Calgary Folk Festival.
16. Based on 2010 figures ("Post-Analysis" 2010: 4).
17. The "Monster Murals" are large "whiteboards" with images for children to color using erasable markers. They are a part of the "Friends of the Environment" display at every festival.
18. Gastown also neighbors Vancouver's notorious Downtown Eastside, one of Canada's poorest and most troubled neighborhoods..
19. It is worth noting that this kind of promotion of ethnic and cultural diversity has historically been a similar priority for Canadian federal, provincial, and municipal government funding organizations.
20. Adam Fine, former artistic director of the Halifax Jazz Festival suggests that at the smaller festivals with fewer regular staff, the AD will be expected to fulfill more roles within the organization, and therefore will likely be expected to work more directly with the sponsors. Nevertheless, even at the small festivals, the sponsors do not dictate programming (Fine 2010).
21. The Friends of the Environment claim (cited in Post-Analysis 2010) that the festival bicycle parking lots provide parking space "free of charge for festival-goers" does verge on greenwashing. While the lots are convenient, and do encourage attendees to cycle to the festival, bicycle parking is always free, so the TD FEF lots are not the cost-saving measure that the marketing description seems to imply.
22. Evidently British Petroleum, not Shell, was responsible for the spill in the Gulf of Mexico. Nevertheless, Shell has been to blame for environmental disasters in other parts of the world—especially in Nigeria. See, for instance, the November 2013 Amnesty International report "Shell's false claims on Niger Delta oil spills exposed" (http://www.amnesty.org/en/news/shell-s-false-claims-niger-delta-oil-spills-exposed-2013–11–07).

Bibliography

"About Us," *TD Toronto Jazz Festival* (Accessed 11 February 2011. http://torontojazz.com/about.

Adler, Nancy. Leading Beautifully: The Creative Economy and Beyond." *Journal of Management Inquiry* 20 (2011): 208–21.

Baumann, Max Peter. "Festivals, Musical Actors and Mental Constructs in the Process of Globalization." *The World of Music* 43 (2001): 9–30.

Brethour, Patrick. "Exclusive Demographic Picture: A comparison of key statistics in the DTES, Vancouver, B.C. and Canada," *The Globe and Mail.* February 13, 2009 (Accessed April 28, 2011) http://v1.theglobeandmail.com/thefix/.

"Charitable Donation Tax Credit Rates," *Canada Revenue Agency* (Accessed March 5, 2011) www.cra-arc.gc.ca.

Condon, Sean. "Sobering Statistics: Downtown Eastside Survey Paints Grim Picture," *The Dominion: News from the Grassroots* 54 (August 25, 2008) (Accessed April 28, 2011) http://www.dominionpaper.ca/articles/1996.

Convery, Alan. Interview with the author (December 7, 2010).

"Corporate Profile," *TD Bank Financial Group* (Accessed March 6, 2011) www.td.com.

Dahl, Richard. "Greenwashing: Do You Know What You're Buying?" *Environmental Health Perpsectives* 11 (June 2010): A246–A252.

Debord, Guy. *The Society of the Spectacle*, trans. Donald Nicholson-Smith. New York: Zone Books, 1995.

de Certeau, Michel. *The Practice of Everyday Life*, trans. Steven Rendall. Los Angeles: University of California Press, 1984.

Eberly, Philip K. *Music in the Air: America's Changing Tastes in Popular Music, 1920–1980.* New York: Hastings House Publishers, 1982.

"Economic Impact Study," *TD Toronto Jazz Festival* (Accessed February 11, 2011) http://torontojazz.com/economic%20impact.

Elson, Chris. Interview with the author (October 14 2010).

Fine, Adam. Interview with the author (October 4 2010).

Frank, Thomas. "Closing Salvo: Dark Age," *Commodify Your Dissent: Salvos from the Baffler*, ed. Thomas Frank and Matt Weiland. New York: W.W. Norton, 1997.

Friedman, Milton. *Capitalism and Freedom*. Chicago, Il: University of Chicago Press, 1962.

Hall, Stuart. "Encoding and Decoding in the Television Discourse," CCCS stenciled paper no. 7. Birmingham, UK: Centre for Contemporary Cultural Studies, 1973.

"History," *montreauxjazz.com* (Accessed February 12, 2011) www.montreauxjazz.com.

Gilroy, Paul. *Darker than Blue: On the Moral Economies of Black Atlantic Culture*. Cambridge, MA: Harvard University Press, 2010.

"Greenwashing," *Greenpeace* (Accessed March 8, 2011) stopgreenwash.org.

Grossman, Josh. Interview with the author (May 26, 2010).

"Jazz Festivals," *The Encyclopedia of Music in Canada* (Accessed March 5, 2011) www.thecanadianencyclopedia.com.

JWT Broadcast Business Affairs Records. 1966–67. Box 2 of 2. Folder "Kraft—Perry Como." John W. Hartman Center for Sales, Advertising, and Marketing History, Duke University.

Kallio, Tomi J. "Taboos in Corporate Social Responsibility Discourse," *Journal of Business Ethics* 74 (August 2007): 165–75.

LindenSmith, Dustin. Interview with the author (August 10, 2010).

MacLeod, Nicola E. "The Placeless Festival: Identity and Place in the Post-Modern Festival," in *Festivals, Tourism and Social Change: Remaking Worlds*, ed. David Picard and Mike Robinson. Clevedon: Channel View, 2006. 222–37.

Marable, Manning. *How Capitalism Underdeveloped Black America: Problems in Race, Political Economy, and Society*, Updated Edition. Cambridge, MA: South End Press, 2000.

Martin, Michele. Interview with the author (November 4, 2010).

McDonald, D'Arcy. Interview with the author (November 25, 2010).

———. Interview with the author (December 7, 2010).

Miller, Mark. *Cool Blues: Charlie Parker in Canada 1953*. London, ON: Nightwood Editions, 1989.

Pasternak, Sean B. and Doug Alexander. "Royal Bank, Scotia Bank Climb Ranks as U.S. Banks Fall," *Bloomberg* (Accessed March 6, 2011) www.bloomberg.com

"Post-Analysis," *TD 2010 Music Festival Sponsorship*. 2010. "Sharing the Vision," *TD Toronto Jazz Festival* (Accessed February 11, 2011). http://torontojazz.com/return-investment.

"Sharing the Vision", *TD Toronto Jazz Festival* (Accessed February 11, 2011). http://torontojazz.com/return-investment.

Silverstein, Barry. "Toronto-Dominion Bank: Safe Deposit," *brandchannel* (Accessed March 9, 2011) www.brandchannel.com

Simard, Alain. "Festival International de Jazz de Montréal Timeline," *History* (Accessed March 5, 2011) www.montrealjazzfest.com.

Smith, Mike. Interview with the author (July 19, 2010).

Starr, S. Frederick. *Red and Hot: The Fate of Jazz in the Soviet Union*. New York, NY: Oxford University Press, 1994.

Taylor, Patrick and Aileen Le Breton. Interview with the authors (October 21, 2010).

Taylor, Timothy. "Music and Advertising in Early Radio," *ECHO: A Music-Centered Journal* 5 (Fall 2003): 1–28.

———. *The Sounds of Capitalism: Advertising, Music, and the Conquest of Culture*. Chicago: University of Chicago Press, 2012.

Thompson, Francis. "The Changing Face of Tobacco Marketing in Canada: New Federal Rules, New Industry Tactics", *Non-Smokers Rights Association* (Accessed March 5, 2011) www.nsra–adnf.ca.

Turner, Victor. *The Ritual Process: Structure and Anti-Structure*. Chicago, Il: Aldine Publishing, 1969.

Wakeham, Hugh. Interview with the author (October 27, 2010).

Waterman, Stanley. "Carnivals for the Elites?: The Cultural Politics of Arts Festivals." *Progress in Human Geography* 22.1 (1998): 54–74.

Wein, George. *Myself Among Others: A Life in Music*. with Nate Chinen. Cambridge, MA: Da Capo Press, 2003.

"Welcome," *TD Friends of the Environment Foundation* (Accessed March 6, 2011) www.td.fef.com.

Wherry, Aaron. 'A great day for jazz', *National Post*. Don Mills, Ont. (October 31, 2003) PM.09.F.

Žižek, Slavoj. *The Sublime Object of Ideology*. New York: Verso, 1989.

6
CONCLUSION

Improvisation is a human right.

Muhal Richard Abrams, Guelph Jazz Festival
(September 10, 2010)

Jazz is not the only genre that advertisers, marketers, and branding teams have used in their promotional efforts. For that matter, it is not even the most prominent genre. Like everything in the advertising industry, the vogue for a particular music is extremely short-lived as advertisers move quickly to try to capitalize on—or to create—the next musical trend. As David Fleury explained to me,

> Through the years, a track will come out that's absolutely amazing. The Mission, Morricone's The Mission came out. Before that it was Chariots of Fire—there's an amazing track by Vangelis in Chariots of Fire, and everybody puts it in commercials. You hear it a thousand, thousand times. Then it was [Coldplay's] "Clocks." You know, whatever. Everybody cuts to "Clocks." "Can we do something like 'Clocks'?" Oh, Jesus. Please no. They'll glom on to great tracks. . . . That'll be the flavor of the month.
>
> (Fleury 2010)

In 2010 and 2011, in Fleury's view, you were far more likely to hear a raspy-voiced woman or man accompanying her- or himself on the ukulele imitating singer-songwriter Jack Johnson than a jazz tune. In 2014, while the Jack Johnson sound endures in certain categories of advertising (especially, it seems, for family-oriented products like laundry detergent and breakfast cereal), many advertisements have started to borrow the synth melodies and wobble bass that typify the dubstep sound of EDM artists like Skrillex, Avicii, and Deadmau5.

Nevertheless, as we have seen, jazz has been a pervasive presence in every form of advertising from the earliest moments of mass-mediation. The music came of age alongside the advent of radio and the mass-circulated magazine. It became (and continues to be) the generic *lingua franca* for jingle writing. Jazz's apex in popularity coincided with both the golden age of car culture and the proliferation of television. And the genre continues to reappear in advertisements for a diverse array of commodities. Advertisers have recognized it as an extraordinarily flexible signifier: it can lend a patina of luster, sexuality, and sophistication to an aspirant luxury car; it can link a diet soft drink to the ideas of agency, cultural diversity, youth, and sensual indulgence; and it can allow a leviathan, international bank to demonstrate its community engagement, appreciation for cultural diversity, and environmental activism. Jazz has endured through the *long durée* of advertising history. As TD Toronto Jazz Festival CEO Pat Taylor suggests, "Jazz is . . . timeless, so you can pick a piece from the '30s and make it relevant today in today's market, so that again has advertisers' interest" (Taylor and Le Breton 2010).

At the same time, however, the articulation of jazz to all of these different commodities has contributed to the musical diffusion of the genre. Through the alchemy of advertising and marketing, jazz is not just a sound, but also a taste, a scent, and a feeling. Jazz has never been simply a musical practice: as we have seen, it has always been simultaneously a musical practice and a set of cultural ideas—what I have called tropes of meaning. In many ways, however, in jazz-based advertising those cultural ideas seem to have eclipsed the music almost entirely, to the point that in advertising parlance at least, "jazz" has virtually become a floating signifier. From an advertising/marketing perspective, as we saw in every case study, jazz's sound is secondary to jazz's signification. Moreover, when the signification of jazz can be invoked through an image or a word, the music need not appear at all. In this way, jazz risks becoming exactly what Charles Mingus described in his published Five Spot rant: "a . . . deaf scene that has nothing to do with any kind of music at all" (quoted in Saul 2001: 400).

That being said, this book is not meant to be a moralizing *j'accuse* of advertisers and marketers. Rather, my purpose throughout has been to consider the practice of advertising as it pertains to jazz in order better to understand the vexed sociocultural position of the music in consumer capitalism. One of the benefits of an ethnomusicological approach to studying the advertising industry is that the researcher engages the industry not as an undifferentiated mass, but as a heterogeneous network of individuals from a variety of interrelated corporations (ad agencies, marketing divisions, music houses, and film production businesses) that work together to produce an advertising spot. Hence, advertising messages are neither mysterious, nor magical, nor malicious: they are developed through consensus achieved among networks of individuals.

It is partly because of this heterogeneity, both in terms of the individuals involved in the creation of advertisements and in terms of the commodities being advertised, that jazz's significance in advertising is so messy. Different advertisers have different ideas about what jazz signifies, and different commodities demand the activation of different—and often contradictory—tropes of meaning to communicate their respective brand identities. In this way, Pepsi can use jazz to signify feminine agency while Chrysler can use the same word (if not exactly the same music) implicitly to play on the historical subjugation of women in jazz. Conversely, Chrysler can benefit from jazz's history and perceived "timelessness" to acquire a patina for its putative luxury car, while TD Bank and Pepsi can use jazz to position their brands as youthful, fresh, and vital.

Because jazz is not a singularity, this book does not have a singular conclusion about jazz's significance in advertising. On the contrary, I have argued that jazz simultaneously signifies a multiplicity of tropes of meaning. There are, however, three principal themes that I hope have emerged through the preceding case studies and analyses. First of all, I contend that since these tropes of meaning are grounded in the historical discourses of the music—even in instances when advertisers seek to efface that history for branding and marketing reasons—a responsible consideration of jazz's use in advertising demands attentiveness to jazz's history. As Amiri Baraka suggests in "Jazz and the White Critic", jazz is a cultural practice that serves as a vital index of both African American history, and of African American ways of being in the world:

> It is the philosophy of Negro music that is most important, and this philosophy is only partially the result of the sociological disposition of Negroes in America. There is, of course, much more to it than that. . . . A printed musical example of an Armstrong solo, or of a Thelonious Monk solo, tells us almost nothing except the futility of formal musicology when dealing with jazz. . . . The notes mean something, and the something is, regardless of its stylistic considerations, part of the black psyche as it dictates the various forms of Negro culture.
>
> (Baraka 1999: 258)

By fracturing the idea of jazz from its history, advertisements threaten to mask—if not erase—this all-important surplus of cultural and historical meaning, and thereby its political resonance.

Indeed, as we have seen, the tropes of meaning that advertisers and marketers seek to activate in the articulation of jazz to commodities are frequently predicated on moments and ideas in jazz history that are deeply vexed, particularly in terms of race and gender: the marginalization of women in jazz, the myth of hypersexual blackness, and the related myth of black male deviance. Hence, the use of the idea of jazz as an advertising or marketing tool, or the adoption of the word "jazz" as a brand name is neither purely innocent nor harmless. Ernesto

Laclau has described the hegemonic violence that can be committed through the ostensibly mundane act of naming:

> [If] the unity of the object is the retroactive effect of naming itself, then naming is not just the pure nominalistic game of attributing an empty name to a preconstituted subject. It is the discursive construction of the object itself. The consequences of this argument for a theory of hegemony or politics are easy to see. . . . [If] the process of naming objects amounts to the very act of their constitution, then their descriptive features will be fundamentally unstable and open to all kinds of hegemonic rearticulations. The essentially performative character of naming is the precondition for all hegemony and politics.
>
> (Quoted in Žižek 1989: xiv)

By articulating jazz to commodities through a brand name, an advertising soundtrack, or a sponsorship strategy, advertisers and marketers do not solely benefit from linking to jazz's tropes of meaning; the articulations also reconstitute the music. Chrysler Jazz, Pepsi Jazz, and TD Jazz are all predicated on jazz history but, at the same time, they become three new frames through which jazz music and jazz history are conceptualized.

Secondly, I contend that jazz music is always in dialogue with consumption and capitalism. Born in large part through the capitalist drive to exploit African American labor through which Western European colonists brought Africans to North America, and raised alongside the development of the North American culture industries, jazz cannot be considered apart from capitalism and the culture of consumption. Consumption and capitalism, therefore, are crucial frames for any thickly contextualized studies of jazz music that acknowledge the situatedness of the idiom in the stream of 20th and 21st century culture, society, and economics. Conversely, jazz offers an invaluable lens through which to scrutinize capitalism and the culture of consumption. An analysis of consumption in terms of jazz illuminates the contradictions that underlie "common sense" discourses of both advertising and of "high art"; it demonstrates the fundamental limitations of the well-meaning but intrinsically flawed practices of politicized consumption and "ethnic" target marketing; and it reveals the racism and sexism that continue to structure white supremacist patriarchy in North America and Western Europe.

Indeed, when jazz *is* used in advertising, it contributes to the general glossing of these traumatic ruptures in the capitalist façade. Simply put, if we think too hard or too frankly about the calamitous global consequences of capitalism and consumer culture (particularly in its current neoliberal guise)—if we were to somehow viscerally experience the human squalor and degradation or the ecological ruin that are among the consequences of structurally inequitable wealth distribution and the relentless, psychopathic plundering of human and natural resources—it seems inconceivable that we would allow these conditions to persist. For the last century and a half, however, most of us in the northwestern quadrant of the world have accepted the twin ideologies of capitalist plenty and limitless consumption, masking the real sociocultural traumas of capitalism. Rendered torpid and inert by our own bourgeois comfort, we eagerly accept the advertising narrative that capitalism is working; that everything will be all right in the end, so long as we continue to prop up a bankrupt socioeconomic system by harvesting more resources, accruing more debt, and acquiring more and more and ever more stuff.

As we have seen throughout this book, jazz works in advertising in part because its widely-accepted countercultural status helps obscure the stark realities of consumer capitalism enough to make a patently absurd capitalist narrative seem credible. By articulating jazz to commodities and brands, advertisers help us believe that our consumer choices can somehow be a rejection of the "mainstream," a radical expression of our individuality and our agency. By opting for a Pepsi Jazz over a Coke, or a Honda Jazz or Volkswagen Jetta over a Ford, we are performatively refusing the titans of mainstream capitalism—those colossal, hegemonic brands—in favor of purportedly outsider, countercultural options that seem more dynamic and vital, even as the actuality of our consumptive behavior continues to sustain the capitalist system that we are pretending to reject.

Instead of shopping, as consumers of jazz-oriented products we claim to be *improvising*—or advertisers position us as *improvisers*, as the case may be. Pepsi drinkers were invited to "*Improvise* with Jazz" in the original, abortive slogan for the diet soft drink; drivers of the Honda Jazz, Plymouth Valiant, and Volkswagen Jetta can turn the open road into a personal playground, limited only by the extent of the driver's imagination; TD Bank's clientèle can take advantage of extended branch hours—part of the "comfort" brand identity—to bank flexibly and spontaneously (even if the counterpart of those extended hours of consumption is extended hours of labor for bank employees). In every case, advertisers have used the jazz articulation to underscore this kind of improvisatory flexibility and spontaneity as a crucial characteristic of the respective brand identities. In this way, we learn that we are improvisers not only in our role as consumers—not only do we have "freedom of choice" in our consumer decisions—but also that improvisation is an element of the core "use value" of the commodities that we acquire.

The issue of improvisation has become increasingly important as individuals in hyper-technologized, post-industrial societies feel that they are working harder than ever and have severely diminished leisure time, often in spite of technology that was intended (and marketed) as a means of increasing flexibility and freeing up time. Numerous popular books have explored this phenomenon, from Juliet Schor's best-selling *The Overworked American: The Unexpected Decline of Leisure* (Basic Books, 1992) to more recent releases such as Jill Andresky Fraser's *White Collar Sweatshop: The Deterioration of Work and Its*

Rewards in Corporate America (W.W. Norton, 2001), and Brigid Schulte's *Over-whelmed: Work, Love and Play When No One Has the Time* (Sarah Crichton Books, 2014)—a top seller according to the *New York Times* and Amazon as I write this concluding chapter. The commercial success of these and other related books speaks to the prevalence of this concern in the popular consciousness. Indeed, as we have seen, numerous advertisers have played to this concern by developing advertising narratives that link commodities to leisure time—recall the comments by OMD's Gail Stein about the "moment," especially in advertising directed at women.

To a considerable degree, of course, the concept of leisure time itself is a condition of consumer capitalism. Capitalism is necessarily predicated on a balance between work and leisure: commodities and services that are produced and/or sold during working hours can only be consumed during leisure hours. Leisure time is therefore a critical element of the socioeconomic sustainability of capitalism. Arjun Appadurai has discussed this notion in *Modernity at Large: Cultural Dimensions of Globalization* (building on E.P. Thompson's ideas about capitalism and the experience of time, discussed in Chapter 2):

> [O]nce time is commodified [i.e., through the industrial regulation of the "work day," and the capitalist equation between time and money], it affects consumption in new ways. . . . "Free" time, whether for workers, professionals, or school-children, is seen as quintessentially the time of consumption, and because discretionary consumption calls both for free time (time freed of commodified constraints) and free money, at least to some degree, consumption becomes a temporal marker of leisure, of time away from work.
>
> (Appadurai 1996: 79)

Indeed, every advertising and marketing campaign that I have considered engages with the idea of leisure through consumption to some extent: the Chrysler Sebring offers moments of contemplative solitude, together with control over the sonic and tactile environment (and implicitly, of Diana Krall's body) within the automotive bubble; the Volkswagen Jetta and Honda Jazz tantalize drivers with the improvisatory freedom and flexibility of the open road; a Pepsi "Jazz moment" gives busy women an indulgent break during the middle of the work day; and the TD jazz festivals are two-week long celebrations of music and community, generated by consumption, and fomented through consumption.

In all of these cases, consumers are asked to accept that despite being conditioned by capitalism, consumptive leisure still retains the possibility of individual agency and collective community building. These advertisements tell us that while consumption occurs within a socioeconomic topography that is determined by hegemony, consumers are free to choose where they will consume, what they will consume, and how they will "make do" with what they acquire. As a mode of artistic expression that has commonly been discursively positioned as if it were outside of—or at least, antagonistic to—capitalism, jazz improvisation not only serves as a potent metaphor for the consumer experience; it also serves the needs of advertisers who wish to demonstrate the expressive and liberatory potential of consumption. The theme of improvisation helps us believe that our consumer choices are free, and by extension, that some kernel of our human subjectivity remains untouched by the social, cultural, and economic structures of a capitalist world.

Indeed, Muhal Richard Abrams, co-founder of the iconic Chicago-based collective Association for the Advancement of Creative Musicians (AACM) argued that improvisation does retain this emancipatory potential in his keynote remarks at the 2010 Guelph Jazz Festival in Guelph, Ontario, Canada—the talk from which the epigraph to this chapter was taken. It is worth considering that brief quote in its fuller context:

> Now, the commercial aspect of things, they are a fact. Human beings have various types among themselves. So there's all kinds of things. There's blues, there's rap, there's this. It all has to exist because all those kinds of people exist. Whether art or any production of art has to make money, that becomes questionable. What is it for? What's the purpose of it? Why is it being put out? And . . . that's what we're talking about. That's what we're talking about. What is it that is happening to us as human beings? The idea of asserting yourself, and being an individual within yourself, that's a human right. Not just for musicians. Improvisation is a human right [audience claps]. Thank you. Improvisation is a human right. Improvisation starts with just the average person. Improvisation is a necessity. It comes about as a result of a necessity by human beings.
>
> (Abrams *et al.* 2010)

For Abrams, improvisation *can* transcend capitalism: Improvisation is precisely *how* human beings can potentially self-actualize; it is *what we aspire to do* to fulfill our expressive potential by refusing to be subjugated by the norms, codes, rules, and pathways of capitalist society. Evidently, Abrams is not speaking only of musical improvisation. For him, improvisation is a cultural—potentially even a biological—imperative that cuts across artistic practice and the myriad practices of everyday life.

What we learn from jazz advertising, however, is that there is nothing necessarily or inherently emancipatory about improvisation, nor is jazz music the intrinsically anti-capitalist phenomenon that we so often believe it to be. That is by no means to reject the contention that Abrams and so many others have made that jazz and improvisation *can be* radical practices of human freedom; rather, it is to underscore the contingent nature of that radical potential.

For what we have seen in the preceding chapters is that jazz and improvisation can equally serve the interests of capital, buttressing the sociocultural, ideological status quo by masking the traumas of reality; by offering a shimmering glimpse of a way out that is actually just a way back in. For those among us who are committed to disrupting the status quo and who aspire to realize Abrams's optimistic vision, it is essential that we recognize how fragile that vision is, and how easy it is to confuse the spectacle of expressive freedom with the genuine article. After all, in many ways it is far easier, safer, and more comfortable to *feel* like we're breaking the rules than it is to actually break them.

Bibliography

Abrams, Muhal Richard, George Lewis, and Roscoe Mitchell. "Chicago Slow Dance: The AACM in Conversation," *Improvisation, Community, and Social Practice*, 2010. (Accessed August 23, 2013) http://www.improvcommunity.ca/research/panel-chicago-slow-dance-aacm-conversation.

Appadurai, Arjun. *Modernity at Large: Cultural Dimensions of Globalization*. Minneapolis: University of Minnesota Press, 1996.

Baraka, Amiri. "Jazz and the White Critic," *Down Beat*. August 15, 1963, *Keeping Time: Readings in Jazz History*, ed. Robert Walser. New York: Oxford University Press, 1999.

Fleury, David. Interview with the author (May 14, 2010).

Saul, Scott. "Outrageous Freedom: Charles Mingus and the Invention of the Jazz Workshop," *American Quarterly* 53 (September 2001): 387–419.

Stein, Gail. Interview with the author (May 27, 2010).

Taylor, Patrick and Aileen Le Breton. Interview with the authors (October 21, 2010).

Žižek, Slavoj. *The Sublime Object of Ideology*. New York: Verso, 1989.

INDEX

Note: 'N' after a page number indicates a note; 'f' indicates a figure.

AACM. *See* Association for the Advancement of Creative Musicians (AACM)

Abrams, Muhal Richard 234

Adelphoi Music 117–18

Adorno, Theodor 11, 219; "On Jazz" 44, 80n5

adulthood 117. *See also* young adults

advertising: "affinity" 20–21; African Americans as excluded from 104–5; author's experience of jazz and 1–2; based on social anxiety 8; and class status 9; and counterculturalism 20; as differentiator of identical products 5; humor in 111–12; as Ideological State Apparatus (ISA) 5; "indirect" 13–14; and interpellation 5; mass media programming supported by 13, 16–17; music in 12–22; psychological dimensions of 5–8, 17; and race 9; and rise in consumption 4; and social citizenship 10; as text and praxis 31; traditional, vs. corporate sponsorship 180–81; "vignette approach" 17. *See also* brand identification; corporate sponsorship

affinity advertising 20–21

African Americans 230; in auto industry labor force 105; Black Capitalists 159; as car buyers 85–86; commentators on

jazz 47; creativity of, in jazz 48–49; distrust of capitalism 47–48; exclusion of, from ads 104–5; and "Great Escape" ad (Volkswagen) 76–77; interpellation of, as consumers 23; jazz as cultural practice of 26, 46–47, 230; and Mailer's conception of counterculturalism 19–20; middle class 53; socioeconomic self-determination of 62–63; and soft drink market 159–60

agency 134, 166–70, 171, 180

Air Canada Jazz 2

Ake, David 23

Aldridge, Henry B. 102

Althusser, Louis 6, 14; "Ideology and Ideological State Apparatuses (Notes Towards and Investigation)" 5; on interpellation 28; Žižek on 28–29. *See also* interpellation

American national character 89–90

American Tobacco Company 181, 182

Annan, Kofi 210

anti-commercialism: and brand fit with TD Bank 209–10; and "Great Escape" ad (Volkswagen) 75–76, 77; of jazz 40, 46, 47, 49; of Mingus 40–41, 56, 63–64, 68–69, 76. *See also* counterculturalism

Appadurai, Arjun 233

"The Appeal of Primitive Jazz" 88–89

appearances. *See* spectacle concept

Armstrong, Louis 16
Arnold Worldwide 41; "Great Escape" ad (Volkswagen) 70, 75–76, 79. *See also* Volkswagen
articulations, definition of 27
artistic creativity, as male domain 51, 68, 132
assembly lines 3–4. *See also* Ford Motor Company; industrialization
Association for the Advancement of Creative Musicians (AACM) 62, 234
AT&T 20
Attrep, Kara, "The Sonic Inscription of Identity: Music, Race, and Nostalgia in Advertising" 23
authenticity 76, 133–34
auto industry 105, 113. *See also* car advertising; cars
automobiles. *See* cars

Bank, Al 182
Baraka, Amiri 26, 40, 52–53, 66, 80n16; "American Sexual Reference: Black Male" 54–55; Black Arts Repertory Theatre/ School (BARTS) 62; "Black Dada Nihilismus" 54; *Blues People: Negro Music in White America* 53; "The Changing Same: R&B and New Black Music" 56; "Jazz and the White Critic" 230
Barkan, Todd 149
Barris, George 84
BARTS. *See* Black Arts Repertory Theatre/ School (BARTS)
Baudrillard, Jean, *For a Critique of the Political Economy of the Sign* 21
Baumann, Max Peter 207–8
BBDO agency 120–24. *See also* "This Is My Car" campaign (Chrysler)
Beat movement 20, 111
Beecham's Pills 13
Bell, Clive 43–44
Berlant, Lauren 14
Bethlehem Steel 66
"Birth of the Cool" recordings 109
Black Arts Repertory Theatre/School (BARTS) 62
Black Capitalists 159
Black Power movement: and artist-run collective 62; sexism of 52–54
Bluhm+Voss 2
Bott, Fenton T. 43
Bourdieu, Pierre 10
brand identification: and accessibility 8; and anti-commercialism 209–10; and

consumer identity 6; Foster on 120; and prestige value 6–7, 124–25; of TD Bank and Jazz Festivals 194–210; of Volkswagen 41
Brubeck, Dave, *Jazz Impressions of Eurasia* 182, 183f
Bruner, Gordon C., II, "Music, Mood, and Marketing" 24, 25
Bull, Michael 144, 167–68
Butler, Broadus 160
"Buyer's Strike" of 1958 106

Cadillac 84, 85f, 105
Calgary Folk Festival 193, 215, 224n13, 225n15
Cantor, Eddie 148
capitalism: African American socioeconomic self-determination 62; compared to prostitution/pimping 66–67; consumer-citizens in 30; consumer dissatisfaction as driver of 11; definition 3; and environmental issues 212; Ideological State Apparatuses (ISAs) as reinforcing 5; and industrialization 3; and leisure time 233–34; and rise in consumption 4; and slavery 47–48; and spectacle 27–28. *See also* industrialization
car advertising: Chevrolet 96–97; DeSoto (Chrysler) 94, 95f; JWT (J. Walter Thompson) report on 95–96; Plymouth Valiant 107, 108f, 109–13; race politics of 103–5; on TV 95–96; women as key demographic for 97, 99, 118; for young adults 116. *See also* specific car companies
Carby, Hazel 52, 67–68
car culture 99
car-driver concept 84, 110–12, 130
Carmichael, Hoagy 16
Carr, Leon 101
cars: accidents 92; African Americans as buyers of 85–86; "Buyer's Strike" of 1958 106; compact cars 106–7; and freedom 86, 93; in *The Great Gatsby* (Fitzgerald) 87–88, 93–94; and jazz 88; joyriding in 90–92; and masculinity 94; 1950s as "golden age" of 94, 106; ownership of, as political act 86; prestige value of 84–85, 93–94, 109; sales of American vs. European 106; and white flight 98–99
Cassiday, Bruce 97, 104
Cawthra, Benjamin 126

Charles, Ray 224n5
Chazz-Mar, Inc. 62
Chevrolet: and car advertising on TV
    96–97; and *The Dinah Shore Show* (TV
    show) 96–97, 101, 182
The Chicago Defender 48–49
Chrysler 16; Plymouth brand 106–7; PT
    Cruiser 121–22; Sebring convertible
    122–23; "This Is My Car" campaign
    121–30; 300M 123, 127
Chrysler, Walter 107
CIBC (Canadian Imperial Bank of
    Commerce) 191, 224n10
cigarettes 126–27, 181–82, 183, 188–90
citizenship 9–10, 30
civil rights movement 76–77
classical music 15, 201
class status: and advertising 9; and jazz
    festivals 223
Clicquot Club: Eskimos radio program 7;
    Ginger Ale bottle 7f; "relationship"
    advertising 8
Coca-Cola 148–49, 174, 175, 184
Cohen, Lizabeth 30
colas: Coca-Cola 148–49; Diet Pepsi 147;
    and diversity 158–66; flanker products
    145. *See also* Pepsi Jazz
Coleman, Jay 183–84
Coleman, Ornette 57, 61
Collette, Buddy 62
Columbia Records 20, 60
commerce: as feminized domain 67–68;
    and gender 50–54; and jazz festivals 220
commercialization, of jazz 43–44, 47, 49
commodity: anti-commercialism as 68–69;
    jazz viewed as 43–44, 47; women as 54, 67
commodity fetishism 221
community belonging: advertising based
    on 8–9; consumption as path into 9; and
    musical style 18–19; as psychological
    advertising strategy 5–6; and TD Bank
    Jazz Festivals 205–8
communitas 179, 219, 223
commuting, to work 99
compact cars 106–20. *See also* Honda
    Jazz; Plymouth Valiant ad campaign;
    Volkswagen
conspicuous consumption 29
consumers: agency of 29, 166–70, 171,
    180; Hispanic 161; identity of, and
    branding 6; middle class as "inauthentic"
    53, 55; women as 50–55, 67–68, 77
consumption: and adulthood 117;
    advertising as key to 4; and citizenship
30; conspicuous, and social citizenship
    10–11; as engine of capitalism 11;
    Gilroy on 11–12; ideology of 5; as
    individualistic 11–12; and jazz 231; as
    path into mainstream 9; performative
    character of 29; rise in, and mass
    production 4, 92–93
Convery, Alan 184, 185, 197–98, 200–201,
    208–9, 216–17
Conyers, John Jr. 164
Cook, Nicholas 18, 42, 155; "Music and
    Meaning in the Commercials" 22,
    71–72
Cooley, Tim 33
co-optation: of African American music
    49–50; counterculturalism in advertising
    as 20; of jazz, by Euro-Americans 103;
    jazz in advertising as 34
Le Corbusier, *When the Cathedrals Were
    White* 90
Corday, Leo 101
Corporate Social Responsibility (CSR)
    210–11, 223
corporate sponsorship: history of 181–86;
    of jazz festivals 187–88; marketing vs.
    community-building 179, 210, 212,
    215–19; vs. philanthropic donations
    186; of TD Bank Jazz Festivals 178–79,
    184–85; of television programming
    16, 180, 182; by tobacco companies
    189–91, 195–96, 224n9; vs. traditional
    advertising 180–81. *See also* TD
    (Toronto Dominion) Bank
Count Basie Orchestra 46
counterculturalism: and 1960s jazz 19–20;
    and advertising 20; as commodity
    68–69; of improvisation 57–58; of
    jazz 232. *See also* anti-commercialism;
    Mingus, Charles
Cozzens, James Gould 51–52
Creative Music Workshop 195–96
The Crisis 48
Cross, Gary 30
Crouch, Stanley 40
CSR. *See* Corporate Social Responsibility
    (CSR)
Cullen, Countee 51
cultural significance 20–22. *See also* tropes
    of meaning

Dahl, Richard 211
Davies, Pearl 122, 124–25, 134
Davis, Miles 40, 84, 109; *Miles: The
    Autobiography* 67

DDB. *See* Doyle Dane Bernbach (DDB)
DDB (Doyle Dane Bernbach) 41, 75, 106, 111, 144, 153
Debord, Guy 27–28, 175, 220
Debut Records 62
de Certeau, Michel 144, 168, 171, 206
de Crèvecoeur, Jean, *Letters from an American Farmer* 89
Denvir, Steve 120–26, 128, 129, 134, 135, 137
Desmond, Paul 109
DeSoto (Chrysler) 16; ads for, as appealing to social status 94, 95f
de Tocqueville, Alexis 138n2; *Democracy in America* 89–90
Dichter, Ernest 17
Diet Coke Women in Jazz Festival 149
The Dinah Shore Show (TV show): Chevrolet as sponsor of 96–97, 101, 182; end of 104; lack of diversity on 102–3, 104, 138n4; "See the U.S.A. In Your Chevrolet" (song) 101–2; women as key demographic for 99
Dinerstein, Joel 88
diversity: and advertising 158–66; and *The Dinah Shore Show* (TV show) 102–3, 104, 138n4; within jazz 164; of jazz genre 201–2, 207–8, 212–15; spectacle of 171
Dixon, Bill 62
domestic space. *See* public/private division of space
Dorr-Dorynek, Diane 68, 78; "Mingus . . ." 63–64
Douglass, Frederick 63, 159
DraftFCB agency 117
Drake, Nick 71f; "Pink Moon" 70–71
Du Bois, W.E.B. 48
Duke, Vernon 16
du Maurier (tobacco company) 178, 188–89, 191, 194–96
Dunham, Katherine 62

Early, Gerald 15
Ebony magazine 105
educational initiatives: and sponsorship 196–97
Eisenmen, Jed 59
Elias, Leah 154, 162, 171, 173, 174
Ellison, Ralph 166
Elson, Chris 195, 197, 198, 214, 215
emasculation 67, 78. *See also* masculinity
Enrico, Roger 148, 153
Ensign, William H. 6

Enstice, Wayne, *Jazzwomen: Conversations with Twenty-One Musicians* 131, 133, 134
environmental issues: and sponsorship 197–99, 211–12, 218, 225n21
Ertegun, Ahmet 56
ethics 221–22. *See also* Corporate Social Responsibility (CSR)
Evans, Gil 109
Expansion Team 144

Falassi, Alessandro 205
false consciousness 29, 222–23
Farmer, Harcourt 43
feminization: and commerce 67–68; and whiteness 51, 55
Ferle, Carrie La 158
Festival International de Jazz de Montreal 187
festivals. *See* jazz festivals
Finch, Russell 2
Fine, Adam 225n20
Finkelstein, Howard 144, 148, 154, 155, 163, 165, 166, 168, 174
flanker products 145
Fleury, David 123, 132, 228
Flink, James 92
Foote Cone Belding agency 115
Ford, Henry 3–4, 92
Ford Automotive 16
Ford Motor Company 4, 95–96, 182
Foster, Robert J. 6–7, 120
Frank, Thomas 19, 20, 41, 75, 219–20
Frankfurt School 29
Franklin, John Hope 160
Frank Productions, Inc. 16
Fraser, Jill Andresky 232–33
Frederick P. Rose Hall 148
Freedman, Marvin 77; "Here's the Lowdown on 'Two Kinds of Women'" 50–52
Freedman's Savings Trust Company 63
freedom: and cars/mobility 86, 93. *See also* mobility
free jazz. *See* improvisation
Friedman, Milton 210
Frissell, Bill 209
"From Spirituals to Swing" concert 46–47
Fuller, Smith Ross, Inc. 13

Gabbard, Krin 23, 26
Galloway, Jim 188
gender: and commerce 50–54; and economic exploitation 67; and Plymouth Valiant ad campaign 110–11;

and public/private division of space 14. *See also* masculinity; women
gender norms, jazz as threat to 45
General Motors 99. *See also* Chevrolet
Gennari, John 46–47
Gibson, D. Parkes 160
Gilroy, Paul 11–12, 98, 223
Gleason, Ralph 63; "So Revolution is Commercial" 20
globalization 113
Goodman, Benny 181
Gordon, Max 59–60
Gorn, Gerald, "The Effects of Music in Advertising on Choice Behavior: A Classical Conditioning Approach 24, 25
Granelli, Jerry 196
Granville Street Bridge 178f
"Great Escape" ad (Volkswagen): and African Americans 76–77; and anti-commercialism 75–76, 77; and civil rights movement 76–77; "II B.S." (Mingus) used in 41–42, 72–74, 79, 81n21, 81n24, 119–20; improvisation in 74, 75; and masculine creativity 78; psychographic message of 74–77; and temporal dissonance 74–75, 77; women in 77
The Great Gatsby (Fitzgerald) 87–88, 93–94
Great Migration 98
Greenpeace 211
"greenwashing" 211, 225n21
Gridley, Mark 40
Grossberg, Lawrence 27
Grossman, Josh 196, 209, 213–14
Gryce, Gigi 62
Guelph Jazz Festival 234
Guy, Barry 209

Halifax Jazz Festival 195–96, 198, 225n20
Hall, Stuart 27, 31, 180
Hammond, John 46
Haram 207
Haraway, Donna 136
Harlem Renaissance movement 48–50
Harvey, Kathryn 144, 147, 151, 161, 172
"Have You Tried Wheaties" jingle 16
Hawkins, Coleman 84
Hayes, David 124–25, 136
Hentoff, Nat 62, 63; *Jazz Is* 61
Hispanic consumers 161
Hitler, Adolph 106
Hodge, Elizabeth 144, 154, 155, 157, 161, 162–63, 171
homophobia 54–55

Honda 171
Honda Jazz 112f; as compact car 112–13; "Jazz Comes to Town" add 117–18; jazz music as absent in ads for 118–20; naming of 114; "Tetris" ad for 114–15, 118; "Village Green" ad for 115–16
hooks, bell 20, 53; *Ain't I a Woman: Black Women and Feminism* 52; *Wounds of Passion: A Writing Life* 86
Horkheimer, Max 11
Howard, Owen 207
Huggins, Nathan Irvin 48
Hughes, Langston 48–49, 80n8; "The Negro Artist and the Racial Mountain" 50–51; "Note on a Commercial Theater" 49
humor, in advertising 111–12
Hung, Kineta, "Narrative Music in Congruent and Incongruent TV Advertising" 24, 25
Huron, David 18; "Music in Advertising: An Analytic Paradigm" 22

IBM 2
identity, music as expression of 12
Ideological State Apparatuses (ISAs): advertising as 5; magazines as 45; mass media as 14; Shore as 101
Imperial Tobacco 188–89
improvisation 169; and advertising psychology 117–18; and authenticity 133–34; on "The Clown" (Mingus) 57; and consumption of jazz products 232–35; as countercultural 57–58; and female jazz musicians 133; in "Great Escape" ad (Volkswagen) 74, 75; Krall on 132–33
individualism: and conspicuous consumption 11–12; as psychological advertising strategy 5–6
indulgence 172
industrialization 3, 74–75. *See also* capitalism
interpellation: and advertising 5; of African American consumers 23, 26; definition of 28; of male viewers 117; as mimesis 221; of minorities 158; music's role in 12, 18; and Pepsi Jazz ads 152–53, 162, 171; and TD Bank Jazz Festivals 216; of young adults 117; Žižek on 28–29
ISAs. *See* Ideological State Apparatuses (ISAs)

Jazz at Lincoln Center (J@LC) 149–50
Jaines, Sunny Jim 76
Jazz Artists Guild 62
jazz clubs 126–27

jazz dance 92
jazz festivals: and class status 223; commerce of 220; corporate sponsorship of 187–88; Diet Coke Women in Jazz Festival 149; Festival International de Jazz de Montreal 187; and genre debates 213; history of 186–94; JVC Jazz Festivals 183; KOOL Jazz Festivals 183; Newport Jazz Festival 59, 182–83; Newport Rebel Festival 59; and spectacle of community 219–23; TD Bank Jazz Festivals 177–223. *See also* specific festivals; TD Bank Jazz Festivals
Jazz Festivals Canada (JFC) 193. *See also* TD Bank Jazz Festivals
jazz moment 150, 152, 153, 169, 233–34. *See also* temporal dissonance
jazz music: and 1960s counterculturalism 19–20; as absent in Honda Jazz ads 118–20; as African American cultural practice 26, 46–47, 230; African Americans on 47; and American national character 90; as anti-commercial 40–41, 46, 47, 49; authenticity of 76; and cars 88; as commodity 43–44, 47, 49; consumption of, and improvisation 232–35; co-optation of, by Euro-Americans 103; counterculturalism of 232; and culture of consumption 231; diversity of 201–2, 207–8, 212–15; elusive meaning of 2–3, 229; and fast pace of life 88–89, 90; and jingles 16, 229; as lowbrow 15, 42–43; as masculinized 78, 119; and mass production 43–44; moral implications of 15, 45–46, 91–92; and sexuality 44–45, 50; as "social location" 26; symphonic vs. "hot" 15; as threat to gender norms 45; tropes of meaning for 26–27, 126, 137–38, 230; Whyton on advertising and 23–24
jazz musicians: and commercialization of jazz 46; exploitation of, as emasculating 67; as exploited by music industry 64–67; fair wages for 59–61; female 131, 133
Jazz Workshop, Inc. 59, 62, 78
JFC. *See* Jazz Festivals Canada (JFC)
Jhally, Sut 17, 31
Jimmy Choo shoes 129
jingles 15–17, 20–21, 229
Johnson, Jack 228
John W. Hartman Center 31
Jones, Jo 62
Jones, Willie 62

joyriding 90–92
J. Stirling Getchell, Inc. 94, 111
JVC Jazz Festivals 183
J. Walter Thompson Company 6, 15, 31, 182
JWT (J. Walter Thompson) agency 95–96

Kallio, Tomi 211
Karmen, Steve 20
Keeler "Jazz" in-ear diagnostic thermometer 2
Kerouac, Jack 111
Kerr, Robert 190, 193
Klein, Bethany 31; *As Heard on TV: Popular Music in Advertising* 23
Kingsley, Walter 88–89
Konitz, Lee 109
KOOL cigarettes 183
KOOL Jazz Festivals 183
Kraft Foods, Inc. 182
Krall, Diana 173; advertising relationships of 134–35; agency of 134, 136; charitable donations by 136; and improvisation 132–33; "The Look of Love" (song) 123–24; "The Look of Love" (video) 135; marginalization of, as jazz artist 131–34; physical appearance of 128–31, 134; popularity of 124; and Rolex Watch USA 125; and "This Is My Car" campaign (Chrysler) 122–25, 127–30, 134–37
Kuenz, Jane 51
Kvasnosky, Tim 155
Kyser, Kay 181–82

Laclau, Ernesto 230–31
Ladies Home Journal: advertising based on community of consumption 8–9; criticism of jazz in 43; as Ideological State Apparatus (ISA) 45; white, middle-class audience of 9
Lawner, Ron 41
Le Breton, Aileen 189, 194, 208
Lee, Wei-Na 158
Lehrer, Jeremy 76
leisure time 233–34
Leonard, Herman 126, 189, 224n8
Lerner, Alan Jay, "On the Street Where You Live" 16
Levy, Sidney 17, 21
Lewin, Nick 76
Lewis, George E. 26
LindenSmith, Dustin 198, 204, 219
Lipsitz, George 105

Locke, Alain 48; *The Negro and His Music* 49
Loesser, Frank 16
Loewe, Frederick, "On the Street Where You Live" 16
Longoria-Parker, Eva 161
Lucky Strike Orchestra 13, 181
Lutz, Bonnie 163, 165
Lynd, Robert and Helen, "Middletown: A Study in American Culture" 93
Lyon, Richard 20
Lyon Music 20

MacDonald, Dwight 51–53, 77, 80n15
Macklam, Steve 136
MacLeod, Nicola E., "The Placeless Festival: Identity and Place in the Post-Modern Festival" 205
magazines, as Ideological State Apparatuses (ISAs) 45
Mailer, Norman 111; "The White Negro: Superficial Ref lections on the Hipster" 19
management principles 3–4
Marable, Manning 62, 159
Marcus, George 32
marginalized groups 9. *See also* African Americans
Marsalis, Wynton 149
Marsh, Kendall 21
Marshall, T.H., "Citizenship and Social Class" 10
Martin, Michele 179, 185, 192, 198–99, 200, 203, 204–5, 208, 214–15, 218–19, 225n14
masculinity: and artistic creativity 51, 68; and cars 94; in "Great Escape" ad (Volkswagen) 78; and jazz 78, 119; and Plymouth Valiant ad campaign 110–12. *See also* gender
mass media 9, 13. *See also* radio; television
mass production: at Ford Motor Company 4; identical products as consequence of 5; and jazz 43–44; and rise in consumption 4, 92–93
Matlin, Daniel 80n16
McCann, Denyse 187
McClaren, Carrie 20, 21
McCracken, Grant 85f, 127
McDonald, D'Arcy 192, 194, 201–2, 204, 208, 209, 214–15, 216, 218–19
McDonough, John 132
McGee, Kristin A. 103
McGovern, Charles 30

McHarg, Jim 187
McMahon, John 43
McMullen, Tracy 149
media studies 17
Meizel, Katherine 33
Ménard, André 187
Mental Music Productions 21
Mercer, Kobena 52
Michener, Marilyn 190–91, 217
"midcult," definition of 80n15
middle class, as "inauthentic" consumers 53, 55
Miller, Mark 132
Mingus, Celia 78
Mingus, Charles 60f, 171; anti-commercialism of 40–41, 56, 63–64, 68–69, 76, 79; Baraka on 56; *Beneath the Underdog* 64–68, 64f; business ventures of 62–63, 78; on capitalist exploitation of musicians 64–67; *Charles Mingus Presents Charles Mingus* 69; "The Clown" 56–59, 57f; disputes over money 59–60; as entrepreneurial 68–69, 78–79; and female partnerships 78; Five Spot rant 68–69, 79, 229; gendered critique of commerce 64–68; "II B.S." 41–42, 56, 72–74, 79, 81n21; improvisation 57; *The Jazz Word* 68; music used in ads 78. *See also* "Great Escape" ad (Volkswagen)
Mingus, Sue 59–60, 60f, 78, 79; *Tonight At Noon: A Love Story* 60, 78
miscegenation 80n6, 103–4. *See also* race
Mitchell, Deborah J. 17
mobility 85–86, 92, 99. *See also* freedom
Model T 92
Monson, Ingrid 19
Montgomery, George 97, 100, 101, 103, 104, 138n3
moral decline 45–46, 91–92
Mortenson, Peter A. 91
Moulton, Alex 144, 154, 157, 168
multicultural marketing 173
Murray, Albert 144, 165, 175
music: in advertising 12–22; as expression of identity 12; psychological dimensions of 18–19; role of, in interpellation 18
Musical America 43
musical semiotics 24–25
musical style: cultural significance of 20–22; demographic appeal of 18; and moral content 14–15; psychological dimensions of 19
music in advertising: affinity advertising 20–21; and community belonging

18–19; history of 13; jingles 15–16; licensing strategies 21; and mass media 13; research in 22–26; subliminal power of 18

music industry: as exploitative 64–67; as racist 60–61

National Negro Business League (NNBL) 63
Nesbitt, Bryan 121, 122
Newport Jazz Festival 59, 182–83
Newport Rebel Festival 59
Nintendo 115
NNBL. *See* National Negro Business League (NNBL)

object value system 21
Ogerman, Claus 123
Oliver, Richard L. 17
Omni-Americans 165
Orwell, George, "Bookshop Memories" 51

pace of life 88–89, 90
Packard, Vance, *The Hidden Persuaders* 17
Packer, Jeremy 86, 105
Pan American airlines 182
Panassié, Hugues 46, 80n8
Park, Lisa Sun-Hee 10
Parpis, Eleftheria 41
patina concept 127, 133
Pears soap company 6
People magazine 172, 175
Pepsi: and African American market 159–60; Diet Pepsi 147; multicultural marketing 160–62, 173; sign-value of, vs. use value 21–22
Pepsi Jazz: author's experience of 1–2; and consumer agency 166–70; failure of 145–46; image of 151–52; introduction of 142–44; naming of 147–48, 151, 175; and Omni-Americans 165; *People* magazine ad 172, 175; "Sounds of the City" 142–44, 153–56, 162–63, 165–66, 167–69, 170, 172–74
Peterson, Richard A., *Creating Country Music: Fabricating Authenticity* 22
Plymouth Valiant ad campaign 107, 108f; American identity 110; jazz soundtrack of 109–13; and masculinity 110–12; vs. Valiant Wagon ad 111
Pond's soap company 6
Porter, Cole, "It's De-Lovely" 16
Porter, Eric 40, 62

Porter, Lewis 40
power dynamics 60–61
Presley, Elvis 84, 85f
Procter Gamble 17
prostitution 64–67
psychological dimensions: of advertising 5–6, 17, 117–18; of music 18–19, 21; of musical style 19
public/private division of space: as gendered 14; and television advertising 17, 96
Pumphrey, P.H. 13

Quartly, Rob 125–26, 129, 130, 132

Ra, Sun 62
race: and advertising 9; and "hot" jazz 15; politics of, and car ads 103–5; and white flight 97–99
racism 104–5
radio 14, 181–82
rape 54
Redding, Saunders 51
Reid, Jamie, *Diana Krall: The Language of Love* 130
research studies: methodology of current study 30–33; misunderstanding of musical semiotics in 24–25; on music in advertising 22–26; scholarly neglect of 24
Reser, Harry 7–8
Roach, Max 59, 62
Robertson, Thomas S. 17
Robinson, Tony 115–16
RockBill magazine 183–84
Rolex Watch USA 125
Rolfe, B.A. 13, 181
Rolling Stone magazine 184
Rome, Harold 16
Romney, George W. 106
Roper, Elmo 159, 174
Russell, Harvey C. 160

Sales, Grover 40
Samuel, Lawrence 16
Sandke, Randall 103
Sartre, John Paul 90
Saul, Scott 59, 68; "Outrageous Freedom: Charles Mingus and the Invention of the Jazz Workshop" 64
Saxton, Kate 114
Scanlon, Jennifer 9
Schaefer Beer 16

Schlage 2
Scholz & Friends agency 114–15
School of Arts, Music, Gymnastics 62
Schor, Juliet 232
Schulte, Brigid 233
Schwab, Klaus 210
Scott, Lauren 144, 146, 150, 152, 160, 173
Scott, Linda 24; "Understanding Jingles
    and Needledrop: A Rhetorical
    Approach to Music in Advertising" 24
"See the U.S.A. In Your Chevrolet" (song)
    101–2
sexism: antagonism toward female
    consumers 50–54, 68; of Black Power
    movement 52–54
sexual fantasy 172
sexuality: and jazz 44–45, 50; and jazz
    dancing 91–92; and Krall in "This Is
    My Car" campaign (Chrysler) 129–30,
    136
Sheller, Mimi 84
Shepherd, Jean 56–58
Shore, Dinah 96–97, 97f, 100f, 173;
    background 99–101; as Ideological State
    Apparatus (ISA) 101; as "passing" for
    white 103–4; "See the U.S.A. In Your
    Chevrolet" (song) 102. See also The
    Dinah Shore Show (TV show)
Silverstein, Barry 200
Simard, Alain 187
Siraisi, Genji 144, 147, 155–56
Sissle, Noble 47–48
slavery 47–48, 138n2
S.L. Feldman Associates 123
Smith, Bessie 84
Smith, Mike 120–25, 128
social anxiety 8
social citizenship: and advertising 10;
    conspicuous consumption as means to
    10–11; definition of 10; vs. political
    citizenship 9–10
social status: ads as appealing to 94; cars as
    symbol of 84–85, 93–94, 109
"Sounds of the City" 142–44, 153–56,
    162–63, 165–66, 167–69, 170, 172–74
spectacle concept: definition of 27–28;
    and ethics 221–23; jazz festivals and
    spectacle of community 219–23
Spellman, A.B. 61
sponsorship. See corporate sponsorship
Stanbridge, Alan 23
Stein, Gail 75, 144, 146, 147, 150–51,
    169–70, 233

Sterne, Jonathan 19
Stewart, Ollie 47
Stewart, Rex 61
Stillwell, Robynn J. 13, 15; "Music and
    Advertising" 22
Stockhouse, Janet, Jazzwomen: Conversations
    with Twenty-One Musicians 131, 133, 134
Sudhalter, Richard 103
Sullivan, Bill 125, 128
Syed, Nasir 33

tactic 168, 171
Tapscott, Horace 62
Taylor, Billy 164
Taylor, Cecil 59
Taylor, Frederick, The Principles of Scientific
    Management 3–4
Taylor, Pat 187, 188, 190, 213, 229
Taylor, Timothy 6, 15, 20, 23, 31, 70, 184,
    208, 214
TD (Toronto Dominion) Bank: brand
    fit of festivals with 194–210; and class
    status 223; "comfort" in brand identity
    200–208, 223; and environmentalism
    212, 218; expansion of 193–94; as
    jazz festival sponsor 178–79, 184–85,
    191–93; marketing vs. community-
    building 212, 215–19; positive regard
    of audiences for 219. See also corporate
    sponsorship; TD Bank Jazz Festivals
TD Bank Jazz Festivals 206f, 207f;
    and anti-commercialism 209–10;
    branding of 200; core demographic
    of 215–16; description of 177–78;
    educational component of 196–97; and
    environmental issues 197–99; expansion
    of 193–94; and false consciousness
    222–23; Groove and Graffiti program
    196, 197f, 218; limited commercial
    involvement of sponsor 208–9; as
    marketing strategy 193–94; "Monster
    Murals" 225n17; neglect of local
    musicians 217–18; as properties 185; and
    shared community values 205–8; TD
    Bank's sponsorship of 178–79, 184–85,
    191–93; TD Comfort Zone 202–5,
    203f. See also jazz festivals
TD Friends of the Environment Fund (TD
    FEF) 198–99, 199f, 211, 218, 225n17,
    225n21
teenagers. See young adults
television: and car advertising 95–96;
    corporate sponsorship of programming

16, 180, 182; jingles in ads for 16–17; ownership rates (1950s) 96
temporal dissonance 232–33; in ads aimed at women 75; and "Great Escape" ad (Volkswagen) 74–75, 77; and industrialization 74–75. *See also* jazz moment
Terry, Luther 189
Tetris (video game) 114–15
"This Is My Car" campaign (Chrysler): background 121–22; and Krall 122–25, 127–30, 134–37; patina concept 127; sexuality in 129–30, 136
Thomas the Tank Engine 115
Thompson, E.P. 74–75
Thompson, Frank Jr. 164, 174
Thornley, Scott 132
Tin Pan Alley 16
Tobacco Act (Bill C-71) (1997, 1998) 190
tobacco companies 224n7; corporate sponsorship by 189–91, 194–96, 224n9. *See also* cigarettes
Tobacco Products Control Act (1988) 189, 224n6
Toronto Downtown Jazz Society 184
Traktor 153, 154, 155
tropes of meaning: definition of 25; for jazz 26–27, 137–38; multiplicity of, for jazz 230; sophistication vs. playfulness 126. *See also* cultural significance
Troupe, Quincy 67
Tucker, Sherrie 131, 133, 149
Turner, Victor 219

Urry, John 84, 130

Vaziri, Aidin 70
Veblen, Thorstein, *The Theory of the Leisure Class* 29
"vignette approach" 17
Village Vanguard 59
Volkswagen 171; background 106; brand identification of 41; "Drivers Wanted" campaign (1990s) 41–42, 70; "Great Escape" ad 41–42, 72–73,

119–20; "Milky Way" ad 70–71; 1960s popularity of 106; "Think Small" campaign 75
Volkswagen Golf 113–14

Waits, Tom 224n5
Wakeham, Hugh 185–86, 190–92, 194, 215, 224n10
Wakeham & Associates Marketing (WAM) 185, 190–91
Waller, Fats 84
Washington, Booker T. 63, 159
Waterman, Stanley 179, 205
Waters, Ethel 99
Weber, Max, "spirit of capitalism" 4
Wein, George 59, 62, 182–83, 213
White, Irving 17, 21
white flight 97–99
Whiteman, Paul 15, 88, 103, 181, 182; *Jazz* 90
whiteness, feminization of 51, 55
Whyton, Tony 27; *Jazz Icons: Heroes, Myths and the Jazz Tradition* 23–24
William Morris agency 59
Williams, Jerome D. 158
Wolk, Douglas 70
women: as commodities 54, 67; as consumers 50–55, 67–68, 77; in "Great Escape" ad (Volkswagen) 77; as jazz musicians 131; as key advertising demographic 97, 99, 118; and social anxiety 8; temporal dissonance in ads aimed at 75; as victims of jazz 45. *See also* gender
Woodbury's face powder 8, 9
Worker, Mocean 155, 174

Yo Sumo programme 161, 174
young adults: freedom afforded to, by cars 93; improvisation in ads for 117–18; jazz's negative impact on 90–92; as key advertising demographic 116
YouTube 2
Yves St. Laurent 2

Žižek, Slavoj 28–29, 220–21

CPSIA information can be obtained
at www.ICGtesting.com
Printed in the USA
LVOW04s0254041115
461048LV00021B/276/P